THE PURSUIT OF PEACE AND THE
CRISIS OF ISRAELI IDENTITY

LIST OF PREVIOUS PUBLICATIONS

"Israel's Dilemma: Unity or Peace?" *Israel Affairs*, vol. 12, no. 2 (April 2006): 195–220.

"An Incomplete Revolution: Israeli National Identity, Cultural Change and The Camp David II Negotiations," *Israel Studies Forum*, vol. 19, no. 3 (Fall 2004): 140–157.

"Between Isolation and Integration: The Jewish Dimension in Israeli Foreign Policy," *Israel Studies Forum*, vol. 19, no.1 (Fall 2003): 34–56.

"A Dream become Nightmare? Turkey's Entry into the European Union," coauthor Ersel Aydinli, *Current History*, vol. 100, no. 649 (November 2001): 381–388.

"Islam and Turkish National Identity: A Reappraisal," *Turkish Yearbook of International Relations*, no. 30 (2000): 1–22.

"A Tragic Hero: The Decline and Fall of Ehud Barak," *Perceptions: Journal of International Affairs*, vol. 6, no. 2 (June–August 2001): 71–88.

"A Jewish Affair," *World Policy Journal*, vol. 17, no. 4 (Winter 2000/01): 75–82.

"Affirming Shared Citizenship in Israel," *Merchavim: The Institute for Multicultural and Democratic Education for Israel* (June 2000).

"Terrorizing Democracies," *The Washington Quarterly*, vol. 23, no. 1 (2000): 15–19.

"In the Arms of Europe," *The Jerusalem Post* (December 14, 1999).

"Terrorism: The War of the Future," *The Fletcher Forum of World Affairs*, vol. 23, no. 2 (Fall 1999): 201–208.

"Turkey-Israel: A New Balance of Power in the Middle East," *The Washington Quarterly*, vol. 22, no. 1 (Winter 1999): 25–32.

The Crisis of Identity in Post-Kemalist Turkey: Domestic Discord and Foreign Policy, Research Institute for the Study of Conflict and Terrorism, London, U.K. (Conflict Study 311, October 1998).

"From Umma to State: The Iranian Revolution in Perspective," *The Georgetown Compass Journal of International Affairs*, vol. 7, no. 1 (Spring 1998): 53–64.

The Islamic Republic of Iran: Between Revolution and Realpolitik, Research Institute for the Study of Conflict and Terrorism, London, U.K. (Conflict Study 308, May 1998).

Immigration and Identity: A New Security Perspective in Euro-Maghreb Relations, Research Institute for the Study of Conflict and Terrorism, London, U.K. (Conflict Study 302, September 1997).

"Back from the Brink: Resolving Turkey's Political Crisis," *CSIS Watch* (July 1997).

Book Reviews

"Review of *Ideology, Party Change, and Electoral Campaigns in Israel, 1965–2001,*" *Journal of Modern Jewish Studies*, vol. 4, no. 2 (2005): 347–348.

"The Enemy Within: Religious Extremism, Political Violence and the Murder of Yitzhak Rabin," *H-NET Book Review* (January 2004).

"Review of *Israel: The First Hundred Years, Vol. II. From War to Peace?*" *Middle East Quarterly*, vol. 9, no. 4 (2002): 73–74.

"Review of *Israel: The First Hundred Years, Vol. III. Israeli Politics and Society since 1948: Problems of Collective Identity,*" *Middle East Quarterly*, vol. 9, no. 4 (2002): 74.

"Review of *The Sabra: The Creation Of The New Jew,*" *Commentary Magazine*, vol. 112, no. 3 (2001): 84–86.

"Conspiracy Mania: A Review of *The Hidden Hand: Middle East Fears of Conspiracy,*" *SAIS Review: A Journal of International Affairs*, vol. 19, no. 1 (1999): 267–271.

The Pursuit of Peace and the Crisis of Israeli Identity

Defending / Defining the Nation

Dov Waxman

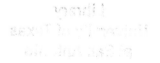

THE PURSUIT OF PEACE AND THE CRISIS OF ISRAELI IDENTITY
© Dov Waxman, 2006.

First published in 2006 by
PALGRAVE MACMILLAN™
175 Fifth Avenue, New York, N.Y. 10010 and
Houndmills, Basingstoke, Hampshire, England RG21 6XS
Companies and representatives throughout the world.

PALGRAVE MACMILLAN is the global academic imprint of the Palgrave Macmillan division of St. Martin's Press, LLC and of Palgrave Macmillan Ltd. Macmillan® is a registered trademark in the United States, United Kingdom and other countries. Palgrave is a registered trademark in the European Union and other countries.

ISBN-13: 978–1–4039–7458–7
ISBN-10: 1–4039–7458–6

Library of Congress Cataloging-in-Publication Data

Waxman, Dov.
    The pursuit of peace and the crisis of Israeli identity : defending / defining the nation / by Dov Waxman.
        p. cm.
    Includes bibliographical references and index.
    ISBN 1–4039–7458–6
        1. National characteristics, Israeli. 2. Jews—Identity—Israel.
    3. Arab-Israeli conflict. 4. Israel–Politics and government . I. Title

DS113.3.W39 2006
956.9405'4—dc22   2006041586

A catalogue record for this book is available from the British Library.

Design by Newgen Imaging Systems (P) Ltd., Chennai, India.

First edition: September 2006

10 9 8 7 6 5 4 3 2 1

Printed in the United States of America.

CONTENTS

Preface and Acknowledgments

This book is about the politics of national identity in Israel and the impact this has upon Israel's foreign policy and, above all, its pursuit of peace with the Palestinians. The politics of identity and the Israeli-Palestinian conflict have long been subjects of great interest and concern to me. But it was not until I spent a year conducting research in Israel that the linkage between these two subjects became clearly apparent to me. I arrived in Tel Aviv in the summer of 1999 expecting to find a country brimming with optimism as it finally secured its place in the Middle East. A new era of peace beckoned, and with it the promise of security, prosperity, and increasing Arab-Israeli cooperation. The Oslo peace process seemed unstoppable, despite the repeated attempts by hardliners on both sides to derail it. Israeli-Palestinian peace was surely something that all but a handful of extremists would enthusiastically welcome, even if it entailed some difficult concessions. Like many observers of the peace process, I confidently expected a happy outcome.

What I discovered over the course of that year in Israel and in numerous visits since, was a far less rosy situation. On the ground, Israel's occupation of the West Bank and Gaza continued, with Israeli settlements, checkpoints, and bypass roads making life for most Palestinians as difficult (if not, harder than) as it was before the signing of the Oslo Accords. Israeli-Palestinian relations continued to be marked by mutual suspicion and hostility, and neither side seemed ready or able to significantly alter their old attitudes toward each other. All of this came as a shock to me, and filled me with despair over the prospects for lasting Israeli-Palestinian peace.

But what surprised and disturbed me the most was the fact that many of the Israelis I spoke with did not seem to care all that much about this. Contrary to the impression one often receives in foreign news reporting on Israel, the peace process did not consume the attention of Israelis. In fact, they seemed far more worried by their own internal disputes—especially concerning the place of Judaism in public life—than by their conflict with the Palestinians. The issue that aroused by far the most intense reactions and generated heated debates was the deteriorating relations between religious and secular Jews in Israel. Both secular and religious Israeli Jews directed more scorn and animosity toward each other than they did toward Palestinians, who seemed for the most part far removed from daily life in Israel.

Even when they discussed the ongoing peace process, Israelis appeared more troubled by their own differences of opinion than by the wider gulf that separated their views from that of the Palestinians. Such discussions had an air of unreality about them, as Israelis debated amongst themselves the concessions that should be made for peace, with little or no reference to what the Palestinians actually wanted. It struck me that the domestic debate in Israel over the Oslo peace process was not really about Israeli-Palestinian relations at all. It was about Israeli-Israeli relations. It was an intra-Jewish debate (the voices of Israeli Palestinians were rarely heard) in which one's attitudes to the occupied territories served to demarcate which side of a broader cultural divide one was on. What was fundamentally at issue in this debate was not land or the state's borders, but Israeli identity—how Israelis saw themselves as a nation and how they wanted to be seen. It was this realization that led me to write this book in the hope not only of understanding why this was the case, but also to comprehend more generally the role that domestic identity politics—a growing phenomenon in many states today—can play in international relations.

This book has benefited from the advice and support of many people. To name just a few, my special thanks go to Charles Doran, Joel Migdal, Ilan Peleg, and Mike Aronoff for providing valuable feedback on different parts of the manuscript. I am grateful to all those who generously gave of their time for the interviews I conducted in Israel. They are, in alphabetical order, Yossi Ahimeir, Moshe Arens, Shlomo Brom, Dore Gold, Eitan Haber, Tamar Hermann, David Kimche, Ephraim Lapid, Alon Liel, Ron Pundak, and Itamar Rabinowitz. I would like to acknowledge the institutional support I have received from the School of Advanced International Studies of Johns Hopkins University, the Moshe Dayan Center for Middle Eastern and African Studies at Tel Aviv University, the Chaim Herzog Center for Middle East Studies and Diplomacy at Ben-Gurion University, Bowdoin College, and Baruch College of the City University of New York. Finally, I would like to thank my parents, Denis and Carole Waxman, to whom I owe, by far, my greatest debt of gratitude for all they have given me.

INTRODUCTION

We are fragmenting and globalizing at the same time. We spin out as from a centrifuge, flying apart socially and politically, at the same time that enormous centripetal forces press us all into more and more of a single mass every year . . . . The fundamental and decisive conflicts grow ever sharper over the hard stuff of wealth, access to sources of energy and raw materials, over production, food, trade and military power. These are the conflicts that will decide the fate of the world and its peoples. But these conflicts continue to be ribbed and shaped and fleshed by the soft stuff of group identities, by the ways people see themselves and are seen, how they feel about themselves and about others, and how these feelings cause them to behave.[1]

—Harold Isaacs

An Unhappy Birthday

In April 1998, Israel turned fifty. This was a momentous milestone in Israeli history, if not in the entire history of the Jewish people. After millennia of statelessness, not only did Jews have their own state, but also they had achieved this against what appeared to be great odds. Fifty years earlier, on the evening of Friday, May 14, 1948, when David Ben-Gurion declared the establishment of the State of Israel, its existence was in danger of being brutally short-lived. It was home to only about 600,000 Jews—many of them newly arrived refugees from postwar Europe—and it faced a violent struggle for control of the land with its Arab neighbors. The very next day five Arab armies invaded the fledgling state. But the Jewish state survived; and over the course of the next five decades, it thrived despite five major wars, innumerable terrorist attacks, an economic embargo, and international isolation. After fifty years, it had become home to five million Jews, and was by far the most prosperous and militarily powerful state in the Middle East, with an arsenal of nuclear weapons, an internationally competitive high-tech industry, and living standards rivaling those of Western Europe. Although Israel had still not achieved peace with the Palestinians and all its Arab neighbors, a peace process was at least underway. As it proceeded, albeit shakily, Israel was able to cast off its earlier international isolation and finally take its place as a respected member of the international community.

Israel's fiftieth anniversary should surely have been cause for joyous celebration by Israelis, or, more precisely, by Israeli Jews (since, for close to one million Palestinian citizens of Israel, the event marked their *Nakhba*, "catastrophe," when hundreds of thousands of Palestinians became refugees during the 1948 war).[2] They had plenty of reason for hope and pride, as the official slogan of the anniversary proclaimed: "Together in hope, together in pride." But for Israeli Jews hope was scarce, pride was muted, and togetherness was notably absent that year. There was little of the jubilation and joy that one might have expected. Israelis it seemed were in no mood for exuberant celebration.[3] A cover story in *The Jerusalem Report* gave the reasons for the widespread public apathy: "Added to the economic woes are the tension between religious and secular, Ashkenazi and Sephardi, the ultra-Orthodox and everybody; uncertainty over the government's plans for redeployment in the West Bank—you name it. There's little sense of unity, and not much agreement over what it means to be Israeli or Zionist. The country has hit middle age, and seems to be undergoing a crisis."[4] This crisis was a crisis of national identity.

By 1998, Israeli society had become deeply divided along religious, ethnic, and political lines. The fault lines within Israeli society were manifested in the many disputes that erupted over the festivities and public ceremonies planned for Israel's fiftieth anniversary. One public controversy was over "Tekumma" (Rebirth), a 22-part television series covering the country's history, commissioned by Israel's Broadcasting Authority to mark the occasion. An episode that challenged the traditional Israeli view of the fate of the Arab population in Israel after its foundation in 1948, and the Palestinian refugee problem since 1948, was fiercely denounced by right-wing critics. The minister of Communications from the right-wing Likud party tried to cancel the episode, and its director even received hate calls and death threats from right-wing Jewish extremists. The political division between right- and left-wing Israelis was also clearly on display in the rival protests staged on Independence Day on a hilltop on the outskirts of Jerusalem by Jewish settlers demanding more rapid construction of a Jewish housing project in occupied East Jerusalem (on a site known in Arabic as Jabal Abu Ghneim and in Hebrew as Har Homa) and supporters of the leftist "Peace Now" movement, with Israeli police keeping the two groups apart. The jubilee celebrations were also marred by the rift between religious and secular Jews. Dancers from Israel's premier modern dance company pulled out at the last minute from the gala event marking the anniversary to protest demands by religious Jews to change a segment in their performance in which they strip to their underwear during a song mentioning God. Prior to the scheduled performance, the public arguments over it had led Israel's President, Ezer Weizman, to mediate a compromise in which the dancers would have worn skin-colored body-suits rather than undress completely. But the dancers decided—after their show had already begun—not to surrender to what they viewed as religious censorship; and instead they left the stage in protest. Elsewhere that day, black flags were hung from the roof of a Jewish seminary in an ultra-Orthodox Jewish neighborhood in Jerusalem, and Israeli flags were torn from cars driving through the neighborhood in protests by ultra-Orthodox Jews against the creation of a Jewish state (which they regard as a blasphemy before the coming of the Messiah).

There was little euphoria and much discord in Israel, therefore, during the country's fiftieth year. The general public mood was one of prolonged sober introspection.[5] Israel's fiftieth birthday became an occasion of serious reflection rather than revelry. This reflection was overwhelmingly concerned with the same issue that had steadily consumed public attention in the 1990s: Israeli national identity. This was not an esoteric subject being discussed by a small clique of intellectuals, but a subject at the heart of a national debate in which many voices were speaking, often loudly and cantankerously. Indeed, by 1998 the debate over Israeli national identity had come to dominate Israel's political agenda, dictating the manner in which both Israel's domestic and foreign policies were being considered. Above all, the debate shaped public attitudes toward the ongoing Oslo peace process between Israel and the Palestinians begun by the Rabin government five years earlier.

No issue aroused greater domestic controversy in Israel in the 1990s than the Oslo peace process. It was the centerpiece of Israeli foreign policy throughout this period, significantly changing not only Israel's relations with the Palestinians, but also Israel's relations with other Middle East states and the world at large. But despite its promise of peace and security for Israelis, the Israeli public and political system were bitterly divided over it. The division centered, as it had for so long, on the question of the future of the territories—the West Bank and Gaza—occupied by Israel since the 1967 war. This question, however, was less a strategic one for Israelis than a cultural one. Whatever security value these territories held for Israel—always questionable—their ultimate significance (the West Bank's in particular) was symbolic, rather than strategic. As the site of the biblical Jewish kingdom and the cradle of early Jewish civilization, Judea and Samaria (the West Bank) have a religious and nationalistic significance for many Israeli Jews, not merely for a devout minority. A focus on the security implications of an Israeli withdrawal from the territories ignores this central fact. For this reason, any attempt to understand Israeli attitudes toward the occupied territories and the Oslo peace process solely in terms of their security concerns misses the mark. While such concerns may well be invoked by Israelis, as they often were during the years of the Oslo peace process, they are not at the root of the dispute between Israelis over the future of the occupied territories.[6] It was Israeli national identity, rather than defensible borders or territorial depth, which was perceived to be at stake for Israelis as they contemplated withdrawing from the West Bank and Gaza. To grasp the real nature of the domestic debate in Israel over the Oslo peace process, one must, therefore, examine the way in which it was intertwined with a broader societal debate over the definition of Israeli national identity. Animating the division over the Oslo peace process and the future of the occupied territories were profound differences over the definition of Israeli national identity, and it was these differences that inflamed passions and made the debate over the peace process so intense.

It is only through an awareness of the politics of national identity in Israel that one can comprehend the passionate and protracted Israeli debate over the peace process. Understanding this debate is, in turn, essential for anyone concerned with the future of the Israeli-Palestinian peace process. A successful peace process and a stable, lasting peace depends upon the willingness of both societies, not just their political leadership. The absence of a strong societal consensus in favor of peace and the concessions it undoubtedly entails will doom any peace process to failure, as the collapse of the Oslo peace process makes tragically clear. In Israel's case, this consensus was—and continues to be—difficult to achieve and sustain. The reason for this lies, this book argues, with the crisis of Israeli national identity.

This book claims that the debate in Israel over the Oslo peace process was fundamentally about Israeli national identity—who Israelis are and who they should be. The two sides in this debate are identified in the book as "Israelis" and "Jews," the former adhering to a civic conception of Israeli national identity and the latter to an ethno-religious conception. These competing conceptions of Israeli national identity were associated with very different foreign policy orientations and attitudes toward the peace process. Thus, rather than employ the now hackneyed division of Israelis into "hawks" and "doves," this book introduces a new division based upon collective identities and interprets critical events in Israel in the 1990s in terms of the competition between these identities. By viewing Israeli domestic politics and foreign policy through a different lens—identity—instead of the narrower lens of security, as is typical of many existing accounts, this book argues that the peace process involved more than a historical accommodation between Israel and the Palestinians and the final setting of Israel's territorial borders. It also involved a redefinition of Israeli collective identity.

As a result, the peace process became entangled in the politics of national identity in Israel. As the peace process continued, the public linkage between it and identity politics within Israel led to an escalating cultural war between "Israelis" and "Jews." Prime Minister Yitzhak Rabin was a casualty of this war, and his 1995 assassination underscored the danger of continued polarization between Israeli Jews. In response, in the years after Rabin's murder, Israelis became increasingly preoccupied and concerned with their internal divisions. In surveys, more Israeli Jews gave importance to strengthening national unity than to achieving peace with the Palestinians or improving their economic welfare. Thus, the pursuit of peace between Israelis came to rival, if not displace, the pursuit of Israeli-Palestinian peace as the leading item on the national agenda. This book helps us to understand the peace process' demise by showing how domestic identity politics affected Israeli foreign policy toward the Oslo peace process, and how Israeli policy-makers reacted to this scenario.

But this book is not just another postmortem of the Oslo peace process. It seeks to answer a larger question and one with wide relevance for contemporary international politics: Why did Israeli foreign policy become so entangled in identity politics? In answering this question, this book helps us to understand the impact that identity politics can have upon the foreign policies of states, which all-too-often are believed to be dictated by *Realpolitik* considerations of security and power. According to the widely held "realist" view of International Relations, states are solely motivated by their need for power and security in order to survive in the anarchic conditions of the international system. For realists, security concerns underlie both the foreign policies of states and the violent conflicts between them. While this exclusive focus on security and conflict has often been criticized for slighting other important aspects of international politics (such as international cooperation and international trade, to name just two), it also fails to take into account the role that identity politics can play in shaping states' foreign policies and in fuelling conflicts, both within and between states—a serious omission for a perspective that is principally concerned with issues of national security.

In fact, the politics of collective identities (national, ethnic, religious, etc.) drive many violent conflicts around the world.[7] These "identity-based conflicts" tend to be especially protracted and hard to resolve.[8] Increasingly, scholars and practitioners in the field of conflict resolution now emphasize the necessity of addressing and reconciling the identity needs of both sides in a conflict.[9] Failure to take into account the importance of collective identities, according to this line of thinking, will doom peace negotiations and the settlement of intractable conflicts. It has even been argued that changes in collective identities are necessary in order for a protracted conflict to be fully transformed into a peaceful relationship,[10] and that true reconciliation between enemies requires the development of new collective identities.[11]

The case of Israel presented in this book offers an instructive example of the difficulties and risks this entails. The collective identity of Israeli Jews was forged in the midst of Israel's long-running and seemingly intractable conflict with the Palestinians. The conflict both shaped this identity and helped sustain it. Ending the conflict, therefore, required Israelis not only to make territorial concessions (according to the formula of "land for peace"), but also identity concessions. They had to revise their own national narrative and self-image. The extent to which Israelis have done this (and the internal resistance this has engendered) is one of the subjects of this book. In particular, in examining the attempt in the early 1990s by the late Israeli Prime Minister Yitzhak Rabin to revise Israeli collective identity in accordance with his peace policy toward the Palestinians and the domestic opposition this aroused, this book contributes to our understanding of the extent to which collective identities are resistant to change and the ways in which they can complicate peacemaking efforts.[12]

This book sets out to do three things—to explain the bitter domestic controversy in Israel over the Oslo peace process; to analyze the impact of Israeli national identity upon Israeli foreign policy; and to offer Israel as a case study from which we can glean broader insights about the relationship between national identity and foreign policy, so that we can better appreciate the importance of national identities in global politics.

The Persistent Power of National Identities

We live in an age in which the politics of identity is all-pervasive. It extends from the global to the personal, from the behavior of states to those of individuals. The language of identity permeates our daily lives as we seek to understand and define who we are and what we want, both as individuals and as collectives. It also permeates our political discourse as an ever-growing number of social groups around the world mobilize on behalf of common identities.[13] Everywhere, it seems, individuals and groups are engaged in asserting their identity, defending it, changing it, searching for it, or debating it. Sometimes these activities have little consequence except for those directly involved, but at other times the consequences can be far-reaching and dramatic. Since the end of the Cold War, the world has witnessed a veritable explosion of ethnic, nationalist, and religious conflicts in many different places, from the Balkans, to Central Asia, to South-East Asia, to Central Africa—all of which have been fueled, if not caused, by the politics of identity. Genocide, ethnic cleansing, religious fundamentalism, and neo-nationalism, all testify to the devastating and deadly potential of appeals to identity. Clearly, the politics of identity is a central feature of contemporary global politics.

Contrary to popular perception, however, although increasingly ubiquitous, the politics of identity is not a new phenomenon.[14] It would be historically myopic to view identity politics as simply the result of the end of the Cold War or current globalization. "Identity politics has been part and parcel of modern politics and social life for hundreds of years," writes social theorist Craig Calhoun.[15] Undoubtedly, the most dominant and successful form of identity politics over the last few centuries has been nationalism. Since its emergence in Europe at the end of the eighteenth century, the doctrine of nationalism has taken hold in almost every corner of the globe, and with it has come the assertion of national identities. National identities have become such a common and basic fact of social and political life that we tend to take them for granted. But what exactly are they? Precisely because national identities seem so obvious, we often fail to consider what they really entail.

It is essential for the purposes of this book, however, to clarify at the outset the meaning of the nebulous concept of national identity. A national identity is a nation's self-image or self-conception, that is, the socially shared set of ideas that make up how a nation imagines itself.[16] It comprises the collective memories, norms, values, beliefs, and ideals (not all of which need to be endorsed by all the members of the nation all the time) that are generally believed to distinguish members of the nation from non-nationals. A national identity accentuates what members of the nation share, and exaggerates differences with non-nationals.[17] Both similarity and difference are the fundamental bases of national identities, as they are with all collective identities. This points to the essential role of the "Other" in defining national identities. The Other is instrumental in helping to define national identities since a nation is defined partly in terms of whom it excludes or opposes.[18] Hence, a nation's interaction with and relationship to Others (i.e., other nations, states, etc.) may heavily influence its national identity.[19]

A national identity is by no means the only collective identity available to individuals. There are many collective identities and these do not necessarily have a clear or permanent hierarchy in relation to each other. In addition to nationality, some of the most prominent collective identities are those based upon gender, ethnicity, religion, social class, and race. Indeed, the forms of collective identity available to us are in theory almost infinitely open. Nevertheless, of all contemporary forms of collective identity, national identity is often the most powerful.[20] It has generally been able to "trump" other collective identities in its claim to political allegiance and loyalty (class being the foremost example[21]). National identities have exhibited an unparalleled emotional, cultural, social, and political power in the modern era. They have motivated acts of heroism and nobility, as well as acts of barbarism and depravity. Millions have died in their name, and no doubt more will continue to do so. Countless more lives are affected by them in a myriad of ways both large and small.

There are many reasons for the power of national identities.[22] Without entering into the long-running debate among scholars of nationalism over this issue, most scholars agree that a major reason for the strength of national identities is the role that states play in sustaining them (through public ceremonies and festivals, for instance, and in its memorabilia, symbols, and monuments).[23] States deliberately foster and promote national identities out of a need to ensure their popular legitimacy and the loyalty of their citizens. As Anthony Smith observes: "There is nothing very dynamic about citizenship or loyalty to most modern states, and most rulers are well aware of this. They, therefore, try to fuse state loyalty with national solidarity, making the latter the mainspring of political obligation."[24] As a result: "The appeal to national identity has become the main legitimation for social order and solidarity today."[25] The frequent portrayal of nationalism today as something that is either limited to the periphery (i.e., non-Western contexts), or else as something whose occurrence is exceptional, obscures the abiding importance of national identities in established nation-states.[26] Even in so-called postmodern Western societies, where the process of globalization is most advanced, people are continually reminded of their national identity in political discourses, cultural products, the media, and a host of other ways.[27]

It has become fashionable among intellectuals to claim that national identities are now endangered in today's globalized world. By encouraging and facilitating the development of global and local identities, globalization is undermining prevailing national identities from above and from below.[28] Hence, national identities are gradually being superseded by new supranational and subnational identities promoted by globalization.[29] This argument, however, mistakenly represents the relationship between national identities and supranational and subnational identities in a zero-sum manner, and thereby seriously overstates the degree to which the proliferation of such identities actually displaces national identities.[30] Instead, it is important to recognize that multiple identities can simultaneously coexist within individuals. Many people do not feel the need to choose between their national identity and a global and/or local identity; instead they possess all three (and many more), with the importance of each varying at different times and in different circumstances. Since multiple identities can coexist, "the issue is not the outright disappearance of the nation-state and of national identities but rather the proliferation of other identities alongside the nation-state."[31] It is, therefore, premature to announce the imminent demise of nations and nationalism. Such announcements have been made numerous times before, only to be contradicted by the continued salience of national identities. National identities have proven themselves to be remarkably resilient and, without disputing the power of globalization to transform identities and dissolve cultural boundaries, they look set to endure and remain a focus of political allegiance and emotional attachment for the foreseeable future.

National Identity and Foreign Policy

Even in the midst of contemporary globalization, therefore, national identities remain pervasive and powerful. Yet, despite the importance of national identities, scholars of International Relations have seldom taken them into account.[32] They have tended to either ignore them entirely or else relegate them to an epiphenomenal status, as an appendage of states. But it is surely essential that scholars attempt to understand the role of national identities in international politics.[33] This book joins a recent and ongoing scholarly effort to investigate this role.[34] In particular, it is concerned with examining how a national identity affects a state's foreign policy. Understanding the impact that a national identity can have upon foreign policy is critical to our understanding of international politics in the past, present, and future. The fact that many states do not simply define themselves as states but as "nation-states" has had profound implications for the manner in which they formulate and conduct their foreign policies.[35] The impact of the emergence of nationalism upon foreign policymaking in the nineteenth century is captured well in the following passage by Rodney Bruce Hall: "In the nationalist era, statesmen were no longer speaking with the voice of a prince, a dynastic house, or of a kingdom, or empire . . . Nor did they any longer articulate these interests and goals. The statesmen of nation-states began speaking in the voice of a sovereign people, a collective actor possessed of a collective identity and collective interests and goals, in the context of both domestic and international social interaction."[36]

Lest we think that such nationalist rhetoric belongs to an earlier age, it is worth recalling President George H.W. Bush's declaration upon announcing that the United States was sending military forces to Saudi Arabia at the outbreak of the Gulf crisis in August 1990: "In the life of a nation, we're called upon to define who we are and what we believe."[37] In a similar manner, President George W. Bush solemnly told the American public in a radio address four days after the terrorist attacks against the World Trade Center in New York and the Pentagon in Washington, D.C., on September 11, 2001: "Great tragedy has come to us and we are meeting it with the best that is in our country, with courage and concern for others. Because this is America. This is who we are. This is what our enemies hate and have attacked. And this is why we will prevail."[38] In effect, the president was saying that the attack on September 11 was directed against American identity, and that the ensuing "war on terrorism" would be a war in defense of this identity, and the values and qualities that define it. Such rhetoric powerfully evokes the national identity and discursively links the state's foreign policy to it. In this sense, foreign policy represents "the nation" to the rest of the world, it expresses who "we" are, what "we" value, and what "we" abhor.

A few scholars have noted the role of national identity in legitimizing a state's foreign policy. William Wallace, for instance, writes that: "Nationhood and national identity represent necessary myths which underpin foreign policy. They constitute the distinction between the 'national community,' which the government represents, and the foreigners with whom it deals; more than that, they legitimize the actions of government in defense of the national interest."[39] Similarly, Ilya Prizel argues that: "Foreign policy with its role as either the protector or the anchor of national identity, provides the political elite with a ready tool for mass mobilization and political cohesion . . . . All countries frequently use national identity to articulate their foreign policies and in turn, rely on foreign policy as a foundation of their legitimacy."[40]

The state's claim to represent the national identity of its population in its foreign policy, however, can be both an asset and a liability. Just as the national identity may legitimize a state's foreign policy, it can also delegitimize it if that foreign policy is perceived to contradict or harm the national identity. National identities can make some policies seem legitimate and desirable and others not so, and a foreign policy that is perceived to be contrary to the national identity is likely to arouse domestic opposition. National identities can, therefore, circumscribe the kind of foreign policies that states can undertake.

The "double-edged sword" that national identity represents in the realm of foreign policy is described in William Bloom's pathbreaking book, *Personal Identity, National Identity and International Relations.*[41] Bloom argues that no government can propose foreign policies which could be perceived as threatening to the national identity, since to do so would be to risk being perceived as itself a threat to national identity, thereby losing it popular support.[42] According to Bloom: "The mass national public will always react against policies that can be perceived to be a threat to national identity. The mass national public will always react favorably to policies which protect or enhance national identity."[43] As such: "Every government must be concerned about how its actions are perceived by the mass national public in relation to the national identity dynamic. A government's foreign policy may thus be dictated by internal domestic political realities as much as by the actual nature of its international relations."[44] National identities can, therefore, influence upon foreign policymaking due to a government's need to gain public approval for its foreign policies. They can act as a constraint upon the kinds of foreign policies that states can pursue since policy-makers are likely to lose public support if their foreign policies are seen to be contrary to the national identity. Thus, a national identity can exert an influence upon foreign policy by limiting the kinds of foreign policies policy-makers can pursue.

There is a second way in which a national identity can influence a state's foreign policy. That is by helping to constitute the interests that states pursue in their foreign policies. A growing body of theory in International Relations known as "constructivism" emphasizes the role of identities in constituting state interests.[45] State interests, according to constructivism, are derived from prior conceptions of identity.[46] As Alexander Wendt, a leading constructivist scholar writes: "Interests presuppose identities because an actor cannot know what it wants until it knows who it is . . . ."[47] An identity influences an actor's preferences by shaping what s/he regards as appropriate, intelligible, and/or desirable.[48] In line with this argument, a national identity can shape the definition of national interests that, in turn, determine a state's foreign policy and, by extension, behavior. Thus, it is by means of shaping national interests that a national identity influences foreign policy. Rarely, however, does a national identity determine particular foreign policy actions or behavior because a number of specific policies or actions may be compatible with the national identity.

The central argument of this book, therefore, is that national identities can shape states' foreign policies. This argument will be empirically supported through an in-depth case study of the way in which Israel's foreign policy has been profoundly influenced by Israeli national identity. Israel offers an excellent case study with which to demonstrate the relevance of national identity in foreign policy since it is located in a dangerous and unstable region and has faced long-standing security threats. If issues of identity are a "luxury" afforded to those whose security is not severely endangered, as some have charged, then identity issues should not enter into an Israeli foreign policy seemingly overwhelmingly concerned with pressing issues of security. But if Israeli foreign policy is more than just a response to the strategic imperatives arising from the external environment in which Israel is located; if it is shaped in important ways by Israeli national identity; then it offers persuasive evidence that national identity even influences the foreign policies of states which have traditionally been interpreted as quintessentially "realist."[49]

When analyzing the influence of a national identity upon a state's foreign policy, one has to be careful to avoid reifying the national identity (taking it as naturalized). National identities, like all collective identities, are socially constructed. They are accomplishments rather than givens. They do not simply exist, they have to be created. The construction of a national identity involves the active creation of an image or representation of the nation, which is typically conveyed through nationalist symbols and discourse, and widely propagated through a variety of cultural channels (such as the media and the educational system). In addition to analyzing how a national identity shapes a state's foreign policy, therefore, we must also pay attention to the construction of the national identity. This involves showing how the national identity has been discursively constructed, how it is understood, and how this understanding gives rise to the national interests that guide the state's foreign policy.[50] The construction of a national identity is not a one-off event. National identities are dynamic and open to change. They are never fixed, but always subject to being re-constructed and re-defined. At different times, national identities may be inscribed with quite different meanings. To fully examine the relationship between a national identity and a state's foreign policy, then, we need to know the definition or particular meaning of that identity at a particular time. This book will therefore examine the changing meaning of Israeli national identity as a result of domestic and international developments, and it will relate changes in the definition of Israeli national identity to changes in Israel's foreign policy priorities and behavior.

The meaning of a national identity is not only subject to change and revision, it can also become subject to intense debate and contestation. Political actors and domestic groups actively compete over the national identity in an attempt to establish their particular interpretation of, and the meanings associated with, the national identity. As Edward Said notes: "We need to regard society as the locale in which a continuous contest between adherents of different ideas about what constitutes the national identity is taking place."[51] While disagreements over what defines the national identity are a constant feature of political and cultural life, there are times (especially during periods of rapid social, economic, and political change) when debates over national identities become especially vociferous. In recent years, the sustained and passionate debates on national identities that have been taking place in many countries around the world suggest that national identities are now more fiercely contested and disputed than ever before. What are the political implications of this? More specifically, what is the impact on foreign policy when the definition of a national identity is contested? Are domestic debates over the national identity of any consequence for the state's foreign policy?

Israel offers an illuminating case study by which to answer this question since Israeli national identity has been the subject of extensive domestic debate and discord. Especially in the 1990s, it was clearly apparent that Israelis sharply disagreed about who they were and who they wanted to be. Indeed, this disagreement was so pronounced and so deep that many observers, both inside and outside the country, claimed that Israelis were suffering from an identity crisis.[52] A national identity crisis can be said to occur when the level of societal debate and conflict over the national identity becomes particularly extensive, intense, and divisive. It does not mean that previously the definition of the national identity went unchallenged. Nor should it be understood as suggesting an abrupt dissolution or collapse of the national identity. Rather, a crisis of national identity may gradually evolve over time and involve a growing awareness that the dominant conception of national identity is no longer sustainable or appropriate. In the words of Lucian Pye (who took the concept from the work of the psychologist Erik H. Erikson and introduced it into political science[53]): "[A]n identity crisis occurs when a community finds that what it had once unquestionably accepted as the physical and psychological definitions of its collective self are no longer acceptable under new historic conditions."[54] An identity crisis cannot be defined by objective criteria since, in the words of Pye: "It is . . . the interpretations a society gives to its experiences that govern the extent to which it enters into an identity crisis."[55]

In Israel's case, the belief that there was a crisis of Israeli national identity was widespread in the 1990s and regularly expressed by politicians, pundits, and ordinary citizens. Instead of being insulated from the crisis of Israeli national identity, Israel's foreign policy became hostage to it as the internal divisions over Israeli national identity were played out in divisions over Israeli foreign policy. In particular, Israel's attempt in the 1990s to make peace with the Palestinians became embroiled in the debate over Israeli identity. The domestic debate over the Oslo peace process was inseparable from the debate over Israeli identity. Hence, the fierce domestic controversy over the peace process in the 1990s fundamentally stemmed from the inability of Israelis to agree upon the definition of their collective identity. In such circumstances, it was impossible to achieve a public consensus over the peace process.

Plan of the Book

Now that the argument of this book has been sketched out, the next chapter presents a historical narrative of the construction of Israeli national identity, starting with the emergence of Zionism in Europe in the nineteenth century and concluding with the electoral victory of the Likud party in the

1977 Israeli general elections. In chapter 2, I discuss how Israel's foreign policy has been shaped by Israeli national identity, especially its Jewish component. I also describe the effort by Likud prime ministers, Menachem Begin and Yitzhak Shamir, to secure Israel's control over the West Bank and Gaza, and the repercussions within Israel of the Lebanon War and the first Palestinian Intifada. In chapter 3, I focus on the Oslo peace process between Israel and the Palestinians, examining how this "revolution" in Israeli foreign policy came about and how it was related to Israeli identity. Having established the linkage between Israeli national identity and the Oslo peace process, I analyze in chapter 4 the debate in Israel over the peace process in terms of a conflict between adherents of "civic" versus "ethno-religious" definitions of Israeli national identity. I also briefly discuss some of the other domestic debates and controversies that occurred in Israel in the late 1990s—over multiculturalism, religious-secular relations, the military draft, the Law of Return, the status of Palestinian Israelis, and post-Zionism—as symptoms of the crisis of Israeli national identity. Chapter 5 deals with the premierships of Ehud Barak and Ariel Sharon. I examine the key positions that Barak took during the negotiations with the Palestinians at the Camp David summit in July 2000; and the domestic reverberations within Israel of the failure of the Camp David summit and the subsequent outbreak of the second intifada in September 2000. Finally, in the conclusion, I summarize the book's argument, consider the critical domestic challenges facing Israeli society in the years ahead, and put the crisis of Israeli national identity into wider perspective as an example of a global trend.

CHAPTER 1

THE CONSTRUCTION OF ISRAELI
NATIONAL IDENTITY: FROM JEWS
TO ISRAELIS AND BACK AGAIN

*We will disappoint the Zionist movement and miss the mark if suddenly we
should begin philosophizing about who I am and what I am.*[1]

—David Ben-Gurion

What are we first and foremost, Jews or Israelis?[2]

—Gershom Scholem

Introduction

The politics of modern Israel is par excellence the politics of identity. Well
before the phenomenon gained the sustained attention of academics and
intellectuals, identity politics had shaped Israel's political landscape and
cultural discourse. Since the beginning of the Zionist movement, issues of
identity have engendered prolonged and agonizing debate, aroused intense
passions, and fueled bitter divisions. Indeed, the emergence of Zionism was
itself due in large measure to identity politics—both that of the Jews of
Europe in the late nineteenth century and that of the Christian European
populations in which they lived.

This chapter presents a historical narrative of the construction of Israeli
national identity. It begins with the birth of the Zionist movement in
Europe in the nineteenth century as a result of the crisis of Jewish identity
in the wake of the Enlightenment and the emancipation. Zionism was a secular, nationalist response to this crisis as it sought to transform a religious
Jewish identity into a modern, secular, national one. But despite Zionism's
avowed intention to break from the Jewish past, it selectively drew upon the
Jewish tradition in its discourse and symbols. While it sought a wholesale
transformation of traditional Jewish life, culture, and identity; it also promised a revitalization of the Jewish nation and a renewal of the glorious Jewish
national past. It simultaneously emphasized both continuity and change.

This dialectical relationship with the Jewish past shaped the way in which Zionist ideologues imagined the new Jewish nation that would emerge in its reclaimed homeland. On the one hand, they aspired to create a new nation, wholly different from Jews in the Diaspora. On the other hand, to do so would undermine Zionism's fundamental tenet that Jews were one nation, and jeopardize the vital link between Jews in Israel and those in the Diaspora. This dilemma bedeviled the Zionist project of nation-building. Initially, in the years before and in the first decade after Israel's founding, Judaism was not a central element in Israeli society, and Israeli national identity was defined more by civic ties to the state than by primordial ethnic and religious criteria. The classic sabra personified this new, secular Israeli national identity. A series of developments in the 1950s and 1960s (the Eichmann trial, the mass influx of more traditional Jews from the Middle East and North Africa and the state's failure to assimilate them, the Six Day War of 1967, and the political ascendancy of the Likud party), however, brought about a resurgence of Jewish traditionalism and the rise of an ethno-religious Israeli national identity in place of the previously dominant civic national identity—Jewishness replaced Israeliness in defining Israeli national identity.

The Identity Crisis of Modern European Jewry

Identity has been a perennial issue for Jews. From the time of their second exile from *Eretz Israel* ("The Land of Israel") by the Romans in 70 CE, Jews have faced the task of preserving their distinct identity in the midst of foreign and frequently hostile populations. That they have done so for almost three millennia is a singular achievement. This success, however, came at great cost as untold numbers of Jews gave up their lives rather than forsake their identities as Jews. Yet for all the anguish and misery that Jews have endured in preserving their identity, the issue of identity that Jews in the Diaspora traditionally faced had a stark simplicity to it: to observe the rules and rituals of Judaism (even if secretly as the *Marranos*—Jewish converts to Catholicism—did in the wake of the Spanish inquisition), or to assimilate and adopt the customs and habits of their gentile neighbors. What it meant to be Jewish, what the transmission of Jewish identity to succeeding generations entailed, was seldom, if ever, in doubt. Jews were defined by their adherence to religious Jewish law, and religion formed the bedrock of their identity. The questions, "who is a Jew?" and "what are the Jews?" were answered with reference to religious strictures by rabbis whose authority was unchallenged.

By the late eighteenth century, however, these questions increasingly came to occupy Jews in Europe for whom religious strictures and rabbinical authority no longer appeared absolute and uncontested. In time, they became the questions around which modern Jewish politics revolved, questions which increasingly appeared to permit no easy answer. Jewish identity became an issue in the wake of the European Enlightenment of the eighteenth century. Indeed, the issue of identity has been a defining characteristic of modern Jewish history, a period whose beginning is generally considered to have been marked by the French Revolution of 1789.[3] When Clermont Tonnerre stood in the French National Assembly in 1789 and urged that as individuals Jews should be granted equal rights, the so-called Jewish question was born. Ostensibly the question was one of loyalty—in order to have the rights and responsibilities of full citizenship Jews had to affirm their unswerving political loyalty to the state in which they resided—but it was essentially a question of identity since in order to do so they had to renounce any separate national consciousness or belonging. They were formally asked to do this in 1807 when Napoleon gathered an assembly of rabbis and Jewish notables in Paris (the *Sanhedrin*). They responded by declaring that the Jews of France were not a separate nation but members of the French nation who simply practiced the religion of Judaism. In this manner, the Jews gained equal rights in France and other states in Western Europe, a development known as the "emancipation."

The European Enlightenment and the emancipation of the Jews to which it gave rise marked a watershed in Jewish history,[4] and resulted in a profound identity crisis for European Jewry in the nineteenth century. It enabled Jews to assimilate into European societies as they had not been able to do before, and in the process secularized many of them. The identity crisis of European Jewry was born out of assimilation and secularization. As Michael Meyer has written: "It was the European Enlightenment [that] inaugurated the identity crisis for modern Jewry, as it drew them to new perspectives from which they began to question the content of their Jewishness."[5]

The identity crisis of European Jewry in the nineteenth century was met with a number of different and competing responses. Some aimed at combining the Enlightenment with personal adherence to the Jewish religion—notably the modern Orthodox movement founded by Samson Raphael Hirsch, the Conservative movement founded by Zacharias Frankel, and the Reform movement founded by Abraham Geiger. Others attempted to develop a secular Jewish identity based upon common ethnicity rather than religious belief. This attempt, labeled by Gideon Shimoni as "ethnicism," was particularly associated with the Jewish intelligentsia in Eastern Europe.[6] Suspended between the opposing poles of tradition and modernity, they sought to develop a synthesis that would allow them to maintain their particularistic Jewish identity within the context of modernity. The efforts of this group to articulate and sustain their Jewish identity in ethnic rather than religious terms generated a Jewish cultural nationalism, which, in turn, led to a full-blown nationalism in the form of Zionism. For the secular Jewish intelligentsia of Eastern Europe, Zionism was an attempt to reinvigorate and modernize Jewish identity, free from the shackles of religion. Zionism, then, was one response to assimilation and secularization.

But Zionism arose not only out of the activities of the Eastern European Jewish intelligentsia, but also out of the disillusionment experienced by some within the Jewish intelligentsia of Western Europe. Unlike their Eastern European counterparts for whom emancipation remained a distant and elusive prospect, the Jewish intelligentsia of Western Europe were already benefiting from emancipation. Many had no qualms about shedding their particularistic Jewish identities in favor of fully integrating into their host societies as equal national citizens. When the growth of modern anti-Semitism in the countries of Western Europe appeared, to certain members of this intelligentsia, to block this integration, however, their despair over their prospects for individual assimilation led some of them to turn to Zionism, as a means of *collective* assimilation.[7] What Jews could not achieve as individuals, they reasoned, could be achieved as a nation with their own homeland.

Zionism: One Movement, Divided

The Zionist movement, therefore, emerged out of the confluence of two separate but related developments.[8] They are related because both were the result of the processes of emancipation, modernization, and secularization that came in the wake of the European Enlightenment. They are separate because they originated, by and large, in different geographical domains and, by extension, out of different social and economic contexts. They are also separate because they had diametrically opposed motivations and goals. Whereas the Eastern European Jewish "ethnicists" sought to counter assimilation amongst secular Jews by articulating and creating the conditions for the development of a secular Jewish identity; the Western European Jewish "integrationists" sought to promote assimilation by creating the conditions for the "normalization of the Jewish people."[9] The former were concerned with the problem of Jewish identity rather than anti-Semitism, the latter were concerned with the problem of anti-Semitism rather than Jewish identity (toward which they were largely indifferent).

The difference between the two approaches was expressed most cogently by the Russian Hebrew writer Asher Ginsburg, who wrote under the name Ahad Ha'am, and was the leading spokesperson of the ethnicists. Writing two years after the groundbreaking publication of *The Jewish State* in 1895 by Theodore Herzl (who founded the Zionist Organization at the first Zionist Congress in Basle in 1897 and was the preeminent spokesman of the integrationists), Ha'am argued in his essay *The Jewish State and the Jewish Problem*: "The eastern form of the spiritual problem is absolutely different from the western. In the West it is the problem of the Jews; in the East, *the problem of Judaism*. The first weighs on the individual; the second, on the nation. The one is felt by Jews who have had a European education; the other, by Jews whose education has been Jewish. The one is the product of anti-Semitism, and is dependent on anti-Semitism for its existence; the other is a natural product of a real link with a millennial culture, and will remain unsolved and unaffected even if the troubled of the Jews all over the world attain comfortable economic positions, are on the best possible terms with their neighbors, and are admitted to the fullest social and political equality."[10]

Judaism was almost entirely absent from Herzl's thinking—demonstrated most clearly by the fact that he first considered a mass baptism for Jewry as a solution to anti-Semitism. In his utopian novel *Altneuland* (Old New Land), Herzl portrayed a society that was secular, progressive, cosmopolitan, and pluralist, guaranteeing full equality for both Jews and non-Jews, who were partners in a cooperative venture. Ha'am vehemently criticized Herzl's vision in *Altneuland* for ignoring the distinct character of the Jewish national spirit, and simply wishing to copy Western culture. In his scathing review of the book, he posed a question that continues to reverberate in Israel through to the present day: "Wherein is the Jewishness of this cosmopolitan society of Herzl's imaginings?"[11] The conflict between Ha'am's "cultural Zionism" and the "political Zionism" championed by Herzl underlined the profound divisions within the nascent Zionist movement.

These divisions took on concrete form at the sixth Zionist Congress of 1903 in the "Uganda episode." Motivated by the simple necessity to find a safe haven for the Jews at a time of mounting anti-Semitism in Europe (45 Jews had just been massacred and over 600 wounded in the Kishinev pogrom of April 1903), Herzl proposed to the Congress' delegates that they accept the British offer of a Jewish state in Uganda. Herzl's proposal was supported by the West European and religious delegates (the latter opposing Jewish settlement in Palestine on the religious grounds that this had to wait until the messianic age), but was fiercely opposed by the Russian Zionist delegation led by Chaim Weizmann who insisted that only Palestine could serve as the Jewish national home. As a result, Herzl was eventually forced to back down.[12] After the Uganda episode, mass Jewish settlement in Palestine became the Zionist movement's overriding goal, and its efforts were directed toward encouraging Jewish emigration primarily from the

Russian Empire (where the majority of European Jews lived) and Eastern Europe and creating the conditions for a viable Jewish national home in Palestine.

The division between cultural and political Zionism was by no means the only division within the Zionist movement. Three distinct ideological streams emerged within it—"Labor Zionism," "Revisionist Zionism," and "religious Zionism." Labor Zionism, which originated in Russia during the first decade of the twentieth century, synthesized socialism and Jewish nationalism in arguing that the creation of a Jewish working class was necessary for achieving Jewish national and economic independence in its historic homeland.[13] Labor Zionists emphasized *Halutziyut* (pioneering) involving physical labor and settlement of the land. They established *kibbutzim* (agricultural communes), the main Zionist militias (the Haganah and Palmach), and the Mapai party (Israel Workers' party—later merged into the Labor party), which dominated the institutions of the *Yishuv* (the name given to the Jewish community in British Mandatory Palestine).

Revisionist Zionism, championed by Vladimir Ze'ev Jabotinsky, was Labor Zionism's chief ideological rival. Influenced by the currents of romantic nationalism in which he grew up, Jabotinsky articulated a vision of integral nationalism and stressed militaristic values. Revisionist Zionists rejected the socialist utopia preached by the advocates of Labor Zionism. Their model individual was not the pioneering Jewish worker, but the heroic Jewish fighter. What particularly distinguished Jabotinsky's Revisionist Zionism from other varieties of Zionism was its staunch insistence upon maintaining the territorial integrity of *Eretz Israel*. Jabotinsky's overriding political objective was to establish a Jewish state with a Jewish majority on both sides of the River Jordan. Any political settlement that did not recognize Jewish sovereignty over the entire *Eretz Israel* was inadequate and thus rejected outright. Jabotinsky and his followers, therefore, consistently rejected proposals to partition Palestine into an Arab and a Jewish state. Whereas Labor Zionists believed that compromise with the Arabs was both possible and desirable, Revisionist Zionists maintained that it was neither possible nor desirable. The Revisionists' approach to the Arab-Jewish conflict over Palestine was fundamentally fatalistic, stressing the inevitability of a conflict between Jews and Arabs that would ultimately be decided through the force of arms. These views formed the basis of a right-wing ideology, which was later represented by the Herut party (which eventually merged into the Likud party).

The third main ideological stream within the Zionist movement was religious Zionism, whose spiritual leader was Rabbi Avraham Yitzhak Kook, the first chief rabbi of the Ashkenazi Jewish community in British Mandatory Palestine. Contrary to most Orthodox Jews at the time who regarded secular Zionism as a heretical movement that defied the will of God by trying to end Jewish exile from *Eretz Israel* before the arrival of the messiah, Kook supported the secular Zionists in the belief that the return of Jews to their homeland represented the beginning of the process of divine redemption. He argued that secular Zionists, the pioneers who had begun emigrating from Europe to Palestine, farming the land, and building settlements, were carrying out God's will—albeit unknowingly—and would eventually return to religion. Kook, therefore, justified the participation of religious Jews in the Zionist national project, and deemed cooperation with antireligious pioneers, physical labor, and modern education to be religious requirements, necessary to ensure the ultimate Jewish spiritual restoration in Zion.

The Zionist movement, therefore, was never united. It was composed of competing factions, advancing different, even contradictory, principles, visions, and strategies, according to their various ideological perspectives. Yet for all their differences and disagreements, all Zionists shared one fundamental belief—that the Jews constituted a nation and had always done so (there was no agreement, however, on the nature and characteristics of the Jewish nation, especially concerning its relationship to Judaism). Despite the fact that Jews were geographically dispersed, spoke different languages, practiced different customs, maintained different social and political allegiances, and possessed different histories and traditions, Zionists insisted that they constituted one nation.

The Zionist claim of Jewish nationhood specifically rested upon the emerging national consciousness of Eastern European Jews in the late nineteenth and early twentieth centuries. This was historically novel, largely a result of the rapid demographic expansion and urbanization of Jews in Eastern Europe during the course of the nineteenth century. In particular, the concentration of a vast number of Jews in an area known as the "Pale of Settlement," and the social, cultural, and economic life that developed therein facilitated the emergence in the late nineteenth century of a national consciousness within a critical mass of Eastern European Jews. However, and contrary to Zionism's claim, the national sentiment that steadily developed amongst Eastern European Jews was not shared by Jews elsewhere (or, at least, not nearly to the same extent or in the same manner). Hence, Zionists were faced with the task of developing a nationalist consciousness and constructing a national identity.[14]

In fact, despite discursively portraying their endeavors as bringing about a national revival and renewal, leading Zionists were well aware that the Jewish nation of which they spoke had yet to really come into existence. In 1892, for instance, Ahad Ha'am, one of the most influential Zionist thinkers, lamented that: "We are not yet a people; we are only [individual]

Jews."[15] Years later, in a meeting with Israeli writers and intellectuals shortly after Israel's establishment in 1948, Prime Minister Ben-Gurion stated: "This nation will be built from many tribes. It is necessary to melt down the debris of Jewish humanity which is scattered throughout the world and will come to Israel, in the melting-pot of Independence and national sovereignty."[16] He also stated during the 1951 election campaign: "I see in these elections the shaping of a nation for the state because there is a state but not a nation."[17] The Zionists were not only engaged in creating a state for the Jews, they were also engaged in creating a nation for the state.

The Zionist Nation-Building Project

Recent studies of nations and nationalism have emphasized their modern, constructed, and invented character. Benedict Anderson's characterization of the nation as an "imagined community,"[18] and Eric Hobsbawm's reference to the "invention of tradition," have become leitmotifs in academic, and even popular, discussions of nationalism.[19] It is strange, therefore, that whilst the modernity of nations and nationalism is now widely recognized, the Jews are still commonly regarded as a perennial nation, indeed perhaps the oldest extant nation in history. But as Uri Ram points out: "The national features imputed to Jewishness by Zionism were not initially taken for granted or widely accepted by Jews in general, and therefore their later almost universal acceptance should be considered as an outcome of invention and persuasion (and eventually Nazi persecution) rather than as a 'natural' and inevitable evolution of Jewishness as such."[20] What did this process of "invention and persuasion" involve? How was the Jewish nation "imagined" by Zionists? What characteristics did they impute to it, and why? These are questions that go to the heart of the Zionist project of nation-building. They imply that this project was not dissimilar from that of other modern nationalisms, and that, contrary to its own self-depiction, the Zionist project did not just involve bringing about the "return" of the "Jewish nation" to its ancestral "homeland," but also involved endowing these notions with new meaning and political force. This crucial aspect of the Zionist project is frequently obscured in accounts of Zionism and the creation of the State of Israel that simply see them as the culmination of Jewish history.

To argue that Zionists, like nationalists elsewhere, were engaged in nation-building and the construction of a national identity does not mean that they simply invented a nation ex nihilo, or that their efforts were pure fabrication. Although nations and nationalism are historically novel phenomena, some nations emerged from older, premodern ethnic communities or "ethnies," characterized by cultural affinities such as common historical memories, symbols, myths, and rituals, rather than actual physical kinship ties.[21] These preexisting ethnic identities and histories impose limits on what can be done in the name of the nation. Ethnic traditions, memories, myths, and symbols shape nationalist discourse since nationalists must appeal to the masses, and in order to do so they regularly draw upon the ethnic past to appear "authentic." Nationalists, therefore, are often engaged in the "rediscovery" and "re-appropriation" of tradition, and not simply its "invention." A national identity, then, is a social construction, yet it utilizes raw materials: the historical reservoir of popular traditions, memories, myths, and symbols, which form the building blocks for its construction. This clearly applies to the case of the Zionist construction of a new secular Jewish national identity as it extensively utilized preexisting Jewish traditions, memories, myths, and symbols.

Zionism was a secular Jewish nationalist movement, which sought to transform a traditionally religious identity (albeit one with ethnic dimensions) into a modern secular national identity. As one scholar has written: "What we see in Israel, and in the Zionist movement which created it, is a deliberate attempt to create secular nationalism and a secular identity out of a collective history which is totally marked by religion."[22] Zionism was conceived of and celebrated as a radical departure from the Jewish tradition. Secular Zionists were fiercely hostile to the Jewish religion, which they frequently derided as irrational, regressive, and repressive. At best, Judaism (as a religion) was seen as a means to preserve Jewish identity in exile. Hence, the end of exile proclaimed by Zionism meant that Judaism was redundant. The early Zionist pioneers who established Jewish settlements in Palestine were "emphatically secular, anti-religious and even anti-traditional."[23] Ideologically and practically, they stressed agriculture and settling the land, activities that were explicitly secular and viewed as efforts to take charge of their own fate in contrast to the "holy" activity of religious Jews whose time was spent studying religious texts. Yet, ironically, the language with which secular Zionists extolled these "pioneering" activities was infused with Jewish religious terminology (e.g., "redemption of the individual," "redemption of the land"). Indeed, Zionist terms like "redemption," "return," and "the end of exile" conveyed eschatological meaning, pointing to the messianic element within secular Zionism. Most paradoxically, the land to be settled was the biblical "Promised Land" ("Zion") to which Jews in the Diaspora had prayed to return for millennia.

Despite its antipathy to Judaism, secular Zionism reconstructed and reinterpreted traditional Jewish religious texts, symbols, celebrations, practices, and myths to suit its interests.[24] Zionism's nationalistic appropriation of the Jewish tradition is clearly evident in its use of the Bible, which was instrumental in the construction of Israeli national identity. "Before the

Holocaust," writes Baruch Kimmerling, "the Bible served as the central core narrative and the most powerful constitutive myth of the new collectivity."[25] David Ben-Gurion, Israel's founding father and first prime minister, himself recognized the important role the Bible played in forming Israeli national identity, writing in his book *Iyunim Ba'Tanakh* (Biblical Analyses): "The Bible was, without doubt, one of the central agents in the shaping of our nation."[26] This was due to the Bible's role in Zionist historiography, which involved a "Biblicalization of Jewish history and identity."[27] The Bible was used in Zionism's construction of a national narrative, which was essential for its representation of the Jews as a nation. A national narrative is a key ingredient in the formation of a national identity, providing a common "story line" for the nation (regardless of its historical accuracy), describing its origins and seminal experiences and depicting it as a "unified group moving through history."[28] The difficulty faced by Zionist ideologues in constructing a national narrative for the Jews, however, was that through most of history they were not unified. How could there be a common "story line" for a people that had been dispersed around the world for thousands of years? As Ram writes: "Jewish national ideologues faced a serious problem weaving different episodes, experienced by different groups in distinct periods and distant locations, into a single collective biography. That these episodes do converge into the biography of a single historical subject was far from obvious. The resolution of this fundamental quandary became the major purpose of the invented national narrative."[29]

Zionist historiography proposed a new narrative of Jewish history, divided into distinct periods corresponding to periods of activity and heroism and periods of submission and passivity. The two periods of heroism were the period before 135 CE, when the last Jewish rebellion against the Romans ended, and the period after 1880, when Zionist settlement activity in Palestine began. The intervening years (1,745 in total) were dismissed as years of submission and passivity and ones that should be erased from the collective memory. Zionism's representation of Jewish history after the Biblical period—the period of "exile"—was highly negative. Typical was Ben-Gurion's description of the period of exile as consisting of "persecution and legal discrimination, the Inquisition, and pogroms; of self-sacrifice and martyrdom."[30] The Zionists' denigration of the period of exile was adopted from their predecessors in the *Haskalah* (the Jewish "enlightenment"). But the Zionists went further in their criticism of the exile, disparaging both the exile (expressed in the concept of *shelilat ha'galut*—"negation of the condition of exile") and those who were its products (*shelilat ha'gola*—"condemnation of those people who live in exile"). The Jew of the Diaspora became the Other against which the new national identity was defined. Rhetorically, the distinction between the Diaspora Jew and the "new Jew" that Zionism intended to produce was represented in the Zionists' use of the term "Hebrew" (which was later replaced by the term "*sabra*" to refer to the native Jew of Palestine).[31] As Ben-Gurion declared in March 1949: "It is necessary to create a Hebrew character and style, which did not exist, which could not have existed, in the Diaspora, among a people without a homeland, without Independence and national freedom."[32] The widespread use of the term "Hebrew" during the pre-state period—as in "Hebrew work," "Hebrew youth," and the like—established symbolic continuity with a purportedly glorious ancient national past and discontinuity with the period of exile.[33]

The Zionists' ideal of the new Jew or "new Hebrew" was born in opposition to the negative stereotype of the "Diaspora Jew." The idealized physical image of the new Hebrew—youthful, slender, tall, muscular, healthy—his renowned bravery, camaraderie, nonchalance, and patriotism were all emphasized in direct contrast to Zionism's representation of the Diaspora Jew as old, sickly, weak, cowardly, rootless, and neurotic. The fact that the characteristics of the new Hebrew were defined in dialectical opposition to those of the "Jew" is clear in Jabotinsky's description of the Zionist project of creating the new Hebrew: "Our starting point is to take the typical Yid [the derogatory Russian term for Jew] of today and to imagine his diametrical opposite . . . because the Yid is ugly, sickly, and lacks decorum, we shall endow the ideal image of the Hebrew with masculine beauty. The Yid is trodden upon and easily frightened and, therefore, the Hebrew ought to be proud and independent. The Yid is despised by all and, therefore, the Hebrew ought to charm all. The Yid has accepted submission and, therefore, the Hebrew ought to learn how to command. The Yid wants to conceal his identity from strangers and, therefore, the Hebrew should look the world straight in the eye and declare: 'I am a Hebrew!' "[34] This highly disparaging portrayal of the Diaspora Jew clearly resembled anti-Semitic stereotypes, and suggests the degree to which Zionists had internalized the prevalent anti-Semitic perception of the Jew. Zionists viewed the Jews of the Diaspora with scorn and derision (despite the fact that they themselves were born and raised in the Diaspora). Their attitude toward Diaspora Jews is expressed in the famous Hebrew poem "In the City of Slaughter" written in reaction to the Kishinev pogrom in 1903 by Chaim Nachman Bialik, the "poet laureate" of the *Yishuv*. The poem contained these lines describing the behavior of the Jewish victims:

> It was the flight of mice they fled
> The scurrying of roaches was their flight;
> They died like dogs, and they were dead![35]

The analogy of the Jewish victims with mice, roaches, and dogs conveys the entirely unsympathetic manner with which they were regarded by Jews in the *Yishuv*. This was a common theme in the Hebrew literature of the *Yishuv*, in which Diaspora Jews were invariably portrayed as helpless victims, as "objects rather than subjects."[36] The implication was clear, only in Palestine could the Jew cease to be a passive victim and regain his subject-hood and pride.

But it was not enough to simply emigrate from the lands of the Diaspora and settle in *Eretz Israel*. According to Labor Zionists such as Nahman Syrkin and Yosef Chaim Brenner, the condition of the Diaspora could only be overcome by rejecting the "dead weight" of the past and constructing a new "Hebrew culture" on its ruins. After enduring millennia of debilitating exile, the Jewish people needed to be "reborn" in their homeland. In this sense, "Zionism proclaimed a contradiction: a nation which must be preserved through being transformed."[37] This aspect of the Zionist project is frequently overlooked in accounts that stress national self-determination as Zionism's end-goal. Yet the creation of a new Jew, as much as the demand for statehood, was central to the Zionist project. As Amnon Rubinstein has written: "Zionism is not content with returning the Jewish people to its lost sovereignty and never-forgotten homeland; it also seeks to be the midwife who helps the Jewish people give birth to a new kind of man. This revolution—no less than the political craving for independence—is the very basis of Zionist philosophy"[38] Thus, Micha Yosef Berdichevsky, a member of the Eastern European Jewish intelligentsia in the late nineteenth century and an influential Zionist thinker, argued that the new Hebrew had to make a decisive choice: "To be the last Jews or the first Hebrews," to be "the last Jews—or the first of a new nation."[39] Brenner went even further, arguing that the new Hebrew/Jew could sever all ties to the Jewish religion and culture. As he bluntly put it: "The new Jews . . . have nothing to do with Judaism."[40]

Secular Zionism, therefore, proclaimed a wholesale rejection of millennia of Jewish life, culture, history, and identity. Anything associated with Jewish life in the Diaspora was rejected, such as rabbinical Judaism, the Yiddish language (in its place, Zionists revived and modernized biblical Hebrew),[41] and even traditional Jewish names (which were replaced with Biblical names or totally new Hebrew ones).[42] Thus, according to one scholar, the "almost total rejection of Diaspora traditions is the cornerstone and capstone of the new Israeli identity, the most tangible product of Zionist ideology."[43] Yet for all their pronounced hostility toward the Jewish religious tradition and disdain for the heritage of the past, the early Zionists were profoundly ambivalent at heart, unable to escape the fact that they were themselves products of that heritage, and thus to discard it meant abandoning some part of themselves. This ambivalence was powerfully conveyed by Berdichevsky when he wrote: "When we defeat the past, we ourselves are defeated—and on the other hand, if the past is victorious, then again we and the sons of our sons are vanquished."[44] Elsewhere, he expressed his inner turmoil and anguish: "Sometimes all my thoughts, all my meditations and the values I have destroyed, turn upside down before me . . . Sometimes I feel I am killing myself."[45] In a similar vein, Brenner rhetorically asked: "How shall we be us without us?"[46]

The Age of the Sabra: A New Israeli Identity

This question hung over the Zionist project to create the new Hebrew and foster a new national identity. In essence, it raised the issue of how much Jewish tradition, religion, history, and culture should inform the new national identity. That is, the issue involved the degree of continuity between Hebrew/Israeli identity and earlier Jewish identity and what the content of that identity should be. The issue was raised, for example, in October 1949 during a lengthy discussion between Ben-Gurion and a number of Israeli writers and intellectuals, when the writer Eliezer Steinmann asked: "The question is, what are we carrying over from Judaism into Israeliness? What do we consider the solid values and what is secondary, which of the old things are we willing to give our lives for, and which are we not? . . . We are deeply stirred and anxious to discover the new form that we are taking, the new, Israeli core which is forming inside us, what links us to the Jewish culture and what to that of other nations, how far can we go from our sources without endangering our distinction and even our existence?"[47] Zionism provided no clear guidance on this issue. As Gershom Scholem observed: "Zionism has never really known itself completely— whether it is a movement of continuation and continuity, or a movement of rebellion. From the very beginning of its realization, Zionism has contained two utterly contradictory trends . . . . It is clear that the conflict between continuity and rebellion is a determining factor in the destiny of Zionism."[48]

Despite Zionism's ambivalence toward the relationship between Jewish identity and Israeli national identity, it always regarded the latter as ultimately inseparable from the former. Although the Zionist discourse of the "new Hebrew" implied a dramatic contrast to its "Jewish" predecessor, Zionists rejected a total rupture between the two.[49] "Canaanism," however, an ideology that emerged in the *Yishuv* in the late 1930s and early 1940s amongst a small group of intellectuals, artists, and writers, completely rejected the link with the Jewish past and Judaism.[50] The so-called Canaanite movement (also known as the "Young Hebrews"), whose central figure was the poet Yonatan Ratosh,[51] espoused a secular nativist ideology that sought a total separation between the emerging Hebrew nation and Jews in the Diaspora.[52] In a sense, Canaanism represented a reductio ad absurdum of Zionism's dismissive attitude toward the culture of the Jewish Diaspora. Canaanism asserted that the new Hebrew did not just represent a transformation of a long-existing Jewish identity (as Zionists claimed), but a completely new identity founded a territorial-linguistic basis rather than an ethno-religious one (although new, this Hebrew identity, according to Canaanism, had an ancient basis in the Hebrew-speaking civilization of pre-biblical times[53]). Whereas the Zionists' "new Hebrew" was a transformed Jew, but a Jew nonetheless, the Canaanites' "new Hebrew" was no longer Jewish at all.[54] As Ratosh unequivocally declared in articulating the main principles of the Canaanite movement in 1944: "Whoever is not a native of this land, the land of the Hebrews, cannot become a Hebrew, is not a Hebrew, and never was. And whoever comes from the Jewish dispersion, its times and its places, is, from the beginning to the end of days, a Jew, not a Hebrew, and he can be nothing but a Jew . . . . And a Jew and a Hebrew can never be the same. Whoever is a Hebrew cannot be a Jew, and whoever is a Jew cannot be a Hebrew."[55] The new Hebrew nation that Canaanism championed was defined by geography and language. This meant that non-Jews (e.g., Arabs and other non-Arab minorities) as well as Jews could become part of the Hebrew nation, as long as they spoke Hebrew and assimilated into Hebrew culture.

For Zionists, Canaanism was esoteric and heretical; and the Canaanite movement never gained more than a small number of adherents (at the peak of its influence, it had no more than about two dozen active, official members[56]). The Canaanites were of marginal importance politically, but as a literary and artistic avant-garde they gave expression to a wider cultural attitude in Israeli society and offered a radical answer to the problematic issue of the relationship between Jewish identity and Israeli national identity. As an anti-Zionist secular territorial nationalist discourse, Canaanism was culturally influential, particularly among young, native Israelis.[57] It openly expressed a popular nativist sentiment at the time, involving a feeling of estrangement from Diaspora Jewry and rebelliousness against the Jewish tradition. As the literary and cultural critic Baruch Kurzweil wrote in his influential 1952 essay on the Canaanite movement: "The spokesmen of this movement state openly what a large section of the youth in this country think secretly."[58] Thus, although Canaanism never came close to challenging Zionism's overwhelming ideological dominance, its development and cultural influence in the 1940s and early 1950s testified to the growing divide between Hebrew/Israeli identity and Jewish identity. According to Akiva Orr, the Canaanite movement represented: "the first assertion of the unbridgeable cultural gap between Jewishness and Israeliness."[59]

The appearance of Canaanism on the Israeli cultural scene in the 1940s, therefore, is a revealing indication of the tension between Jewishness and Israeliness in Israeli national identity.

After the establishment of the State of Israel in May 1948, the emergence of a new Israeli identity appeared to be almost inevitable. Writing in 1949 after visiting the new state, Arthur Koestler expressed his belief that an Israeli nation distinct from Jews elsewhere was likely to emerge in Israel. "One thing seems fairly certain," Koestler wrote, "within a generation or two Israel will become an entirely un-Jewish country."[60] A few years later another astute observer, Isaiah Berlin, predicted the development of "a new type of man and citizen" in Israel, commenting that: "If a new nation is born which differs from the Jews of the outside world, if a gap occurs—if the Israeli nation gradually becomes almost (never wholly) as different from the Jews of the outside world as other nations are, we should have no ground of complaint."[61]

The sabras—those who were born and grew up during Israel's formative years (roughly the period between 1930 and 1960)—seemed to many to be the representatives of this new Israeli national identity.[62] The leading members of this group (who were no more than a few hundred) became a reference group or "cultural archetype" for their generation and subsequent generations of Israelis.[63] These "classic Sabras" appeared as the harbingers of the new Israeli identity and were responsible for developing an array of cultural symbols, styles, and practices which then became identified as "Israeli." As Oz Almog writes in his sociohistorical portrait of the sabra generation: "Even though the Sabras were proportionally a small part of society, they were not perceived by the broader public as a marginal sector of singular aspect, but rather as representatives—in their character, style, language, and values—of the new Israeli identity."[64]

The idealized sabras were renowned for their courage, idealism tempered with pragmatism, and self-sacrificing patriotic devotion to the homeland and the Zionist enterprise, a devotion they displayed through physical labor on the *kibbutzim* and through their acts of heroism on the battlefield in the 1948 war, which broke out immediately upon the proclamation of the new State of Israel. More than anything else, it was the 1948 war that immortalized the sabras in Israel's collective consciousness as the image of the fallen soldier in Israeli culture became identified with the mythological image of the sabra.[65] The sabras were also famed for their strong sense of camaraderie, sociability, and solidarity, qualities expressed and reinforced through a variety of cultural practices, such as the popular *Hora* dance, public singing, and campfires (*kumzitz*), all of which became part of the new Israeli national tradition.[66] The stereotypical sabra was popularized in the 1940s and 1950s as he appeared in Israeli fiction, poetry, songs, painting, sculpture, cinema, theater, and entertainment.[67]

The sabras were, therefore, the bearers of the new Israeli identity, one that was starkly at odds with traditional Jewish identity. They embodied, both metaphorically and literally, the new Hebrew that Zionism aspired to create in opposition to its Other—the Diaspora Jew.[68] The rise of an indigenous Israeli identity, however, although widely regarded as a testament to the success of the Zionist project, raised serious problems for a state which claimed to represent not merely its citizens, but Jews all over the world and which was established on the basis of the claim that all Jews, wherever they were, constituted a single nation. If a separate Israeli nation was emerging, one in which Judaism was increasingly remote, would this not undermine Zionism's fundamental tenet? And if Israeli Jews began to see themselves as unrelated to Jews in the Diaspora, would this not jeopardize Israel's self-declared mission to represent the interests of Jews worldwide and gather them all within their ancestral homeland? Moreover, how would Diaspora Jewry—on whose political and economic support Israel depended—react if Jews in Israel regarded them as altogether alien and different? In the first two decades of Israel's existence such questions were far from hypothetical. A survey of Israeli high school students carried out in the mid-1960s, for instance, found that about 50 percent of students surveyed regarded Diaspora Jews as a "different people."[69] The alienation felt by Israeli Jews toward those in the Diaspora was also revealed in a survey which showed that almost one-third of Israeli parents and students believed that the main cause of anti-Semitism lay in the characteristics of Diaspora Jews themselves.[70] These statistics clearly support one scholar's statement that: "Until the 1960s . . . Israeli Jews seemed increasingly indifferent if not alienated from their Jewish past."[71]

From Israel's establishment through the 1950s and early 1960s, Judaism was not a central element in Israeli society, and the new Israeli collective identity was defined more in terms of "Israeliness" than "Jewishness." Under this more civic than ethno-religious conception of Israeli national identity, at least in principle, non-Jews could also be considered "Israeli" and part of the new Israeli nation. Thus, Ben-Gurion declared in December 1947: "In our state there will be non-Jews as well—and all of them will be equal citizens; equal in everything without exception; that is: the state will be their state as well."[72] Similarly, the "Declaration of the Establishment of the State of Israel" on May 14, 1948, stated: "The State of Israel . . . will foster the development of the country for the benefit of all its inhabitants . . . it will ensure complete equality of social and political rights to all its inhabitants irrespective of religion."[73]

In line with this civic discourse, those Palestinians who remained in Israel after the 1948 war were given the right to vote, to serve in the Knesset (which they did from the very beginning), and were granted Israeli citizenship in 1950.[74] But despite the official guarantee of equality before the law with Jews, the reality for Palestinians in Israel was far from one of enjoying equal citizenship with their Jewish counterparts. Until the end of 1966, most lived under military rule, and were subject to strict curfew, with severe restrictions on their physical mobility and on their permitted political activity.[75] This was done on the official grounds that "Israeli Arabs" (as they were designated by the state) posed a potential security threat to the fledgling state (since they could act as a "fifth column" within Israel in the context of the ongoing Arab-Israeli conflict). As a result, they were almost completely segregated from Israeli Jews, and they had little opportunity to participate in the political, economic, cultural, and social life of the new state. No attempt was made by Israel's leaders to integrate them into Israeli society. The prevailing ideology of the "melting pot" was not applied to Palestinian citizens. Whilst the government attempted to overcome the cleavages between religious and secular Jews, and between Ashkenazim (Jews originally from Europe) and Sephardim (Jews originally from the Middle East and North Africa, also known as Mizrahi ["Eastern"] Jews); no real efforts were made to overcome the cleavage between Arabs and Jews in Israel. On the contrary, this cleavage was sustained and even intensified as a result of the military government. As Ilan Peleg writes: "The Military Government not only 'marked' the Arabs as second-class citizens; it declared them to be an unmeltable, unintegratable minority, people of a different kind, the 'ultimate other.' The physical separation of the Arabs, their ghettoization via the Military Government, thus became not merely a fact of political significance, but a reality of far-reaching psychological importance."[76]

The fact that the "Israeli Arab" community was treated by the state as a hostile minority and was widely regarded as such by Israeli-Jewish society clearly indicates that Israeli national identity was not purely civic during Israel's first decades. Jewishness, although not dominant at this time, was still an integral component of Israeli national identity. The boundaries of national belonging were drawn around the Jewish community and excluded Palestinian Israelis.[77] Yet, for most Israelis, Israeli national identity was still understood to be civic, despite the restrictions placed upon the country's Palestinian citizens.

Behind the rise of a new, civic-oriented (though also exclusionary) Israeli identity lay a strong state with Ben-Gurion at its head (he was prime minister and defense minister from 1948 to 1963, with only a brief interregnum). In its first two decades, the Israeli state was powerful, and effectively controlled society.[78] In fact, the state was almost hegemonic in its relations with society.[79] The state used its immense influence over the Israeli population in order to accomplish the task of nation-building. It helped foster the new Israeli nationalism by establishing national holidays, commemorations, ceremonies, and symbols. It disseminated national myths and values through its dominance of the media and popular culture. The educational system and the military (the "Israel Defense Forces" [IDF], the successor to the pre-state Jewish underground militia, the Haganah) were especially important instruments in the nation-building project. The educational system was ideologically mobilized with the explicit goal of instilling ideals and values and not just knowledge.[80] Likewise, the army was used not just for the purposes of defense and national security, but as a means of socialization and national integration. Ben-Gurion described the army as "a pioneering, educating force, nation-building, wilderness-redeeming . . . molder of the nation's leaders, the cultural instrument of the ingathering of the exiles, their unification and spiritual uplifting."[81] He saw the army as a means to build the nation and explicitly advocated this role for it. In a speech to the Knesset, for example, he stated: "I have been a Zionist all my life and I do not deny the existence of Israel, heaven forbid . . . but . . . even the English nation was not always that nation . . . but was composed of different tribes . . . fighting one another. And only after a development of hundreds of years did they become one nation . . . . We do not have hundreds of years, and without the instrument of the army . . . we will not soon be a nation . . . . We must guide the progress of history, accelerate it, direct it . . . . This requires a framework of duty . . . a framework of national discipline."[82]

For Ben-Gurion, the state was the primary agent of nation-building. He sought to transform and unify a heterogeneous Israeli society through the power and prestige of the state and through the political dominance of his Mapai party which acted as an arm of the state.[83] The importance and centrality of the state for Ben-Gurion was encapsulated in his doctrine of *mamlachtiyut* (statism).[84] In the narrow sense, *mamlachtiyut* meant that the state should take control of functions that had previously been provided by political parties or sectarian interests. Ben-Gurion's disbanding of the Etzel and Palmach militias in 1948, and the abolition of the Labor Zionist stream of education in 1953 are examples of the application of this doctrine. But these decisions were not just motivated by a need for order and governmental efficiency; rather they had a direct ideological purpose. In justifying centralized state control over education, for instance, Ben Zion Dinur, the minister of education, argued during the Knesset debate preceding the enactment of the 1953 Law of State Education that it was essential for the state's survival that there be "full and complete" identification with it, and that "each one of its citizens regard the state as a part of his own personal being."[85] Thus, in its broader sense, *mamlachtiyut* "reflects the effort to transform the state and its institutions into the central foci of loyalty and identification . . . . [It] gives rise to values and symbols that point to the state, legitimate it, and mobilize the population to serve its goals."[86] Moreover, according to Charles Liebman and Eliezer Don-Yehiya: "In its more extreme formulation statism cultivates an attitude of sanctity toward the state, affirming it as an ultimate value."[87] This was exactly what Ben-Gurion was accused of doing by the outspoken religious philosopher Yeshayahu Leibowitz, who denounced Ben-Gurion for elevating the state to a value in itself, something Leibowitz saw as entirely alien to the Jewish tradition.[88]

The charge Ben-Gurion repeatedly faced in his advocacy of *mamlachtiyut* was that it made the state an end in itself, rather than a means toward achieving a larger goal. Opponents of *mamlachtiyut* argued that the new state needed a mission or guiding purpose, over and above its own self-preservation and the welfare of its citizenry. Once the Jewish state had been successfully established, the vexing question of what larger purpose it would pursue was immediately raised. National self-determination for the Jewish people had been Zionism's overriding political goal. Once this had been achieved, what was left to strive for? This question was posed to Ben-Gurion by the philosopher S.H. Bergmann in a meeting in October 1949 involving a number of Israeli writers and intellectuals: "I feel that we are in the throes of a great crisis of values, a profound spiritual crisis . . . . Zionism has given the people of Israel, the Jewish people which had been severed from its spiritual resources, a new content and purpose. Zionism filled the hollow space which had opened in the Jewish people, and enabled it to go on existing spiritually for several generations, because it was a goal for which it could strive. And now this goal has been achieved, in its first and most important phase. And once again we have to face the question: What is Judaism, what does it stand for, and what is a Jewish State?"[89]

Ben-Gurion was well aware of the need to imbue the state with a larger purpose. For him, this purpose lay primarily in what he called "the ingathering of the exiles." Despite his emphasis upon the state and the importance he attached to it, the state was never simply an end in itself for Ben-Gurion. Rather, a sovereign Jewish state was a precondition for free *aliya* (going up—the Zionist term referring to Jewish immigration to Palestine and later the State of Israel).[90] He consistently stressed the importance of *aliya* and on many occasions asserted that it took precedence over all other goals. In 1950, for instance, Ben-Gurion declared: "Neither security nor development of the land [two other goals he regularly stressed] are the essence of the state, they are merely necessary conditions for the final goal . . . . The ingathering of the exiles is the *raison d'être* of Israel . . . ."[91] In the same year, the Knesset passed the "Law of Return" proclaiming the inalienable right of every Jew to immigrate to Israel.[92] The law was, and still remains, the foremost legal manifestation of Israel's Zionist mission.

Unrestricted Jewish immigration to Israel, however, could not by itself constitute a sufficient rationale for the state. After all, why should Israelis welcome Jews from the Diaspora, and bear the economic burden that this entailed, especially when they were widely perceived to be so alien to the emerging Israeli nation? On what grounds could free Jewish immigration to Israel be justified? *Aliya* did not solve the issue of Israel's ultimate purpose, instead it begged the question. Given the largely negative attitudes of Israeli Jews toward Diaspora Jews and the growing sense of alienation from them that they felt, they had to be provided with a powerfully persuasive reason to accept these "foreigners" into their midst. That reason was the Holocaust. It became, in the words of Eliezer Schweid, "[T]he answer found to the question 'Why be a Jew?,' to the question 'Why live in the State of Israel?' and to the question 'Why serve in the IDF and absorb aliya?' "[93]

Israeli Collective Memory and the Trauma of the Holocaust

The Holocaust is undoubtedly a central event in Israeli collective memory.[94] Yet this was not always the case. In the late 1940s and 1950s, a silence surrounded the Holocaust and public discussion of it was completely muted. It was not taught in schools or researched in universities, nor did it feature in Israeli literature and the arts. This remarkable silence was due in part to the state elite's official reluctance to embrace the Holocaust as part of Israeli collective memory, as they preferred instead to memorialize and emphasize national glories and victories.[95] Indicative of this official reluctance is the fact that the establishment of Yad Va'Shem (Martyrs' and Heroes' Remembrance Authority) and a fixed day for commemorating the Holocaust did not occur until 1953, and it took a further six years until another law was introduced making observance of this memorial day mandatory. Even these measures displayed Israeli ambivalence toward the Holocaust during this time. The memorial day was termed "Holocaust and Heroism Remembrance Day," and the chosen day (the twenty-seventh of the Hebrew month of *Nisan*) was the same day on which fighting during the Warsaw Ghetto uprising reached its peak, making the uprising the focal point of commemoration. Thus, Yael Zerubavel notes that: "During those years [the late 1940s to the 1960s] Israeli collective memory showed a clear tendency to commemorate the 'heroic' aspects of the Holocaust and suppress the 'nonheroic' past."[96] Moreover, it was only the armed resistance of the ghetto fighters and partisans (with whom Israelis could identify) that was perceived as "heroic" and separated from the "Holocaust," which became, by implication, "nonheroic."

Although the initial attitude of the state and much of Israeli society toward the Holocaust was deeply conflicted—torn between the necessity to remember and the desire to forget—the Holocaust became a dominant event in Israeli collective memory as it provided strong support for Zionism. Most Zionists perceived the destruction of European Jewry and the helplessness of the Jews there as a powerful though tragic confirmation of their assumptions. The Holocaust was seen as the most profound testament to the necessity of Zionism and the Jewish state it sought to build. Lacking a state of their own, the persecuted and terrorized Jews of Europe had nowhere to turn. Without their own place of refuge or means of protection, they were totally vulnerable and defenseless. But with a Jewish state in existence that would serve as the protector and defender of world Jewry, the tragedy of the Holocaust would never happen again.

Thus, the Holocaust became the fundamental legitimization for the Jewish state. This was clearly expressed in Israel's Declaration of Independence, which stated that: "The Holocaust . . . in which millions of Jews in Europe were forced to slaughter again proved beyond doubt the compelling need to solve the problem of Jewish homelessness and dependence by the renewal of the Jewish state in the land of Israel, which would open wide the gates of the homeland to every Jew."[97] As the Holocaust was increasingly represented as the ultimate justification for the State of Israel, it became a seminal event in Zionist historiography, reflected in the emphasis placed upon it in the teaching of Jewish history in schools.[98] The memory of Holocaust was also kept alive through rituals such as school visits to Yad Va'Shem and through the annual Holocaust Remembrance Day (which is followed in the same week by the Memorial Day for the Fallen of the IDF and ends with Independence Day—the proximity of these three national events conveying "a contemporary saga of exodus from enslavement to freedom and from subjugation to redemption").[99] According to Eliezer Schweid, the official memorialization of the Holocaust and the emphasis placed upon it in Israeli-Jewish education "was a deliberate and planned development [by the state leadership], intended to provide an answer to the danger of a 'holocaust of assimilation,' of obscuration of the national cultural image and the loss of will to identify with the people, with Zionism, and with the state as a Jewish state."[100]

The Holocaust's function in legitimizing the State of Israel led to the gradual erosion of the anti-Diaspora ethos that had prevailed in the *Yishuv* and the early years of the state. As Robert Wistrich and David Ohana write: "Its [the Holocaust's] role in the Israeli collective memory underlined the degree to which the Zionist rupture with the Diasporic past of Jewry was beginning to break down. The image of the Holocaust as the nadir of Jewish powerlessness in *Galut* (exile) and the stigma attached to it, gave way to an increasingly strong symbolic identification with this traumatic memory.[101] In fact, the empathy that Israeli Jews felt toward European Jews in the

Holocaust was such that, according to Amos Elon: "The Holocaust was an event many native Israelis felt they had experienced vicariously, as it were, irrespective of age, origin, or education."[102]

The trial of Adolf Eichmann, the Nazi war criminal responsible for the deportation of European Jews to the concentration camps who was captured by Israeli agents in Argentina, increased the identification of Israelis with the victims of the Holocaust. During the much publicized trail, which opened in Jerusalem on April 11, 1961 and lasted nine months, the court heard from over 100 witnesses.[103] The heart-wrenching personal testimonies of survivors, some of whom were overcome by emotion during the court proceedings, profoundly changed the attitude of Israeli society toward the Holocaust. From the early 1960s on, the attitude of Israeli Jews toward those in the Diaspora gradually shifted from one of alienation, if not contempt, to increased identification. This shift in attitudes signaled an even more fundamental change in Israeli attitudes toward the Jewish past, from an emphasis upon discontinuity to one of continuity. "Underlying this renewed emphasis on historical continuity is the perception of a great threat to Jewish survival throughout Jewish history, which also applies to the State of Israel," writes Zerubavel. "Israeli collective memory has thus lost much of its oppositionist stance vis-à-vis traditional Judaism, now embracing a lesson deeply ingrained in Jewish memory: the experience of a persecuted group struggling to survive against all odds."[104]

The Return of the Jew: The Judaicization of Israeli National Identity

This development effectively marked the end of the secular Zionist effort to construct an Israeli identity contrasting sharply with the identity of Diaspora Jewry. Instead of a new "post-Jewish" Israeli identity, from the 1960s onwards Israeli national identity became increasingly "Jewish." Rather than being disdained as they had once been, Judaism and the Jewish tradition were steadily embraced both by the general population and by the leadership of the state.[105] For the latter, this involved a recognition that the prevailing ideology of *mamlachtiyut* was insufficient for the task of nation-building. *Mamlachtiyut*— the emphasis upon state values and civic attachment to the state—was originally intended by the state leadership to unify an Israeli population divided by geographic origin, political affiliation, and religious observance. But the state alone was insufficient to provide a common focus of unity, allegiance, and identification; and the only other common denominator that could potentially unite the Jewish population in Israel was the Jewish religion.

During the course of the 1950s and 1960s, therefore, religion and religious values were gradually integrated into what was previously "secular"

Zionism. Significant in this regard was the introduction of a "Jewish Consciousness Program" in secular public schools in 1957. This was an early sign of a shift toward Jewishness (and away from Israeliness) in defining Israeli national identity, and of Judaism's steady move from the social and political periphery to the center of Israeli identity.[106] The state leadership purposefully bolstered the role of Jewishness in the definition of Israeli national identity in order to shore up Israeli Jews' identification with Diaspora Jewry, and unify Israel's Jewish population. This meant, in the words of one scholar, "a reorientation of the basic principles of legitimation of Israel: a trend away from secular Zionism, especially its pioneering socialist variety, towards a neo-traditionalist Jewish nationalism which, while it reinforces the primordial links among Jews both within Israel and the Diaspora, de-emphasizes the modern, civil character of the state."[107] As a result, Jewishness became an increasingly dominant element in Israeli national identity, and the sharp divide that had emerged between Israeli identity and Jewish identity narrowed.

This *Judaicization* of nationalism in Israel—as Jewishness became a central element of Israeli national identity—simultaneously entailed the further *nationalization* of Judaism. Traditional religious rituals and rites became infused with new national meaning. As Bernard Susser observed: "An idiosyncratic pattern of religious practices, beliefs, and attitudes has become broadly constitutive of the Israeli national ethos. Whether or not one is 'religious' in the familiar sense of the term, these practices and beliefs are perceived as among the defining marks of Israeli national belonging."[108] The Jewish religious tradition was steadily nationalized through a selective interpretation of history and text. In Charles Liebman's words: "The religious tradition, once rejected by Zionist leaders, has become an important component of Israeli life. In the process, the tradition itself underwent a measure of transformation and assumed a more nationalistic content."[109] What took place, however, was not exactly a revival of religion. It was Jewish traditionalism, not religiosity as such, that was on the rise. The two are distinct, as Liebman and Susser make clear: "Traditionalism, in a word, possesses the protean character of popular, ethnocultural folkways that derive from religious sources; often utilizes religious symbols, practices, and language—and yet is fundamentally not a religious phenomenon. It is, rather, a form of national self-identification expressed through the immemorial language of the Jewish tradition."[110]

A number of factors were together responsible for this change (some already alluded to). First, the state elite refused to countenance the development of an entirely new Israeli national identity, since this would undermine Zionism's core belief that Jews all over the world were members of a single nation, and would jeopardize the crucial relationship between Diaspora Jewry and the

State of Israel.[111] Second, the mass immigration of Eastern European Jews after the Holocaust and Jews from the Middle East and North Africa after the establishment of the state radically changed the new state's demographic composition. Many of the new immigrants, especially those from the Middle East and North Africa, were far more religious and attached to Jewish traditions than those who had been born or entered the country in the years of the *Yishuv*.[112] Judaism, therefore, served as a means to integrate this population into Israeli society and foster their allegiance to and identification with their new state, a task that *mamlachtiyut* could not by itself achieve. Third, the increasing centrality given to the Holocaust in Israeli collective memory and in legitimizing the existence of the state (especially in the context of continued Arab attempts to delegitimize Israel) fostered an emotional identification with Diaspora Jews, and a belief that Israeli Jews continued to face threats to their existence on account of their Jewishness.

A fourth factor driving the Judaicization of nationalism and the nationalization of Judaism in Israel was the ideological failure of Labor Zionism to perpetuate itself after the establishment of the state. Despite Mapai's prolonged political dominance, its value system was not shared by the majority of Israelis, particularly by the young.[113] In a 1945 survey of students in Jewish high schools in Palestine, for example, when asked what was the most important occupation for the future of the *Yishuv*, 75 percent responded that it was agriculture, echoing the official Labor Zionist ideology of the *Yishuv*. But when asked how many of them intended to become farmers, only 12 percent expressed this desire.[114] Another example indicating the dissonance between the ruling Labor Zionist ideology and the attitudes of the general population was a 1963 opinion poll which found that only 28 percent of members of the Mapai-controlled Histadrut ("the General Federation of Labor") joined the organization for ideological reasons.[115] The ideological vacuum created by the decline of Labor Zionism was filled by "neo-traditionalist Jewish nationalism."[116] As Aharon Megged, a leading Labor Zionist intellectual, wrote in the pages of *Davar* (the influential daily newspaper published by the Histadrut): "Every vacuum—as we have learned—must fill up. Gone is the socialist religion of work and its place is being taken by our father's religion. Is this so bad? Is this worse than total emptiness?"[117]

Although their cumulative impact was not immediate, all of these factors were at work from the 1950s onwards. But it was the Six Day War of 1967 that catalyzed the already ongoing Judaicization of nationalism and nationalization of Judaism in Israel. If the 1967 war was like a volcano suddenly creating a new domestic political and cultural landscape in Israel, then the forces that it unleashed had been simmering like magma under the surface of Israeli life for some time. Israel's secular, universalist, civic ethos had already been fraying; it was then to be torn asunder by Israel's stunning military victory in the 1967 war. In only six days, Israel had taken control of the entire city of Jerusalem, the Sinai Peninsula, the Golan Heights, the Gaza Strip, and the West Bank (the biblical territories of Judea and Samaria). When Israeli paratroopers triumphantly entered the gates of the Old City of Jerusalem and arrived at the Western Wall (Judaism's holiest site), few, if any, Israeli Jews were not filled with a sense of the miraculous, of a feeling that divine providence had returned "the children of Israel" to their holy city and the lands of their biblical ancestors. The spectacle of battle-weary, hardened Israeli soldiers reverently bowing their heads before the hallowed stones of the Western Wall, eyes filled with tears and wonder, is perhaps the most resonant symbol of the rapprochement that took place between the "new Jew" created by secular Zionism and the Jewish tradition: the new in awe of the old and reconnecting with their once-buried Jewishness.

The religious sentiments kindled by Israel's conquest of Jerusalem and the West Bank were, however, only transient for the majority of Israeli Jews.[118] There was no general renaissance of religious observance (despite the impression created at the time by the much-publicized conversion to Orthodox religious life of a small number of well-known Israelis) though there was a greater public appreciation of Jewish history and tradition. But the impact of the 1967 war was profound and long-lasting upon those Israeli Jews who were already religiously observant and who were members of the religious Zionist movement (as opposed to ultra-Orthodox religious Jews who were not Zionist). For these people, Israel's victory in the war appeared to be a clear indication that the messianic process of redemption was moving forward and that the dawn of a new messianic age was imminent. The heart of the sacred land that God had promised Abraham— Hebron, the hills of Samaria, the Old City of Jerusalem—had been triumphantly restored to Jewish rule and would never again be relinquished, since to do so would be a violation of God's will (as revealed in the 1967 war), and would mean forfeiting divine redemption. Imbued with new confidence and an unshakable conviction in historical inevitability, religious Zionists became more politically active and assertive.

In the 1950s and early 1960s, religious Zionists had been preoccupied with ensuring their existence and continuity in the face of pressures from both the secular and non-Zionist ultra-Orthodox worlds. Their political strategy was basically defensive, aimed at safeguarding their separate institutions and the conditions that allowed religiously observant persons to participate in national life (by ensuring, for example, Sabbath and *kashrut* observance at public institutions). By the early 1960s, religious Zionists had already become more confident, as it seemed that their efforts to prevent the "desertion" of their youth to the secular or ultra-Orthodox societies (through religious education and the religious youth movement) were largely successful, and the growing participation of their youth in distinguished army units elevated their status in Israeli society.

But the decisive change in their attitude and political behavior came as a result of the 1967 war. They were ideologically galvanized and went on the political offensive. This was apparent in the behavior of their political representative, the National Religious party (NRP), which abandoned its previously docile and subservient attitude in the formulation of Israeli foreign policy and began intervening in foreign policy debates, notably those concerning the future of the territories captured in the 1967 war. As a result, the NRP steadily swung to the right. The political activism of the religious Zionist public reached its climax with the formation and activities of the extra-parliamentary movement Gush Emunim (Bloc of the Faithful) which was set up in 1974 to act as the spearhead of the new settlement movement in the "liberated" territories of Judea and Samaria. More generally, religious Zionists, and especially their political leadership (who were increasingly infiltrated by younger Gush Emunim activists) were vociferous advocates of a stronger Jewish content in Israeli national identity. They were also politically well-positioned to champion this since the governing Labor Alignment (Mapai's successor and the predecessor of the Labor party) depended upon the NRP's parliamentary support. Indeed, at the end of 1976 it was the NRP's refusal to vote with the government on a motion of no-confidence (over the alleged desecration of the Sabbath in connection with a ceremony at an Air Force base) that led to early elections in May 1977. Its subsequent defection from its "historic coalition" with Labor, then allowed for the formation of the first ever Likud-led government under Menachem Begin.

The political maneuvering of the NRP was, however, only partly responsible for the Likud party's rise to power in 1977. It was the votes cast by large numbers of Mizrahi Jews that did most to put the Likud into office. They were equally, if not more, important (due to their far greater number) than militant religious Zionists in promoting the rise of Jewishness within Israeli national identity. Although the Mizrahim had arrived in Israel en masse from the countries of the Middle East and North Africa in the late 1940s and early 1950s, during the first two decades of statehood their cultural and political impact was marginal due to the social, political, and cultural dominance of Ashkenazim (Jews of European-origin). But as the proportion of Mizrahim in the population gradually rose (due to their higher birth rate), and they acquired social and political skills,[119] they began translating their demographic weight into political power—culminating in their shift of electoral support from Labor to Likud to produce Likud's 1977 election victory. At the time, this was widely seen as a "protest vote" on the part of the economically and politically marginalized Mizrahi population against the dominance of the Labor establishment, which was overwhelmingly composed of Ashkenazi Jews. But the fact that Mizrahim have dispropor-tionately voted for the Likud in every election since 1977 suggests that it was more than just a protest vote.[120] Rather, the explanation for the large Mizrahi electoral support given to the Likud party in the 1977 election (and in every election thereafter) lies in their preference for Likud's definition of Israeli national identity. The Likud's (and especially Begin's) emphasis upon Jewishness and the Jewish tradition appealed to the Mizrahi public as it appeared to assure their inclusion and acceptance within the boundaries of the Israeli collective. By voting for the Likud, Mizrahim were expressing their desire to "belong" within the Israeli nation.

As noted previously, Mizrahi Jews tended to be more traditional than their Ashkenazi counterparts, and their Jewish identity tended to be stronger. As such, the more that Jewishness defined Israeli national identity, the more Mizrahim would be accepted within the boundaries of the Israeli nation, and would themselves feel a part of it. By contrast, when secular Israeliness rather than Jewishness dominated in the definition of Israeli national identity—as it did in the 1950s and early 1960s—the Mizrahim's ability to belong in this Israeli nation was highly tenuous and conditional. It was tenuous because Mizrahi Jews did not share the characteristics then associated with being an Israeli, as embodied in the sabra ideal. In both appearance—ideally, tall, blond and blue-eyed—and attitudes—secular, antitraditional—the sabra was implicitly Ashkenazi (no doubt due to the fact that its creators were themselves Ashkenazim).[121] The Mizrahim's acceptance within the bound-aries of the Israeli collectivity was also conditional, as they were required to shed their own cultures and traditions, which were dismissed as primitive. In the early years of the state, disdain for the Mizrahim was widespread throughout the Ashkenazi-dominated political and cultural establishment. Typical of the elite's attitude toward Mizrahim was Ben-Gurion's comment: "Those [Jews] from Morocco had no education. Their customs are those of Arabs . . . . The culture of Morocco I would not like to have here. And I don't see what contribution present [Jewish] Persians have to make . . . . We do not want Israelis to become Arabs."[122] The integration of the Mizrahim into the Israeli nation, therefore, "was based on efforts to upgrade the 'back-ward primitives' and to reshape their entire being and thinking in the European image."[123] This left a legacy of resentment and hostility amongst the Mizrahim against what they perceived as the patronizing and discrimi-natory attitude of the Labor elite toward them—sentiments which fueled the electoral rise of the Likud. The Likud, by contrast, provided Mizrahim with a sense of psychological equality vis-à-vis the Ashkenazim, helping them overcome their abiding sense of marginality within the Israeli collective.

Likud's dramatic electoral victory over the Labor Alignment in the 1977 general election became popularly referred to by Israelis as the *mahapach* (upheaval) as it brought to an end Labor's long-standing political dominance (under different names, it had been the senior party in every coalition government since the state's establishment).[124] Although the Likud's victory surprised many both in Israel and abroad, this "electoral earthquake"[125] was the result of two interrelated long-term trends—the gradual erosion of the ideological dominance of Labor's interpretation of Zionism, and a cultural shift that began in the 1950s and accelerated after 1967 that essentially involved the "reassertion of [Jewish] tradition."[126] The political "upheaval" of 1977, therefore, was a product of ideological and cultural changes that had been underway for decades. The magnitude of these changes was obscured as long as the Labor party remained the preeminent party in Israel's governing coalitions. Hence, it was not until the 1977 election that their significance became fully apparent. The election brought to power a right-wing party whose nucleus (Herut) was committed to Revisionist Zionism and its brand of militant Jewish nationalism.

Menachem Begin, its leader, became the new prime minister. After being politically ostracized by Ben-Gurion (who even refused to address him by name) and spending years in the political wilderness, losing election after election, Begin's rise to power was a staggering success. This success was due in no small measure to Begin's ability to personify Jewish traditionalism. He publicly presented himself as a pious traditional Jew as well as a staunchly patriotic Zionist. Despite receiving a secular education and not being religiously observant himself, Begin felt a deep attachment to and respect for the Jewish tradition and religious orthodoxy. His political rhetoric was heavily laden with references to Jewish history and tradition, and he extensively drew upon traditional Jewish concepts and imagery. Thus, one author described him as: "The only Israeli leader who can talk with equal force in the language of traditional and secular Jewish nationalism."[127] Another writes that Begin was a man who "identified himself primarily as a Jew and then as an Israeli."[128] Moreover, far from being a sabra, in both his appearance and demeanor, Begin appeared to be the stereotypic Diaspora Jew once mocked and reviled by secular Zionists. His ascendancy to the premiership, therefore, was laden with significance in so far as it symbolized the victory of Jewishness over Israeliness in defining Israeli national identity.

This development was to profoundly affect not only relations within Israeli society, but also Israel's foreign relations. Indeed, it was the state of these relations, as much as the domestic processes discussed in this chapter, that was responsible for the ascendancy of an increasingly particularistic, ethno-religious Israeli national identity in the first place. The next chapter examines the relationship between Israeli national identity and Israeli foreign policy, and the impact that Likud's rise to power had upon Israeli foreign policy.

CHAPTER 2

BETWEEN ISOLATION AND INTEGRATION: FOREIGN POLICY AND ISRAELI NATIONAL IDENTITY

Two basic aspirations underlie all our work in this country: to be like all nations, and to be different from all nations.[1]

—David Ben-Gurion

We Fight, Therefore We Are.[2]

—Menachem Begin

Introduction

"This state will in some ways be a glass house, and every time we yawn, and anything we do, big or small, will be photographed by the entire world," remarked Pinhas Lavon, then the general secretary of the Histadrut, in early 1948.[3] This remark was certainly true then—as the attention of the world was focused on the escalating conflict between Jews and Arabs over the territory of British Mandatory Palestine—and it has remained true until today. Coverage of Israel in the international media far surpasses that of many other far larger and more populous countries. In addition to the reams of journalistic writing about Israel, there is also a wealth of scholarly literature covering almost every conceivable aspect of the country.

Given this cornucopia of commentary and analysis, it is striking how little attention Israeli foreign policy has received from scholars of International Relations.[4] Only a small number of books and articles have explicitly examined Israeli foreign policy through the lens of International Relations theories.[5] Of these, most have used realist theory to explain Israel's foreign policy.[6] The choice is an obvious one. Realism's depiction of foreign policy as geared toward state survival in an anarchic, ruthlessly competitive inter-state environment in which military power and the threat or resort to force is the primary tool of statecraft, appears to characterize Israeli foreign policy as it seeks to defend Israel's existence in a region where diplomatic niceties and international norms are all-too-often regarded as dangerous luxuries, where violence—both internal and external—is a regular feature of political life, and where the security of states, and the individuals within them, is often highly precarious. Israel's security predicament mirrors that postulated by realism, and neorealism in particular. Thus, Shibley Telhami writes that: "For many realists, Israel presented a prime example of a vulnerable state whose security concerns drove its foreign policy."[7] Hence, according to Telhami, in much of the literature on Israeli foreign policy: "[I]t was argued that Israel's security calculations in the context of its hostile environment are, by themselves, sufficient, to explain the dominant tendencies in Israeli foreign policy."[8] Avner Yaniv, for example, has claimed that: "[T]he Jewish state's conduct, like that of her adversaries, remains motivated chiefly by the patently anarchic nature of the regional and the wider international environment in which it has existed since its inception."[9]

In contrast to this neorealist view of Israel's foreign policy being determined by the country's external circumstances, other scholars have argued that Israel's internal environment has been equally, if not more, important in shaping Israeli foreign policy. A host of domestic factors have been held responsible for the conduct of Israeli foreign policy, such as the personalities and beliefs of individual political leaders,[10] the bureaucratic or partisan nature of foreign policymaking in Israel,[11] and Israel's socioeconomic structure.[12] Analyses of Israeli foreign policy in terms of Israel's domestic politics, particularly with reference to inter-party and intra-party divisions, are common in journalistic coverage and in some academic studies.[13] Here the emphasis is upon the competing ideological perspectives toward the Arab-Israeli and Israeli-Palestinian conflicts of those on the right and left of the political spectrum—commonly termed "hawks" (associated with the right-wing Likud party and its allies) and "doves" (associated with the left-wing Labor party and its allies), respectively.[14] It is claimed that these domestic ideological and partisan divisions exert a major impact on the formulation of Israeli foreign policy (especially due to the parliamentary character of Israel's democracy and the reliance of its governments on numerous parties in coalition).

The account of Israeli foreign policy that I present here also emphasizes the importance of internal ideological and partisan divisions in shaping Israeli foreign policy. But it does not explain the conduct of Israeli foreign policy only in terms of Israel's domestic politics. Rather, I emphasize the importance of Israeli national identity—which is a product of both domestic and international processes—in shaping Israeli foreign policy. I interpret Israeli foreign policy through a constructivist theoretical lens, and argue that Israeli national identity, and the debates and divisions surrounding it, exert an important influence upon it. I claim that the interests and goals Israel pursues in its foreign policy, the means it adopts to accomplish them, and the perceptions and beliefs that underlie these choices, are all related to Israeli national identity.

In this chapter, I begin by examining the interaction between the Jewish component of Israeli national identity and Israel's foreign policy. I focus on this relationship because of all the components of Israeli national identity, the Jewish component is by far the most relevant to Israeli foreign policy since it has undoubtedly had the greatest impact. "Jewishness" has profoundly influenced the worldview of Israeli Jews, their threat perception, their attitudes toward the value of diplomacy and the use of force, and their belief in the primacy of security—all essential ingredients in the formulation of Israeli foreign policy. The occasionally acute sensitivities, anxieties, and fears of Israeli politicians and the Israeli public at large are simply inexplicable without reference to their Jewish identity and the collective historical memories associated with it—above all, of the Holocaust. To disregard this, to interpret Israel's foreign policy through a neorealist lens as solely a response to persistent external threats would be a woefully deficient understanding of Israeli foreign policy. Without disputing the constraints that Israel's external environment has placed upon the conduct of Israeli foreign policy, I argue that the perception of an unremittingly hostile environment and the attribution of specific motives to Israel's adversaries have been shaped by the Jewish component of Israeli national identity and the beliefs, attitudes, and perceptions it has given rise to amongst Israeli policy-makers and the general public. This was especially true of Prime Minister Begin, whose foreign policy was decisively influenced by his perception of Israel as the collective Jew fighting to survive in an anti-Semitic gentile world, and by his firm belief that the occupied territories belonged to the Jewish people and could, therefore, never be abandoned. For this reason, I pay particular attention to his foreign policy in this chapter. I also discuss the Likud's attempt under Prime Minister Shamir to build a new national consensus in the wake of the Lebanon War around its goal to retain the occupied territories, and the affect that the first Palestinian Intifada had in this regard.

The Jewish Dimension in Israeli Foreign Policy

The most important component of Israeli national identity that has influenced Israeli foreign policy has been the Jewish component. It has shaped the perceptions, beliefs, values, and attitudes that have driven Israeli foreign policy. The most obvious example of this has been the consideration Israeli decision-makers have given to the interests and welfare of Jews abroad.

Israeli foreign policy is not just concerned with securing the interests of its own citizens, but also Jewish citizens of other countries. As Ben-Gurion told a meeting of Israeli ambassadors on July 17, 1950: "So long as there exists a Jewish Diaspora . . . Israel cannot behave as other states do and take into account only its own geographic and geopolitical situation or limit its concerns to its own citizens and nationals only. Despite the fact that the Jews living abroad are in no legal way part and parcel of Israel, the whole Jewish people, wherever it resides, is the business of the State of Israel, its first and determining business. To this Israel cannot be neutral: such a neutrality would mean renouncing our links with the Jewish people."[15]

Israeli policy-makers, therefore, feel obliged to consider the potential impact their policy toward another country might have upon the Jewish community residing there. Hence, the existence of a Jewish community in a particular country has always exerted an influence on Israel's attitude and policies toward that country. The clearest instance in which considerations of the welfare of local Jewry affected Israeli foreign policy toward another state was in Israel's relations with the Soviet Union (USSR). Although it is difficult to gauge the extent of its impact upon Israeli policy toward the USSR, the large number of Jews residing there was definitely a factor that Israeli policy-makers had to take into account, especially because the welfare of Soviet Jewry was highly precarious (they were subject to numerous restrictions by the Soviet regime, most notably, the ability to freely leave the country). Shimon Peres, for instance, stated in 1966: "When it comes to Soviet Jewry the consideration of local Jewry is dominant—because of the real danger to their survival."[16]

Declarations of concern for the welfare of Jews abroad by Israeli policy-makers do not, of course, mean that their actual foreign policies have always, or even mostly, been predominantly guided by this concern. Above all else, Israeli policy-makers have sought to defend and advance the interests of the State of Israel. If there is a conflict between the interests of a particular Jewish community and those of the State of Israel, the interests of the latter will prevail in determining policy. But the preference accorded to Israel's interests by Israeli policy-makers finds its justification in their belief that the interests of Israel are ultimately identical with those of world Jewry, since the survival of the former ensures the survival of the latter. As Ben-Gurion stated: "It was *always* my view that we have to consider the *interests* of Diaspora Jewry—any Jewish community that was concerned. But there is one crucial distinction—not what *they* think are their interests, but what *we* regarded as their interests. If it was a case vital for Israel, and the interests of the Jews concerned were different, the vital interests of Israel came first—because Israel is vital for world Jewry."[17] There is no reason to suspect that this is simply a rationalization for the narrow pursuit of Israel's interests. Numerous statements by Israeli policy-makers attest to the sincerity of their conviction that the welfare of Jews around the world is inextricably tied to the welfare of the Jewish state. Ya'acov Herzog, the director-general of the Prime Minister's Office under Levi Eshkol, Golda Meir, and Menachem Begin sums up this view: "The Israeli elite looks upon Israel as the bastion of the collective Jewish group and, as such, it takes into account the interests of its part. But it places primary value on the whole and, to that end, the survival and enhancement of the bastion."[18]

A less direct, but no less profound influence of the Jewish component of Israeli national identity upon Israeli foreign policy has been through shaping the worldview of both Israeli policy-makers and the Israeli public at large. A number of scholars have identified a link between the Jewish identity of Israelis and their foreign policy perceptions. In his book, *The Foreign Policy System of Israel: Setting, Images, Process*, Michael Brecher analyzed the "attitudinal prism" of Israeli policy-makers—the psychological lens through which they view the world.[19] This attitudinal prism is shaped above all by their sense of Jewish identity. "The consciousness of being Jewish," Brecher writes, "creates a unique Attitudinal Prism for members of the High Policy Elite [Israeli policy-makers], as for most Israelis."[20] This sense of Jewish identity "pervades thought, feeling, belief, and behavior in the political realm."[21] It gives rise to a belief in a "two-camp thesis," according to which the world is divided into Jews and non-Jews, with the former considered Israel's only reliable ally.[22] This belief that world Jewry was Israel's only dependable ally was expressed on a number of occasions by Ben-Gurion. As he once put it: "Do not forget that although Israel enjoys the friendship of many nations it is the only country which has no self-governing 'relatives' from the point of view of religion, language, origin or culture . . . . The only *permanent loyal* "relatives" we have is the Jewish people."[23]

The Jewish component of Israeli national identity generated suspicion and mistrust of the gentile world, a legacy of the hatred and persecution that Jews had endured at the hands of gentiles through the ages. "One of the most fundamental aspects of Israel's diplomatic tradition," writes Sasson Sofer in his book on Zionist diplomacy during the pre-state period, "is its attitude towards the outsider and foreigner. While Zionism sought constantly to attain international recognition, it was afflicted at the same time by deep, sometimes obsessive, misgivings regarding the intentions of foreign individuals and governments. Anti-Semitism played a dominant role in molding the dichotomous perception of a world divided up into Jews and Gentiles."[24] But while memories of anti-Semitism affected early Zionist diplomacy, such memories became far more poignant and powerful in the wake of the Holocaust. The memory of the Holocaust gradually came to cast a dark shadow over Israel's relations with the rest of the world, especially from the 1960s onwards. Important in this respect was the growing historiography of the Holocaust, which revealed that, contrary to their immediate post–World War II claims of ignorance, many Western countries were aware of the genocide against the Jews taking place in Nazi-occupied Europe, but did virtually nothing to help them. As knowledge of the Western countries' passivity in the face of the Holocaust grew, so too did their culpability in Jewish eyes. The Holocaust increasingly took on metaphysical proportions, perceived not only as a German atrocity committed against the Jews, but as the culmination of centuries-long gentile persecution of Jews. Israelis also feared that another Holocaust could happen. A survey of public attitudes carried out during the Eichmann trial in 1961 revealed that 22 percent of respondents thought that a future Holocaust was possible in all countries, and 58 percent believed that it could occur in some countries. The fact that these were not passing attitudes was demonstrated in another study undertaken twenty years later (in 1982) in which 18 percent thought a future Holocaust was possible in all countries, and 52 percent in some countries.[25]

Such statistics testify to the deep impact of the Holocaust upon Israeli Jews' perceptions of gentiles and the surrounding world. From the 1960s onwards, Israelis increasingly perceived the rest of the world as anti-Semitic. This profoundly affected their attitudes toward foreign policy and the international system. As Ofira Seliktar writes: "the re-interpretation of anti-Semitism and the Holocaust contributed to a highly Hobbesian perception of international order in Israel."[26] Such a perception is clearly apparent in Begin's book *The Revolt* where he writes: "The world does not pity the victims; it respects the warriors. Good or bad—that is how it is."[27] The *Realpolitik* that Israeli policy-makers frequently evinced in their foreign policy discourse, therefore, emanated (at least in part) from their tragic view of the history of the Jewish people.

The world was often viewed by many Israeli policy-makers, and by much of the Israeli public, as an inhospitable place, at best indifferent toward the welfare of the Jewish state, at worst outright hostile. This view of the world was expressed by Abba Eban, the veteran Israeli diplomat, in his description of Israel's predicament on the eve of the 1967 war: "When we looked out at the world we saw it divided between those who wanted to see us destroyed and those who would not raise a finger to prevent it from happening."[28] A corollary of this negative worldview was a deep sense of loneliness and isolation. Asher Arian, who has studied the attitudes of Israeli Jews over a thirty-year period (from 1963 to 1994), writes that: "There is a fundamental belief that in the final analysis the world will do nothing to protect Jews, as individuals, as a collectivity, as a state."[29] He claims that

Israeli Jews share a common belief system that he labels the "People Apart Syndrome."[30] According to Arian, this "permits rejecting the outsider and thereby increases solidarity within the community by casting together the lot of all."[31] Thus, the sense of international isolation felt by many Israeli Jews facilitated internal cohesion and national unity among them, whilst simultaneously alienating and distancing them from the rest of the world. It promoted a basic divide between "us" and "them" that both bolstered Israeli national identity by clearly delineating an in-group and an out-group (central to the constitution of any identity), and fueled the anxieties of the Israeli public as they perceived themselves and their state to be the object of international persecution and discrimination. These sentiments were most famously articulated in the popular Israeli song of the late 1960s and early 1970s entitled, "The Whole World Is Against Us."[32]

Describing "the weight of Jewish history" that influences Israeli foreign policy, Aaron Klieman writes that: "At the level of attitudes and perceptions, nineteen centuries from Masada to Maidanek still profoundly influence Israeli international conduct . . . . This weight of Jewish history lies heavily on both leaders and public. It is one of the primary sources for Israel's underlying insecurity and perceived isolation."[33] Israeli policy-makers themselves were well aware that their memories of Jewish history bore down upon them. Asked by a reporter whether Israel suffered from a "Masada complex," for instance, then Prime Minister Golda Meir responded: "We do have a Masada complex. We have a pogrom complex. We have a Hitler complex."[34] Similarly, Pinhas Sapir, then a senior cabinet member in Golda Meir's government, stated: "We have a Warsaw ghetto complex, a complex of the hatred of the Jewish people, just as we are filled with a Masada complex."[35]

The belief, which became increasingly widespread from the late 1960s onwards, that Israel had not "escaped" from Jewish history, that it too was being victimized and persecuted by a hostile gentile world, influenced both the national mood and the tenor and conduct of Israeli foreign policy. It had a direct bearing on Israeli threat perceptions, on Israel's emphasis upon self-reliance, and on Israeli policy-makers' skepticism toward diplomacy and preference for military activism. The Jewish component of Israeli national identity magnified the perception of threat from the Arab world. When Arab leaders declared their intention to destroy Israel and "drive the Jews into the sea," Israeli Jews, including those responsible for making Israeli foreign policy, did not dismiss these threats as bombastic propaganda. Instead they took them seriously, all too aware that not long before a similar threat of destruction had been issued by Nazi leaders in Germany but was not taken seriously enough by large numbers of European Jews until it was too late. The traumatic memory of the Holocaust made Arab threats of destruction credible, and cast the conflict with the Arabs as one of basic survival, aimed at preventing a second Holocaust.

The acute threat perception of Israelis was also a result of their tendency to view the Arab world as a homogenous bloc. This view was also influenced by the Jewish component of Israeli national identity, as Ben-Gurion's comment to George Antonius, the historian of the Arab nationalist movement, in 1936 suggests: "As a point of departure the proposition must be accepted that the issue is not one between the Jews of Palestine and the Arabs of Palestine . . . . Instead, we must view the Jews as one world entity and the Arabs as one world entity."[36] This perception of the conflict as an Arab-Jewish one, rather than an Israeli-Palestinian one, was widely shared by Israeli policy-makers and the general public. It completely overlooked the distinct identity and aspirations of the Palestinians. In the dominant discourse in Israel, Palestinians both within and outside the "Green Line" (the pre-1967 war borders of Israel) were referred to as Arabs (in the case of those within the Green Line as "Israeli Arabs" or "Arab Israelis"). The term "Palestinians" was completely absent from this discourse. The denial of a separate and distinct Palestinian identity was most famously expressed in 1969 by then Israeli Prime Minister Golda Meir when she stated: "There was no such thing as Palestinians. When was there an independent Palestinian people with a Palestinian state? . . . It was not as though there was a Palestinian people and we came and threw them out and took their country from them. They did not exist."[37]

The failure or refusal to acknowledge the Palestinians' distinct identity, in turn, generated Israeli incomprehension of their claim to Palestine. The Arabs already had a huge amount of land, Israelis often wondered, why were they so uncompromising about such a small patch of territory (i.e., Israel/Palestine)? As Levi Eshkol expressed it as Israel's prime minister in July 1963: "Israel has regained her independence in a tiny patch of 8,000 square miles, about the size of Wales. There are now a dozen Arab states, none of them independent before the end of the First World War, occupying territories covering a total of four and a half million square miles. Is there any sense in countries with such vast spaces . . . to begrudge us this small corner which is the basis for our independence?"[38] Since they could not understand the Arabs' unwillingness to allow the Jews their national homeland, Israelis frequently attributed it to irrational motives, notably anti-Semitism. Instead of viewing the conflict with the Arabs as a struggle for power and territory, it was interpreted through the lens of Jewish history, especially recent history, and framed as an unrelenting existential struggle in which Jewish survival was at stake. This interpretation was bolstered by the fact that Arab enmity to Israel was frequently expressed through virulent anti-Semitic discourse.[39]

In so far as the Arabs were seen as implacably hostile to Israel, it was believed that to make concessions to them would be viewed by them as a sign of Israeli weakness, thereby encouraging them to pursue their goal of destroying Israel. The only available policy for Israel, therefore, was a policy of strength and resilience, which would ultimately force the Arabs to become reconciled to Israel's existence.[40] This was eloquently conveyed by Moshe Dayan, then IDF Chief of Staff, in his eulogy for a fallen soldier delivered in May 1956: "Beyond the furrow that marks the border is a sea of hate and the desire for revenge, hate that is lying in wait for us the day when the calm will dull our readiness . . . . This is the fate of our generation. The only choice we have is to be armed, strong, and resolute, or else our sword will fall from our hands and the thread of our lives be severed."[41] According to this conception of the conflict, Arab-Israeli peace could not be achieved through Israeli concessions. Instead, it would only come once the Arabs finally accepted that they could not destroy Israel. As Ben-Gurion put it: "Peace cannot be achieved until the Arabs, or rather the Arab leaders, will be persuaded they cannot destroy Israel either by economic boycott or by political pressures or by military offensives."[42]

This belief ensured the primacy of security in guiding Israeli foreign policy. Security was the overriding goal of Israeli foreign policy, and all other considerations were made subservient to it. Furthermore, since Israelis had little faith in international treaties and guarantees as a means of ensuring their security (after all, they remembered that they did not prevent the dismemberment of Czechoslovakia in 1938, or more immediately the "War of Attrition" launched by Egypt after Israel's withdrawal from the Sinai peninsula after the 1956 Suez War), they preferred to rely upon themselves for their security, and especially their military power. As Yitzhak Rabin stated in an interview when he was Chief of Staff of the IDF: "The analysis of the facts proves that essentially what has assured Israel's existence, and will continue to do so, in the face of the hatred around it and the will to destroy it, is primarily Israel's comprehensive power, with military might as the decisive element."[43] Diplomacy, therefore, was given short shrift by Israeli policy-makers and the public alike, whereas force was highly esteemed. The combination of self-reliance and military power as the ingredients of Israeli security was encapsulated in the statement made by the then Prime Minister Rabin following the 1973 war (which dramatized Israel's vulnerability and fortified the conviction of Israelis that their survival was at stake): "Israel shall dwell alone and only our military might guarantees our existence."[44]

Unlike Jews in the Diaspora who had been powerless to defend themselves in the face of attack, Israeli Jews had a powerful state to defend them, with military force at its disposal. Their military might, and their willingness to use it, would distinguish Israeli Jews from their less fortunate forebearers. They would not suffer the same ignoble fate as those Jews who had perished without a fight in the Holocaust. Efraim Inbar has described how Israel's use of force has been regarded by members of Israel's political elite as symbolizing a rejection of traditional modes of Jewish behavior in the Diaspora.[45] Hence, Israel's readiness to use military force, even preemptively—as it did most dramatically in 1967—was, at least in part, a result of both the perception that Israel was facing threats to its survival as Jews had before, and the desire to respond to these threats in a manner unlike that of Jews before. This was most apparent during the Begin government. For Begin, "the use of force constituted . . . a part of the Jewish quest for assertiveness and respectability."[46] On the eve of Israel's invasion of Lebanon in June 1982, for instance, Begin told his cabinet ministers: "The blackguards and the world must know that the Jewish people has the same right of self-defense as any other people."[47] The rejection of the image of weakness and passivity associated with Diaspora Jewry was also evident in a Knesset debate over the war in Lebanon, in which Begin rhetorically declared: "Can we allow the shedding of Jewish blood to go unavenged? Can we allow an ambassador of the State of Israel, representing Israel's glory, honor, and sovereignty, to be murdered?"[48] Similarly, in another Knesset debate on the war in Lebanon, Geulah Cohen, a representative from the right-wing Tehiya party argued that those Israelis who were critical of Israel's invasion of Lebanon and who had reservations about the use of force suffered from a lack of boldness and martial initiative due to their inability to escape from the Diaspora mentality.[49] During the same debate, Hanan Porat, another member of the Tehiya party, declared: "The days of pogroms, persecutions, forced baptism and blood-libels are gone forever. Now, since our return home to build the House of Israel, a life without shame and degradation, a life of honor, has returned to us."[50] The war in Lebanon, then, was discursively associated with Jewish honor and pride. It was depicted as a repudiation of the Diaspora Jewish mentality, and an affirmation of a new assertive Jewish identity in its homeland.

The Jewish component of Israeli national identity has affected the worldview and foreign policy perceptions, beliefs, values, and attitudes of Israeli policy-makers and the general public. This influence can be traced from the beginning of Zionist diplomacy in the pre-state period through to the foreign policy of every government of the State of Israel. But it has waxed and waned, dependent upon shifting domestic and international conditions. The more Israelis felt rejected and condemned by the international community, the more they were reminded of the Jewish past and their inheritance of it. Conversely, the more Israelis felt accepted and welcomed by the international community, the more confident they became that they had moved away from their Jewish predecessors and the fate that had befallen them, coming to see themselves as "a nation like all the nations" as early Zionists like Herzl had originally intended them to be.

In this sense, the international community functioned as a "generalized other" for Israelis.[51] This term comes from the theory of symbolic interactionism in sociology associated with the work of George H. Mead.[52] Mead put forward a view of the Self as a "looking-glass self," a product of an ongoing synthesis of self-definition and the definitions of oneself offered by others and by the "generalized other"—the organized community or society to which an individual belongs. Symbolic interactionism, therefore, emphasizes the impact of external actors upon our definition of identity. Identities emerge out of social interaction. Applying this idea to collective identities suggests that how a group is viewed and treated by others, especially by "significant others," exerts an influence upon how the group sees itself.[53] Thus, the attitude of the international community toward Israel, or, more precisely, Israelis' perception of this attitude, influences the way in which Israelis see themselves. That is, the definition of Israeli national identity, and especially the role of Jewishness in this identity, is affected by how Israelis interpret the attitude of the international community toward them. When Israelis perceive the international community to be anti-Semitic, this elevates the Jewish component of Israeli national identity. The more they believe that they are being treated as Jews—in the hostile manner with which Jews had earlier been treated by the non-Jewish world—the more Jewishness dominates their conception of Israeli national identity.

The strength of the Jewish component in Israeli national identity, therefore, is affected by the perceived attitude of the international community toward Israel. Hence, it is no coincidence that in the 1950s and early 1960s when the world appeared to stand by and support Israel (which was widely perceived to be a "plucky little country" struggling against immense odds), Jewishness was relatively marginal in Israeli national identity—it was more civic than ethno-religious. But from the late 1960s onwards, as world public opinion seemed to turn against Israel (increasingly viewing it as the oppressor rather than the oppressed), Jewishness became increasingly dominant in defining Israeli national identity, which in turn increased the impact of Jewishness upon Israeli foreign policy. After 1967, many Israeli Jews perceived the growing international condemnation of Israel's occupation of the territories it had seized in the 1967 war (expressed in numerous critical resolutions in the United Nations [UN] and other international forums—culminating in the notorious 1975 UN General Assembly Resolution equating Zionism with racism) as a manifestation of anti-Semitism. According to this perception, anti-Semitism was now being directed against the State of Israel, as the representative of the Jewish collective. Anti-Zionism became synonymous with anti-Semitism in the minds of many Israelis. As a result, Israeli Jews increasingly came to see themselves and their state as sharing the same fate that had long afflicted their ancestors in the Diaspora. The Jewish State was being shunned and made into a "pariah state" much like the Jews had been a pariah people. Thus, Rabin, in his first term as Israel's prime minister, reacted to the UN resolution equating Zionism with racism by declaring: "The whole world is against us—when was it not so!"[54]

The role of Jewishness in defining Israeli national identity and, by extension, in shaping Israeli foreign policy was therefore related to international developments as well as developments within Israel. The more "Jewish" Israeli national identity became as a result of changes in Israel's domestic and international environment, the more Israeli foreign policy was influenced by Jewish historical memories and traumas. In the preceding chapter, I argued that Jewishness gradually came to supersede Israeliness in Israeli national identity, and that it became steadily less civic and more ethno-religious over time. A civic Israeli national identity arose in tandem with a strong state under the leadership of Ben-Gurion. As Israel's prime minister, Ben-Gurion emphasized the importance and value of the state through his doctrine of *mamlachtiyut*. This doctrine had implications for Israeli foreign policy, as much as it did in Israeli domestic politics. According to Shmuel Sandler: "In foreign affairs *mamlachtiyut* was the desire to develop a conception of a normal state that interacts like all the states, and a nation like all the nations, rather than a state that behaves according to the traditional conception of a Jewish particularistic destiny."[55] This statist approach to foreign policy was reflected in a number of important foreign policy decisions during the period 1949 to 1967, such as Ben-Gurion's decision on January 3, 1951 to seek and accept German monetary reparations for the Holocaust (which then led to the forging of an arms relationship with West Germany during the late 1950s), and Golda Meir's decision in the early 1960s to favor maintaining good relations with France over assisting the emigration of North African Jews.

The decline of *mamlachtiyut* and its associated civic conception of Israeli national identity, resulted in Jewishness exerting a stronger influence upon the formulation and conduct of Israeli foreign policy. This was most pronounced during Begin's tenure in office between June 1977 and September 1983 (when he resigned). As I argued in the previous chapter, Begin's rise to power marked the triumph of an ethno-religious discourse of national identity that emphasized Jewishness in defining Israeli national identity. This had dramatic repercussions for Israeli foreign policy under Begin. Although the Jewish dimension had never been absent from Israeli foreign policy, it had been tempered by statist considerations under Ben-Gurion and his Mapai heirs. The difference between the approaches of Ben-Gurion and

Begin to Israeli foreign policy clearly emerges in their contrasting attitudes toward the sensitive and controversial issue of German reparations. Ben-Gurion adopted a highly pragmatic attitude, approaching the issue in terms of Israel's dire economic need (arising as a result of the long and costly 1948 war, its high military expenditures, and the need to absorb the massive immigration then underway). For Ben-Gurion, the interests of the state were paramount, and he insisted that it should use all the resources and tools at its disposal, even when this meant doing business with a country that only a few years before had ruthlessly murdered millions of Jews. For Begin, the issue of German reparations was primarily an issue of national honor, and he vehemently condemned Ben-Gurion's decision, personally leading the opposition to it. In a public demonstration organized by Begin's Herut party prior to the opening of the Knesset debate on the reparations issue on January 7, 1952, Begin declared to the crowd with his traditional inflammatory rhetoric: "A government which negotiates with the Nazis is not a Jewish government but a tyranny which is supported by bayonets"— note the reference to "a Jewish government" rather than to an Israeli government.[56] Later that day, during his speech in a stormy Knesset debate, Begin argued that accepting reparations would only increase the contempt in which the Jewish people and Israel were held by the rest of the world, and undermine Jewish national dignity: "The goyim [gentiles] not only hated us, not only murdered us, not only burnt us, were not only jealous of us— it was especially contempt that they felt for us. And in this genera-tion, . . . in the generation when we gained a position of honor, in which we came out from slavery to liberty—you [Ben-Gurion] come, and because of a few million defiled dollars, because of foul goods, and throw away the little bit of dignity which we have earned for ourselves . . . you endanger our honor and independence. How we shall be scorned."[57] Begin demanded that Ben-Gurion hold a national referendum on the question of accepting German reparations (convinced that the majority of Israelis were against it). He even went so far as to threaten a violent civil war against the government (which resulted in a three month suspension from the Knesset).

Begin's approach to Israeli foreign policy was a product of his own life experiences. The violent anti-Semitism he encountered as a youth in the ethnically mixed city of Brest-Litovsk (under Russian and then Polish rule), and his proximity to the Holocaust—which took the lives of his parents and older brother—instilled in him a sense of pervasive, intractable, and frequently deadly anti-Semitism in gentile society. His intellectual and political com-ing of age during the turbulent and ominous period of the 1930s (he turned eighteen in 1931) was to prove decisive in shaping his personal identity and worldview. In his later life, Begin commonly viewed events through the prism of the 1930s, and he often drew analogies with events in this period.

The contemporary problems of the Middle East were equated with those of Central Europe in the 1930s—during a dinner table discussion in the winter of 1978 with the Egyptians and Americans, for instance, he argued against Palestinian self-determination by referring to Hitler's abuse of the principle in advocating it for the Sudetenland Germans as a means to destroy Czechoslovakia.[58] Above all, the trauma of the Holocaust marked Begin's political outlook.

The Holocaust was a continual reference point for Begin, and his speeches while he was prime minister were littered with references to it. The Arabs were regularly likened to the Nazis, he referred to the Palestinian national covenant as *Mein Kampf*, to the Palestinian Liberation Organization (PLO) as "the Arab SS," and described PLO leader Yasser Arafat as a Hitler. The Holocaust not only shaped Begin's political rhetoric, but also the actual conduct of his foreign policy. Begin was explicit about this when he explained that his decision to order the bombing of Iraq's nuclear reactor in 1981 was prompted by his fear of a new holocaust that Israel's enemies could accomplish. Responding to massive international criticism following Israel's bombing of the Iraqi nuclear reactor on June 7, 1981, Begin held a press conference two days later in which he declared: "We have a special reason to guard our people: a million and a half children were poisoned by a gas called Cyclon B. There is no difference between poisons. Radioactivity is also a poison . . . . Two, three years, at the most four years, and Saddam Hussein would have produced his three, four, five bombs, what should, what could we have done in the face of such a present, direct, horrifying peril? Nothing. Then this country, and this people, would have been lost, after the Holocaust. Another holocaust would have happened in the history of the Jewish people. Never again, never again."[59] Similarly, in a speech to his cabinet on the eve of Israel's 1982 invasion of Lebanon, Begin justified the war in the following terms: "In the Land of Israel we are condemned to fight with all our soul. Believe me, the alternative is called 'Auschwitz.' We are determined to do everything to prevent another Auschwitz."[60] There is no reason to believe that Begin was insincere in this instance or the many others in which he drew upon the Holocaust to explain his policies.[61]

The Holocaust was the major factor in conditioning Begin and his associates' general attitude toward the non-Jewish world, which was marked by pronounced distrust and suspicion. Accommodation with, and integration into, the outside world was totally rejected on the grounds of it being both impossible and undesirable. Such a view was clearly expressed by Ya'acov Herzog, the Director-General of the Prime Minister's Office under Begin, when he stated: "We are not a normal people, we are not free from the *Galut* ['Exile'] burden and we are not accepted by the world . . . . Political

Zionism maintained that the concept of 'people who dwell alone' is, in fact, an abnormal condition. In reality, the concept of 'people who dwell alone' is the *natural* condition of the Jewish people."[62] The impossibility of normalizing Jewish existence, according to this perspective, stems from the anti-Semitic nature of gentiles, manifested most catastrophically in the Holocaust. Anti-Semitism was viewed as an immutable, irrational force—one that had no specific causes and was tied to no particular historical period. The timeless and all-pervasive nature of anti-Semitism provided the Begin government with a simple and convenient explanation for the frequent international condemnation it received. Rather than having to identify specific causes for Israel's isolation, Begin and his associates saw it as a continued manifestation and proof of anti-Semitism now directed against Israel as the representative of the Jewish people. Foreign criticism of Israeli policies and actions during Begin's administrations, whether from individuals, organizations (such as the UN), or foreign governments were frequently denounced as motivated by anti-Semitism. When asked to explain his government's part in the Phalangist massacre of hundreds of Palestinians in the Sabra and Shatila refugee camps on September 17, 1982, for instance, Begin labeled the very inquiry a "blood libel"—alluding to the traditional anti-Jewish accusations that Jews killed Christian children in order to use their blood for baking Passover *matzoh* (traditional unleavened bread).[63] He also declared: "Goyim [a derogatory term for non-Jews] kill goyim . . . and they blame the Jews."[64] In Begin's discourse, Israel was represented as the collective Jew, its experience mirroring and replaying that of individual Jews throughout the millennia. His frequent allegations of anti-Semitic discrimination by the gentile world against Israel served, therefore, to affirm and emphasize the Jewishness of Israelis.

Thus, during Begin's premiership, the Jewish dimension of Israeli foreign policy reached its height, just as the Jewish dimension of Israeli national identity was also ascendant. The linkage between these two dimensions was nowhere more direct than on the issue of the future of the territories occupied by Israel in the 1967 war. This issue came to dominate Israel's foreign policy agenda after 1967. As Sandler notes: "No foreign policy issue preoccupied the agenda of the State of Israel in recent years as much as that of the territories . . . . The territories became identified with the essence of Jewish statehood and nationhood, peace and war, and the result was that the territorial issue became a new cleavage, dividing Israeli society and its polity."[65]

The long-running and heated political debate in Israel over "the territories" went well beyond issues of security and strategy. As Shlomo Avineri writes: "Anyone trying to understand both Israel's foreign policy—and the internal debate in Israel about it—only in terms of security and strategic considerations, will fail to grasp either the intensity of the debate or its nuances."[66] Perhaps nobody has been able to more eloquently describe the underlying nature of this debate than the Israeli novelist Amos Oz. In his numerous works of nonfiction, Oz chronicles the many divisions within Israeli society and conveys the deep-seated identity crisis from which it suffers, involving questions of "who we are, what we want to be, and what our source of authority should be."[67] In one such work, he writes: "The real argument that divides the nation today ceased long ago to be a dispute about territories, political parties, security, ancestral rights, and borders. This is an argument about the nature of Judaism and the image of man. The question is not whether these Palestinians are really a people or perhaps just a hodgepodge of laborers, hewers of wood and drawers of water by day and terrorists and murderers by night. The question is not: Who are the Palestinians? The question is: Who are we?"[68] Elsewhere, Oz expressed his concern over the failure of Israelis to recognize that their debate over the territories was really a debate over Israeli identity. "I see a mortal danger," he wrote, "in the continued repression of the internal rift over the character of Israeli society and its camouflaging as a division over the location of the frontiers."[69]

The ability of Israelis and their political leaders to repress this "internal rift" and to camouflage the real nature of the debate over the territories steadily diminished in the 1980s and 1990s until, by the middle of that decade, the territories themselves were no longer the main focus of debate. Instead, the debate was explicitly over Israeli identity, and though the territories were often invoked in the course of this debate, few could deny that they were really symbols wielded in a battle over the definition of Israel as a state and the Israelis as a nation. Furthermore, it was a battle that openly manifested a profound crisis of Israeli identity. In order to understand how a foreign policy debate over the future of the territories became a debate over Israeli identity, and how this resulted in Israeli foreign policy becoming entangled in identity politics, it is necessary to examine Begin's foreign policy and the fierce domestic controversy this aroused.

The Quest for Greater Israel

As Jabotinsky's ideological successor, Begin maintained the Revisionist claim to Jewish sovereignty over *Eretz Israel* in its entirety (although this was directed toward the West Bank and Gaza, rather than the east bank of the Jordan River as it had been under Jabotinsky). For Begin, Israeli possession of the West Bank (Judea and Samaria, in his terminology) and Gaza was based upon the historical rights of the Jewish people. These areas were the ancestral home of the Jewish nation, and hence its inalienable birthright.

To forfeit these territories would undermine Israel's basic raison d'être and the entire legitimacy of the Zionist project of settlement in Palestine/*Eretz Israel*. Begin defended his approach to the question of the territories in a Knesset address on October 18, 1982:

> I know full well that if I open the discussion with historical-moral argumentations the scoffers will be quick with their mockeries. What of it, will the so-called "realists" ask, those who allegedly have their feet firmly planted on the ground, if in those parts of Eretz Israel there was once a Jewish Kingdom? What of it from whence we once came the cradle of our faith, where our civilization was created and developed and which we took with us on our global wanderings, its greatness within us, and with which we turned home? All that happened many generations ago. Are we going to live with the past whose testimony is dusty books and yellowing pages?
>
> Surely we must turn to the vibrant, living, ever-changing present. Surely we have to accommodate ourselves to the new times, to the new conditions, forged in such tumult and propaganda and money and blood.
>
> It is my duty to warn the citizens of Israel against such contrived "realism." Let each person ask his friend and his neighbor: what are we without our history? From whence derives our right to any part of Eretz Israel? Do not our worst detractors deny us the right to Eretz Israel, to every single part of it? Shall we lend them support in obliterating our past, which is the foundation—and there is no other—of our rights?[70]

For Begin, the ancient past of the Jewish people was of abiding importance. It was not to be dismissed as irrelevant to the policies of the modern State of Israel. On the contrary, it was integral to Israel as the Jewish state and to Israeli national identity. Begin's conception of the relationship between the territories and Israeli national identity is clearly apparent in the following statement: "As far as Judea and Samaria and the Gaza district are concerned, where we have a perfect right to live and to stay, there we were born as a nation—nobody should forget it and nobody should tell us that this belongs to ancient history. Our people lives on its history. What would we be without our great past?"[71]

Since the territories were tied to Jewish history, and this history was a constitutive element of Israeli national identity, it followed that, for Begin, to forsake these territories would be to forsake Israeli national identity (defined exclusively in terms of Jewishness). The maintenance of Israeli national identity was, therefore, discursively linked by Begin to the maintenance of Israel's control over the territories. Begin's political stance toward the territories was ultimately determined by his conception of Israeli national identity as being completely synonymous with Jewish national identity, and of Israel as being the state of the entire Jewish people, and not merely its own citizens (who, of course, were not all Jewish). As Israel's prime minister, Begin saw himself as speaking and acting on behalf of the Jewish nation all over the world. This was evident in another speech he delivered in the Knesset during the debate on the Reagan Plan of September 1982, in which he declared: "If anyone will seek to take us from Judea and Samaria, we will say to him: Judea and Samaria belong to the Jewish people for all the generations. Yes for the sake of Zion I will not be silent and for the sake of Jerusalem I will not rest. This is the announcement of the Jewish nation, in its overwhelming majority, in the homeland and the Diaspora. I only speak for it."[72]

Begin's foreign policy throughout his period in office emanated from these ideological convictions. It was consistently animated by one key concern: to maintain Israeli control over the territories through a process of de facto annexation of the West Bank and Gaza which, it was hoped, would eventually pave the way toward formal, de jure annexation. Recognizing that outright annexation of the territories was not feasible in the short term due to the international and internal opposition this would provoke, as well as the demographic facts in the territories (overwhelming Palestinian numerical superiority), Begin directed his efforts toward gradual annexation through neutralizing the opposition to this policy. First, he sought to remove Egypt's opposition by signing the Camp David Accords (September 17, 1978) and the Egyptian-Israeli peace treaty (March 26, 1979). The significant concessions Begin made to the Egyptians in the Camp David Accords and Egyptian-Israeli peace treaty (returning all of the Sinai peninsula with its valuable oil resources and evacuating the Israeli settlement at Yamit) were chiefly motivated by his ideological commitment to eventual annexation of the territories. Hence, the Camp David Accords and Egyptian-Israeli peace treaty were not conceived as the prelude to a comprehensive peace, but were rather a maneuver designed to facilitate the eventual incorporation of the West Bank and Gaza into Israel. By removing the most powerful Arab state from the conflict, reducing international (mainly American) pressure for Israeli concessions on the issue of the territories, and prolonging inconclusive talks on Palestinian autonomy, Begin was "buying time" for his government's annexation activities in the territories. These activities included a government-sponsored Jewish settlement effort, legal and administrative reforms in the territories, and land control techniques, all aimed at ensuring total Israeli control over the area in order to impose future annexation on the Palestinian population.[73]

When the Begin government came to power in 1977 there were twenty-four Jewish settlements in the West Bank and Gaza, inhabited by 3,200 people. By the time of Begin's retirement in 1983, there were 106 settlements (98 in the West Bank, and 8 in Gaza) with the number of residents increasing to 28,400.[74] This represented a massive settlement drive in the territories orchestrated by the Begin government, and aimed at eventual annexation or, at least, undermining the prospects for a future territorial compromise. Not only did the number of settlements and settlers increase, but also the type and location of settlements changed during this period, as well as the actual type of settler. Under previous Labor governments (particularly in the period 1967 to 1975), settlement activity in the territories was largely restricted to chains of very small agricultural settlements in strategically located areas (along the Western bank of the Jordan river, and on the Eastern slopes of the Samarian mountains), with the major exception of Jerusalem. This settlement pattern was in line with the recommendations formulated by Yigal Allon (in the "Allon Plan"), a prominent Labor leader and foreign minister during the Rabin government (1974–1977), who regarded settlements as a means to guarantee militarily defensible borders (according to topographic conditions), but who favored the eventual return of most of the West Bank to Jordan.

Beginning in 1975 with the illegal settlement activity of Gush Emunim, which then received official backing from the Begin government when it came to power in 1977, settlement activity in the territories took on entirely new dimensions. In its first phase, the fiercely ideological settlers of Gush Emunim, with financial, organizational, and ideological support from the Begin government, established a large number of settlements in central locations in the West Bank, and in close proximity to local Palestinian populations—an area that would form the basis of any territorial compromise. Since the number of ideologically motivated settlers was demographically insufficient, however, in a second later phase, the government encouraged nonideological settlers through the provision of economic incentives (more land and cheaper housing) to establish nonagricultural semi-urban or suburban communities (near the Tel Aviv and Jerusalem metropolitan areas). In both phases, the Begin government's overriding objective was to create enough "facts on the ground" to effectively forestall the possibility of future territorial compromise.

Creating "facts on the ground" in the occupied territories, however, would not be enough to guarantee against the possibility of a future territorial compromise. No matter how many Jewish settlements were established, as long as they were regarded by the majority of Israelis as lying outside the legitimate borders of the State of Israel, their existence would remain precarious and they would be at risk of one day being traded away. For the Begin government's annexationist goal to succeed, therefore, it was necessary to redraw the "mental map" of Israelis so that the territories would be considered an integral part of the State of Israel. It was, in other words, necessary to create new "facts in the minds" of Israelis, as well as new "facts on the ground" in the territories. This meant overturning the hegemonic status of the Armistice lines of 1949—"the Green Line."

Until 1967, Israel's 1949 boundaries were accepted and taken for granted by the vast majority of Israelis as the state's permanent and legitimate borders. Indeed, in the period 1949–1967, Herut's irredentist program of expanding the borders of the Jewish state to include the entire Land of Israel (which during this period also referred to the territory of Transjordan) held very little appeal to the Israeli public. Although Israel's capture of the West Bank and Gaza in the 1967 war undermined the hegemonic status of the Green Line in Israeli consciousness, it did not result in majority support for the annexation of the territories. Instead, after 1967, there was simply no national consensus on the location of the state's borders. In order to fulfill its annexationist project, therefore, Begin's government had to create a new consensus on the legitimate borders of the state, one that regarded the territories (Judea and Samaria) as indivisible from the rest of Israel. Thus, the Begin government, in concert with its messianic religious Zionist allies (represented by the NRP and Gush Emunim) attempted to make the Land of Israel (expanding the state's borders to include the West Bank and Gaza) hegemonic in the public consciousness.[75] They did this through "policies in the educational, broadcasting, judicial, and administrative spheres designed to accelerate the disappearance of the Green Line from the practical life and ordinary language of all Israelis."[76] "The long run purpose of these policies," writes Ian Lustick, "was to transform Israeli beliefs, allegiances, and interests—to re-shape the cognitive map of Israelis to conform with an image of the country which included the territories as no different from other regions of the state. If this were accomplished all future governments would be prevented from publicly entertaining 'land for peace' options with respect to the West Bank and Gaza Strip."[77]

The War in Lebanon: Israel's Vietnam

Although the goal of annexing the territories consistently drove Begin's foreign policy, there were still significant differences in the conduct of Israeli foreign policy in Begin's first and second terms in office. Begin's foreign policy can be divided into two distinct periods: a period of relative moderation from 1977 to 1979 when the Camp David Accords and Egyptian-Israeli peace treaty were signed; and a period of radicalization from 1980 to 1983, when the annexation of the Golan Heights, the bombing of the Iraqi nuclear reactor, and the invasion of Lebanon took place. The period of radicalization corresponds to a change in the ruling political elite, marked by the departure of the moderates—Foreign Minister Dayan (who resigned in October 1979) and Defense Minister Ezer Weizman (who resigned in July 1980)—and the rise of Yitzhak Shamir as foreign minister and Ariel Sharon as defense minister. Led by these more hawkish personalities, the second Begin government was more radical than the first.[78] Dayan and Weizman had both been influential in moderating Begin's conduct of foreign policy.[79] With their influence gone, Begin was left to pursue a more dogmatic and aggressive foreign policy. Indeed, he was actively supported in this by his new Defense Minister, Sharon, who, in the words of Amos Perlmutter, "encouraged Begin's most extreme and cherished ambitions, principally the destruction of Palestinian nationalism in any form, and, specifically, the total destruction of the PLO."[80] Thus, Perlmutter wrote in 1982 that: "The second Begin government is without a doubt the most hawkish government in Israel's history."[81]

This had dramatic consequences for Israel's policy toward the territories. The first Begin government, although opposed to Palestinian statehood and the principle of territorial compromise, offered the Palestinian population of the West Bank and Gaza a form of genuine autonomy instead. The second Begin government dropped even this slightly more accommodating position as outright annexation became the main policy goal. To advance this goal, the second Begin government adopted two main strategies aimed at undermining the power and influence of the main Palestinian opposition, the PLO. The first aimed at establishing a patronage-based system in the West Bank by co-opting village leaders (through a system known as the "Village Leagues") and marginalizing and undermining the urban Palestinian nationalist leadership (almost all of whom supported the PLO). The government's intention was to foster a new pliable leadership in the West Bank, which would comply with Israel's annexationist activities.

When this attempt at cultivating a new Palestinian leadership failed (due to its lack of popular support and PLO intimidation), the Begin government adopted its second strategy—launching a war in Lebanon to destroy the PLO's military capabilities and, by extension, its political power in the territories.[82] By destroying the PLO's base in Lebanon the government hoped to undermine its political influence in the territories, an influence which was preventing the Palestinian population there from accepting Israeli domination under the guise of Begin's autonomy plan. Israel's war against the PLO in Lebanon was, therefore, a by-product of the Begin government's policy toward the territories. This was clearly stated by Rafael Eitan, the IDF Chief of Staff during the war in Lebanon: "Our war here is a war over Eretz Israel, not over Beirut and not for the Christians," he declared. "We want the terrorists out of here. That is the aim. If we can manage that, the struggle over Eretz Israel will look different . . . . We have come for the struggle over Eretz Israel."[83]

Although the war in Lebanon was aimed at ensuring Israel's permanent control of the West Bank and Gaza, this was not what the Israeli public was told by the war's planners—principally, the triumvirate of Prime Minister Begin, Defense Minister Sharon, and Chief of Staff Eitan. At its outset, it was presented to the Israeli public as a limited military incursion into the PLO-controlled territory of southern Lebanon (dubbed "Fatahland" in the Israeli media) in order to remove the threat of terrorism posed to the communities residing along Israel's northern border (who had regularly endured Katyusha rocket attacks and armed infiltrations by the PLO). Justified in this manner, Israel's invasion of Lebanon, which began on June 6, 1982, and was named "Operation Peace for Galilee," initially received wide domestic support, both from the Israeli public and from the main opposition Labor party. When Begin made a statement to the Knesset two days into the war, therefore, he happily declared that: "The entire nation, save one faction [the Israel Communist Party], has united around the IDF, vanquisher of the enemy, victorious, ensurer of the peace of the citizens of Israel. This national unity is one of the finest hours in the history of Israel . . . . It will be remembered for generations to come."[84]

This national unity did not last however. Within a year, Begin's tone had changed from one of triumphalism to desperation as the war in Lebanon became the subject of increasing domestic controversy. Responding to the repeated attacks on the government by the opposition (who had reversed their earlier support for the war), Begin made a speech before the Knesset on June 1, 1983, in which he implored: "When as a result of fighting the situation becomes difficult from a national point of view, must there be an outcry? . . . Why should we create the situation that we are divided among ourselves? . . . Today I call on all factions that are loyal to the State to stand together in this trial as we have stood in other times . . . I ask that the same measure of unity which existed at the start of the fighting should continue until we reach the yearned for peace."[85]

But Begin's exhortations for national unity fell upon deaf ears. The left openly challenged the justice of Israel's war in Lebanon. Hundreds of public demonstrations and assemblies were held; most notable was the one organized jointly by the Labor Party and *Shalom Achshav* ("Peace Now," founded in 1977) on September 25, 1982, in Tel Aviv which drew an estimated 400,000 people, around 5 percent of the Israeli public—the largest attendance ever at a political rally in Israel.[86] In uproar over the massacre by Israel's Phalangist allies of innocent Palestinians in the Sabra and Shatila refugee camps and indications of Israel's acquiescence in this atrocity, the protesters demanded that the government set up an independent investigating committee to examine the government's responsibility for the massacre. The mass demonstrations staged both for and against the government in the midst of the war were unprecedented in Israeli history. Even more unusual was the public refusal of some Israelis to fight in it (for example, the much-publicized resignation of Colonel Eli Geva who refused to participate in the attack on Beirut, and the establishment by soldiers and officers of *Yesh Gvul* ["There is a Limit"], a social movement of conscientious objectors).

Although there had always been dissenting voices raised during Israel's previous wars, the widespread public protest against the war in Lebanon was a new phenomenon in Israel. Never before had an Israeli government faced such open defiance of its foreign policy and military strategy. This was recognized by Moshe Arens who succeeded Sharon as defense minister after he was forced to resign in the wake of the Kahan commission's report on the Sabra and Shatila massacre (which found Sharon to be morally, but not criminally, culpable and negligent in his ministerial duties). In a newspaper interview in May 1983, Arens commented: "I see here a phenomenon . . . and it is new in Israeli society—opposition spokesmen and article writers who ask whether the achievements [from the Lebanon War] are worth the price in blood we have paid . . . no such question had been asked throughout the history of the State of Israel—and justifiably so."[87]

Why did the war in Lebanon generate such unprecedented domestic controversy? At the time, the Begin government viewed criticism of the war as politically motivated, blaming it on the Labor party and its left-wing supporters in the media who, they charged, still chafed at Likud's electoral victories in the 1977 and 1981 elections. The media, in particular, became a target for the government's wrath. Journalists' criticisms of the government were assailed as being part of a "leftist conspiracy," and the government directly blamed the media for undermining the national consensus and the morale of the IDF.[88] The government attempted to censor critical reporting of the Israeli conduct of the war and to strictly control the flow of information that the Israeli press received about events in Lebanon. Journalists who did not adhere to the official government line were even removed from their posts. Resentment at the way the Israeli media was reporting the war led some Likud members to suggest even more drastic measures. Meir Cohen-Avidov, a Likud member of the Knesset, proposed that the government should take over television under the terms of the 1965 Broadcasting Act in order to stop "the lies and calumnies."[89] Another Likud member of the Knesset, Dov Shilansky, declared in the Knesset that the media showed "a lack of critical sense and national responsibility," alleging that, "it encouraged and served as a spur to the enemy."[90] Although Israel's media was, most likely, staffed by a disproportionate number of liberal and left-leaning individuals who were probably not inclined toward sympathy for the Begin government, media bias is insufficient in accounting for the widespread domestic unpopularity of the war in Lebanon. As much as they were shaping public opinion, the media were giving voice to it, and thus the explanation for the contentiousness of the war lies elsewhere.

Part of the explanation has to do with the nature of the war itself. The war in Lebanon constituted a departure from Israel's traditional foreign and security policy. Whereas previously Israel had essentially been a "status quo" power in the Middle East, resorting to war only as a defensive measure, with the invasion of Lebanon, Israel's approach shifted from defensive to offensive, aimed not so much at securing the status quo as establishing a new political order in the region.[91] War was no longer conceived of as a last resort, instead it became a means by which Israeli military superiority could be used to accomplish political objectives. Thus, in 1981, Chief of Staff Eitan pushed for war against the PLO, arguing that Israel's war machine should be put to good use (implying that deterrence was not enough).[92]

This offensive military strategy motivating Israel's war in Lebanon suffered from a serious flaw—it failed to take into account Israeli national identity, and the accompanying attitude of Israeli society toward war. Despite having fought many wars, valorizing military virtues, and esteeming their military prowess, Israelis did not see themselves as a bellicose nation. On the contrary, they believed they were naturally pacific, and thus reluctant fighters, engaging in war only as a defensive necessity. This self-conception as "defensive warriors" found expression and support in the popular concept of *milchemet ain breira* ("war of no choice").[93] This concept was a central element in Israeli political discourse articulated on both the left and right of the political spectrum until the Israeli invasion of Lebanon in 1982.[94] The common depiction of all of Israel's wars as having been forced upon Israel by its Arab neighbors absolved Israel of any moral responsibility for the outbreak of the war and the subsequent deaths incurred on both sides. It thus bolstered Israelis' sense of moral righteousness. War was presented in a fatalistic manner entirely beyond Israel's control. Israeli actions were purely reactionary and defensive and, hence, just.[95]

Israel's invasion of Lebanon challenged this prevailing Israeli attitude toward war. Initially, Begin attempted to present the war in Lebanon to the Israeli public as a "war of no choice," by claiming that the PLO's military presence there constituted an existential threat to Israel that had to be destroyed. However, a number of factors militated against such an interpretation of the war. First, as Begin himself admitted, the PLO did not pose an immediate threat to Israel's existence in 1982. Second, diplomatic means to reach a solution had not been exhausted prior to the invasion. Third, and perhaps most decisively, the Israeli conduct of the war went well beyond its stated goal of eliminating the PLO artillery threat to the northern settlements to encompass more ambitious political goals—removing the PLO and Syrians from Lebanon and establishing a friendly Maronite regime there. The Begin government was, therefore, gradually forced to abandon its attempt to present the war in Lebanon as a "war of no choice" in the face of strong criticism from the left who argued that the concept was not applicable to Israeli actions in Lebanon. Conceding that the Lebanon War was a "war by choice," Begin claimed that the 1956 and 1967 wars had also been wars of this type.[96] Such wars were in fact preferable, Begin argued, because they minimized Israeli casualties since Israel, rather than the Arabs, had the initiative.[97] As he declared on one occasion: "There is no divine mandate to go to war only if there is no alternative. There is no moral imperative that a nation must, or is entitled to, fight only when its back is to the sea, or to the abyss. Such a war may avert a tragedy, if not a Holocaust, for any nation; but it causes it terrible loss of life."[98]

Begin's attempt to legitimate Israel's "war by choice" in Lebanon, however, was unsuccessful. It "conflicted with the prevalent tendency to see war as something forced upon Israel, rather than chosen."[99] It also conflicted with Israelis' self-identity as a peace-loving, fundamentally moral people. In the eyes of many (both in Israel and abroad), Israel's war in Lebanon was not only unnecessary, it was also callous and brutal. The suffering of Lebanese and Palestinian civilians, particularly during the extensive Israeli bombing and siege of Beirut, was witnessed on television sets in Israel and around the world. Israeli soldiers no longer appeared as brave defenders of their homeland, but as invaders of another's homeland. It was an uncomfortable spectacle for many Israelis, and they laid the blame for it squarely on the doorstep of Begin's government.

The unprecedented domestic contentiousness over the war in Lebanon was also due to the changes Israeli society had undergone and was continuing to undergo in the wake of the Camp David Accords and the Egyptian-Israeli peace treaty. Sociologists have long suggested that an external conflict tends to increase a society's internal cohesion. George Simmel, in his book *Conflict*, for instance, claimed that wars promote patriotism and distract people's attention from internal conflicts toward a common goal.[100] Social psychology also supports this argument. Research in social psychology has demonstrated that the greater the level of intergroup conflict, the greater the level of intragroup solidarity. When groups are in conflict, their members face greater pressures to conform to the values and practices of the group.[101] When the level of conflict diminishes, the group members are under less pressure to conform to the group, and hence, the solidarity and social cohesion of the group diminishes in line with the reduction of conflict.

Applying this to Israeli society suggests that the Arab-Israeli conflict had a unifying effect upon it, bolstering social solidarity (specifically, amongst Israeli Jews). Thus, the Camp David Accords signed between Israel and Egypt in 1978 and the Israeli-Egyptian peace treaty signed the following year, heralded a major challenge to the preservation of Israeli national unity.

By substantially reducing the external threat Israelis faced and breaking the ring of hostility surrounding Israel, peace with Egypt promoted the gradual dissipation of Israelis' sense of siege, which had hitherto been so instrumental in fostering social cohesion. This was appreciated at the time by Yitzhak Rabin, who in his 1979 memoirs written in the wake of the Camp David Accords, anticipated the potential risks that peace held for the inner strength and cohesion of Israeli society.[102] Amidst an atmosphere of general Israeli euphoria, Rabin sounded a cautionary note concerning the recent peace treaty with Egypt, writing: "We have not yet begun to calculate the psychological and social impact upon us of peace. I have no doubt that the imminent threat from the outside was the most powerful force uniting the people of Israel. Now we live in a time of both peace and war, and we have never experienced anything like it before. No one can predict how it will affect the motivation of our people, their readiness to bear heavy burdens."[103]

The Lebanon War put social solidarity in a more secure Israel to the test, and the result was a collapse of national unity. No longer feeling that they had to subdue their voices and withhold their demands for the sake of collectively resisting a common enemy in an existential struggle, many Israelis felt free to vent their outrage and opposition. To be sure, the end of national unity had long been in the making as political polarization steadily increased after the 1967 war, and especially after 1973, as the debate in Israel over the future of the territories became increasingly heated and vitriolic. In a sense, then, the war in Lebanon was a "tipping-point" that pushed Israeli society over the edge and into the abyss of domestic discord and disharmony. Whatever remained of the national consensus on Israeli foreign policy disintegrated. During the war, extra-parliamentary groups proliferated and attained greater political weight, as did ideological splinter parties on both the left and right. Both the extreme right and the extreme left increased their electoral support as a result of the war.[104] The Lebanon War, therefore, accelerated the processes of political radicalization and polarization underway in Israeli society. The war also undermined the public's faith in the government (since not only the Knesset but even the cabinet had little involvement in the conduct of the war), and politicized the IDF.

The domestic impact of Israel's war in Lebanon was similar to that of the United States' war in Vietnam.[105] Indeed, Ephraim Lapid, who was the IDF's spokesman and member of the General Staff during the latter stages of the Lebanon War, describes it as "Israel's Vietnam."[106] Both wars became highly controversial domestically, and the widespread opposition they generated was a major factor in the decision to end them. In both cases, this opposition also led to the downfall of the political leader in charge of the war—President Johnson in the United States, and Prime Minister Begin in

Israel (who resigned on September 15, 1983). Both men retreated from public life psychologically broken, their reputations tarnished, and their prior achievements overshadowed by the wars they oversaw (in Begin's case, his outstanding achievement in office was the 1979 peace treaty with Egypt). The parallels between the domestic impact of Israel's war in Lebanon and the United States' war in Vietnam go further. Both wars intensified existing domestic cultural and political divisions, giving rise to a public perception of a dangerously fractured polity. Opposition to the wars also initiated new generations into political activism. For many of the Israeli youth who came out in protest against the war or refused to participate in it, their defiance of official policy inaugurated a prolonged commitment to advocating a negotiated peace with the Palestinians, involving Israel's withdrawal from the territories.[107] For them, and many others, the Lebanon War proved the futility of attempting a military solution to the Israeli-Palestinian conflict and the necessity of mutual compromise. As Shimon Peres, who became a leading political advocate of this view, wrote about the Lebanon War: "In the shade of the cedar trees, and beneath the cherry blossoms, the seeds of . . . Israeli recognition of the need for bilateral talks [with the Palestinians] were planted."[108]

Besides demonstrating that there was no military solution to the Israeli-Palestinian conflict, the war in Lebanon also demonstrated—to the shock and dismay of many—that Israel was not always righteous, its military actions not always just, and its leaders not always honest to their own public. As Michael Keren writes: "It was in the muddy terrain of Lebanon, that Jewish nationalism had to confront its own myths."[109] By increasing public skepticism, if not outright suspicion, vis-à-vis the assertions and promises of the government, the Lebanon War promoted public questioning of official Israeli foreign policy and encouraged public opposition to it. This facilitated the rise of numerous protest movements—most notably, the peace movement, spearheaded by Peace Now—and contributed to the expansion and development of civil society in Israel.[110]

Over time, this also engendered a questioning of Israel's dominant national narrative. After all, if Israel's wars had not all been wars of self-defense as the official narrative maintained, what else of this narrative was false? How else had Israel's public been misled or deceived by official propaganda? These were questions that were taken up by a new generation of Israeli intellectuals and academics, many of whom came of age in the heated atmosphere of Israel's war in Lebanon, intent upon shattering Israel's "myths" and "deconstructing" and revising its national narrative. They were to become known as Israel's "New Historians" and "critical sociologists," and their work was to have a profound affect upon Israeli society's sense of its own history and identity as they challenged Zionism's core beliefs. Thus, the war in Lebanon had long-lasting and deep consequences for Israeli society and politics.

The Lebanon War also had major regional and international repercussions for Israel. Although Israel did succeed in expelling the PLO from Lebanon, the long-term outcome of the war was very different from the Begin government's intentions. The PLO was not destroyed, it relocated its headquarters to Tunis, its political status remained intact, and its popularity amongst Palestinians in the West Bank and Gaza continued. More generally, the salience of the Palestinian issue in the Arab-Israeli conflict was increased as a result of the war and the extensive media coverage it received. This had a pronounced effect upon American public opinion, generating increased support for a Palestinian state. This in turn was reflected in President Reagan's peace plan of September 1, 1982.[111] The war in Lebanon also damaged Israel's relations with Egypt and bolstered Syria's presence and influence in Lebanon. Worst of all perhaps, the Israeli invasion aroused the hostility of the Lebanese population, particularly of the Shi'ites in the south, leading to the formation of numerous groups, most notably Hizbullah ("The Party of God"), dedicated to violent attacks against Israeli soldiers in Lebanon and Israeli civilians living along Israel's northern border. Over time, Hizbullah's presence in southern Lebanon became a greater menace to Israel than the PLO's had ever been.

In Search of National Unity

The Lebanon War increased the already fractious nature of Israeli politics. As a result, after the 1984 general election, more parties entered the Knesset than ever before (fifteen in total).[112] The outcome was parliamentary deadlock with neither Likud nor Labor able to form a coalition with its satellite parties. Faced with the choice of calling for new elections or joining parliamentary forces, Likud and Labor settled on forming a national unity government with a rotation of the premiership between Likud leader Yitzhak Shamir and Labor leader Shimon Peres. The national unity government that was formed following the 1984 elections, however, was not merely a matter of political expediency. It represented a sincere attempt on the part of the Labor and Likud leadership to find common ground and to project an image of national unity, which they hoped, would set an example to the wider society. Both Peres and Shamir repeatedly emphasized this goal. A few days after establishing the national unity government, for instance, Prime Minister Peres elaborated on the reasons for its formation in a speech on September 16, 1984, stating: "We are so used to being divided, to argue, to attack each other, that we feel almost at a loss to sit together, and try to deal with the major issues of our lives. And then we reached the simple conclusion: Why not try and have a democracy, and a Jewish democracy, which instead of being so much polarized, fragmented, misunderstood by each other to the point of becoming weak and revolting, why not try our hands, and come to terms together, and serve our people as one government."[113] Similarly, upon assuming the premiership in 1986 according to the national unity government's rotation agreement, Prime Minister Shamir made a statement to the Knesset in which he reiterated the purpose of the national unity government as unifying Israeli society: "The national unity is not just a matter of parliamentary convenience. Those who conceived the idea of the unity government hoped and desired that by virtue of its very formation and existence, that government would project a message of unity, of drawing closer together, of love of Israel, and of true cooperation among the country's political leadership and between all the strata of the population in the country . . . The government I head will indeed make the unity of the nation its chief concern."[114] Shamir made the same point after the 1988 elections when another national unity government was formed, declaring to the Knesset: "At the present chapter in our nation's history, we urgently need national unity, a united appearance on international platforms and national consensus on basic and existential matters."[115]

The formation of two national unity governments in the 1980s, therefore, was motivated, at least in part, by the desire of Israel's political leadership to promote wider national unity. This desire stemmed from two overriding concerns. The first was the growing fear that deepening political polarization and radicalization could result in a civil war between Israeli Jews. The killing of a young protestor, Emil Grunzweig, during a Peace Now demonstration in Jerusalem against the war in Lebanon appeared to many a dangerous portent of things to come if the inflammatory political rhetoric and mutual vilification between left and right continued unabated. Fears of a civil war erupting over the issue of the territories began to be frequently expressed in the mid-1980s by journalists, academics, and politicians.[116] In an interview in June 1985, for instance, when asked about the possible danger of a civil war in Israel over the issue of the territories, the then Prime Minister Peres responded: "I am very disturbed . . . by the matter of polarization. What is the solution? I say that the solution is to guard the nation's unity, to also guard unified frameworks and, from this aspect, I think the national unity government, with all its problems, is contributing to the nation's unity . . . . This is a contribution of prime importance, in a situation of polarization."[117] Peres thus justified Labor's participation in a national unity government with the Likud as a means to strengthen national unity and avoid threats to Israeli democracy and even civil war. The general public also seemed to share this concern about a possible civil war. Fifty-eight percent of respondents, for instance, answered "yes" to a

June 1989 poll asking: "Could the exacerbation of domestic controversies lead to civil war?"[118]

The second major concern prompting Israel's leadership to attempt to bolster national unity was their belief that domestic disunity and division posed an existential danger to the state since it undermined Israel's military power and ability to withstand prolonged conflict with the Arabs. This danger was underlined by the war in Lebanon, which, it was believed, ultimately could not be won because of the domestic opposition to it. This sparked fears that Israeli society's willingness to bear the costs of continued war with the Arabs could no longer be taken for granted. Defense Minister Moshe Arens, for instance, stated in the midst of the Lebanon War: "Everyone knows—on the right and the left—that our ability to survive is first of all contingent on one thing, and that is our willingness to go and fight when it is necessary. If the enemy will begin thinking that in the next round we will not stand up and be counted, then our situation will be very serious."[119]

In addition to the basic need in any democracy to ensure public backing for government policy, Israeli policy-makers have to keep their society constantly mobilized to deal with the security threats facing the country. In particular, the IDF's reliance upon mass conscription and a large reservoir of reserve soldiers means that its military posture and strength crucially depend upon the larger Israeli society. As a "citizen's army," the IDF cannot be insulated from societal discord. Its ability to function depends upon the willingness of Israelis to serve in its ranks, and to make sacrifices—physical and economic—on its behalf. A national consensus and social cohesion are, therefore, crucial elements in Israel's ability to sustain its huge defense burden. Given this, the exacerbation of sociopolitical divisions, and the further erosion of the national consensus on Israeli foreign policy as a result of the Lebanon War were dangerous developments that had to be rectified. The lesson was simple and straightforward—large-scale future military action by the IDF had to be conducted within the boundaries of a national consensus. In a radio interview in May 1984, for instance, Shamir was asked: "Is there any personal lesson from this war, from the way it was handled, from everything relating to national consensus which was broken as a result of the war?" To which he responded: "I can say that a national consensus is a most important element in every step of this kind that a government decides upon. To our great disappointment, this element didn't exist in full—at the beginning in part, later totally not—and this is very sad and a deficiency."[120]

As Israel's prime minister from 1986 to 1992, Shamir attempted to rebuild a national consensus on Israeli foreign policy. In election campaigns, the Likud and its allies promoted themselves as comprising "the national camp," implying that those who did not agree with their policies and ideas—specifically, those who favored territorial compromise and did not support *Eretz Israel*—were not part of the national community.[121] Yet, despite this claim, the Likud and its allies on the right were never able to establish a national consensus surrounding their primary goal of retaining *Eretz Israel* in its entirety.[122] A majority of Israelis did not share the right's ideological commitment to Jewish sovereignty over the whole of the Land of Israel. The Likud under Shamir, therefore, attempted to appear more moderate and pragmatic, even though Shamir's ideological commitment to *Eretz Israel* never wavered.[123]

The Likud's effort to present a more moderate face to the Israeli public, and to the international community, whilst simultaneously avoiding alienating its more right-wing constituency was apparent in the argument advanced by Foreign Minister Moshe Arens and his protégé Benjamin Netanyahu (who was ambassador to the UN from 1984 to 1988 and then deputy foreign minister until 1990) that Israeli control of the territories was essential for Israeli security.[124] According to this pragmatic security-oriented conception, the territories formed a protective belt around the state and provided necessary strategic depth. Moreover, negotiating with the PLO was completely ruled out on the grounds that it was a terrorist organization implacably committed to the destruction of Israel. Palestinian terrorism, whether by the PLO or any other Palestinian group, was used as a means to delegitimize Palestinian political demands. In the words of one author: "The leadership of the Likud sought to shore up its ideologically inspired policy of settling and retaining Judea and Samaria by emphasizing the scourge of terrorism at home and abroad and thereby delegitimizing the PLO as a future partner in negotiations."[125] The Likud was therefore able to avoid entering into negotiations over the future of the territories due to Palestinian terrorism and the fear and animosity this instilled in the Israeli public toward Palestinians in general and the PLO in particular. Hence, in its firm rejection of negotiations with the PLO and the establishment of a Palestinian state in the territories, the Likud was able to claim that it represented the national consensus. By the end of the decade, however, that claim was far more tenuous, and the Likud appeared far less moderate.[126] A major reason for this change was the Palestinian uprising—the "Intifada"—that broke out in Gaza on December 8, 1987, and quickly spread to the West Bank.

The Intifada: The Moral Cost of Occupation

The Intifada presented Israeli policy-makers with a novel challenge. Arab armies were not massing at Israel's borders and issuing threats of destruction; instead masses of Palestinian civilians in the territories, many of them children and adolescents, were taking to the streets demonstrating against "the Occupation," and their weapons—if they had any—were stones, not guns. Taken by surprise, and without any consensus within the national unity government on how to respond to the unfolding events, Israel's reaction was hesitant and confused. Israeli policy-makers debated over whether to classify the Intifada as a war or just an extreme form of civil disorder, and hence, whether to send in the army or the police.[127] A compromise was reached—the army would be used, but its use of force against the demonstrators would be restricted and moderated.[128] The decision to send in the army rather than the police carried with it symbolic significance, as Yaron Ezrahi makes clear: "Inasmuch as the army (unlike the police) usually represents the use of force vis-à-vis external enemies, the use of the army against the Intifada suggested that Israel was unwilling to treat it as a mere civil disorder in its own territories. Rather, the Palestinians—and the occupied territories—were still treated as *external*, thus reinforcing a perceptual distinction between most of the West Bank and internal Israeli space."[129] This, together with the fact that Israelis (with the obvious exception of the Jewish settlers) ceased visiting, or even traveling through the territories during the Intifada (since it was considered too dangerous for them to do so), had a long-term affect upon Israelis' perception of the territories. As Mark Tessler writes: "An important consequence of the Palestinian uprising has been the resurrection of the green line in the consciousness of most Israelis."[130] The Intifada, therefore, effectively overturned the efforts of the Likud and others on the right to erase the Green Line in the minds of Israelis. Over time, the distinction bolstered by the Intifada between "Israel" (within its pre-1967 borders) and "the territories" was to become instrumental in enabling Israelis to entertain the possibility of a territorial compromise with the Palestinians.

The unsettling implications of the Intifada for Israeli national identity were also instrumental in moving Israelis toward the option of territorial compromise with the Palestinians. The Intifada, like the Lebanon War, constituted a major challenge to Israeli identity. In both cases, the actions of the IDF were particularly important in challenging the self-image of Israelis, due to the prominent role played by the IDF in representing Israeli national identity. The Lebanon War, as stated earlier, undermined Israelis' belief that the IDF only fought defensive wars. The Intifada, in turn, undermined their belief that the IDF's military conduct was always in accordance with the principle of "purity of arms" (*tohar haneshek*).[131] It was hard to reconcile this cherished belief with the actions of the IDF during the Intifada (actions which were widely reported in the domestic and international media). The high social prestige of the IDF was also undermined in the

Intifada, as it appeared incapable of adequately responding to the uprising. The IDF was forced to carry out a role with which it was unfamiliar and unprepared to deal with. This, together with the criticism it received both domestically and internationally, eroded military morale and led to concern by the political echelon about the impact of the Intifada on the IDF.[132]

The Intifada challenged many different aspects of Israeli national identity. One aspect that was challenged was that of being a liberal and enlightened people. The values of secular Israelis were largely drawn from the tradition of the European Enlightenment, and as such, Israelis identified themselves as civilized and humane.[133] In the course of the Intifada, this self-image was threatened since, in the words of Ezrahi: "The liberal-humanistic-universalistic self-image we Israelis have held for so many years was hardly consistent with our practice."[134] Another aspect of Israeli identity threatened by the Intifada was Israelis' sense of belonging to the West. Although Israelis had always been ambivalent toward the West—a legacy of the Holocaust and anti-Semitism—they nevertheless saw themselves as members of the West, since many had originally come from Western countries, Israel shared the same democratic political system as Western countries, participated on the same side in the Cold War, and the culture which held the greatest appeal and attraction to many of them was that of the West (whether European or American). But as critics of Israel in the West denounced the heavy-handed way in which it dealt with Palestinian demonstrators and stone-throwers, Israeli leaders responded to this criticism in the same manner they had reacted to earlier criticism of Israel—by viewing it as an indication of bias against the Jewish state.

Such a view was regularly expressed during the Intifada. Three months after it began, for instance, Rabin responded to international criticism over his order in the Intifada's early stages for Israeli soldiers to use clubs against Palestinians to break up demonstrations by stating: "In general, beating a Jew is unimportant in the eyes of the world. But when a Jew beats somebody, then it is news."[135] The following month, in March 1988, Prime Minister Shamir declared in the Knesset: "One cannot escape the impression that this nation and this country are put to a constant test of moral standards that no nation and no people faces or can pass, yet we are impudently asked to meet such demands."[136] In June of that year, President Chaim Herzog even went so far as to denounce: "The irrational attitude of the Western world toward Jews, Judaism and, in our case, the Jewish state."[137] International condemnation of Israel during the Intifada, therefore, gave rise to widespread feelings of being discriminated against and persecuted. This was reflected in a survey of the attitudes of a representative sample of Israeli Jews in 1987 in which 68 percent of respondents agreed with the statement that "world criticism of Israeli policy stems mainly from anti-Semitism," 69 percent believed that "Israel is and will continue to be 'a people dwelling alone'," and 51 percent agreed that "the whole world is against us."[138] Former Defense Minister Ezer Weizman bluntly summed up the national mood in the late eighties: "There is too much disbelief in peace, a feeling that everyone is out to screw us."[139] This increased Israelis' feelings of alienation from the West and hostility toward it and, as it had before, aroused their traditional sense of Jewish identity.

But the IDF's behavior in the Intifada also challenged the Jewish component of Israeli national identity. One abiding and deeply rooted aspect of Jewish identity was the self-perception of being a uniquely moral people—arguably, a secularized version of the traditional religious belief in Jewish "chosenness." The victimization that Jews suffered was traditionally interpreted as emanating from the gentiles' resentment of Jewish righteousness.[140] A legacy of this attitude was that Israeli Jews long believed that they were essentially "righteous victims" in their conflict with the Arabs and Palestinians.[141] This reassuring self-image, however, was disabused in the Intifada. To many, both inside and outside the country, Israelis appeared as the victimizers not the victims, and as immoral not righteous. The stories and pictures of Israeli soldiers beating Palestinians with clubs, shooting them at close-range (often resulting in fatal injuries as rubber bullets were only intended to be fired from a distance), and physically and verbally abusing them, were deeply unsettling for Israeli Jews (and for those in the Diaspora). They conveyed an image of the IDF—and, by extension, of Israeli society as a whole—as a "bully" who "picked on" defenseless Palestinians. The image of Israel as "David" battling the Arab "Goliath," which had already declined in foreign perceptions of the country after 1967, was now being sullied in the minds of Israelis themselves. This was evidently not a conflict in which Israel was outnumbered or outgunned. Nor was it one in which the survival of the state seemed to be at stake. Instead, the Intifada was fundamentally a violent protest by Palestinians who, living under the yoke of Israeli occupation (many of the protesters had, in fact, grown up under it), became increasingly frustrated with the lack of diplomatic progress in resolving their plight, and with the continued expansion of Israeli settlements and the appropriation of their natural resources (i.e., land and water).

Another popular Israeli belief that was challenged by the Intifada was the belief that the Palestinians, led by the PLO, were intent upon violently destroying Israel. Almost a year after the Intifada's outbreak, the PLO officially accepted UN Resolution 242, which amounted to implicit recognition of Israel, at the Palestine National Council's (PNC) nineteenth meeting held in Algiers on November 12–15, 1988. The PNC also issued a statement calling for a UN-sponsored international conference based on

Resolutions 242 and 338 involving Israel and the PLO with the participation of the five permanent members of the UN Security Council. A month later, in a speech before the UN General Assembly on December 13, 1988, PLO leader Yasser Arafat denounced terrorism and reiterated his call for Israel to begin peace negotiations with the PLO. This opened the way for the beginning of an official U.S. dialogue with the PLO. As a result, calls for negotiating with the PLO became more frequent in Israel and were publicly voiced by more "mainstream" elements of Israeli society, including prominent Labor leaders such as Moshe Shahal, Uzi Baram, and Mordechai Gur. Even the head of Israel's military intelligence branch, Amnon Shahak, advocated negotiations with the PLO as the only means to end the Intifada.[142]

The Israeli public also began to adopt a more compromising stance toward the Palestinian issue. In public opinion surveys, greater numbers of Israeli Jews showed a readiness to exchange "land for peace" and negotiate with the PLO.[143] Even amongst Likud voters, the prospect of negotiating with the PLO was no longer a taboo. In a March 1989 survey, for example, 49 percent of Likud-leaning voters expressed a willingness, under certain conditions, to talk with the PLO.[144] Reacting to this shift in Israeli public opinion toward accepting the perceived necessity of negotiations with the PLO, Shamir was forced into narrowing his formulation of the national consensus. "We don't want to negotiate with the PLO," he stated in a newspaper interview on Israel's Independence Day in 1989, affirming Likud's long-standing position. But he went on to defend this position not on the traditional grounds of what the PLO is (i.e., a terrorist organization), but on the grounds of what it wants (i.e., Palestinian statehood): "What does the PLO want? A Palestinian state, immediately. But we say we oppose a Palestinian state, this is the national consensus. So what will they talk to us about?"[145] In fact, even public opposition to a Palestinian state was eroding, as opinion polls showed.[146] The issue of the future of the territories, therefore, acquired much greater urgency as a result of the Intifada. Thus, whilst the issue received relatively little attention in the 1984 election campaign, in the 1988 election (held roughly eleven months after the outbreak of the Intifada) the situation in the territories was by far the most important issue.[147]

The Intifada substantially increased international—and, especially American—pressure upon Israel's national unity government to formulate a political initiative to quell the Palestinian uprising and work toward a resolution of the Israeli-Palestinian conflict. Prime Minister Shamir, however, was unmoved by the mounting international pressure. When asked in an interview how he felt about the fact that "the whole world, in some degree or another, is talking to the PLO," Shamir responded by saying: "This is perhaps our historical destiny, to swim against the tide. But we keep on swimming, we have not drowned yet."[148] Like his Likud predecessor Begin, Shamir was dismissive of international public opinion toward Israel. A few months after the outbreak of the Intifada in the midst of international criticism of Israel's handling of the uprising, Shamir defiantly stated in the Knesset: "We reject the condemnations, and have no use for the preachings."[149] On another occasion he insisted: "I don't need anyone's approval that Eretz Israel is ours."[150] Like Begin, Shamir believed that Israel as the Jewish state was destined to be alone. As he stated in a television interview when rejecting widespread calls for Israel to begin a dialogue with the PLO: "The people of Israel has a long tradition of being alone."[151] Since he believed that Israel, as the collective Jew, was always the object of discrimination and persecution, he was highly distrustful of international forums, particularly the UN.[152] He was therefore adamantly opposed to Israel's participation in an international conference to solve the conflict with the Palestinians (as proposed by the PLO, the Soviets, and the Europeans). "I will never trust any decision made by the UN or by any UN institution," Shamir asserted, "because we know in advance that any UN body, no matter what its composition, will be against us."[153]

What eventually led Shamir to finally propose a peace initiative in the spring of 1989, in conjunction with Defense Minister Rabin (who had by then given up on the "Jordanian option"),[154] was his mounting concern over the divisions that beset Israeli Jews as well as those in the Diaspora over Israel's policy in the territories.[155] The Intifada aggravated domestic divisions in Israel over Israeli policy in the territories, and threatened to create a rift between Diaspora Jewry, particularly American Jews, and Israel.[156] As a result, Shamir's ideological commitment to Jewish sovereignty over the entire *Eretz Israel* came into conflict with his commitment to ensure unity both between Jews in Israel and between Diaspora Jewry and Israel. According to his close aide Yossi Ahimeir, Shamir was aware of this conflict and was very troubled by it, and he was willing to make some compromises for the sake of unity.[157] Thus, in presenting his and Rabin's four-point peace plan (elections in the territories to nominate Palestinian representatives to conduct negotiations for a transitional period of self-rule, and later for a permanent settlement) to the Knesset on May 17, 1989, Shamir emphasized that: "The government is saying to the nation in Israel, to our neighbors—first and foremost to the Arabs of Eretz Israel—and to the countries of the world, that we are united in our aspiration for peace, we are united in proposing the channel for this, and we are of course united in recognition of the security requirements of Israel and its inhabitants"; and he went on to say that the need for Jewish and national unity was one of the "primary motives" for the formulation of his peace initiative.[158]

The Shamir-Rabin peace plan soon fell victim to infighting within the Likud party. Although the plan stipulated that Israel opposed the establishment of a Palestinian state in the West Bank and Gaza, Shamir's rivals within the Likud (principally, Sharon, David Levy, and Yitzhak Moda'i) attacked the plan, arguing that this would be its eventual, if unintended, outcome. Faced with fierce opposition from within the Likud, Shamir chose to back away from the plan, leading to the collapse of the national unity government as Labor withdrew its support. With Labor unable to form a governing coalition; a narrow Likud-led government was established on June 11, 1990, headed by Shamir and backed by the right-wing and religious parties. This government was voted out of office just over two years later in the 1992 elections. The new Labor-led government under Rabin that came to power in 1992 was to initiate a revolution in Israeli foreign policy, one that had dramatic repercussions for Israeli national identity. At the center of this foreign policy revolution was the Oslo peace process that the Rabin government began with the PLO. This development, and its relationship to Israeli national identity, will be the subject of the next chapter.

CHAPTER 3

OUT OF THE GHETTO: THE OSLO PEACE PROCESS AND ISRAELI NATIONAL IDENTITY

The world is no longer against us.[1]

—Yitzhak Rabin

We will not exist for long if we become just another country that is mostly devoted to the welfare of its residents.[2]

—Yitzhak Shamir

Introduction

The Oslo peace process that the Rabin government embarked on with the PLO in 1993 was a watershed in Israeli foreign policy. It came about due to major changes in the international system as well as in the Middle East regional subsystem due to the end of the Cold War, the collapse of the Soviet Union, and the Gulf War. But these external changes, though necessary, were not sufficient to alter Israel's long-standing policy of not negotiating with the PLO. I argue in this chapter that the critical event that enabled the Oslo peace process to occur was the election of a Labor-led government under Yitzhak Rabin in the 1992 election. Had Shamir and the Likud party remained in office, the Oslo Accords would never have been signed. Hence, in order to understand what brought about the Oslo peace process, it is necessary to investigate why Labor won the 1992 election.

I explain Labor's victory in terms of a triumph of individualism over collectivism. In contrast to the traditional Zionist collectivist ethos that viewed the needs of the nation as being more important than the needs of the individual, individualism upheld the primacy of the individual's needs and desires (e.g., self-fulfillment, personal autonomy, professional success, material well-being). The rise of an individualistic ethos in Israeli society meant that fewer Israelis were willing to make personal sacrifices for the sake of national goals, such as maintaining the entirety of *Eretz Israel* under

Israeli rule. It also meant that growing numbers wanted the government to provide them with economic opportunities and personal security, rather than dedicate itself to the pursuit of collective goals. The Labor party capitalized on this "me, now" sentiment by emphasizing its commitment to addressing the domestic social and economic concerns of Israelis that had been neglected by the previous Likud government. It was this that drew electoral support away from the Likud to the Labor party.

After discussing the 1992 election, I analyze some of Prime Minister Rabin's major speeches in office. Rabin stressed the interests of individual citizens, in accordance with the individualistic ethos that brought him to power. He also highlighted Israel's transformed international environment and the positive consequences this had for Israeli security. Both of these aspects of his discourse had implications for Israeli national identity, in so far as they contradicted elements of the prevailing ethno-religious conception of Israeli national identity. This was not accidental. Rabin believed that Israeli national identity needed to be refashioned in a post–Cold War, globalizing world in which Israel was no longer a pariah state. This changed perception of the world as no longer hostile to the Jewish state also animated a more activist and confident Israeli diplomacy.

The Oslo peace process was the centerpiece of Israel's new foreign policy. But it was bound to be domestically controversial since it involved a complete redefinition of Israel's policies toward its historical enemy (the Palestinians), the organization representing them (the PLO), and the occupied territories (the West Bank and Gaza). The Rabin government anticipated this and both Rabin and Peres attempted to publicly legitimize the peace process by linking it to different constructions of Israeli national identity. I end this chapter by showing how they defined Israeli national identity in ways that would make a withdrawal from the territories appear legitimate and desirable to the Israeli public.

From Despair to Hope

Israel entered the 1990s in disarray. The national consensus on foreign policy—captured in the popular axioms that "there is no one to talk to," that Israel's wars were "no choice wars," and that an "iron wall" was necessary to ensure the country's survival—had disintegrated, and was replaced by a polarizing debate between those advocating Israel's withdrawal from the territories and those refusing to countenance such a possibility on either national-religious or strategic grounds. The attempt by Israel's political leadership on both the left and the right to regenerate a sense of national unity by their joint participation in a coalition government failed, ending with acrimonious recriminations on both sides.

With a public bitterly divided, reflected in a deadlocked political system with no party able to secure majority support for its policies, the prospects for Israeli foreign policy to meet the challenges ahead for the country appeared bleak. There was no end in sight to the political stalemate. Nor did there appear to be much chance of ending the Intifada in the territories or the guerrilla war that the Shiite Lebanese group Hizbullah was waging against Israeli forces bogged down in southern Lebanon. The two seminal events of the previous decade—the Lebanon War and the Intifada— continued to take their toll upon Israel, both in terms of the physical casualties they inflicted (the number of dead, missing, and injured soldiers slowly rising month by month), and the psychological impact they had upon the national self-image of Israeli Jews. At the country's helm sat a narrow right-wing government composed of the Likud and its allies on the far right and the religious parties. Such a government appeared to offer little hope to Palestinians in the territories, or to moderate, secular Israelis who wished to see their country extricate itself from the morass in which it had languished during the 1980s. Outside Israel, the world seemed to be entering a period of momentous change with the fall of the Berlin Wall and the demise of the Soviet Union. The end of the Cold War, and the proclaimed victory of democracy and capitalism, looked set to usher in a period of widespread peace and prosperity. Yet Israel was still at war and its economy stagnant, with unemployment at 8.9 percent—the highest level in almost twenty-five years (the positive economic effects of the structural adjustment program introduced in the mid-1980s were yet to materialize).[3]

This bleak picture was soon to be overturned. Within a few years, Israel's prime minister was shaking hands with the leader of the Palestinians on the lawn of the White House at the signing ceremony of a landmark agreement between Israel and the PLO. The Israeli-PLO "Declaration of Principles on Interim Self-Government Arrangements" (DOP)—referred to as the "Oslo Accords" after the Norwegian capital where the agreement was hammered out after months of secret meetings (beginning in July 1992)—signed in September 1993, set into motion an incremental process to resolve the century-old Israeli-Palestinian conflict. As a first step in what became known as the Oslo peace process, in return for the PLO's renunciation of violence and promise to combat Palestinian terrorism against Israel, Israel was to withdraw from most of the Gaza Strip, except for the Jewish settlements, and from the West Bank city of Jericho. Further Israeli redeployments from the West Bank would follow, and a newly established Palestinian Authority (PA) would take full or partial control over these areas.

Although the Oslo Accords deferred the start of negotiations toward a comprehensive peace treaty (during which the thorniest issues of permanent borders, Palestinian refugees, Jewish settlements, and Jerusalem would be taken up) to a later date on the grounds that both parties needed to first develop trust in each other, hopes were high that such a treaty would eventually come about; and even before it did, it was confidently expected that Israelis and Palestinians alike would begin to enjoy the fruits of peace and prosperity. For Israel, the Oslo Accords heralded the Palestinians' acceptance of the Jewish state's existence, thereby allowing it to finally live at peace with its neighbors and the world at large. For many Israelis, the signing of the DOP on September 13, 1993, by Israel's Prime Minister Yitzhak Rabin and PLO leader Yasser Arafat, was a truly momentous event, whose significance was perhaps only surpassed by the UN General Assembly's famous vote in favor of the partition of Palestine and the creation of a Jewish state in November 1947.

The Oslo Accords came about due to many developments and events within Israel, the Occupied Territories, the Middle East region, and the world at large. These have been described in painstaking detail by numerous journalists, scholars, and the negotiators themselves, so that another narrative here would be superfluous.[4] Hence, rather than provide an exhaustive account of the "road to Oslo," the following analysis will concentrate on the importance of three events in bringing about the Oslo Accords: the first Gulf War (January 17 to February 28, 1991); the ensuing Middle East Peace Conference in Madrid (October 30 to November 3, 1991); and the electoral victory of Rabin and the Labor party over Shamir and the Likud on June 23, 1992. The Oslo peace process would not have happened without these events. What makes them so critical is the effect they ultimately had upon Israel's willingness to negotiate with its long-time enemy, the PLO. It was Israel's new willingness to negotiate with the PLO that was the decisive development that led to the signing of the Oslo Accords.[5]

A Window of Opportunity Opens

The paralysis and vacillation that characterized Israeli foreign policy from the mid-1980s onwards looked set to continue in the 1990s. But what made this impossible was Iraq's invasion of Kuwait on August 2, 1990. After the UN Security Council imposed sanctions on Iraq, and the United States began mobilizing a coalition of European and Arab states to wage a military campaign to remove Iraq from Kuwait, Iraqi leader Saddam Hussein began threatening to attack Israel with missiles. These threats were not hollow. On January 18, 1991, the day after the United States-led "Operation Desert Storm" began,[6] Iraq launched eight Scud missiles into Israel. These missile attacks continued throughout the war (thirty-nine missiles were launched in total against Israel, resulting in two direct fatalities). Under intense

American pressure not to retaliate in order to maintain the coalition against Iraq, the Shamir government could do little but make oblique references to its willingness to use Israel's nuclear arsenal against Iraq if the latter used non-conventional weapons against Israel, and instruct a fearful population on an almost nightly basis to remain in sealed rooms with gas masks on.

Although some within Israel's political elite urged Shamir to retaliate, fearful that a failure to do so would erode Israel's deterrent capability,[7] Shamir's policy of restraint was supported by a vast majority of the Israeli public (opinion polls conducted during the war showed almost 90 percent popular support for Israeli inaction).[8] The Gulf War, therefore, was the first war in which Israel was attacked but did not retaliate. This passivity, and the acute sense of vulnerability that accompanied it, was another blow to the self-image of Israelis. Like the war in Lebanon and the Intifada, the Gulf War challenged Israeli national identity. Their self-reliance, military might, and willingness to defend themselves at all costs—characteristics that had long distinguished them in their eyes from Diaspora Jews—were suddenly thrown into doubt. Moreover, the fear of Iraqi poison gas attacks evoked Israelis' memories of the Holocaust, when millions of Jews had been gassed to death.[9] The parallels with the tragic experience of Diaspora Jewry were deeply disconcerting for Israeli Jews, especially since a striking two-thirds of them during the Gulf War believed "to a great extent" that Saddam was out to get them "as a Jew."[10] Equally disturbing, especially for those within Israel's political and security establishment, were the scenes of tens of thousands of residents of Tel Aviv and its suburbs fleeing to safer places in the country or leaving Israel entirely. For Rabin, this behavior (and the unapologetic manner with which these Israelis spoke of it in television interviews) was "shocking" and "unprecedented," as he compared it to the steadfastness of the city's residents under Egyptian bombing (which claimed over thirty civilian casualties) in the 1948 war.[11] "We have changed," he lamented, implying that Israelis had lost some of their former perseverance and determination.[12] The proud national self-image of Israelis as a nation of courageous fighters was therefore undermined by the behavior of the government and some Israelis during the Gulf War.

The Gulf War, however, had little impact on Israeli public opinion concerning foreign policy and national security.[13] Despite underlining the new strategic danger that Israel faced—in the form of missiles which could be equipped with weapons of mass destruction—and the fact that the possession of territory was of little, if any, use in defending against this danger (thereby reducing the strategic significance of the West Bank as a land buffer), the Gulf War did not increase political support in Israel for a territorial compromise with the Palestinians. It did, however, force Shamir to engage in direct negotiations with the Palestinians in the context of the Middle East Peace Conference convened in Madrid in the wake of the war.[14] After the Palestinians and all the Arab states (except Iraq) agreed to participate in the conference (either directly or as observers), Shamir had no choice but to reluctantly accept the joint U.S.-Soviet invitation to the conference.[15] In the words of the Israeli diplomat and former director-general of the Foreign Ministry David Kimche, Shamir was "dragged to Madrid."[16]

However half-hearted, the Shamir government's participation in the Madrid peace conference and in subsequent rounds of talks in Washington DC was highly significant in terms of Israel's policy toward the territories, although for symbolic rather than practical reasons. Not only did it break the domestic Israeli taboo on direct negotiations between Israel and the Palestinians, but also it paved the way for Israel's later direct negotiations with the PLO under the Rabin government.[17] Although the Shamir government insisted that the Palestinian delegation to the conference be independent from the PLO (it consisted only of Palestinians from the West Bank and Gaza who were not formally PLO officials), in reality the Palestinian delegates took their instructions from PLO headquarters in Tunis. Thus, while Israel was still officially refusing to negotiate with the PLO, it was effectively conducting informal and indirect negotiations—a fact that Israeli negotiators were well aware of.[18] Consequently, when Rabin's Labor-led government came to power in the 1992 election, it abandoned this pretense and initiated a series of direct, albeit clandestine, negotiations with the PLO leading to the Oslo Accords.

The Madrid Conference, which opened on October 30, 1991, was a watershed event in the Israeli-Palestinian conflict (as well as the larger Arab-Israeli conflict). It inaugurated the peace process between Israel and the Palestinians and established its ground rules—direct, bilateral negotiations on the basis of UN Resolutions 242 and 338 and the principle of land for peace that they incorporated. Yet, for all its historic importance, the Madrid Conference and the subsequent bilateral negotiations in Washington DC that went on for eighteen months produced no concrete results. This was exactly the outcome that Shamir wanted. Shamir agreed to negotiate with the Palestinians solely in order to ease international and, especially American, pressure upon Israel. He had no interest in making a territorial compromise with the Palestinians and relinquishing Israeli control over the West Bank and Gaza, and his only goal at Madrid and in the subsequent talks was to drag out the negotiations and ensure that they were inconclusive.[19] As he candidly admitted soon after leaving office: "I would have carried on autonomy talks for ten years. Meanwhile we would have reached half a million Jews in Judea and Samaria."[20]

Thus, although American pressure brought Shamir to the negotiating table, he adamantly refused to make a deal with the Palestinians and give up his dream of a united *Eretz Israel* under Israeli sovereignty. Shamir's intransigence prevented any real progress from taking place in the negotiations between Israel and the Palestinians during his premiership. The momentous international and regional developments that occurred between 1989 and 1992 while Shamir was prime minister—the end of the Cold War, the collapse of the Soviet Union, and the Gulf War—did not incline him toward compromise on the issue of the territories. Shamir's perception of the Middle East and Israel's position in it remained unaltered. According to his former aide Yossi Ahimeir, Shamir saw the end of the Cold War as "belonging to another world," and as far as he was concerned, the "rules of the game" in the Middle East remained the same.[21]

The end of the Cold War, the withdrawal of Soviet support for Israel's adversaries, the division within the Arab world as a result of Iraq's invasion of Kuwait, the financial bankruptcy of the PLO after it sided with Iraq in the Gulf War, and the "Pax Americana" established in the region in the wake of the war, all tilted the global and regional balance of power strongly in Israel's favor and against the Arab states and the Palestinians. Nonetheless, Shamir continued to believe that Israel was engaged in an existential struggle and that its survival remained as precarious as ever. "There is a constant threat to our existence," he affirmed in a newspaper interview shortly after the Gulf War.[22] In his Independence Day message on May 7, 1992, he declared that: "[T]he dangers facing us and the threats to our security have not abated. A host of terrorist organizations continue to attack Israel, its citizens, and missions abroad. And Arab governments are making every effort to acquire massive quantities of arms and weapons of mass destruction. In spite of the end of the Cold War, our region has not become safer."[23] It was not only Shamir's perception of the Middle East as a dangerous and volatile region (or, as he once described it, "an ocean of shifting sands, with very few islands of relative and even transient stability") immune from trends elsewhere in the world, that accounted for his belief that the end of the Cold War, the collapse of the Soviet Union, or the Gulf War were of little, if any, significance for Israel. It was also his conception of Israel's historical past and future that accorded little, if any, significance to events outside of Israel within the non-Jewish world. His narrative of Jewish history was essentially self-contained, isolating Jewish history from world history, or the history of the gentiles. According to this narrative, the existential condition of Jews was constant. Their estrangement from gentile society was absolute and unchanging. Israel as the collective Jew would thus be unable to integrate into international— non-Jewish—society and make peace with its neighbors whatever the prevailing international conditions. The end of the Cold War, the collapse of the Soviet Union, and the Gulf War were, therefore, essentially irrelevant to this national narrative. They did not mark a historical rupture, and they could not alter the Jewish fate, and that of the Jewish state.[25]

The end of the Cold War, the collapse of the Soviet Union, and the Gulf War, therefore, did not shake Shamir's convictions that Israel faced an existential threat from the Arab world, and that territorial compromise with the Palestinians and Arab states would merely be a prelude to further Arab aggression against the country. These major international developments, however, did significantly affect the thinking of Rabin who, as the leader of the Labor party (after his defeat of Peres in a contest for the leadership in February 1992), became Shamir's main political rival. For Rabin, unlike Shamir, the Cold War's end, the Soviet Union's collapse, and Iraq's devastating defeat in the Gulf War, greatly improved Israel's security predicament.[26] Rabin believed that the United States' victory in the Cold War and the fall of the Soviet Union shifted the international balance of power strongly in the United States' favor, and that this strengthened Israel's position since it was a close ally of the United States. The regional balance of power had also shifted dramatically in Israel's favor, according to Rabin, as its main regional adversaries were weakened. Syria was weakened as it lost its superpower ally, the Soviet Union. Iraq was weakened as its military capabilities were decimated in the Gulf War. Jordan was weakened, financially and diplomatically, as it sided with Iraq in the Gulf War. The PLO was weakened; financially, as it sided with Iraq in the Gulf War and so lost its funding from the Gulf states; politically, as its leadership over the Palestinians was challenged by the rise of the Islamist group Hamas in the territories; and diplomatically, as it lost the support of the Soviet Union. The Arab world as a whole was also weakened due to its divisions over the Gulf War.

While the end of the Cold War and the Gulf War improved Israel's security situation in the short term, for Rabin, both events raised greater dangers for Israel in the long term. Rabin was aware that in a post–Cold War international system the importance of small allies, such as Israel, for the United States could diminish over time as they lost their previous role in contributing to the containment of the Soviet Union.[27] Therefore, the United States might become less supportive of Israel, in the future (a support which Rabin had long deemed to be crucial for Israel's security).[28] The second risk Israel faced in the long term came from the proliferation of weapons of mass destruction in the Middle East, a risk that the Gulf War accentuated. The very real possibility that in the future Israel's adversaries could attack the country's major population centers with missiles, and chemical, biological, and potentially nuclear weapons, posed the risk that a future war would result in large-scale Israeli civilian casualties (Iran and Iraq were most menacing in this regard, and became the locus of Israeli threat perception). Compounding this threat was the continued spread of Islamic radicalism in the Middle East and beyond which threatened to topple moderate Arab and Muslim regimes, and bring Islamic militants to power who might seek to wage war against Israel, possibly with the use of weapons of mass destruction.

The danger this posed to Israel, however, was not just that Israel's enemies could come into possession of these weapons, but that Israelis would panic and even flee en masse in the face of such a threat. Eitan Haber, Rabin's long-time advisor, claims that Rabin's concern about the proliferation of ballistic missiles in the Middle East was not really a strategic or military concern at all, but rather a concern about how Israeli society would respond to such a threat. Rabin knew that Israel could develop the technological capacity to counter a ballistic missile threat, but he was much less sure about whether Israeli society had the willpower to withstand the threat. In Haber's words: "It [ballistic missiles] was a social question not a military question."[29] This was because: "Rabin was worried about the collapse of Israeli society's morale."[30] The most important event that shaped Rabin's view of Israeli society's morale and willpower was the Gulf War and the flight from Tel Aviv of many of its residents. According to Haber, the behavior of Israelis during the Gulf War raised the alarming prospect for Rabin of a mass panic in the event of a future missile war. He was aware that the Syrians possessed hundreds of missiles, and wondered what the public reaction would be if the Syrians launched an attack on Israel. Nor was it only the behavior and attitude of Israeli civilians that worried Rabin. A "spill-over" effect from the civilian domain to the all-conscript IDF threatened to undermine soldier's morale and willingness to endure sacrifices. Thus, according to Haber, Rabin's evaluation of the growing weakness of Israeli society was the prime factor motivating his new strategic prognosis.[31]

In sum, the end of the Cold War, the demise of the Soviet Union, and the Gulf War led Rabin to believe that international and regional conditions were more favorable to Israel in the short term than they would be in the long term. This belief, together with his assessment that the willpower of Israelis to withstand additional war(s) was diminishing, lay behind his use of the concept of a "window of opportunity," suggesting a time constraint and the need for urgent action.[32] In line with this understanding, Rabin advocated greater Israeli activism than before in the pursuit of peace. This was reflected in the reversal of his position regarding negotiating with the PLO. Having long opposed this (like most Israelis, Rabin abhorred the PLO and viewed it as a terrorist organization dedicated to Israel's destruction),[33] Rabin finally came to accept the necessity of directly negotiating with the PLO. It was this acceptance that later enabled the informal meetings in Oslo between PLO representatives and two Israeli academics

(Yair Hirschfeld and Ron Pundik) to become official back-channel negotiations between Israel and the PLO (by the dispatch of Israeli government employees, Uri Savir and Joel Singer, to join the secret Oslo meetings).

Thus, changes in the global and regional security landscape altered Rabin's attitudes and beliefs, but not Shamir's. Hence, the main impact of these external changes upon Israeli policy toward the territories came with Rabin and the Labor party's defeat of Shamir and the Likud in the 1992 elections. Israeli domestic politics was, then, the essential factor in enabling the agreement between Israel and the Palestinians represented in the 1993 Oslo Accords. Without Labor's electoral triumph in 1992 these accords would not have been reached. The victory not only resulted in a dramatic change in Israeli foreign policy toward the territories and the Palestinian issue, but also a dramatic change in the discourse of Israeli national identity. It is, therefore, worthwhile analyzing what brought this victory about.

The 1992 Election: "Me, Now!"

The general election held on June 23, 1992 was a political watershed in Israel. Just as the 1977 election that brought Begin and Likud to power represented a domestic political "upheaval," so too did the 1992 election. The parties on the left collectively defeated those on the right, winning 56 seats in the Knesset compared to 49 seats.[34] The Labor party alone received twelve more seats than its Likud rival. After nearly a decade of political deadlock with support for both parties almost evenly balanced, this result was, in the words of one writer, an "electoral earthquake."[35] For the first time in eighteen years, a Labor government came to power in coalition with Meretz and Shas, the Sephardi ultra-orthodox political party.[36] A multitude of factors contributed to this outcome; particularly important amongst them the defection of a significant number of Mizrahi voters from Likud to Labor, the votes for Labor and Meretz from about half of the new immigrants from the former Soviet Union (who made up 9 percent of the voting public), and the shift in electoral support of Israeli Arab voters from Arab nationalist parties to Labor and Meretz.[37] No doubt, each of these groups had its own specific concerns influencing its vote (e.g., for the newly arrived immigrants from the former Soviet Union, it was their lack of employment and absorption difficulties which mattered most). Nevertheless, overall the issue of the territories was prominent in influencing the vote—in a survey prior to the election, 81 percent stated that it would influence their vote greatly or very greatly.[38]

This was so, neither because Israelis had a newfound empathy and understanding of the plight of the Palestinians prompting them to acknowledge the right of the Palestinians to national self-determination, nor even because they feared the demographic consequences of annexing the territories and sought to preserve Israel as a Jewish state,[39] but because many centrist Israelis were swayed by Labor's argument that Likud's settlement policy in the territories had consumed too much of Israel's scarce resources, resources which were better spent elsewhere. In its election campaign, Labor framed the issue of the territories in terms of pragmatism rather than principle. It differentiated itself from Likud on the issue of the territories with regard to its priorities rather than its principles—claiming that its different set of priorities involved investing more money in infrastructure, education, welfare, and job creation in Israel, rather than channeling funds to the settlements in the West Bank and Gaza.[40] Labor's electoral campaign successfully reflected the Israeli public's desire for a reordering of government budget priorities, in favor of jobs, education, and health. These domestic social and economic concerns now mattered more to most Israelis than maintaining the entirety of *Eretz Israel* under Israeli rule.

The ideological commitment to Israel's possession of the entirety of *Eretz Israel*, long-championed by the Likud and its right-wing allies, had steadily receded within the Israeli public. This development was not limited to one social group within Israeli society, but was a trend that encompassed all social groups. As Asher Arian reports on his survey of the changing attitudes of Israeli Jews: "The percentage that responded that Israel had a 'right to the land' [as the main reason to hold onto the territories] dropped steadily between 1986 and 1993 in all demographic categories; there was also a uniform increase in the percentage of those willing to return the territories for peace and security in all demographic categories. Moreover, even those who retained their view about Israel's 'right to the land' generated a growing rate of readiness to return the territories over the years. Something systemic was going on, quite different from explanations stemming from changing demography or polarization."[41]

What accounts for this systemic change? Why did the ideological claim that Israel had a "right to the land" gradually lose its appeal amongst Israeli Jews? One answer to this question lies in the steady rise of individualism within Israeli society. From the beginning of Zionist settlement in Palestine, "a thick culture of collective consciousness" prevailed within the society of the *Yishuv* and later the State of Israel.[42] Israelis were raised to esteem the collective over the individual, and to put the interests of the nation over their own. Individual sacrifice for the sake of the nation was valorized—most famously, in the dying words attributed to revisionist hero Yosef Trumpeldor: "It is good to die for our country."[43] A "heroic-sacrificial ethos" glorifying patriotic sacrifice was only one manifestation of a culture in which supreme value was placed upon the nation rather than the individual.[44] The state itself was conceived of as a vehicle for the promotion of the interests of the nation, as Yaron Ezrahi writes in his penetrating analysis of collectivism within Israeli political culture: "Since 1948, many Israelis have regarded the State of Israel primarily as a collective expression of the Jewish people, not as a creation based on a social contract among free, autonomous individuals. In this view, Israel was founded to secure the survival and self-fulfillment of the Jewish people, and only secondarily and within these premises can it address the issue of individual freedom and welfare."[45]

But for many Israelis in the early 1990s, although they continued to pay lip service to this view, their practical adherence to it was diminished by a rising tide of individualism. Growing numbers of Israelis began to focus on their own interests and aspirations, even if they conflicted with the purported interests of the nation. As Arian notes: "There developed a 'me' generation in Israel as steadily as in the rest of the world; 'all of us for the nation' seemed to be replaced by 'me, and now.' "[46] The ethic of self-sacrifice, and the ideological slogans brandished in support of it, became increasingly worn out.[47] Zionist ideology no longer mobilized Israelis as it once had. "Our people have long since tired of bearing Zionism on its shoulders generation after generation," Yoel Marcus, the Israeli political commentator, later lamented.[48] To be sure, few Israeli Jews explicitly disavowed their commitment to Zionism. Instead, they just ceased to be strongly motivated by it. In the words of Erik Cohen: "[A]lthough many Israeli Jews remain nominal Zionists, Zionism has become largely irrelevant as an ideological context for their opinions and actions with regard to the most burning dilemmas that Israel faces. Nevertheless, even if Zionism has lost much of its practical relevance, for many people, few would openly admit that they have ceased to be Zionists. Such an admission, indeed, would widely be considered close to treason or sacrilege."[49]

The increasing trend toward individualism within Israeli society was both a cause and an effect of the declining power of Zionism.[50] On the one hand, individualism arose to fill the ideological vacuum left by Zionism's gradual demise. On the other hand, individualism contributed to that demise by shifting people's attention away from grand social and political visions to more personal, immediate concerns. Growing numbers of Israelis became more interested in their own pursuit of wealth and happiness than in the pursuit of national redemption. This was well conveyed by Robert Wistrich and David Ohana when they wrote: "It is the stock exchange rather than the Kibbutz, technocracy instead of Zionist visions, and the dream of quick profits not Hebrew prophets, which sets the tone for much of present-day Israeli society."[51]

The economic liberalization policies pursued by successive Israeli governments since the early 1980s, and the consequent privatization of state-owned enterprises in many different sectors (such as the media, agriculture, and health services), transformed Israel's economy from a highly-centralized, statist economy to one increasingly dominated by market forces.[52] In this new market-driven economy, the interests of the individual entrepreneur and consumer were paramount. Individualism was, therefore, promoted by the restructuring of the Israeli economy. This individualism stressed personal freedom and fulfillment at the expense of the collectivist values and ideals espoused by Zionism. Thus, individualism effectively undermined adherence to Zionism, as it did with other collectivist ideologies. In the words of Ezrahi: "Despite, and partly in defiance of, Israeli collectivism, the Israeli individual as a cultural, moral, political and economic actor has come of age. As a private person . . . this individual, joining the increasingly articulate, cacophonous chorus of Israeli voices, has begun to challenge the hold of Israeli collectivist orientations at all levels."[53]

Israeli society's transition from being a highly collectivistic society to an increasingly individualistic one, affected popular Israeli attitudes toward the territories. After capturing the Israeli-Jewish public's imagination in the wake of the 1967 war, the mythic appeal of Judea and Samaria waned in the 1980s and early 1990s.[54] The right's ideological argument in favor of Israeli control over the entire territory of *Eretz Israel* on the grounds that Israel had a "right to the land" lost its power, not so much because Israelis no longer believed this to be true, but because they simply cared less about it and more about other things. Israel's possession of the biblical areas of Judea and Samaria, discursively represented by the right as the culmination of the Zionist dream of the return of the Jewish nation to its homeland, was now deemed less essential by Israelis than their personal need for security and economic well-being. The territories—Judea and Samaria—may well have been the birthplace of the Jewish nation, but they were also a source of constant problems for Israelis, whether in the form of the violence directed against them by Palestinian inhabitants of those areas, or in the form of the money that the Jewish settlements there drained from an already overstretched national budget. More and more Israelis (especially among the younger generation) wondered whether it was really worth risking their economic welfare and their personal security for the sake of maintaining Israel's possession of the territories. If by withdrawing from the territories, Israel could redirect government money toward immigrant absorption, job creation, health, education, and the like, and reduce the risk of terrorist attacks and even war, then this was something that many Israelis came to regard as a worthwhile trade-off. In the words of Arian: "Public opinion wanted personal safety and economic well-being, and was willing to suffer withdrawal from the territories if that was the price it took to achieve those goals."[55] In the 1992 election, therefore, a large segment of the Israeli public eschewed collectivist ideology and voted on the basis of pragmatic self-interest. Hence, Labor's victory in the 1992 election was a result of individualism prevailing over collectivism (a historical irony given Labor's socialist roots).

Toward a New Israel and a New National Identity

The ascendancy of individualism over collectivism in Israel was strikingly apparent in the difference between the newly elected Prime Minister Rabin's rhetoric and that of his defeated rival Shamir during the inaugural ceremony in the Knesset on July 13, 1992 for the new Labor-led government. In his speech to the Knesset introducing his government, Rabin stressed the interests of the individual citizen, declaring that: "We are determined to place the citizen at the top of our concerns."[56] Rabin went on to articulate an individualized notion of security, as opposed to the collectivist notion of security that had previously been upheld: "Security is not only the tank, the plane, and the missile boat. Security is also, and perhaps above all, the person—the Israeli citizen. Security is also a person's education, his home, his school, his street and his neighborhood, the society in which he grew up. Security is also a person's hopes. It is the peace of mind and livelihood of the immigrant from Leningrad, the roof over the head of the immigrant from Gondar in Ethiopia, the factory that employs a demobilized soldier, a young native son. It is integration into our way of life and culture; that, too, is security. You ask how we will ensure this security. We are going to change our national priorities."[57] This statement was intended to "put the individual first," according to Rabin's aide, Eitan Haber, who wrote the speech for him.[58]

Shamir's speech to the Knesset on that day could not have been more different from Rabin's. In his speech, he argued that an ideology and a collectivist ethos were essential to Israel and could not be discarded. As he put it: "For many reasons, stemming from its past, world view and the destiny of the Jewish nation, the Jewish state cannot exist without a unique ideological content. We will not exist for long if we become just another country that is mostly devoted to the welfare of its residents. Starting here [the Knesset], the leaders of the nation must provide the young generation in Israel with an ideology upon which it will be educated and in light of which it will act for the benefit of the nation and society. We must provide our sons and daughters with a motivation of value and challenge."[59] Shamir attacked the new government's program as being bereft of vision and ideology and displaying "alienation from any Zionist or Jewish content," even deriding it as being "similar to a nihilistic philosophy."[60] In this context, he went on to stress the importance of *Eretz Israel*: "Eretz Israel is not another piece of land, it is not just a place to live. Above all, Eretz Israel is a value; it is holy. Any conscientious Jew aware of his roots will never be able to treat Eretz Israel as a commodity that could be traded on the stock exchange or in political negotiations, however important they may be." The implication of this statement was clear—those who were willing to carry out "land for peace" (i.e., Rabin and his associates) were not "good" Jews. Shamir also conveyed in his speech his perception that Israel remained a country under siege: "Many around us, near and far, are harassing our country, questioning our right to it, aspiring to cut off parts of it to give them away to others. We, however, can and have to remain loyal to this precious deposit [*Eretz Israel*] we have been given and guard it with all our might."

Rabin's speech contrasted sharply with Shamir's bleak characterization of Israel's situation and his uncompromising ideological commitment to *Eretz Israel*. When outlining his government's approach to foreign policy in his speech Rabin described the new opportunities available to Israel in the post–Cold War period, and clearly signaled his willingness to compromise and make peace with the Palestinians and surrounding Arab states. Noting the dramatic changes that had occurred in international politics as a result of the end of the Cold War and the process of globalization that was underway, Rabin emphatically declared: "We are no longer an isolated nation, and it is no longer true that the entire world is against us. We must rid ourselves of the feeling of isolation that has afflicted us for almost fifty years. We must join the campaign of peace, reconciliation, and international cooperation that is currently engulfing the entire globe, lest we miss the train and be left alone at the station."[61]

Shamir and Rabin offered two very different messages to the Israeli public. Shamir's message was that nothing had really changed, that Israel remained isolated and endangered, and that Israelis could not forsake their historical responsibilities to their ancestral homeland and the Jewish people at large. In short, Israelis were beholden to a collective national endeavor that was neither finished nor secure. Rabin's message was that everything had changed, that Israel was no longer isolated and endangered, and that Israelis did not have to sacrifice their personal interests to the state, but that the basic purpose of the state—and, by extension, the government—was to serve their interests as citizens. Implicit in these contrasting messages were two fundamentally different conceptions of Israeli national identity. Shamir espoused the familiar Israeli-Jewish identity of an isolated, victimized, yet proudly defiant and stoic nation whose historical fate was to be "a people apart." Rabin, on the other hand, offered Israelis the prospect of becoming a normal, liberal, prosperous nation, much like those in the West with whom it rightfully belonged. Peace would be the catalyst for this transformation. Political accommodation and compromise with the Palestinians and surrounding Arab states would usher in a new era for Israel, one in which the pervasive demands of "security" would no longer prevail at the expense of other domestic needs. As the state of war and sense of siege was lifted, Israelis would finally be able to live their lives as they wished, freed from the fear and anxiety that had hung over them.

The hopeful message that Rabin expressed in his inaugural speech as prime minister was frequently repeated over the next three years of his premiership. He consistently emphasized optimism in place of the pessimism that had overtaken Israelis in the 1970s and 1980s. As he stated on one occasion: "I believe that we are strong. We can believe in our capability to defend ourselves. The world is open. The fear of generations of Jews living in the *galut* [Exile] should not be repeated here. Hope, not fear, should be the motor force that drives us."[62]

This optimistic attitude even carried over to how Rabin dealt with the traumatic memory of the Holocaust, a memory that had played such an important role in fueling Israelis' distrust toward the gentile world. In a speech in Warsaw at the memorial ceremony to mark the fiftieth anniversary of the Warsaw Ghetto uprising, Rabin declared: "We have come to tell you and ourselves that, even if man betrayed us in this place in the Warsaw Ghetto, even if our faith in mankind proved false then, we believe—and will continue to believe—in the spirit of the human race. We still believe that people, and countries, can change and treat others (in the words of our ancestors) with a 'new heart and new spirit.' "[63] This was a poignant message, and one that had obvious contemporary resonance—applying as much to the attitude of Israeli Jews toward the Palestinians as it did to their attitude toward those responsible for the Holocaust. The theme of reconciliation with historic enemies was prominent in both cases. Indeed, it was a theme that animated the Rabin government's conduct of Israeli foreign policy. Uri Savir, who was director-general of the Foreign Ministry at the time, has written in his account of the Oslo peace process of this significant change in attitude affecting Israeli foreign policy during the Rabin government: "At the end of the twentieth century, the leaders of the State of Israel acted on the premise that enemies may not be eternal; that we may be strong enough to transform them into partners; that we need not be perpetual victims; and that we may even, because of our mistakes, become victimizers . . . . We had to learn to ignore imaginary dangers and work with our neighbors on the basis of mutual understanding and interests. We were now a modern nation-state, not an institutionalized ghetto. It was up to us to forge a different future by influencing trends and attitudes in the region."[64]

The belief that Israel could influence trends and attitudes in the Middle East constituted a major change from the fatalism and despair with which earlier Israeli governments (especially Likud-led governments) had approached the region. This attitude change was part of "a far-reaching diplomatic revolution" that Israeli foreign policy underwent in the early 1990s.[65] Whereas previously Israeli foreign policy was basically reactive and defensive in nature, marked by a constant rearguard effort aimed at "damage control," the foreign policy of the Rabin government was much more proactive.[66] Motivating this "activist" foreign policy was the changed perception of Israeli policy-makers and much of the Israeli public toward the outside world.[67] In the words of then Deputy Foreign Minister Yossi Beilin, the new perception was of an Israel that was a part of the "community of nations," and an Israel for whom "the world is important."[68] Instead of conceiving Israel as a unique state—a Jewish state—with a unique destiny, Israeli policy-makers now regarded Israel as a normal state whose fortunes were tied to global trends as a member of the international community of states.

According to this conception, Israel could, if it wished, finally integrate itself fully into this community, rather than regard itself as destined to remain apart. This meant that, unlike in earlier decades when Israelis had tended to view the rest of the world with a large degree of suspicion and pessimism, Israeli policy-makers in the Rabin government felt a new sense of optimism and confidence in Israel's ability to integrate itself in the international community. This change in attitude was conveyed by Shimon Peres, then foreign minister, when he told a gathering of foreign diplomats in Israel that: "[We] are . . . less in fear of the so-called world diplomatic community."[69] As Israel received increasing international recognition and legitimacy during the period of the Rabin government (1992–1995) as a result of the peace process,[70] a "positive feedback process" was set in motion whereby "[e]ach act of rapprochement—between Israel and individual sister-states, between Israel, and international agencies, between Israel, the media and world opinion—assumes symbolic importance, but also contributes to a deeper psychological healing process."[71] This, in turn, generated greater Israeli appreciation for the role of diplomacy,[72] rather than force, which then further bolstered Israel's international standing. Traditionally, Israeli policy-makers were highly dubious about the value of diplomacy, preferring instead to rely upon the use or threat of military force to protect their country's national interests. As Israelis policy-makers elevated the value of diplomacy and international cooperation, they displayed a greater willingness to support the involvement of international actors in the Middle East, and to experiment with cooperative and regional security arrangements. This was evident, for instance, in Israel's changed approach to arms control measures, which it showed little interest in before the Rabin government. Thus, in 1993, Israel signed the Chemical Weapons Convention (although at the time of writing it has still not been ratified), and began to report its arms sales to the UN arms registrar; and in 1994, it agreed to ban the export of antipersonnel landmines.

As the peace process facilitated a far-reaching rapprochement between Israel and the international community (both with individual states and with international organizations—particularly with the UN and its specialized agencies[73]), Prime Minister Rabin made many references in his speeches to the end of Israel's isolation and its improved international status. He declared in a major speech at the National Security College on August 12, 1993: "The world is no longer against us . . . . States that never stretched their hand out to us, states that condemned us, that assisted our bitterest enemies . . . regard us today as a worthy and respectable address . . . . This is a new reality."[74] He reiterated this in a speech before the Knesset in 1994: "Even before comprehensive peace . . . we are witnessing a new wind blowing throughout the world regarding its relationship with the State of Israel: the claim that the 'whole world is against us' has dissipated in the spirit of peace. The whole world is not against us. The world is with us."[75]

By regularly and emphatically contradicting the long-held popular Israeli belief that the "whole world is against us," Rabin was effectively undermining the Jewish component of Israeli national identity. In the preceding chapter, the deep sense of isolation and insecurity felt by Israelis was related to their Jewish identity and the historical memories and traumas associated with it. I argued that Israel's international standing—the extent to which it was supported or condemned by the international community—affected the salience of Israelis' Jewish identity. That is, Israeli Jews were inclined toward suspicion and distrust of the gentile world as a historical legacy, and the more the gentile world appeared to confirm these feelings by its attitude toward the Jewish state, the more dominant they became as the Jewishness of Israelis became accentuated. In short, a dialectical relationship existed between Israeli Jews' perception of the non-Jewish world and their sense of Jewish identity. Thus, in challenging Israelis to look upon the world in a new way, to see it as friendly rather than hostile toward Israel, Rabin was simultaneously challenging the Jewish component of Israeli national identity. If Israel was no longer being treated as the "pariah" state, Israelis were less likely to identify themselves with the traditional pariah people—Jews.

Rabin's discourse challenged the dominance of Jewishness in constituting Israeli national identity in other ways while he was in office. As prime minister, Rabin appealed to, and spoke in the name of, Israeli citizens, rather than the collective Jewish people (in contrast to Begin and Shamir, whose political rhetoric tended to refer to the Jewish people across time and space). Rabin's discursive focus upon Israeli citizens conveyed a more civic conception of Israeli national identity rather than an ethno-religious one (since non-Jews were also citizens). His discourse effectively elevated the value of Israeli citizenship, and defined the boundaries of Israeli collective identity more in terms of civic than ethno-religious ties. In other words, membership of the Israeli collective—national belonging—was conferred on the basis of citizenship, not primordial criteria.

This more civic orientation toward Israeli national identity was evident in Rabin's approach to the Israeli Arab community. He made a number of significant gestures indicating his government's desire to integrate this community within the Israeli body politic. For example, he abolished the office of Advisor to the Prime Minister on Arab Affairs, which had effectively marked Arab citizens out from other citizens, and had been perceived by them as paternalistic. He also appointed two Israeli Arabs as deputy ministers, and important Knesset committee assignments were given to the Arab parties. After decades of under-funding, state resources allocated to the Arab sector were also substantially increased (especially in the areas of education, health, and welfare benefits[76]). No doubt, these improvements in the status of the Israeli Arab community under the Rabin government were prompted in part by the fact that the survival of Rabin's government depended upon Arab parliamentary support. But Rabin's curt response to right-wing attacks that denounced his government's dependence on the votes of Arab Knesset members (MKs) also suggests his preference for a more civic conception of Israeli national identity: "It is time, once and for all, to decide whether the Israeli-Arab public is an integral part of Israel. Those who claim that it is not should come out and apologize to those Arabs whose votes they had solicited."[77] Yet despite this apparent endorsement for regarding Israeli Arabs as full members of the national community and legitimate participants in the domestic decision-making process, Rabin would not bring any of the Arab parties into his government coalition as full-fledged partners. This would have violated an informal rule against having Arab parties in government, something that Rabin dared not challenge. Thus, although Rabin went further than any other Israeli prime minister before him in reaching out to the Israeli Arab community, there was still a limit to how far Rabin was prepared to go.

Rabin's civic-oriented discourse was one element in his broader effort to refashion Israeli national identity. Rabin believed that it was necessary to change and update Israeli national identity by discarding those elements of it which had become anachronistic or dysfunctional.[78] During his premiership, he talked about Israeli national identity on numerous occasions in his speeches and interviews, and discursively associated it with the Israeli-Palestinian and Israeli-Arab peace processes. He openly criticized many of the beliefs and attitudes that had formerly shaped how Israelis viewed both themselves and the rest of the world, repeatedly telling Israelis that they should no longer see themselves as "a people apart," and that they had to shed their traditional defensiveness and sense of international isolation. In doing so, Rabin wanted to change Israeli national identity in line with the changes he believed were taking place in the world. He expressed this most clearly in his speech at the National Security College in August 1993.[79] In it, Rabin outlined how Israeli national identity had developed, and how it should continue to develop in the present circumstances.

Rabin began by describing his image of the traditional Jew: "For me, as a native of this land, the Jew, in the collective sense, and the Diaspora were always represented by the image of the bent-over Jew possessed of meager bodily strength and immense mental powers . . . the picture of the world engraved upon the memory of members of our generation is of a Jew with fear in his eyes, a leaf being wafted about." This accurately captures the stereotypic and derogatory manner in which Diaspora Jews were represented in the discourse of secular Zionism, especially during the pre-state period. Rabin then went on to describe the change in this image brought about by Israel's creation: "The establishment of the State of Israel gave birth to the image of a new Jew—the sabra, the strong person, a fighter, standing upright, rooted, one who beats back all who rise up against him, a David who overcomes Goliath. And around the new Jew developed the image of the Israeli 'superman,' omnipotent, resourceful, sophisticated, victorious." Again, Rabin echoes the discourse of secular Zionism, as it depicted itself as giving birth to the "new Jew" in the form of the sabra.

But then Rabin departs from this by-now familiar script. He proceeds to challenge this identity by pointing to its failure to bring peace and security to Israelis, asserting that: "[T]he stronger we were, the more we were attacked." This brought with it negative psychological repercussions for Israelis, according to Rabin: "We lost trust in others. We were suspicious of everyone. We developed a siege mentality. We lived in a kind of political, economic, and mental ghetto. We secluded ourselves. We distanced ourselves. We became skeptical and harbored reservations. We developed patterns of obstinacy and of seeing the world in somber colors." In this manner, Rabin conveys the dour state-of-mind prevalent among Israeli Jews from the 1960s onwards. Although characterizing a somber state of affairs, Rabin also recognized that: "The truth is that there were advantages to the siege atmosphere," namely, the national unity it encouraged among Israeli Jews. Nevertheless, Rabin argued that such an atmosphere was no longer appropriate given the momentous international changes that were taking place in the 1990s. He then connected the new emerging international environment to the construction of a new Israeli identity and a new foreign policy, declaring that: "In the face of the new reality of the changing world, we must forge a new dimension to the image of the Israeli. This is the hour for making changes: for opening up, for looking around us, for engaging in dialogue, for integrating, for making friends, for making peace."

Thus, in this keynote speech, Rabin presented a narrative of Israeli national identity. It was a narrative that incorporated the conventional, existing one—according to which the proud and courageous Israeli Jew (the sabra) had replaced the weak and cowardly Jew of the Diaspora—but revised and updated it by narrating the rise of a suspicious, insular Israeli psyche. In so doing, the triumphalist, if not boastful, depiction of Israeli identity was displaced by a more critical, less salutary depiction. Moreover, Rabin's narrative of Israeli national identity emphasized the changes it had undergone, and hence represented it as something that was essentially dynamic and fluid rather than fixed and unchanging. This implied that further changes could legitimately be made, although Rabin did not specify exactly what changes he had in mind. Rabin's narrative of Israeli identity was also a personal narrative. He was born (in 1922) and grew up at a time when the Zionist project to create a "new Jew" was at its height, he commanded the Israeli army to its greatest victory in 1967, and he entered politics and came to power when Israelis felt most isolated and distrustful. Thus, as the classic sabra whose individual biography mirrored that of the nation at large, Rabin personified the Israeli national identity he advocated, much like Begin had earlier personified the Israeli national identity he articulated.

Rabin's ability to embody Israeli national identity, to be the exemplary Israeli, gave his words power, and his actions deep symbolic resonance. This was put to great use during the signing ceremony of the Israel-PLO Declarations of Principles on the White House Lawn on September 13, 1993—a landmark event witnessed by almost every Israeli as well as by many millions around the world. Rabin's aide, Eitan Haber, claims that Rabin purposefully represented the new Israeli identity he wanted when he chose to shake Arafat's hand during the ceremony: "The new image of the Israeli was one shaking hands, rather than holding a gun."[80] This image was meant for both domestic and foreign consumption. According to Haber, Rabin wanted to change not only how Israelis saw themselves, but also how the rest of the world saw Israelis: "He [Rabin] decided to change the image of the Israeli from one who appeared with kalashnikov and tzitzit [a religious Jewish garment] to a peace face, a negotiable face." Rabin intended, in Haber's words: "To show the world that we are not only soldiers, not only conquerors." The famous Rabin-Arafat handshake was, therefore, loaded with symbolism. By shaking Arafat's hand, Rabin was signaling not only the beginning of a new era of peace and reconciliation between Israelis and Palestinians, but also the birth of a new Israeli national identity. It was a physical display to Israelis, and to the world at large, of the arrival of a different Israel and a different Israeli national identity.

Legitimizing the Peace Process

However much Rabin wanted to change Israeli national identity and however much his words and actions challenged it, Israeli national identity could not be instantaneously transformed. The adoption of a new Israeli national identity would be a slow and difficult process, lasting years, perhaps even decades. But the Oslo peace process with the Palestinians could not wait. In order for it to succeed, a still wary Israeli public had to be persuaded to support it. Generating this support would not be easy. Rabin, Peres, and their associates anticipated that the Oslo peace process would be highly controversial, and would be vociferously opposed by a substantial segment of the Israeli public.[81] Oslo's architects were well aware at the outset of its potential to exacerbate an already polarized domestic political climate. This awareness is reflected in the account given by Savir, Israel's chief negotiator at Oslo, of his feelings upon returning to Israel after his first secret meeting in Oslo in May 1993 with PLO representatives:

> Suddenly I felt anxiety that a process in which I believed in deeply would be seen by others . . . as a suicidal surrender. Though I believed that a reconciliation with our enemy would fulfill the very idea and goal of a strong, modern Jewish state, there were many others who felt that if the walls came down, we would be vulnerable to external and internal enemies, that the coherence of Israeli society depended on resisting a common enemy and the penetration of what they saw as pernicious external influences. Was it possible in Israel to bridge these two worlds? Probably not. Peace with the PLO would widen the abyss between those who believed in the possibility and desirability of a new relationship between a strong Israel willing to face the future and its neighbors, and those who believed that eternal hostility demanded not only external vigilance but extreme suspicion of our neighbors . . . . The peace process would therefore be a crucial struggle not only with the Palestinians but with ourselves.[82]

How could the internal struggle over the peace process be won? How could the Rabin government gain public support for an Israeli withdrawal from the territories (as required by the Oslo Accords) when many Israeli Jews would construe this action as tantamount to a betrayal of Zionism's goal of returning the Jewish people to their historic homeland? Rabin and Peres, who as prime minister and foreign minister respectively bore greatest responsibility for the Oslo peace process, knew that the Oslo Accords would be seen in the eyes of its opponents as contradicting the entire purpose of Zionism and of Israel as the Jewish state. Thus, to counter the argument of those who would depict the Oslo Accords as a repudiation of Israel's Jewish and Zionist identity, they claimed that their intention was actually to defend Israel's Jewish and Zionist identity, and they attempted to present withdrawal from the territories as the only way of ensuring this identity.

In presenting their peace policy to the Israeli public, Rabin and Peres frequently couched it in the language of identity. Their political rhetoric was laden with references to Israeli and Jewish identity, as they discursively linked the peace process to these identities. In this context, the point made in this book's introduction concerning the role of a national identity in legitimizing a state's foreign policy should be recalled. Put simply, a national identity can make some policies seem legitimate and desirable, and others not so. Thus, Rabin and Peres' references to Israeli and Jewish identity were designed to achieve domestic support and backing for their peace policy.[83] They sought to demonstrate that the peace process was consistent with Israeli national identity in order to publicly legitimize it. This required them to define Israeli national identity in a way that made a withdrawal from the territories appear desirable and legitimate to the Israeli public.

In his discourse, Rabin emphasized the liberal and humanistic qualities that characterized Israelis. By defining Israeli national identity in these terms, Rabin was attempting to make withdrawal from the territories appear desirable and legitimate to the Israeli public as he argued that relinquishing Israeli control over the territories was the only way to preserve the nation's liberal and humanistic qualities. Those Israelis who opposed the peace process, by implication, were endangering these precious moral qualities. The fiercest opponents of the Oslo peace process—the religious right and the settlers—were depicted by Rabin as threatening the nation's moral character. This was most apparent in Rabin's statement to the Knesset following the "Hebron massacre" in which twenty-nine Muslim worshippers were gunned down by the Jewish settler Baruch Goldstein on February 25, 1994: "Maybe more than any other nation in the world today, Israel is fighting for its life in a bloody struggle which has continued for generations . . . . And we continue onward, as we struggle, all the long while, over our image as a nation which gave the world the values of morality and culture. It is not easy for a country engaged in an endless war to protect its humanity and its moral composure." In this statement, Rabin rhetorically casts the political struggle between supporters and opponents of the peace process as a moral struggle over the national character. To support the peace process was to uphold the nation's morality, whereas to oppose the peace process was to be an accomplice to the nation's moral degeneration. Rabin also presented Goldstein and his cohorts as an anathema to Zionism, Judaism, and democracy. He drew the boundaries of the Israeli collective in these terms, putting Goldstein and the settlers outside the boundaries of the democratic, Zionist, and Jewish collective. As he categorically stated: "To him [Goldstein] and to those like him we say: You are not part of the community of Israel. You are not part of the national democratic camp to which we in this house all belong, and many of the people despise you. You are not partners in the Zionist enterprise. You are a foreign implant. You are an errant weed. Sensible Judaism spits you out. You placed yourself outside the wall of Jewish Law. You are a shame on Zionism and an embarrassment to Judaism."[84]

Like Rabin, Peres also discursively related the peace process to Israeli national identity. But unlike Rabin, it was the Jewish dimension of Israeli national identity that Peres appealed to most often. Whereas Rabin spoke primarily of Israeli identity, Peres spoke more about Jewish identity. Peres' frequent references to Jewish history suggest that for him, Israeli national identity was basically an extension of Jewish identity. The aspect of Jewish identity that Peres emphasized in the context of the peace process was that of a humane people, who having suffered victimization themselves had a moral imperative not to victimize others. In a speech at the UN World Conference on Human Rights in Vienna in 1993, Peres stated: "Anti-Semitism brought untold suffering to the Jewish people . . . . We are on the side of all victims, whether black or white, whether they are Muslims, Christians, Hindus, Jews; whether they are Turks, Bosnians, or Somalis . . . . Jewish history would never permit domination of another people; neither in the past nor in the present, neither Palestinians or Arabs."[85]

In Peres' discourse, the history and values of the Jewish people meant that they were sympathetic to all victims and would not dominate over another people. As he told members of the diplomatic community stationed in Israel: "[W]e do not want to become a dominator of another people against their wish. Nations have interests. I believe nations have also values, and for us the Jewish people, the values are occasionally our interests, and we cannot overlook it. We don't want under any circumstances to become a dominating people or an occupying country."[86] Peres, therefore, argued that Israeli withdrawal from the territories was mandated by the historic values of the Jewish people, whereas occupation of the territories was incompatible with those values. He was even more explicit about this in his speech at the signing ceremony of the Israel-PLO agreement in Cairo on May 4, 1994: "Our position stems from a moral call: Govern yourself, don't rule others. The agreement today is not a submission to threats of weapons. It is a return to the values of our heritage."[87]

Peres' discourse represented a serious challenge to the nationalist-religious right. By justifying Israel's withdrawal from the territories with reference to the Jewish heritage, Peres was effectively disputing the nationalist-religious right's claim to exclusively represent this heritage. Instead of opposing their argument that Israel as the Jewish state could not forsake *Eretz Israel* on non-ideological, pragmatic grounds (as Labor did in its 1992 election campaign), Peres directly countered this argument in terms of Jewish identity, history, and values.[88] Like the nationalist-religious right, he drew upon the Jewish tradition, but to advocate a policy furiously opposed by them. When he stated: "Israel is not only a matter of geography. Israel is also faith," he was expressing a view that Shamir, Begin, and other right-wing ideologues had long championed.[89] But his definition of that "faith," and his conception of what the Jewish tradition required of Israel, was completely at odds with that of the nationalist-religious right. Indeed, his argument implied that those who sought to maintain Israel's domination over the Palestinian people (by keeping the territories under Israeli control) were, in fact, the ones who were being unfaithful to the Jewish tradition. Those who claimed to represent that tradition were really abusing it, while those accused by the nationalist-religious right of abandoning the Jewish heritage were its true defenders and champions.

Israeli national identity, then, was a prominent element in the discourse of Rabin and Peres as they attempted to publicly legitimize the peace process. They represented this identity in ways that were not only consistent with a withdrawal from the territories, but actually entailed it. The peace process was "framed" in terms of a Jewish, democratic, humanistic, and liberal Israeli identity.[90] It was both an expression of this identity, and a means to reinforce and promote it. This was an attractive argument for some Israelis—particularly those on the left—as they had experienced a series of challenges to their national identity in the 1980s and early 1990s. As the preceding chapter argued, the Lebanon War and the Intifada both undermined important aspects of Israeli national identity. Each challenged the positive self-image of Israelis as a peace-loving, humane, enlightened nation who were the innocent victims of Arab aggression, by conveying an image of Israelis as a domineering, war-like, even amoral nation that brutalized, tortured, and killed innocent civilians. This highly negative national image was propagated within Israel by parts of the media (both domestic and foreign), and by left-wing domestic political activists and intellectuals who vehemently condemned "the Occupation," as well as the injustices, abuses, and limitations of Israel's political and legal system.

The discrepancy between the nation's purported values and self-image and its actual behavior was widely publicized, and it was this discrepancy that Rabin and Peres claimed the peace process would rectify. They, together with their colleagues and supporters on the "Zionist left," believed that the source of Israel's moral corruption, that which had sullied their national self-image, was Israel's occupation of the territories.[91] It was this that was responsible for both the Lebanon War and the Intifada, and it was this that had fueled the rise of a militant, messianic, religious right, which threatened Israeli liberalism and democracy. The solution was simple and obvious—end the occupation of the territories. This would remove the stain upon the nation's moral character. Israel's withdrawal from the territories, therefore, would rehabilitate the positive national identity of Israelis. This motivation was openly acknowledged by Peres in a speech soon after the signing of the DOP agreement between Israel and the PLO when he stated that: "We were not just in conflict with the Palestinians and the Arabs, we were in conflict with ourselves. The Jewish people in their four thousand years of history have never dominated another people. And we felt strongly that we had to follow this moral commitment—never, never to dominate another people. It's a mistake, and we wanted to liberate ourselves from it."[92] For Peres, therefore, Israel's withdrawal from the territories would enable Israelis to re-align their behavior with their national identity and values.

For many of its Israeli supporters, the Oslo peace process was more about rectifying Israel's self-image and restoring their national identity than it was about the rights of the Palestinians. As Amnon Raz-Krakotzkin argues: "The new policy was accepted, not because a new consciousness [toward the Palestinians] had evolved but because it seemed the only way to fulfill the long-standing political aspirations of Israel and to salvage the self-image which defined Israeli culture. Paradoxically, the terms of the Oslo Accord and the shift in the attitude towards the PLO were accepted by many Israelis because it helped them to preserve their identity and political goals."[93] That the Oslo Accords did not result in any real change in Israeli attitudes toward the Palestinians is confirmed by a survey conducted in 1994 in which most Israelis reported that their attitude toward the Palestinians had not changed as a result of the Accord signed the year before.[94] Many Israeli Jews were accustomed to regarding the Palestinians— long their collective enemy—with suspicion and even hatred (and vice versa).[95] For the most part, this continued even after the onset of the Oslo peace process. Despite the important shift in Israel's official attitude toward the Palestinians—from denying their existence as a nation to recognizing it—informal Israeli attitudes were slower to change. Palestinians continued to be the object of Israeli animosity and fear, while sympathy for their collective plight remained scarce.[96] To make peace with the Palestinians, however, Israeli attitudes toward them had to change.

This would inevitably affect Israeli national identity. From the outset, Israeli national identity had developed under conditions of conflict with the Palestinians, and over time this conflict had become a constitutive element of that identity. As their collective "Other," the Palestinians had helped to provide Israelis with a collective sense of "Self."[97] The Oslo peace process meant that Israelis would now be deprived of the "Other" against which they had defined themselves for so long. As the Israeli psychologist, Dan Bar-On, wrote: "Many Israelis will have to question and let go of that part of their self-definition that has been achieved mainly through the negative use of the [Palestinian] Other."[98] But would Israelis be able to do this, and if so, how would they define themselves without the "Other"? How would Israeli collective identity be maintained once the collective enemy was gone? Writing in September 1993 after the signing of the Oslo Accords, the Israeli author, David Grossman, conveyed the challenge and opportunity that lay ahead: "This [peace] is a condition in which—years from now—the two sides [Israeli and Palestinian] will be able to give themselves a new kind of definition—not one contrasted with an enemy, but one that turns inward. One dependent not on the fear that they might be destroyed but instead on the natural development of a nation, on its system of values and the various facets of its character. This is a decisive change . . . . I can definitely see that such a process of defining ourselves, the Israelis, will bring about tremors and changes. It will require a painful assessment of our definition of ourselves today in relation to our Jewish heritage. It will force us to confront our complicated history anew, and to consider the possibility of choosing a new way of relating to the world outside us."[99]

The loss of the Palestinian Other represented a profound test for Israeli national identity. In the face of this, many Israelis feared the total disintegration of Israeli national identity, or at least an erosion of its importance. Others welcomed the chance for Israelis to finally tackle the long-deferred questions of their identity. But whatever view one took, the peace process with the Palestinians threw Israeli national identity into doubt. In the process, many of its unresolved tensions and dilemmas came to the fore. Hence, the challenge facing the Rabin government went deeper than that of convincing the Israeli public that a withdrawal from the territories was consistent with Israeli national identity. No matter how much Rabin and Peres discursively cast the peace process as a means to restore and revitalize Israeli national identity—one that was Jewish, Zionist, liberal, and humanistic—the peace process entailed a threat to the existing Israeli national identity. As a result, Israeli national identity became the focus of intense public debate. This debate was widely interpreted as symptomatic of a national identity crisis. This crisis of Israeli national identity, and the Pandora's box of identity issues it opened, will be the subject of the next chapter.

CHAPTER 4
THE CRISIS OF ISRAELI IDENTITY

We're like a 3,000-year-old people with a teenage identity crisis. To live here is to not know who you are.[1]

—David Hartman

Israel is undergoing today the worst identity crisis since its inception.[2]

—Naomi Chazan

Introduction

Peacemaking is as much a domestic challenge as it is a foreign policy challenge. Both warring parties must negotiate with each other while simultaneously ensuring domestic support for the negotiations and the concessions they may lead to.[3] The Declaration of Principles (DOP) signed by the Rabin government and the PLO in September 1993 represented a historic agreement between Israel and the Palestinians, as both sides finally recognized each other and agreed to resolve their conflict through peaceful bilateral negotiations. But this was only the first step toward peace. Accords still needed to be reached on the process of Israel's withdrawal from the West Bank and Gaza and the transfer of governing authority to the Palestinians; and eventually the issues at the heart of the Israeli-Palestinian conflict would have to be tackled. Moreover, all this would have to be done under intense public scrutiny, in contrast to the secret talks that led to the signing of the DOP.

Whatever concessions the Rabin government was prepared to make for the sake of Israeli-Palestinian peace mattered little if the Israeli public did not consent. To make peace with the Palestinians, the Rabin government had to have the backing of a solid majority of Israelis. This chapter begins by describing the challenge the Rabin government faced in gaining this public support. It proved to be too great a challenge. Although many Israelis enthusiastically supported the Oslo peace process, many others were just as strongly opposed. The Israeli public was split almost evenly between supporters and opponents of the peace process. In this chapter I examine why the Rabin government failed to get a decisive majority of Israelis to support its peace policy. I argue that a major reason for this failure was the lack of societal consensus over the nature of Israeli national identity. Beneath the social division over the peace process lay a deeper division between adherents of a civic conception of Israeli national identity whom I label "Israelis," and adherents of an ethno-religious conception whom I label "Jews." These competing conceptions of Israeli national identity were associated with very different foreign policy orientations and attitudes toward the peace process. I analyze the origins and development of the cultural conflict between "Israelis" and "Jews," and I interpret Prime Minister Rabin's assassination in 1995 and Benjamin Netanyahu's electoral victory in 1996 as consequences of this escalating conflict over Israeli national identity.

The division between "Israelis" and "Jews" over the peace process was by no means the only manifestation of bitter societal discord over Israeli national identity. In fact, in the late 1990s, the intense debate over the peace process gave way to a host of other domestic controversies over religious-secular relations, the military draft, multiculturalism, the Law of Return, the status of Palestinian Israelis, and post-Zionism. I discuss these controversies later in this chapter and argue that the politics of national identity was apparent in all these different issues and that they were all symptomatic of a crisis of Israeli national identity. Identity politics increasingly dominated the national agenda in Israel, as it did in many other countries. Part of the reason for this was the new public prominence of numerous subnational identities. This highlighted the heterogeneity of Israeli society, and called into question the common characteristics that supposedly defined Israeli national identity. The "tribalism" that appeared to characterize Israeli politics and society in the 1990s gave rise to a widespread sense of internal fragmentation and cultural anxiety.

Also generating this cultural anxiety was the burgeoning cosmopolitanism of Israelis' new consumption and leisure habits. This was one of the many consequences brought about by globalization as it transformed not only Israel's economy,[4] but also the lifestyle of many Israelis. Israel's integration into the global economy (beginning in the mid-1980s and accelerating with the end of the Arab economic boycott after the Oslo Accords) ushered in a consumerist culture, marked by higher private consumption and an increase in possession of luxury items such as private cars, personal computers, televisions, videos, and mobile phones.[5] Global consumer culture penetrated the daily lives of ordinary Israelis, influencing how they dressed, what they ate, where they shopped, where they vacationed, what music they listened to, and what television programs they watched. In light of this, many Israelis feared that globalization would obliterate whatever was distinctively "Israeli," and further erode Israeli national identity. "Israeli identity, the reason behind the entire Zionist project, is indeed suffering from a serious and prolonged crisis," wrote the commentator Yair Sheleg. "The identifying marks of this identity—the Hebrew language, the connection to this particular place, and the connection to the history of the Jewish people (including its modern-secular version) are becoming more and more blurred. The 'global village,' with the enormous power of its mass culture . . . is erasing this identity."[6] Similarly, an editorial in *The Jerusalem Post* on Israel's fifty-first Independence Day in 1999 noted that: "The loss of identity stemming from absorption into a global, modern, information-age society tends to increase with Israel's success."[7] Such expressions of unease with what was perceived as the culturally homogenizing tendency of globalization were certainly not unique to Israel. Similar reactions were being voiced throughout the world. In this sense, the crisis of Israeli identity described in this chapter had both global and distinctly local origins.

The Peril of Peacemaking

By embarking upon the Oslo peace process with Israel's longtime enemy, the PLO, the Rabin government undertook an enormous challenge. Resolving the conflict between Israelis and Palestinians would require difficult compromises on both sides, a relinquishing of historic dreams, a willingness to trust former foes and, perhaps above all, a determination to overcome the many obstacles that were bound to arise. What made it an even bigger challenge was the fact that, since Israel was a democracy, the government needed the backing of the Israeli public. Gaining public support for the peace process was by no means guaranteed. For one thing, the Israeli public was intensely interested in foreign policy issues, and the Israeli media covered foreign policy much more extensively than media in many other countries. Hence, the actions and decisions of Israeli foreign policy-makers were subject to constant public scrutiny and discussion, much of it critical.[8] For another thing, although Israelis longed for peace and security, there was no public agreement over how best to accomplish this. Since Israel's occupation of the territories after the 1967 war, the old national consensus on foreign policy had steadily unraveled. The Lebanon War and the Intifada in the 1980s further exacerbated this trend, leaving the Israeli public bitterly divided. This greatly complicated Israeli foreign policymaking, as one scholar notes: "Israeli statesmen must deal . . . with a fragmented constituency, and encounter enormous difficulties in achieving solid support and legitimacy for a given policy, whether of the left or the right."[9]

To make matters worse, the acrimonious domestic debate that developed over the future of the territories was more than just a debate over foreign policy. It was also a debate over the definition of Israeli national identity. The question of whether Israel should rule over the West Bank and Gaza—a question that Israelis had grappled with since 1967—was not simply a question of national security, or economics, or morality (though all three were implicated in some degree); it was essentially a question of identity—who Israelis were and who they should be. Its resolution ultimately depended, therefore, on the ability of Israelis to agree upon the definition of their national identity. As one analyst wrote: "The fundamental question for Israelis has to do with finding and agreeing on an identity commensurate with their actual circumstances. This will mean coming to grips with the presence and claims of the Palestinians in the midst of whom Israel was established . . . . In this sense, defining their own identity now and reaching accommodation with the Palestinians are one and the same problem and quest for Israel."[10]

Given the monumental challenge it faced, it is hardly surprising that the Rabin government was unable to secure widespread legitimacy for its policy of peacemaking with the Palestinians both amongst the general public and in the Knesset. Although both Oslo agreements ("Oslo I" and "Oslo II") were supported by a majority of the general public, in both cases the margin of support was very narrow.[11] Between 40 to 50 percent of the Israeli public consistently opposed the Oslo Accords,[12] and even more expressed dissatisfaction with the Oslo peace process over time. According to a comprehensive public opinion survey conducted in March 1995, for instance, 62 percent of Israelis expressed dissatisfaction with the peace process, compared to only 11 percent who felt satisfied.[13] The situation was the same in the Knesset, where the Rabin government received only minimal majority support for the Oslo Accords. It was barely able to ratify the Oslo I and Oslo II agreements, and did so only with the help of an Israeli Arab party and the mostly Arab ex-communist party.[14]

Instead of legitimizing the Oslo Accords, the Knesset votes ratifying them only highlighted the extent of the opposition, and the fact that the government lacked a so-called Jewish majority. This contributed to delegitimizing the Rabin government in the minds of its opponents. They were already being accused of "an act of national treachery" by negotiating with Israel's archenemy, the PLO, and by offering to hand over parts of the Jewish people's homeland to this enemy, who the right believed were still intent upon Israel's destruction.[15] By relying upon non-Zionist and non-Jewish votes in the Knesset, they were condemned by opponents of the Oslo Accords for ignoring the wishes of the Jewish, Zionist public.[16] This bolstered the opposition's argument that the Oslo Accords were a betrayal of Israel's Jewish and Zionist identity. As Yehiel Leiter, the spokesman for the settler's organization *YESHA* (the Judea, Samaria, and Gaza Council), put it: "Holding on to Yesha [Judea, Samaria, and Gaza] and building it forces a particular identity on the nation, one which emphasizes the uniqueness of the Jewish people—one that many in Israel's current left-wing government [the Rabin government] and the people they represent are trying to escape."[17] Thus, in the same manner that Rabin and Peres claimed that the Oslo peace process was consistent with Israeli national identity in order to publicly legitimize it, its opponents claimed that it contradicted Israeli national identity in order to delegitimize it.

In the eyes of its critics, the Rabin government's signing of the Oslo Accords was an act of defeatism, signaling national weakness and even spiritual bankruptcy. Withdrawing from the West Bank and Gaza, they charged, was contrary to the fundamental purpose of the Zionist project—the return and resettlement of the Jewish people in its homeland. It was also dangerously misguided in their opinion, since it would mean that the security of Israelis would depend upon the peaceful intentions of the PLO. The PLO and, above all, its leader Yasser Arafat could not be trusted in this regard. In this vein, Likud leader Benjamin Netanyahu stated: "We did not return to our homeland to live in ghettos, behind barbed wire, and at the mercy of our enemies."[18] Opponents of the peace process in Israel argued that Israel's withdrawal from the territories would only increase the dangers Israel faced by creating a Palestinian state that would allow terrorists and foreign armies to enter Israel. In making this argument, they pointed to the continuing acts of terrorism committed against Israelis by Palestinians as proof that territorial compromise with the Palestinians would not bring Israelis peace and security.

Although gaining widespread popular legitimacy for the peace process with the Palestinians was an immensely difficult, if not impossible, challenge from the beginning, the attitude of Rabin and Peres toward the peace process' domestic opponents did not help in this regard. Rabin made little effort to placate his domestic critics. Quite the contrary, he dismissed them as a bunch of extremists insanely intent on perpetuating the state of war between Israel and the Arabs, and he publicly derided the Jewish settlers in the West Bank and Gaza as "crazies" and "propeller-heads." Even in his response to Palestinian terrorist attacks against Israelis, Rabin showed little concern and sympathy. Following a spate of attacks in the spring of 1995, Rabin commented: "These are difficult times, but they are not unique. The nation had known worse times, but knew how to bear the hardships. We must decide now whether we show resolve or act like crybabies."[19] Peres, too, was dismissive of domestic opposition to the peace process. When asked in an interview, for instance, whether he was concerned by opinion polls which showed limited public support for the Oslo peace process, he remarked: "I'm convinced there is a stream of history than even the public polls cannot stop. Suppose we have a majority of people saying we don't like it—so we'll stop?"[20] On another occasion, Peres stated: "Leadership, in my judgment, means to be elected by the constituencies of yesterday and to represent the constituencies of tomorrow. We have to answer to a constituency that doesn't exist."[21] Rabin and Peres, therefore, displayed little respect for, or understanding toward, opponents of their peace policy—an attitude that further enraged their domestic critics.[22]

The Backlash: Israelis versus Jews

The Oslo peace process demolished any last semblance of national unity in Israel, and exposed the depth of the rifts within Israeli society. As Hillel Halkin wrote: "Like a man in great torment who breaks psychologically in two, Israel . . . went, or was dragged, to Oslo as two nations, each willing to risk what the other was not and unwilling to risk what the other was; neither able to communicate with or to understand the other but only to blame the other rancorously; thesis and antithesis, each half of the now-fractured personality of the Jewish people in its homeland."[23] This vivid depiction of the Israeli population as being split into two over the Oslo Accords is supported by numerous opinion polls, which showed an almost equal division of supporters and opponents of the Accords within the Israeli public. It had long been customary to describe this division as one between hawks and doves, but such a description was misleading when applied to the debate over the Oslo peace process, since it was concerned less with questions of security, than with questions of identity. What is Israel's identity? What does it mean to be a "Jewish state," and how can Israel truly remain one? How important should Jewishness be in Israeli national identity? Where does Israel belong internationally, in the Middle East, in the West, in neither or both? All these were fundamentally questions of identity and, while they were by no means new, they assumed an urgency and importance that they did not have before. Hence, instead of the familiar distinction between hawks and doves in the domestic debate over the territories, a new distinction between "Israelis" and "Jews" was popularized in Israel during and after the tenure of the Rabin government. It was a distinction based upon competing identities rather than competing foreign policy orientations, and to many it seemed to reflect a national identity crisis.

The distinction between "Israelis" and "Jews" and the corresponding perception that Israel's Jewish population was split into two dichotomous camps was, like the distinction between hawks and doves, somewhat oversimplified. "Israeli" and "Jewish" were not mutually exclusive identities. An overwhelming majority of Jews in Israel identified themselves as both Jews and Israelis. In surveys, more than two-thirds in 1965 and almost three-quarters in 1974 responded that being Jewish played an important part in their lives, and in those same surveys, 90 percent responded that Israeliness played an important part in their lives. Similarly, in a 1996 survey, a vast majority of Israeli Jews identified themselves as Jewish and Israeli.[24]

In fact, the dominance of an ethno-religious conception of Israeli national identity from the mid-1960s onwards meant that for Jews in Israel, their Jewish and Israeli identities became complementary and mutually reinforcing.[25] Empirical evidence showed that both identities were positively interrelated—the more Jewish one felt, the more Israeli one felt.[26] For many Israeli Jews, "Israeli" was basically synonymous with "Jewish"—indeed, according to one survey, only 45 percent of the Israeli Jewish public considered the term "Israeli" to be applicable to Israel's Arab citizens.[27] As long as the ethno-religious conception of Israeli national identity held sway, there was no tension between Israeli and Jewish identities. What generated this tension and a competition between the two identities was a definition of Israeli national identity in civic, territorial terms. In this sense, "Israeli" signified an identification with a civic, territorially based national identity encompassing all citizens of Israel (Jewish and non-Jewish), whereas "Jewish" signified an identification with a primordial, ethno-religious national identity restricted to those deemed to be Jewish.[28] Understood in these terms, Israeli and Jewish represented alternative and competing foci for the conceptualization of Israeli national identity.

For most Israelis Jews, however, their national identity was an amalgam of both the civic Israeli identity and the ethno-religious Jewish identity. But each identity was given a different priority by different Israeli Jews. For some, their Jewish identity was most important; for others it was their Israeli identity that mattered most. The distinction between "Israelis" and "Jews," therefore, was based upon how these identities were prioritized by different people—"Israelis" prioritized their civic Israeli identity (Israeliness), whilst "Jews" prioritized their ethno-religious Jewish identity (Jewishness). Of course, "Israelis" and "Jews" were not homogeneous groups. Both groups themselves contained subgroups and subcultures. Among those who prioritized their Jewish identity over their Israeli identity, for instance, were many ultra-Orthodox Ashkenazi Jews, traditional Mizrahi Jews, and secular Jewish immigrants from the former Soviet Union.[29] Nevertheless, in general, the demographic profiles of "Israelis" and "Jews" significantly differed. A study on the identity hierarchies of Israeli Jews (which asked respondents to rank different social identities according to the importance of each one to them) found that those who ranked "Israeli" identity highest tended to be secular and Ashkenazi, while those who ranked "Jewish" identity highest tend to be more religious and Mizrahi.[30]

The competition between "Israeli" and "Jewish" variants of Israeli national identity was longstanding. In the course of Israel's history, the fortunes of these two alternative foci of Israeli national identity have waxed and waned. Just as the articulation of a Hebrew identity in the pre-state period signaled a departure from traditional Jewish identity; so too, after Israel's Independence and during the early years of statehood, did the rise of an Israeli identity whose foremost representative was the fabled sabra. Hebrew, sabra, Israeli—all signified a new, territorially based, national identity.[31] But the old Jewish identity did not simply fade away. It continued to shape the meaning of Israeli national identity, and from the 1960s onwards the dominance of a civic definition of Israeli national identity gradually gave way to an ethno-religious definition. This ethno-religious definition of Israeli national identity was predominant throughout the 1970s and 1980s. In different periods, therefore, Jewishness and Israeliness have dominated discourses of Israeli national identity—with Israeliness dominant in the 1950s and early 1960s, and Jewishness in the 1970s and 1980s.

The struggle between these polarities has been played out over specific political issues, most notably in the long-running debates about the relationship between religion and the state and the future of the occupied territories. Underlying the domestic debate over the Oslo peace process, therefore, was an ongoing struggle between Israelis and Jews over the character of Israeli national identity. But in the 1990s, this struggle assumed an intensity that distinguished it from previous periods. For one thing, although there had been constant competition between Jewishness and Israeliness in defining Israeli national identity, in the 1990s this competition became more open and obvious as public awareness of it grew as a result of the sustained media attention it received. But more importantly, the new intensity was due to the fact that while most Israelis continued to hold both Israeli and Jewish identities, increasing numbers came to favor one over the other. Simply put, "Israelis" became more "Israeli" and "Jews" became more "Jewish." The combined Israeli-Jewish identity traditionally held by most Israeli Jews was slowly disintegrating (although it certainly did not disappear) due to the emergence of two separate collective identities: "[A]n increasingly strident and separatist religious Jewish identity, and a secular identity in which the Jewish is becoming progressively weaker."[32]

Two simultaneous processes were behind this development: the increasing secularization of secular Jews and the growing religiosity of religious Jews. Research has indicated that the strength of a person's Jewish identity is positively related to the degree of their religiosity.[33] Thus, Jewish identity is weaker among secular than religious Jews. Conversely, research has shown that Israeli identity is weaker among religious Israeli Jews than secular Israeli Jews.[34]

Overlapping the division between Israelis and Jews, therefore, was a growing division between secular and religious Jews in Israel. It was not that Israeli society was sharply divided between secular and religious Jews (as it was sometimes depicted to be).[35] In addition to the secular and religious (who are themselves divided into ultra-Orthodox and modern Orthodox), there were also traditional Jews (those who observe some religious customs and rituals but are not observant according to strict Orthodox criteria) who made up the majority of the Jewish population. But these Israeli Jews (many of them first, second, and third generation immigrants from North Africa and the Middle East) lacked a clearly defined identity and clearly articulated values, ideas, and goals.[36] Despite their numbers, therefore, their presence in Israeli society was overshadowed by the more vocal and assertive religious and secular camps. They were also slowly shrinking in size, as their children, caught between the two poles of secularism and orthodoxy, tended to gravitate to one pole or another.[37] Although most Israeli Jews continued to observe at least some religious customs and rituals, across generations there was a clear trend toward both stricter religious observance by some and nonobservance by others. Over time, Israeli Jews, were becoming more religious and more secular.

But it was the change taking place within the secular and religious communities, rather than the small but significant decline in the number of traditional Jews, that was most responsible for the growing polarization between "Israelis" and "Jews." Secular Israeli Jews were becoming increasingly estranged from the Jewish religion.[38] In the past, many secular Israeli Jews had been raised in religious households so that even when they ceased to be religiously observant, they retained a personal familiarity with the Jewish religion and a strong sense of Jewish identity. By the 1990s, this was no longer the case as more and more secular Jews came from nonreligious backgrounds. Without personal memories of a religious upbringing and with little religious knowledge, these secular Jews lacked even a sentimental attachment to the Jewish religion and were less likely to have a strong Jewish identity.[39] Their secularism was very different from that promoted by Israel's Labor Zionist founders. The latter involved an ideological rejection of religious forms and authority in favor of a purely national secular conception of Jewish identity. The new secularism, by contrast, was more of a lifestyle than an ideology,[40] and it was individualistic rather than collectivist, and universalistic rather than Jewish (whether religious or nationalist or both) in its orientation.[41] Thus, a secular Israeli identity and culture emerged in the 1990s in which the conglomeration of symbols, customs, and traditions associated with the Jewish religion were largely absent. In the words of one observer: "[T]he Israeli street . . . is penetrated increasingly by concepts, symbols, and values of a cultural nature that are not Jewish. Popular Israeli culture is increasingly universalist and Jewishly neutral."[42]

At the same time that a process of secularization was making some Israeli Jews less "Jewish," an opposite trend toward an intensification of religious observance was occurring amongst the religious (especially within the religious Zionist population), promoting a stronger religious identity and increased separatism, as religious and secular lifestyles became increasingly distinct.[43] Eva Etzioni-Halevy, an Israeli sociologist, summed up these developments: "[W]hen we look at one side of the fence, we see a religious public, a large part of whose second generation is more adamant in its religious adherence than its parents' generation. We also see a public which, increasingly, lives in geographical separation from the secular, within its own, religious, world. Thus, this camp not only harbors a very strong Jewish identity, but is prone, more and more, to conceive of this identity in religious terms. And . . . when we look at the other side of the fence, we see a secular public, whose Jewish identity is weakening from one generation to the next."[44] Moreover, according to Etzioni-Halevy: "These trends are by no means unconnected with each other. The growing religious extremism in the religious camp, leads the secular to be alienated not only from religion and the religious, but also from Judaism and Jewishness, which they see as the latter's domain, and under their hegemony. This also leads to a decline of their own Jewish identity: the more they feel estranged from the religious, the more they feel alienated from their own Jewishness. And the less the secular identify themselves as Jews, the more the religious feel distanced from them."[45] Internal changes within the secular and religious communities, therefore, had a polarizing effect as the social and cultural distance between them increased.[46] And, as the dual processes of secularization and growing religiosity weakened a shared Israeli-Jewish national identity, they strengthened two separate and increasingly antagonistic collective identities: a civic-territorial Israeli identity and an ethno-religious Jewish identity.

This development undermined a crucial source of unity for Israeli Jews. The Zionists' nationalization of the Jewish religion had transformed it into a central element of Israeli national identity, and provided Israeli Jews with a stock of common memories, symbols, and myths (which became part of Israel's "civil religion"[47]). These helped to unify a diverse population of immigrants with very different social and cultural backgrounds and conflicting political orientations. Although the meaning of these Jewish memories, symbols, and myths were continually disputed by Israeli Jews, such dispute took place within a common frame of reference and masked a deeper social bond. As Gershon Shaked points out: "[E]ven polarized interpretations of the same tradition give a group more unity than the loss of the attachment of one of the groups to these links."[48]

Common attachment to the Jewish tradition, therefore, had provided Israeli Jews with a sense of shared identity. This shared identity was steadily eroded by the declining attachment of secular Jews to the Jewish tradition. The "loss of the attachment" of some secular Israeli Jews to the Jewish tradition was evident in a study by the Guttman Institute released in December 1993 on the "beliefs, observances and social interaction among Israeli Jews."[49] Although the study found that 94 percent of Israelis took pride in being Jewish, and that 96 percent felt a connection to Jews in the Diaspora, it also revealed a correlation between these beliefs and levels of religiosity.[50] The most secular Israelis attributed less importance than other Israeli Jews to the value of living in Israel, they identified less with the Jewish people throughout the world, and they were less likely to describe themselves as Zionists.[51]

Despite being a small minority, this group was the best educated within the population, and was vastly over-represented within the Israeli political, cultural, and business elite, probably comprising a majority of the elite.[52] The high-profile activities of this group, therefore, brought popular attention to the emergence of a staunchly secular Israeli identity, even if it was one that in reality was only shared by a small number of individuals. Many members of this group were also at the forefront of the public campaign in support of the Oslo peace process. Since they were among its most vocal and influential supporters, the peace process was identified in the minds of many Israelis with these individuals. As a result, the peace process became associated with the emergence of a new secular Israeli identity, and the conflict between "Israelis" and "Jews" that had simmered under the surface of Israeli politics openly erupted.

Yisrael Harel, a leader of the settler movement and the editor of YESHA's magazine Nekuda, described "the battle between the 'Jews' and the 'Israelis,'" that he believed was taking place in the following manner: "[T]he major barricade is the one that divides the Jews from the Israelis. The Jews are those who want to live, to one degree or another, in accordance with the Bible. The Israelis pay lip service, maybe, to the heritage, but in essence they aspire to be a completely new people here, a satellite of Western culture . . . . I think that the positions of Gush Emunim really do constitute an irritating and alarming threat to the legitimacy of this secular, hedonistic 'Israel-ism.' The existence of Gush Emunim disturbs your experience of modern Western existence, including permissiveness and pacifism and internationalism; it interferes with your attempt to 'adjust' our society to fashionable Western values."[53]

A very different perspective on this division between "Israelis" and "Jews" comes from Akiva Orr, a long-time advocate of a territorially based Israeli national identity: "Israeliness is the local nationalism of people born and bred in Israel . . . . Israeliness is not averse to employment of Arabs in the Israeli economy. It has no religious obsession with sovereignty over every inch of the soil between the river Jordan and the Mediterranean sea. Israelis who hold such views are motivated by security considerations, not by religious ones. Israeliness is aware that living in the Middle East requires a *modus vivendi* with the surrounding Arab world, necessitating territorial compromises with the Palestinians."[54] As these statements suggest, "Israeli" and "Jewish" identities implied strongly divergent political positions and cultural perspectives. In general, "Israelis" were mostly liberal and left-wing, and "Jews" were mostly conservative and right-wing. On defense and foreign policy issues, "Israelis" tended to be dovish, "Jews" tended to be hawkish. On the issue of the territories, in particular, "Israelis" favored Israel's withdrawal and supported the Israeli-Palestinian peace process, whilst "Jews" were more opposed to a withdrawal from the territories and were less supportive of the peace process.[55] More broadly, "Israelis" wanted Israel to become a "normal" country and believed that this was possible, whereas "Jews" felt that this was neither possible nor ultimately desirable. "Israelis" were more cosmopolitan and universalistic than Jews. They viewed the adoption of foreign cultural products and styles in a more positive manner, while "Jews" decried this as a form of "Hellenization" (assimilation into a materialistic Western culture) that would threaten the preservation of their national culture.[56]

These differing attitudes between what Eliezer Schweid has described as "identity-preserving Jews" and "assimilating Israelis" mirrored those within the nascent Zionist movement a century earlier in the debate that took place over its basic orientation and objectives.[57] As discussed in chapter 1, the emergence of the Zionist movement was a result of two different and contradictory political and cultural impulses, both of which were responses to the processes of modernization and secularization that European Jewry underwent as a result of the Enlightenment and emancipation. On the one hand, there was the assimilationist impulse which, once it appeared to some to be unfeasible on the individual level, assumed a collective character in the political Zionists' attempt to "normalize" the collective condition of the Jewish people by means of attaining a Jewish state, or more accurately, a state for Jews. The political Zionism espoused by Western European Zionists like Theodore Herzl essentially aspired toward collective Jewish assimilation. On the other hand, there was the counter-impulse to resist assimilation, one form of which was represented in the cultural Zionism espoused by Eastern European Zionists like Ahad Ha'am.

This early division between political and cultural Zionism contained the seeds for the later conflict between "Israelis" and "Jews" in Israel. In embryonic form, the argument between Herzl and Ha'am over Herzl's vision of a Jewish state in *Altneuland* was the same argument that Israeli Jews had in the 1990s. Herzl's cosmopolitan universalistic vision was a vision that many secular left-wing Israeli Jews championed, whilst Ha'am's condemnation of this vision for its disregard for specific Jewish culture and values and its desire to copy Western culture was also that made by Israel's religious and nationalist right. Would Israel merely be a state in which Jews lived, or a Jewish state with a unique mission and destiny? How important should the preservation of Jewish identity be, and how important should Judaism be in a "Jewish" state? These questions first arose in the fledgling Zionist movement and continually thereafter. At issue is the degree to which Israeli national identity should be informed by Jewishness: Should it continue and preserve traditional Jewish identity, or should it be a radical departure from it?

In the late nineteenth century, notwithstanding all the passion with which they were discussed, these questions were merely hypothetical. In the early 1990s, they were not. The Labor party's decisive electoral victory in 1992, and the signing of the DOP agreement the following year, appeared to herald a new age for Israel. It would be an age of peace and prosperity. An age in which the spirit of liberal individualism would replace the nationalist collectivism of old. An age in which the wealthy entrepreneur would replace the heroic soldier as the model Israeli to be admired and emulated, and an age in which Israel would be famed worldwide for its hi-tech industries rather than its battlefield prowess. And, as the peace process brought an end to Israel's pariah status, the prospect of Israel's normalization—meaning that Israel could become a country much like those in the West—was, for the first time in its existence, within reach. All of this was a prospect greeted with enthusiasm by "Israelis"—and with dread by "Jews," above all by those "Jews" who believed that Jewish sovereignty over all of *Eretz Israel* would usher in the messianic age. This messianic hope was dashed by the Oslo peace process as it involved Israel's withdrawal from the territories. For one young devout Jew, something had to be done to prevent this.

On the evening of Saturday November 4, 1995, Yigal Amir walked up to Prime Minister Rabin, who had just finished addressing a massive rally in support of the Oslo peace process, and fired three shots from a revolver into his back. Rabin died shortly afterwards. Amir was immediately arrested and was later sentenced to life imprisonment for the murder. Amir was not simply a lone, crazed gunman. He came from a devout Orthodox home, grew up in a Tel Aviv suburb, had served in a prestigious army combat unit, and at the time of the assassination, was studying law, computing, and Jewish studies at Bar-Ilan University, a prestigious religious Zionist institution. Amir was not unlike many other right-wing religious Zionists who believed that Rabin had betrayed and endangered the Jewish people by giving up Israeli possession of *Eretz Israel*. Like them, he had listened to the verbal invective directed against Rabin by opponents of the peace process, and had seen the signs depicting Rabin in an Arab headdress and Nazi uniform in rallies against the peace process. And like them, he had heard rabbis denounce Rabin and read their rulings that giving up parts of *Eretz Israel* was a sin against God. It was in response to all this that Amir took it upon himself to murder Rabin.[58] As he later told a Tel Aviv magistrate's court: "Maybe physically I acted alone, but what pulled the trigger was not only my finger, but the finger of this whole nation, which for 2000 years yearned for this land and dreamed of it."[59]

Clearly, Amir saw himself as acting on behalf of the collective Jewish nation, and he justified his action in terms of Jewish law, citing the Talmudic notions of *din moser* and *din rodef*.[60] Thus, as a Jew, Amir represented one extreme in the battle between Israelis and Jews and, in so far as Rabin personified the quintessential Israeli, his assassination symbolized the slaying of the Israeli by the Jew.[61] The assassination of Rabin can therefore be seen as a violent manifestation of the struggle between Israelis and Jews. Indeed, in the eyes of many Israelis, it later came to signify the disintegration of a common Israeli national identity.[62] As one Israeli journalist wrote about the public mood on the annual memorial day for Rabin's assassination: "Gradually the memorial days for Rabin are becoming 'the days of awe' on which many Israelis mourn the corruption of the Israeli character and its break-up, the inability of Israeli society to deal properly with the frantic changes it is undergoing."[63]

Rabin's assassination was a deeply shocking and traumatic event for Israelis. It laid bare the deep division within Israel between Israelis and Jews, supporters and opponents of the peace process, and underscored the danger that this division posed to Israel. The act and its aftermath—in which some Israelis mourned whilst others rejoiced—proved beyond a doubt that national unity was a thing of the past. Israelis were now engaged in a bitter internal political and cultural dispute that could endanger Israel's democratic order, and even lead to a war amongst themselves. As in the mid-1980s, fears arose about the potential for civil war erupting between Israeli Jews. For many secular, left-wing Israelis, the enemy was no longer the Palestinians; but Jewish religious fanatics who sought to impose theocratic rule upon the country. For the religious right, these secular Israelis had succumbed to the lure of gentile culture and were merely "Hebrew-speaking gentiles,"[64] who were jeopardizing the coming of the messianic age by their sacrilegious disregard for *Eretz Israel*.

Despite all the impassioned calls for reconciliation and dialogue between these two opposing camps in the wake of the assassination, the conflict between them continued unabated. Although the inflammatory rhetoric was toned down, the substance of the debate was the same and the division between the two sides remained as wide as ever. Rabin's assassination did not have any long-term affect on public support for the peace process.

Although support for the peace process rose sharply in the immediate aftermath of the assassination, it gradually and steadily declined until stabilizing more or less at the level it had been before the assassination.[65] Hence, according to Yoram Peri: "[T]he assassination succeeded in stopping the escalation of political violence in the context of the process of withdrawal and separation from parts of the Land of Israel, but it did not succeed in repairing the internal disunity."[66]

Indeed, this disunity was even apparent when it came to deciding how to commemorate Rabin's assassination. First, there was a debate over whether to establish an official memorial day for the assassination. Once again, Israeli public opinion was divided, with 59 percent favoring a national day of mourning and 37 percent opposed, and the political nature of this division was apparent in the fact that 84 percent of those who voted for left-wing parties supported the idea, compared to only 48 percent of right-wing voters.[67] Second, there were disputes over the meaning that should be attached to the assassination. Those on the left represented Rabin's death as an act of heroic sacrifice and supreme courage in the pursuit of peace, while those on the right objected to Rabin's mythologization as a martyr for peace, and instead represented his death as the result of national disunity.[68]

If Rabin's assassination was a violent manifestation of the struggle between Israelis and Jews, the 1996 elections were a peaceful manifestation of this same conflict. More than in any other before it, identity politics was at the heart of the elections. Since the 1984 election (the first following the war in Lebanon and the replacement of Begin by Shamir as leader of the Likud), the issue of the territories had grown in importance to become the major electoral cleavage distinguishing the left from the right, and Labor from Likud voters. But in the 1996 election, the future of the territories was not the overriding political issue. Instead, it became part of a larger issue—that of deciding what kind of nation and state Israelis wanted.

Conflict over Israel as a Jewish state was a basic theme of the 1996 elections. At issue was not whether Israel should be a Jewish state or not—this was something that was widely accepted by Israeli Jews—but what the actual meaning and implications of this were. What kind of Jewish state should Israel be? The answer given by many Israeli Jews in the 1996 elections seemed to be that Israel should be a *more* Jewish state. This is suggested by the fact that approximately a quarter of a million nonreligious voters, around 9 percent of the Jewish electorate, voted for religious parties in the election for the Knesset giving them twenty-three seats—more than they had ever had before. In particular, many traditionally minded Mizrahi Jews voted for Shas and the NRP, who together gained seven more seats than in the previous election. Rather than advocating religious legislation, these parties' campaign materials emphasized the need for more Judaism and more Jewishness in Israeli society.[69] That this was something Israeli Jews desired is supported by the results of a survey carried out prior to the 1996 elections in which a record 53 percent of respondents supported the principle of public life carried out according to the Jewish religious tradition. By contrast, in the same survey in June 1992 prior to the election of that year, less than 30 percent of respondents supported this. Since there had been no significant increase in religious observance within the population in the years 1992 to 1996, this "demand for more Jewishness" must have increased within the nonreligious sector of the population.[70]

Whereas the religious parties increased their share of the vote, the combined vote of Labor and Meretz dropped from 44 to 34 percent. This was due to the popular perception among Jewish voters that the policies of both parties were undermining and endangering Israel's Jewish character. In reality, it was only the secular-left Meretz party that openly championed a civic Israeli national identity, and advocated the separation of religion and state in Israel.[71] Nevertheless, Labor's alliance with Meretz since 1992 contributed to the public impression that it was abandoning its Jewish-Zionist heritage (as did some of the statements made and policies advocated by left-wing members of the Labor party). According to Elazar and Sandler: "The fact that Meretz was Labor's principal coalition partner and was given control of the Ministries of Education and Culture and Communications, where Amnon Rubinstein and Shulamit Aloni either pressed for or presided over major steps to both publicly and quietly eliminate signs of Israel as a Jewish state, was seen as an enormous threat not only to those who were themselves religiously Orthodox, but to many Jews who, whatever their own beliefs and practices, felt that Israel's whole *raison d'être* was in peril."[72]

The centrality of identity politics in the 1996 Knesset election was not only due to the intensifying cultural conflict underway in Israeli society, but also to the major change in the electoral system implemented in the 1996 election. The electoral reform passed by the Knesset in March 1992 established separate votes for the Knesset and for the post of prime minister. Its goal was to augment the power of the prime minister by giving him a direct electoral mandate, but its unintentional consequence was to facilitate and promote identity politics by allowing split-ticket voting.[73] By providing voters with two votes—one for the prime minister and the other for the party of their choice—voters were able to overcome the traditional dilemma of having to choose between national and communal interests. They could express their national preferences in voting for the prime minister and their narrower, more particularistic interests (e.g., ethnic and/or religious) in voting for the Knesset. As a result, both Labor and the Likud, which campaigned on national platforms, lost ground to smaller, sectarian parties (especially those representing Mizrahi Jews, ultra-Orthodox Jews, Israeli

Arabs, and the new immigrants from the former Soviet Union)—together, they received only 66 Knesset seats.[74]

Although Labor succeeded in gaining the largest number of seats in the Knesset in the 1996 election, Peres, its leader and the incumbent prime minister following Rabin's assassination, narrowly lost to Netanyahu, the leader of the Likud, in the election for prime minister, enabling the latter to form the new government. Numerous factors accounted for Netanyahu's surprise victory, principal among them a gruesome series of Hamas suicide bombings in central Israel shortly before the election, which increased public support for Netanyahu's proposal for "a secure peace," as opposed to Peres' vision of a "New Middle East" without armies and borders—something most Israelis considered to be dangerously unrealistic.[75]

But the choice between Netanyahu and Peres involved more than who would best ensure the security of Israelis and be tougher in peace negotiations with the Palestinian Authority. It was also a choice between two different possible futures for Israel. In the "New Middle East" that Peres envisioned, Israel would be integrated into a host of regional economic and political structures that would unite the states of the Middle East, just as the once warring states of Western Europe were becoming united within the new European Union. In his book *The New Middle East*, Peres offered a vision of an Israel living at peace with the Palestinians and its surrounding neighbors, cooperating with them to overcome their common problems and common dangers in a joint effort to build a prosperous and stable Middle East.[76] However idealistic, such a vision had hitherto been absent during the period of the Rabin government.[77] But if Israelis were to embrace the peace process, surely they would need some idea of what might lie beyond it? Rabin himself was not a visionary, and he had no conception of Israel's role in a post-peace Middle East.[78] By default, if not by design, then, Peres offered Israelis the only available vision of Israel's future in a post-peace Middle East.

The problem was, even if it were attainable, it was a vision that did not appeal to most Israelis, who continued to look upon the broader Middle East with a mixture of revulsion and contempt. This negative perception of the Middle East was deeply rooted, and the suggestion that Israel was or should be a Middle Eastern country was something that many Israelis had long objected to.[79] Ever since Herzl declared that the future Jewish state would serve as "the portion of the rampart of Europe against Asia, an outpost of civilization as opposed to barbarism,"[80] most Zionists adopted an "Orientalist" view of the Middle East, regarding it as a backward, uncivilized region.[81] In so far as the Middle East was equated with "backwardness," it followed that for Israel to remain technologically, economically, and militarily advanced it must not adopt the negative traits of the region.

As Ben-Gurion once stated: "We do not want Israelis to become Arabs. We are duty bound to fight against the spirit of the Levant, which corrupts individuals and societies . . . ."[82]

Israel, according to this view, belonged to the Middle East only geographically. In all other respects it should remain apart. Peres' proposal for Israel's integration into the Middle East clearly failed to take into account this deeply ingrained opposition to the "Levantinization" of Israel. Integration into the Middle East was simply not something most Israelis wanted.[83] Indeed, if anything, they wanted to separate themselves from the Arabs as much as possible. According to Shimon Shamir (Israel's former ambassador to Egypt and Syria), for many Israelis peace was seen as a means to disengage from the Middle East rather than integrate into it.[84] Thus, instead of attracting domestic support for the peace process (and by extension, for himself as its leading representative after Rabin's death), Peres' "New Middle East" vision alienated some of its erstwhile supporters, and further appalled its opponents.[85]

The mistake Peres made in outlining his vision of a "New Middle East," however, went beyond his failure to appreciate the depth of disdain with which many Israelis regarded the region and its inhabitants. By advocating the creation of a regional community sharing a common market and elected centralized bodies along the lines of the European Union, Peres was effectively proposing an end to the Zionist mission of providing the Jewish nation with its own political and military power. In his own words: "[N]ational political organizations can no longer fulfill the purpose for which they were established—that is, to furnish the fundamental needs of the nation . . . . One day our self-awareness and personal identity will be based on this new reality, and we will find that we have stepped outside the national arena."[86] For a nation still traumatized by the memory of the Holocaust and convinced of the necessity for Jewish power, this revolutionary message was bound to be unpersuasive. Moreover, it only appeared to support the allegation made by the peace process' domestic opponents that Oslo's architects had abandoned the Zionist ideal of a Jewish state.[87] Thus, according to Yoram Hazony (one of Netanyahu's advisors), Peres' "stunning political reversal, at the end of a career spanning five decades in which he was one of Labor Zionism's most important figures, has been a decisive factor in gaining legitimacy for the view that even among leading Zionists, the idea of the Jewish state is dying or dead."[88] Unlike Peres, Netanyahu's support for an independent Jewish state was not in doubt. In stark contrast to Peres' idealism, Netanyahu preached a hard-headed realism in his book, *A Place Among the Nations: Israel and the World*; arguing that if Israel, like Diaspora Jewry before it, failed to be powerful (or was unable to bear the costs of power), it too would invite aggression and ultimately its destruction.[89] He stressed the need for Jewish power, and criticized the "escapist tendencies of Israeli politics [which] stem from this Jewish inability to reconcile oneself to the permanent need for Jewish power."[90]

Not only did Peres question Israel's role as the provider of Jewish power, he also questioned its future role in safeguarding Jewish identity, and appeared to advocate a de-territorialized Judaism instead. As he put it in his 1995 memoirs: "In the five decades of Israel's existence, our efforts have been focused on re-establishing our territorial center. In the future, we shall have to devote our main effort to re-establishing our spiritual center. The Jewish People is neither a nation nor a religion in the accepted sense of those terms. Its essence is a message rather than a political structure."[91] But for many Israeli Jews, a Jewish state was essential for preserving Jewish values, culture, and identity in the face of what was widely perceived to be the already sweeping Westernization or Americanization of Israel.[92] The massive influx of Western, especially American, cultural products, consumer goods, fashions, and the like, as a result of Israel's increasing integration into the global economy generated a growing cultural anxiety, especially among the religious and traditionalist Jewish public. In their eyes, untrammeled globalization threatened to erase Israel's Jewishness. One member of the ultra-Orthodox Shas party even went so far as to declare: "We are in a moral bankruptcy . . . . This Western culture has eroded everything . . . . It's a cancer."[93]

Netanyahu addressed this cultural anxiety by presenting himself as the guardian of "the Jewish heritage" as opposed to the secular cosmopolitanism of the left.[94] Peres, by contrast, appeared as the apostle of globalization and was widely seen as advocating Israel's integration into the Middle East and the world at large, with little or no concern for Israel's Jewish identity. As one observer described it, Peres' "New Middle East" was one in which "Israel would have open borders, a computer in every home, foreign investment, Pizza Hut, the Disney Channel, Blockbuster Video and 50 cable stations and be fully integrated into the global village."[95] Regardless of the accuracy of this perception, it was important in deciding the outcome of the 1996 election in favor of Netanyahu, as he received 12 percent more of the Jewish vote than Peres (56 percent to 44 percent). In explaining the nearly unanimous support of Israel's Orthodox Jews for Netanyahu, the Israeli philosopher Moshe Halbertal writes: "Peres fell into the trap of defining peace in cultural terms. Instead of defining peace as a 'separation' from the Palestinians, he defined it as an 'integration' with the world that would usher in a new, Westernized, Israeli society. And so for Orthodox Jews the peace process became synonymous with a loss of Jewish identity."[96] Similarly, Charles Liebman and Bernard Susser interpreted Netanyahu's victory "as the protest victory of a Jewish identity coalition that felt its traditional and communal values threatened by the forces of dejudaization."[97] Hence, the slogan "only Netanyahu is good for the Jews" that appeared on car stickers and posters all over the country in the days leading up to the election succinctly captured the belief of many Israelis Jews who went to the polls in 1996.[98]

"The Israelis lost, the Jews won," Peres was reported to have remarked the day after his defeat to Netanyahu.[99] Survey data support this view, revealing a clear difference in the ranking of "Jewish" and "Israeli" identities between voters for Netanyahu and voters for Peres. Sixty-eight percent of Netanyahu voters ranked "Jewish" as their first, or most salient, identity, and 29 percent ranked "Israeli" first. The choice of Peres supporters was almost exactly the opposite, with 32 percent ranking "Jewish" first, and 66 percent "Israeli" first. Thus, for Netanyahu voters their Jewish identity was most important, whereas for Peres voters their Israeli identity was most important.[100] The 1996 election, therefore, underscored the division of the Israeli Jewish public into "Jews" and "Israelis." Commenting on the results of the election in *Ma'ariv* newspaper, former Knesset member and prominent peace activist Uri Avnery wrote: "We have not only two political blocs, but two cultures, and in reality two separate nations." These two nations were "Jews" whose "historical memory is that of an oppressed minority," and "Israelis" who are "aware of their Jewish roots the way Americans, Canadians and Australians are aware of Anglo-Saxon roots, but they are part of modern culture."[101] *Ma'ariv*'s own editorial on the election result went even further, declaring that Israeli society: "[W]ill never be one homogenous society, but at least four societies: the religious-traditional world . . . ; the world of 'the round eyeglasses'. . . which relate to Israeli identity as a kind of extra value; the central stream, which aspires to combine Zionist values with a bourgeoisie lifestyle . . . ; and the Arab public, which is trying to settle the conflict between its life experience in the democratic society which the Jews have established and their belonging to the Palestinian people and the Islamic faith."[102]

A Splintering Nation

The assassination of Rabin by a Jewish religious extremist in 1995 and the 1996 prime ministerial and Knesset elections highlighted the deep schisms within the Israeli public over the definition of Israeli national identity. Both events signaled a backlash against the "de-judaicization" of Israel and Israeli national identity that appeared to many to have been underway during the period of the Rabin government between 1992 and 1995. This backlash was violently expressed in Rabin's assassination, and democratically expressed in the 1996 elections which brought to power a governing coalition of the Likud and religious and right-wing parties that was strongly oriented toward the ethno-religious definition of Israeli national identity and hostile toward the Oslo peace process. Netanyahu's surprise election as Israel's prime minister appeared suddenly to throw the continuation of the Oslo peace process into doubt.

Both in Israel and abroad, the peace process' supporters feared (and its opponents hoped) that Netanyahu, backed by a new Knesset dominated by religious and right-wing parties, would abandon the peace process—which he was known to be suspicious of, if not outright opposed to. But, however much Netanyahu may have wanted to desist from continuing negotiations with the PA in the framework of the Oslo Accords (a subject of incessant speculation during his period in office), he was in no real position to do so. For one thing, the international community, led by the United States, strongly backed the peace process and thus Israel risked international outrage, and even isolation, if it did not continue negotiations with the PA. For another, a majority of the Israeli public still supported the peace process and wanted it to continue. Netanyahu was well aware of this. In the run-up to the 1996 elections, for instance, he did not campaign against the Oslo peace process. Netanyahu promised Israelis "peace with security" (the official slogan of his election campaign) and presented himself as someone who would be a tougher negotiator with the Palestinians than his "soft" rival, Shimon Peres. Instead of telling the Israeli electorate that he would scrap the Oslo Accords, he merely told them that he would ensure that Arafat and the PA better comply with them. Drawing public attention to the continuing vitriolic anti-Israeli propaganda in Palestinian schools and the Palestinian media, to the failure of the PA to collect illegal firearms and to limit the growth of their security forces, and to its apparent reticence in combating the radical Palestinian Islamist organizations, Hamas and Islamic Jihad, Netanyahu insisted that Israel would only implement the provisions of the Oslo Accords if the Palestinians did so. Hence, for the most part, the vote for Netanyahu in the 1996 election was not a vote against the Oslo Accords. It was the cultural changes associated with the peace process as promoted by the left rather than the peace process itself that Israeli voters rejected.

As long as a majority of the Israeli public favored a continuation of the peace process, Netanyahu could do little but oblige (at least, if he wished to be reelected—which he surely did). Thus, strong international pressure, coupled with continued domestic support for the peace process effectively forced Netanyahu to continue the Oslo peace process once in office. But although he could not put an end to a peace process he believed to be "deeply flawed,"[103] as prime minister, Netanyahu did his best to stall negotiations with the PA—delaying a meeting with Arafat, for instance, until September 1996, a whole three months after he took office. His goal in the negotiations with the Palestinians was simple: "I wanted to give very little, as little as possible, and force Arafat to give as much as possible," he later explained.[104] During his three years in office, Netanyahu certainly tried hard to give the Palestinians as little as possible—Israel did not implement the three stages of the second redeployment from the West Bank that was supposed to take place according to the Oslo II agreement; it released fewer Palestinian prisoners than it had agreed to; it did not establish the safe passage that was supposed to connect the West Bank and Gaza; it repeatedly delayed the construction of the airport and maritime port in Gaza; and for long periods of time it refused to transfer money belonging to the PA. Most damaging to the peace process was the Netanyahu government's decision in August 1996 to lift the freeze on the expansion of Jewish settlements in the West Bank that had been in place for four years under the previous Labor-led government (Netanyahu promised only to expand existing settlements, not to build new ones). As a result, under the Netanyahu government, the number of settlers living in the West Bank and Gaza Strip rose by 12.4 percent in just 18 months from January 1997 to July 1998.[105]

Although Israeli-Palestinian relations seriously deteriorated and the peace process was largely paralyzed during Netanyahu's tenure, the little that Netanyahu did "give" the Palestinians was nonetheless immensely significant in terms of Israel's domestic debate over the future of the territories. In the Hebron Accord of January 1997, signed by Netanyahu and Arafat after four months of difficult negotiations, Israel agreed to transfer control of the West Bank town of Hebron to the PA, while keeping 20 percent of the town—the central area where more than 400 Jewish settlers lived among 130,000 Palestinians—under Israeli control. Netanyahu's agreement to partially withdraw from Hebron—a town whose biblical and modern history gave it a particular significance to nationalist and religious Jews[106]—was condemned by many of his right-wing supporters, especially by the Jewish settlers for whom it was seen as an act of betrayal. For the first time, a leader of the Likud was officially handing "Jewish land" over to the Palestinians. This was an act of historic importance. Netanyahu had effectively abandoned the principle of full Jewish possession of *Eretz Israel* (even if he still opposed the establishment of a Palestinian state), a principle that had been at the heart of right-wing ideology in Israel since the days of Jabotinsky.[107] Under Netanyahu, the Likud's militantly uncompromising opposition to the partition of *Eretz Israel* between Israelis and Palestinians was irrevocably undermined.[108]

This was made even more apparent with the October 1998 Wye River Memorandum. After 18 months of stalemate in the peace process and increasing Israeli-Palestinian violence, the Clinton administration became increasingly frustrated with Netanyahu's strategy of procrastination and delay. In an effort to salvage the peace process, President Clinton convened a summit with Netanyahu and Arafat at Maryland's Wye River Plantation.[109] The outcome was the Wye River Memorandum in which, under intense American pressure, Netanyahu reluctantly agreed to carry out a further Israeli withdrawal from the West Bank. The first withdrawal took place on November 20, 1998, two days after narrowly being approved by Netanyahu's cabinet (with six votes in favor, five against, and three abstentions).[110]

Not only did Netanyahu continue the peace process while in office from 1996–1999, but also he became the first Likud leader to publicly present a plan that called for an Israeli withdrawal from over half of the West Bank. Based on the plan proposed by former Labor politician Yigal Allon, Netanyahu's "Allon Plus Plan" indicated that Netanyahu was prepared to withdraw from Gaza and roughly half of the West Bank, a move which would effectively mean the abandonment of some Jewish settlements.[111] Indeed, on presenting the plan, Netanyahu referred to the retention by Israel of settlement blocs away from dense concentrations of Palestinian population, rather than all settlements remaining under Israeli control.[112] In addition to advocating a territorial division of the West Bank, Netanyahu and his advisors also talked about accepting a demilitarized Palestinian state within the West Bank and Gaza, albeit one with limited sovereignty.[113] This effectively recast the long-running domestic debate over the future of the territories. The debate was now no longer about whether Israel should withdraw at all, but by how much, how quickly, and in exchange for what. Although there was no agreement over the extent of a future territorial withdrawal, this was just a question of percentages. It was no longer an argument over absolute principles—territorial compromise with the Palestinians versus Jewish sovereignty over the entire Land of Israel. The principle of territorial compromise had now been accepted and implemented by Israeli governments on both the right and the left. The right had lost its battle for *Eretz Israel* and, in an ironic twist, this had occurred under the leadership of a right-wing prime minister.

The waning of the debate over the future of the territories in the late 1990s, however, did not end the broader debate over Israeli national identity. After all, it was this debate that really animated the debate over the territories, fueling its intense passions and divisions. The debate over the territories had long been about more than whether Israel should remain in control of them. Once the issue of the future of the territories finally appeared to be settled, Israelis began to address the issue of their identity and that of their state directly, without recourse to the metaphor of the territories. The domestic debates that occupied Israelis in the late 1990s all involved questions of identity, just as the foreign policy debate had earlier.

Indeed, the identity issues which had always been in the background of the debate over the territories moved into the foreground and came to dominate Israel's new political agenda.

At the top of this agenda was the issue of the status of Judaism in Israel, an issue that gripped Israeli public attention as soon as the debate over the peace process died down. The relationship between Judaism and the state in Israel was originally determined in the "status quo agreement" made between Ben-Gurion and Agudat Israel (an ultra-Orthodox political party) in 1947 just before Israel's founding. This agreement stipulated that the soon-to-be-created State of Israel would recognize the Jewish Sabbath (Saturday) as the public day of rest, ban public transportation on the Sabbath (except in locales, such as Haifa, where there was already public transportation on the Sabbath), observe Jewish dietary laws in government institutions, give exclusive jurisdiction over all matters pertaining to personal status (marriage, divorce, burial, conversion) to the Orthodox rabbinical establishment, provide state funding to religious institutions, and allow men studying in *yeshivot* (Jewish seminaries) and religious women to be exempt from army service. Although this agreement satisfied neither ultra-Orthodox nor secular Jews, it provided for a basic modus vivendi between the two communities. In the 1990s, however, this modus vivendi increasingly came under attack from both sides. Secular Israeli Jews objected to the disproportionate political power of the ultra-Orthodox (due to the ability of ultra-Orthodox parties to hold the swing seats in Israel's coalition governments), and to having so many aspects of public life in Israel governed by Jewish religious law, which to them amounted to "religious coercion" as it limited their personal freedoms.

One of the most contentious and emotive issues in this regard was the rabbinical monopoly on personal status matters. This meant, for instance, that Jews and non-Jews could not marry, that their children would not be considered Jewish if the mother was not Jewish according to Orthodox religious criteria, and that immigrant soldiers who died in combat and who were not considered to be Jewish could not be buried in Jewish cemeteries. The ultra-Orthodox, for their part, resented what they saw as the increasing secularization of Israeli society, evident for example in the growing number of shops, restaurants, and places of entertainment open on the Sabbath. To combat this trend, they attempted to exert their political power to enact legislation that would safeguard Israel's Jewish character (pushing, for example, for laws banning the sale and importation of pork). This effort appeared to many secular Israelis to be part of a broader strategy to force a religious lifestyle upon them and even establish a theocracy.

The mounting tensions between secular and ultra-Orthodox Jews in the late 1990s were widely seen as evidence of a *Kulturkampf*.[114] For instance, a crowd of around 250,000 religious Jews gathered in Jerusalem in February 1999 to demonstrate against the "anti-Semitic" decisions and "judicial dictatorship" of the Supreme Court (in the words of one of the organizers of the demonstration), and some 50,000 secular Israelis held a counter-rally in defense of the Supreme Court. In response, Prime Minister Netanyahu commented, "We all have to be very concerned at this flare-up," and added that a "*Kulturkampf*" is a "synonym for the beginnings of a civil war."[115] Netanyahu was not being alarmist in publicly warning of the danger of a civil war erupting between Israeli Jews. Many Israelis were concerned that the growing cultural conflict between secular and religious Jews could turn into a violent conflict between them. In September 2000, 80 percent of the Israeli population believed that it was accurate to talk about a "cultural war between secular and ultra-orthodox Jews," and 66 percent believed that there would be physical violence between these groups in the future.[116] Thus, the polarization between the secular and ultra-Orthodox "camps" sparked fears of a civil war, as the polarization between "Israelis" and "Jews" over the future of the territories had done earlier.

Israeli national identity was also among the issues at stake in the conflict between secular and ultra-Orthodox Jews. This can be seen in the heated controversy over the exemption from the military draft given to *yeshiva* students.[117] At the time of the "status quo agreement" this exemption applied to only a few hundred students, but by the late 1990s it came to allow roughly 30,000 *yeshiva* students to avoid military service. If these students stopped studying and began working, moreover, their exemptions were no longer valid; therefore, most choose to remain in *yeshivot* and not work, depending instead upon state subsidies to support them and their large families. For many secular Israelis, this was blatantly unfair: why should their sons and daughters have to risk their lives serving in the army, whilst others did not? Moreover, why should their taxes support those who "shirked" their duty to the state?

But the fierce public debate that took place over the induction of *yeshiva* students went beyond issues of equality and fairness. It was also about determining who was an Israeli, who belongs and who does not belong within the national community, and how this was to be decided. The IDF had long been an integral component of Israeli national identity, and service in it traditionally constituted the fundamental rite of passage into Israeli society. This is conveyed in the comments made by Israeli conscientious objectors in interviews eliciting their perceptions of military service. One interviewee bluntly stated: "All in all, the army is an Israeli experience, is experiencing Israeliness, it's part of our culture, that's the way it is . . . ." In the words of another: "Army life is part of our being Israeli . . . it is the price you pay to be Israeli. To be an Israeli means to be in the army and then you go to reserves, whether you want to or not."[118] The relationship between Israeli national identity and the IDF is clearly apparent in these comments. "Israeliness" is directly equated with army service; to be an "Israeli" means to have served in the army as a youth and, for men, to continue to serve in the system of reserves (until one reaches the age of around fifty-five). Military service facilitates a sense of belonging within Israeli society. This entails the conviction held by many Israelis that military service is a precondition for full political participation in the affairs of the "nation."[119] Thus, the boundaries of the national community are effectively demarcated through military service.[120] Those groups who do not engage in military service—the ultra-Orthodox and Palestinian Israelis—are therefore placed outside the boundaries of the Israeli nation, and are socially marginalized.[121] Their "Otherness" in Israeli society is constituted in part by their non-participation in this collective endeavor, as it represents a symbolic divide. Simply put, since being "Israeli" means serving in the IDF, those who do not serve are not "Israeli." By contrast, non-Jewish Israelis who do serve in the IDF, notably the Druze community, are more accepted within the boundaries of Israeli society.[122]

Given the IDF's role in determining the boundaries of the national community, the demand that the ultra-Orthodox serve in the IDF expressed a more fundamental demand that they join the Israeli nation. It represented an attempt to "Israelize" the ultra-Orthodox, to bring them within the bounds of the Israeli nation (significantly, no such demand was made vis-à-vis Palestinian Israelis).[123] By ending their draft exemption, the ultra-Orthodox would become members of the Israeli collective, voluntarily or not. Thus, the debate over the draft exemption for *yeshiva* students was, at least in part, a debate over the boundaries of Israeli national identity: who was to be included and who was to be excluded. Reflecting on this, the Israeli columnist Doron Rosenblum lamented: "[T]he sad anomaly that lies at the heart of the debate over the induction of yeshiva students . . . is the fact that, even after 50 years of independence, the 'rifle'—meaning compulsory military service—continues to enjoy the exclusive status of being the factor that determines and defines Israeli identity."[124] The IDF's role in defining Israeli identity, however, is jeopardized when military service ceases to be a common experience for most Israelis. With growing numbers of Israelis avoiding military service (for whatever reason) in the late 1990s (in this period, the proportion of conscripts from each annual cohort did not exceed 55 percent), it became increasingly difficult to view it as the experience that defined and united Israelis.

The IDF, therefore, risked losing its traditional role in defining Israeli identity. This also explains the demand for the ultra-Orthodox to serve in the army. As Rosenblum writes: "There is the nagging suspicion that drafting ultra-orthodox Jewish males into the IDF has become a highly emotionally-charged issue not only because of injustice and inequality but also because of the fears of a vacuum: In other words, there is a feeling that the elimination of the draft will remove the last straw of identity towards which Israelis have been reaching without success for so long."[125] Without compulsory military service, then, Israelis feared that there would be no common denominator left to define Israeli collective identity.

There was ample reason for this fear. In the 1990s, Israeli society had become openly multicultural, made up of a mosaic of different groups each with their own distinct subculture. Members of these different cultural groups often lived apart from one another in their own enclaves, dressed differently, spoke differently, possessed different collective memories, and had different political orientations. To be sure, Israeli society had always been a multicultural one. Jewish immigrants to Israel brought with them the cultures of their native lands—German, Polish, Russian, Moroccan, Yemenite, Persian, to name but a few. Despite concerted efforts by the state authorities to coax or, on occasion, coerce, new immigrants to forsake these cultures of the Jewish Diaspora, many clung to them tenaciously, albeit often in the privacy of their own homes.

In the 1990s, however, the various subcultures within Israeli society received growing public attention. The change that took place in the 1990s was not so much in the nature of Israeli society—from homogenous to heterogeneous—but in the degree of public awareness and recognition these subcultures received. This came about as the different cultural groups in Israeli society developed their own media and social, cultural, and political organizations, and actively championed their own interests (political, economic, cultural). The most prominent example of this was the greater cultural assertiveness of Mizrahi Jews, whose culture had traditionally been scorned by Ashkenazi Israelis as folkloristic and primitive. In the 1990s, traditional Mizrahi customs and practices (such as the Kurdish *Saharane* and the North African *maimounah* festivals), which had earlier been suppressed, gained new vitality, and Mizrahi music and literature became increasingly popular.[126] The Mizrahim were no longer willing to just integrate themselves into a dominant Ashkenazi culture. Instead they articulated and celebrated a distinct Mizrahi identity and collective memory.[127] So, too, did other marginalized cultural groups—Russians, Ethiopians, Bedouins, Druzes, and Palestinian Arabs. In varying degrees, all engaged in what the philosopher Charles Taylor has described as "the politics of recognition."[128]

As the various subcultures in Israeli society became more public and their members more assertive and more vocal, the existence of a multicultural society in Israel could no longer be denied or ignored. But this cultural pluralism was an unwelcome reality for those who clung to the ideal of a uniform national culture and national identity.[129] As one Israeli intellectual wrote: "A large number of Israelis think and act like pluralists without really wanting to. They know that the diversity of Israeli society is a fact of life, but deep inside, they cherish the dream of 'one Israeli,' not 'many Israelis.' "[130] The increasing recognition of a multicultural Israeli society, therefore, did not necessarily entail acceptance of this fact.[131] Hence, a public debate arose over multiculturalism in Israel, as it did in many other countries.[132] Opponents of multiculturalism stressed "the need to develop a positive national and cultural common denominator," in the words of Yair Sheleg, a writer for the liberal daily *Ha'aretz*.[133] In a similar vein, the authors of a government-sponsored report on cultural policy in Israel published in 2000 recommended that the state should strive "to strengthen the common cultural core and the recognition of a common center and a common system of values."[134]

The growing perception that Israelis lacked a "common denominator" cast new doubt over Israeli national identity.[135] After decades spent arguing over the definition of their collective identity, by the late 1990s, it appeared to many Israelis that they no longer shared a collective identity at all. "Many Israelis have the sense that the concept of a collective identity has vanished," wrote the former minister of Justice and Meretz Knesset member Amnon Rubinstein.[136] Accounting for this feeling of the disappearance of a collective identity was the widespread perception of Israeli society as splintered and "balkanized" into warring "tribes," each vocally advancing their own separate agendas. As one commentator wrote: "You can hardly open a paper in Israel these days without being confronted with the claim that the traditional solidarity of Israeli society has come to an end, having given way to a fragmentation of identity usually referred to as 'tribalism.' "[137]

The escalating identity politics of multiple groups within Israel, therefore, created a popular impression that Israeli society had fragmented, and that what divided Israelis was greater than what united them. There were the secular and the religious, Ashkenazim and Mizrahim, Jews and Arabs, Russians, Ethiopians, and others. "The adjectives (Sephardi, religious, Ashkenazi) outweigh the noun (Israeli)," wrote the Israeli commentator Gershon Shaked.[138] The stereotypic, classic Israeli—the sabra—was clearly a thing of the past, but what, if anything, could take his or her place, Israelis wondered? One question was repeatedly asked in the media: who is an Israeli?[139] For over a year and a half (winter 1996 to spring 1998), for example, the popular newspaper *Ma'ariv* featured a weekly column entitled, "Who is an Israeli?" Each week, prominent Israeli personalities were asked to answer the question and the public was allowed to respond by telephone. The question was one that the column's writer, Tzvi Gilat, believed the "average Israeli is troubled by." According to Gilat: "Today, I think an Israeli is someone who is asking what an Israeli is."[140] This certainly appeared to be the case, at least judging by the number of newspaper articles, books, television talk shows, and even conferences devoted to the issue of Israeli identity in the late 1990s.[141]

By asking "who is an Israeli," Israelis were searching for a clue as to what Israeli national identity was in the 1990s. The old Israeli national identity was clearly in decline; the question was what, if anything, would replace it? What were its supposedly distinctive characteristics or unique traits? If the mythological sabra no longer embodied Israeli national identity, who did? But the identity issues Israelis encountered in the latter half of the 1990s went beyond the problematic question: "who is an Israeli?" They also faced the challenge of how to deal with those citizens who did not regard themselves as "Israeli" at all. This was the case with many members of Israel's growing ultra-Orthodox Jewish community who still fundamentally considered the State of Israel to be a foreign government. The demand for their induction into the IDF was, as argued earlier, a demand for them to become "Israeli."

Many of the approximately 877,000 immigrants who arrived in Israel in the 1990s from the former Soviet Union (making up almost 20 percent of the total Jewish population of Israel) also did not consider themselves "Israeli" (for many, in fact, Israel was not their preferred destination when emigrating from the former Soviet Union). In a survey, 47 percent of these immigrants stated their preferred identity as "Russian," another 45 percent as "Jewish," and only 8 percent chose "Israeli."[142] According to Ron Dermer, an aide to Natan Sharansky (then leader of Yisrael Ba'aliya, the largest political party representing the immigrants from the former Soviet Union), the more recent immigrants from the former Soviet Union, "have a compelling desire to be treated like all Israelis, but not a compelling desire to be Israeli, or to accept the culture."[143] This was reflected in their creation of a separate Russian-language subculture in Israel, with their own Russian cable television station, three hundred Russian bookstores, six major publishing houses, four daily newspapers, over forty weekly publications, and a host of music, dance, and theater venues.[144] Thus one Israeli journalist wrote: "These immigrants may have internalized the Israeli political agenda, but it is doubtful whether they have developed a deep attachment to Israeli society and culture. In joining the ranks of other groups that feel alienated from the Israeli ethos (such as the Arabs, the foreign workers, and some of the ultra-orthodox), they have contributed to the growing sense of disintegration that permeates Israeli society today."[145]

The apparent failure to integrate the so-called Russian immigrants into Israeli society signaled the decline of the traditional Israeli "melting-pot,"[146] and sparked concern over continuing mass immigration to Israel.[147] In the words of one commentator: "The fear of continued mass immigration is, in effect, an expression of the feeling that Israel today can no longer turn its immigrants into Israelis."[148] This led to calls to delay a new immigrant's right to vote until they became integrated into Israeli society, or even to deny new immigrants arriving under the Law of Return automatic citizenship, and instead to require them to first pass examinations in the Hebrew language and Israeli history, geography, and politics.[149] There were even proposals to amend or abolish the Law of Return, the cornerstone of Israel's status as a safe haven for Jews around the world.[150] The Knesset debated the issue and newspaper editorials were devoted to it.

What gave particular impetus to the debate that arose over the Law of Return was the fact that many of the "Russian" immigrants—about 250,000—who arrived in the 1990s under the Law of Return were not classified as Jewish according to Jewish religious law.[151] In 1999, for instance, as many as 57 percent of the new immigrants from the former Soviet Union were not Jewish by this criterion.[152] Furthermore, it appeared that the proportion of non-Jews among immigrants arriving from the former Soviet Union was steadily increasing (as the number of Jews left in the former Soviet Union shrank). Alarmed at this trend, some politicians and government officials advocated various restrictions to the Law of Return designed to reduce the number of non-Jews immigrating to Israel. A report produced, for instance, by officials in Israel's Immigration and Absorption Ministry recommended revising the Law of Return on the grounds that non-Jewish immigrants could eventually align themselves with other non-Jewish citizens within the state and demand to change the Jewish character of the state.[153] This fear was also expressed by a columnist in Ha'aretz: "Hundreds of thousands of non-Jewish immigrants . . . will create a critical mass that will not only pose problems in everyday life but will also raise serious questions as to the country's national identity. The very presence of hundreds of thousands of non-Jews who have arrived here by virtue of the Law of Return will produce large questions marks concerning Israel's identity as a Jewish state as opposed to being a 'state representing all its citizens.' "[154]

What ignited the concern surrounding the influx of non-Jewish immigrants from the former Soviet Union, therefore, was the belief that this immigration could endanger the preservation of Israel's Jewish identity.[155] These immigrants, together with the roughly one million Palestinian Israelis (around 20 percent of Israel's population), could potentially form a politically powerful bloc of voters opposed to the institutions and practices entrenching Israel's Jewish identity.[156] These institutions and practices were already being increasingly challenged by a more assertive generation of Palestinian Israeli politicians. In October 1999, for instance, MKs from the

Hadash and Balad parties (both Palestinian Israeli political parties) announced their intention to introduce bills in the Knesset to abolish the Jewish Agency, the Zionist Federation, the World Jewish Congress, and the Jewish National Fund. One of these MKs, Mohammed Baraka of the Hadash party, provocatively declared: "These institutions are anachronistic and corrupt organizations that completed their role with the establishment of the State of Israel."[157]

By the end of the 1990s, the unresolved issue of the status of Palestinian Israelis within a self-declared Jewish State gained widespread attention.[158] This issue had long been neglected by successive Israeli governments.[159] For decades, Israeli governments and the Jewish public basically ignored the discrimination and exclusion (economic, legal, and political) endured by Palestinian Israelis.[160] Gradually, however, as the Palestinian Israeli community became increasingly politicized, radicalized, and empowered, their collective plight received greater public recognition and, by the late 1990s, it had become a major issue on the public and political agenda.[161] Israeli Jews generally preferred to consider this issue solely in socioeconomic terms—as a problem of underdevelopment—and favored policies aimed at reducing the socioeconomic gap that separated the Jewish and Palestinian Israeli communities.[162]

But for most Palestinian Israelis, this economic gap was only part of the problem. Equally, if not more important, was their awareness of living in a state and society whose "Jewishness" they did not share, thereby excluding them from the national community.[163] This accounted in part for the growing sense of alienation felt by Palestinian Israelis vis-à-vis the Israeli state and society.[164] In the words of one Palestinian Israeli: "Budgets are important, but that's not enough. I have to feel that I belong to this country. When I hear the national anthem now—what does it have to do with me? When I see the flag—what does it have to do with me?"[165] Similarly, another stated: "People have feelings, identity, values. Not all problems come down to a question of one's standards of living."[166] In the opinion of many Palestinian Israelis, the issue of equality and the issue of identity were bound together—as long as Israel remained a Jewish state, they would be "second-class citizens," always subject to unequal treatment.[167]

Hence, over time, the long-standing Palestinian Israeli demand for equal treatment became a demand for Israel to become a "state for all its citizens" rather than a state for Jews, as it was perceived by them to be.[168] This demand represented a fundamental challenge to Israel's identity as a Jewish state. What made this demand even more worrisome to many Israeli Jews was their fear that if Palestinian Israelis were unable to achieve this demand through parliamentary and other democratic activities—and there was little reason to believe that they would given the preferences of a large majority of the Jewish population—this could discredit such activities and lead to a radicalization of both goals and methods on the part of Palestinian Israelis. Consequently, proposals for secession, irredentism (into a future Palestinian state), and even binationalism (encompassing the entire area of mandatory Palestine) could well be voiced in the future by Palestinian Israelis.

The definition of Israeli national identity was also challenged by the heightened salience of the Palestinian Israeli issue. Palestinian Israelis had always remained outside the boundaries of Israeli national identity in so far as "Jewishness" was a constitutive element of it. Excluded from membership in the Israeli nation, increasingly over time they came to identify themselves as members of the Palestinian nation (this began after 1967 when Israel's occupation of the West Bank and Gaza allowed Palestinian Israelis to renew contact with their kin in those territories, and accelerated as a result of the Intifada in the territories beginning in 1987).[169] This process of "Palestinization" increased the marginality, disaffection, and resentment Palestinian Israelis felt vis-à-vis the Israeli state and Israeli-Jewish society, despite the fact that they were also becoming more fully acculturated into Israeli society and more deeply involved in Israeli politics. Thus, since Israeli national identity was limited to Jews, Palestinian Israelis developed a Palestinian national identity.[170] The growth of Palestinian nationalism within the Palestinian Israeli community—reflected in the rise of Palestinian nationalist parties and growing solidarity with Palestinians in the territories—fuelled Israeli Jewish society's suspicion and mistrust of Palestinian Israelis. To reverse the deteriorating relations between the two communities, therefore, there were increasing calls for a revision of Israeli national identity in order to allow Palestinian Israelis to identify themselves as "Israeli." This meant redrawing the boundaries of Israeli collective identity. The only way Palestinian Israelis could possibly consider themselves "Israeli" was if the prevailing ethno-religious definition of Israeli national identity was replaced by a civic, territorial definition. As the prominent Palestinian Israeli writer Anton Shammas appealed to the Israeli Jewish public in 1987: "I'm asking you for a new definition of the word 'Israeli,' so that it will include me as well, a definition in territorial terms that you distort because you are looking at it from the Jewish point of view."[171] Hence, to some it appeared that the only way to overcome the growing alienation of Palestinian Israelis was to have a more inclusive definition of Israeli collective identity.

The Post-Zionist Challenge

This view was advanced most forcefully by a group of Israeli intellectuals who collectively became known as "post-Zionists."[172] The fact that these individuals were in positions of influence within the cultural establishment, academia, and the media, and were mostly members of Israel's quintessential "in-group"—secular Ashkenazim—meant that their views reverberated well beyond their own immediate circle. As a result, these post-Zionists generated much debate and controversy in Israel in the 1990s.[173] Although not an organized political group, what characterized post-Zionists was their willingness to publicly question and criticize cherished Zionist tenets and beliefs. Some post-Zionists argued that Zionism was illegitimate and fundamentally misguided from the outset,[174] others that it had outlived its purpose and become anachronistic.[175] But whether they thought Zionism was inherently flawed or just no longer relevant, post-Zionists shared the belief that Israel should abandon Zionism and cease to be a Jewish state. Hence, they wanted to abolish all the laws, institutions, and national symbols that expressed Israel's identity as the state of the Jewish people (such as the Law of Return, the Jewish National Fund, and the national anthem *Ha-Tikvah* with its Jewish references[176]). The post-Zionists' opposition to Israel's continuation as a Jewish state was based upon what they regarded as a basic contradiction between Israel's simultaneous desire to be a democracy and a Jewish state. To resolve this contradiction, they advocated that Israel become a democratic state for all its citizens (thereby placing its non-Jewish citizens on an equal plane with its Jewish citizens).

Thus, in place of a Jewish state, they called for Israel to become a completely secular state oriented to the universal values of liberal democracy. In such a state, Israeli national identity would be defined solely by civic, territorial criteria, thereby including all Israel's citizens. Boaz Evron was one of the first post-Zionists to explicitly make this demand, writing in his conclusion to a blistering attack on Zionism: "It is necessary . . . to change the basis of the Israeli national definition and found it on the conventional territorial principle—equality before the law of all citizens living within the Israeli territory, irrespective of ethnic origins, race, community, religion, or sex."[177] This demand for a territorial, civic definition of Israeli national identity was advanced in the work of numerous other Israeli writers and intellectuals. They stressed the value of a pluralistic democracy, and the need to bolster a tolerant and open Israeli civil society. Hence, post-Zionism was described by one of its proponents as: "[A] trend of libertarianism and openness, which strives to lower the boundaries of Israeli identity and to include in it all relevant 'others.' "[178] Post-Zionism represented, therefore, another contribution to the ongoing debate over the definition of Israeli national identity. As such, its increasing prominence in Israeli intellectual discourse was seen by some as a symptom of the identity crisis afflicting Israeli society.[179]

The rise of post-Zionism as an intellectual movement in the 1990s was popularly associated with a growing revisionist trend in Israeli historiography and sociology.[180] In a series of books and articles, a younger generation of Israeli historians and sociologists who became known as the "New Historians" and "critical sociologists" respectively, presented new and sometimes provocative interpretations of seminal events and periods in Zionist and Israeli history, especially the events surrounding the war of 1948–1949 and the establishment of Israel.[181] They viewed Israel's past critically, in stark contrast to the rosy lens of nostalgia through which most Israelis had come to view it. According to Uri Ram, a prominent critical sociologist: "[C]laims such as those raised by the New Historians and critical sociologists deconstruct the Zionist national grand narrative and expose its contradictions and instabilities, omissions and lapses, that have marginalized and repressed others."[182]

This critique was most evident in the work of the New Historians dealing with Israel's conflict with the Arabs, in which they debunked many popular Israeli beliefs. Among their iconoclastic claims were that Israeli soldiers had not always been faithful to the "purity of arms" principle (meaning, essentially, that unarmed civilians must not be killed)—in more than one battle, Israeli soldiers committed war crimes, including mass executions, rape, and looting; that not all Palestinians refugees left Israel in response to their own leaders' call—some were driven out by the Israeli army; and that not all Arab countries had always refused to negotiate with Israel—at times, Israel preferred the status quo to negotiations. Collectively, the work of the New Historians represented, in the words of Ilan Pappé, one of the most outspoken New Historians, "an attempt to de-idealize Zionist history."[183]

Needless to say, this attempt was not well-received by some. The New Historians were accused of seeking to tarnish Israel's reputation and delegitimize Zionism and the State of Israel.[184] They were denounced by critics for being motivated by an anti-Israeli political agenda, rather than by a dispassionate scholarly one; to which they responded that they were simply offering a more factually based, demystified account of Israeli history using recently declassified official Israeli government documents.[185] Beginning as a disciplinary conflict among professional historians, the debate over the "new history" steadily entered into the public sphere in the 1990s as the New Historians' revisionist interpretations of Israeli history filtered down from the universities into Israeli high schools. In July 1999, for instance, Israel's Ministry of Education introduced a new history textbook for ninth-graders in which they were presented with a less heroic description of the 1948–1949 war. Describing the causes of the Jewish victory in the war over the Arabs, the textbook stated: "In almost every sector and in every battle, the Jews had the advantage over the Arabs, both with regard to planning, organization and operation of equipment as well as the skilled soldiers who took part in the battle."[186] By attributing the victory of Jewish forces in the War of Independence to the Jews' organizational and logistical edge, this one sentence shattered the Zionist myth of the "few against the many," and was thus particularly grating to the defenders of the traditional historical record. It contradicted the prevailing view of the war as one in which the Jews overcame enormous odds to defeat the invading Arab armies—a view which helped foster Israel's self-image as David battling the Arab Goliath.

The new textbook ignited a storm of public controversy. A group of prominent right-wing intellectuals and politicians published an advertisement in *Ha'aretz* that called on schools to boycott the textbook, declaring: "The book is written in a post-Zionist fashion that weakens the student's feeling of the justice of the Zionist path and the establishment of the State of Israel—to the point of questioning our right to the land."[187] Death threats were even sent to the Education Ministry's inspector for history instruction.[188] The debate conducted in the press between supporters and opponents of the new textbook clearly revealed that there was much more at stake than just the historical accuracy of the author's depiction of the 1948–1949 war. In the opinion of the popular Israeli journalist and television talk show host Dan Margalit: "We are not talking about a dispute over a certain limited issue in history, but rather about a plan to tarnish the image of Zionism."[189] Critics also assailed what they saw as the state's retreat from promoting fundamental Zionist values and beliefs. The fact that the "new history" was actually being disseminated by the state through its school curricula and textbooks and through state-funded universities signaled the state's sanctioning and promulgation of a critical discourse and a revisionist narrative that seemed to some to call into question its very legitimacy.[190] Defenders of the new textbook, however, hailed the willingness to present Israel's history in more honest and less heroic terms as a sign of maturity and self-confidence.[191]

The heated argument between defenders of the traditional Zionist historiography and advocates of the "new history" touched directly on Israeli collective memory and, by extension, Israeli national identity (since a collective memory is a constitutive element of all national identities). Since the birth of the state, and even before, the traditional Zionist narrative shaped Israeli collective memory. It provided Israeli Jews with a common story line that depicted them as a virtuous, heroic nation that had overcome great adversity. Propagated by the state through its educational system and its national commemorations, the dominant Zionist national narrative was instrumental in forging Israeli national identity.[192] By "rewriting" Israel's history, the "new history" subverted the hegemonic Zionist narrative and, in the process, challenged its representation of the nation.[193] If the dominant narrative of the nation's past was misleading and/or false (at least with regard to certain events and episodes), then the national self-image linked to that past was equally problematic and erroneous. Specifically, generations of Israelis had been raised to believe that Israel's origins were pure and just, that its survival had been miraculous, and that their nation was noble and peace seeking. These beliefs were all challenged by the New Historians as their work exposed the historical fictions of Israel's self-congratulatory national narrative. If Israel was "born in sin" (as some of the New Historians contended) and if Israelis had not always acted humanely, then Israel and the Israeli-Jewish nation was really no different from any other nation whose past was marred by conquest and cruelty. Thus, their cherished national uniqueness was exploded as a myth. In this sense, the "new history" contributed to the process of Israel's "normalization" taking place in the 1990s. But it also added to growing crisis of Israeli national identity. As a result of the social, cultural, and political changes in Israel in the 1990s, it was hard enough to define Israeli national identity. As a result of the work of the New Historians, even the past (however selectively constructed) could not provide such a clear definition any longer.

For both its advocates and its critics, the intellectual ascendancy of post-Zionism indicated not only the profound changes that had taken place in the preceding decade, but also the likelihood of even more dramatic changes to come. Whether Israelis liked it or not, Israel was becoming a very different country from the one it had been just a decade earlier. It was a country in which domestic conflicts, rather than the conflict between Israelis and Palestinians, were dominating the public agenda; a country in which the unifying power of a common Zionist ideology was giving way to divisive post-ideological identity politics. Although Israelis had always disagreed over the definition of their national identity, by the end of the 1990s this disagreement was more public and more pronounced than it had ever been before.

Moreover, it was not only the definition of Israeli national identity that was contested in the late 1990s, it was also the existence of Israeli national identity itself that came into question as the proliferation of subnational identities—Mizrahi, Russian, Ethiopian, Arab, and the like—portended the demise of any common identity that could unite Israel's heterogeneous population. Whereas once the existence of a common national identity was assumed and the debate centered upon how it was to be defined, now a common national identity could no longer even be taken for granted. The Israeli public was deeply divided; but instead of the old, neat divisions between hawks and doves, Jews and Israelis, there were multiple divisions, some reinforcing, and some crosscutting. With the arrival of the twenty-first century, Israel's pursuit of peace with the Palestinians and its neighbors in the region appeared to be almost at an end. Israeli-Palestinian peace seemed to be just around the corner; peace between Israelis, however, seemed increasingly remote.

CHAPTER 5
THE RETURN OF THE OTHER

I for one . . . never believed we would really be able to survive here if we were nothing more than Israelis. For our attachment to the land of Israel, our identity with it, comes through our Jewishness . . . .[1]

—Ariel Sharon

Zionism was founded in order to save Jews from persecution and anti-Semitism, and not in order to offer them a Jewish Sparta.[2]

—Yossi Beilin

Introduction

The 1990s had been a decade of momentous changes in Israel's internal and external affairs. The Oslo peace process transformed Israel's foreign relations, turning the country from an international pariah into an accepted member of the international community with burgeoning diplomatic and trade relations with a host of countries that had previously shunned it (including many in the Arab world). By the end of the 1990s, Israelis felt more secure than they had ever done before. The risk of war with Israel's neighbors seemed remote since the military balance of power was overwhelmingly in Israel's favor (not to mention the fact that Israel now had peace treaties with two of its neighbors—Egypt and Jordan), and the fear of terrorist attacks had diminished as their number had substantially declined during Netanyahu's premiership. If peace meant security, as it did for many Israelis, then they were already enjoying it in the late 1990s, even in the absence of a final peace treaty with the Palestinians.

The achievement of a peace treaty between Israel and the Palestinians, moreover, was widely seen as inevitable. Although the Oslo peace process remained a subject of much controversy and argument, it no longer preoccupied Israelis as it had previously. To many, both inside and outside Israel, it seemed that the peace process was unstoppable. Even the advent of a right-wing Israeli government led by Benjamin Netanyahu, a declared opponent of the peace process, did not derail it. Although mistrust and suspicion intensified between Israelis and Palestinians during Netanyahu's premiership, the process of Israel's gradual withdrawal from the occupied territories continued, albeit at a much slower pace than that envisaged in the Oslo Accords. Certainly, there would continue to be ups and downs along the way, but the end result—an Israeli withdrawal from most, if not all, of the West Bank and Gaza and the establishment of a Palestinian state in those areas—was almost certain, however one judged this outcome. This common, largely unspoken, belief allowed Israelis to move on to other matters of importance to them. Above all, Israelis increasingly turned their attention inwards, to the domestic divisions and debates that had simmered for so long under the surface of the debate over the future of the territories. Mounting secular-religious tension, the widening economic gap between rich and poor, the growing radicalism of the Palestinian-Israeli community, the mutual estrangement between native Israelis and the new immigrants from the former Soviet Union, the continuing resentment felt by the Mizrahim toward perceived Ashkenazi hegemony—these were issues which preoccupied Israelis and dominated Israel's political agenda at the end of the millennium. Israeli-Palestinian peace had not yet arrived, but "post-peace" domestic politics had.

This chapter begins with an analysis of the results of the 1999 elections for the Knesset and the premiership. It then proceeds with an examination of Prime Minister Ehud Barak's term in office from 1999 to 2001. I claim that Barak chose to prioritize the pursuit of peace over addressing domestic issues—especially religious-secular relations in Israel. I also contrast Barak's approach to the Israeli settler population in the West Bank and Gaza with that of his mentor, Rabin. I discuss the failure of the Israeli-Syrian peace negotiations under Barak and his decision to unilaterally withdraw the IDF from southern Lebanon. It was only after these events that Barak turned his full attention to the Israeli-Palestinian peace process. Determined to conduct final status negotiations with the Palestinians, Barak persuaded the Clinton Administration to host the talks at Camp David in July 2000. The concessions that Barak offered at Camp David were the most far-reaching concessions ever made by an Israeli prime minister to the Palestinians. I analyze the positions taken by Barak in the negotiations on the issues of Jerusalem, the Temple Mount/Haram al-Sharif, and a Palestinian right of return. These positions were formulated within the limits imposed by Israeli public opinion. On the issue of Jerusalem, I argue that Barak was able to break the long-standing Israeli commitment to the unity of Jerusalem due to a sea change in Israeli culture that occurred in the 1990s, marked by increasing pluralism, a critical reevaluation of Israeli history and society, and a declining public attachment to Zionist myths, symbols, and slogans. But while this cultural change made it politically possible for Barak to propose a division of sovereignty in Jerusalem, Barak could not compromise on the issues of sovereignty over the Temple Mount/Haram al-Sharif and accepting a Palestinian right of return because Israeli Jews would not accept concessions on these issues. The inability of the Israeli and Palestinian delegations at Camp David to reach an agreement on these two issues resulted in the failure of the summit.

This failure and the outbreak of a second Palestinian Intifada in September 2000 brought about the collapse of the Oslo peace process. I discuss the domestic consequences of this in Israel, specifically examining its impact on Israeli public opinion. With their hopes for peace dashed, Israelis elected Likud leader Ariel Sharon as prime minister and sought national unity in the face of escalating Israeli-Palestinian violence. The resurrection of national unity in Israel was most apparent in the popular support for the construction of a West Bank barrier and for a unilateral separation between Israelis and Palestinians. I end this chapter by describing some of the ways in which an ethno-religious definition of Israeli national identity was reasserted and how this brought to an end (if only temporarily) the crisis of Israeli identity.

The 1999 Elections: Post-Peace Politics

Israel's new political landscape clearly emerged in the May 1999 elections. These were the second elections to involve separate votes for the Knesset and the prime minister, and just as they did in the 1996 elections, many voters took advantage of their ability to "split their vote" by voting for the prime minister on the basis of national considerations, while voting for parties on the basis of communal or identity-related considerations. As a result, the outcome of the 1999 elections was decidedly mixed—Ehud Barak, the new Labor party leader (who succeeded Peres after Peres' defeat in 1996), won a landslide victory against the incumbent Netanyahu in the prime ministerial election, but his One Israel party (combining Labor, David Levy's Gesher party, and the dovish-religious party Meimad) won only 26 seats in the Knesset, nearly a quarter less than in 1996. The biggest winners in the Knesset election were a host of small parties representing identity-based groups. All these parties gained seats at the expense of the two largest parties, Labor and Likud, which continued their downward slide.[3]

The restructuring of the political sphere around distinct identity groups, already evident after the 1996 elections, became even more apparent in the 1999 elections. More small parties representing different identity groups in Israeli society gained seats in the Knesset—the two "Russian" immigrant parties (Yisrael B'Aliyah and the newly-formed Yisrael Beitenu) together won ten seats, the three Arab parties (Hadash, Ra'am, and Balad) won ten seats, the ultra-Orthodox Sephardi party Shas won seventeen seats, and the new militantly secular Shinui party won six seats. In total, fifteen parties had seats in the new Knesset, four more than in the previous Knesset. To a greater degree than ever before, the composition of the Knesset reflected the diversity and divisions within Israeli society. Israel's political fragmentation mirrored its social balkanization into feuding sectarian camps.

The bitterest feud was that between secular and religious Jews, and the parties representing these constituencies enjoyed the greatest gains in the Knesset elections. Most spectacular was the success of Shas, which increased its seats from ten to seventeen, just two behind the Likud's nineteen seats. With an ultra-Orthodox leadership and a large number of ultra-Orthodox followers, Shas called for increased funding for religious education, the construction of synagogues and ritual baths, and stricter observance of Jewish religious law by state bodies. These demands were not merely aimed at safeguarding the lifestyle of ultra-Orthodox Jews. Rather, they were part of Shas' broader ambition to elevate the place of Judaism in public and private life in Israel, in order to gradually transform the entire Israeli Jewish society into a religious society and Israel into a theocratic state.

This goal was clearly expressed by Aryeh Deri, Shas' charismatic and immensely popular leader, in an interview in which he described the kind of Israel he wanted to bring about: "There is no doubt that my vision and my dream . . . is that there will be a Jewish state that will follow the laws of the Torah. I, as a Jew, want the laws of the State of Israel to be the laws of the Torah and the halakha [Jewish religious law]."[4] Notwithstanding this far-reaching religious agenda, Shas really owed its electoral success to its provision of social services in predominantly lower class, Mizrahi-populated towns (located mainly in Israel's geographic periphery). Most of its new supporters came from these towns and were former Likud voters (this accounts for Likud's dramatic loss of support). Neither strictly religious nor strictly secular, these traditional, poor and working-class Mizrahi Jews were drawn to Shas through its independent educational and welfare agencies (funded by its control of the Ministries of the Interior, Labor, and Social Welfare during the years of the Netanyahu government). The trial and conviction of Aryeh Deri, who was sentenced to four years in jail for bribery and corruption in April 1999 just one month before the election, also increased the party's support as Deri depicted himself as an innocent victim who was persecuted by Israel's secular Ashkenazi elite. This resonated with many disadvantaged Mizrahim who continued to harbor resentment at what they saw as Ashkenazi political, cultural, and economic dominance.

The other big success story of the 1999 Knesset election was the sudden rise of Shinui, a party formed only three months before the election and led

by Tommy Lapid, a popular former television personality.[5] A one-issue
party, Shinui won six seats on the basis of its strident secularism and anti-
clericalism. Shinui vehemently attacked the power of the ultra-Orthodox
religious establishment and championed the rights of Israel's secular population against what it termed "religious coercion" (an example of which is
the ban on public transportation on the Sabbath, which Shinui wanted
overturned). In doing so, it articulated many of the long-held grievances of
Israel's secular population (the exemption of yeshiva students from military
service, for instance). As the antithesis of Shas, Shinui drew its support from
secular middle-class Ashkenazi Jews. Thus, for the first time in Israeli electoral
politics, a self-defined "secular camp" emerged in the 1999 elections to
directly counter the "religious camp." Also representing this "secular camp"
were the Center party and left-wing Meretz party, together forming a large
new secular bloc in the Knesset of twenty-two seats.[6]

While secular/religious relations and the relationship between religion
and state were major issues in the 1999 Knesset election, the issue of the
territories did not arouse public interest. This was evident in the poor per-
formances of the National Religious Party (NRP) and the National Union
party led by Benny Begin, parties whose central platform was complete
Jewish sovereignty over *Eretz Israel*.[7] The ideological claim to *Eretz Israel*
had already lost some of its popular appeal by the 1992 election—a factor
that, as explained earlier, helped Labor win that election. By 1999, it had
effectively become defunct (except amongst a few die-hard adherents). The
process of partitioning *Eretz Israel* between Israelis and Palestinians was
already underway, and few believed it could be reversed. Moreover, a right-
wing prime minister had now handed territory over to the Palestinians.
More than anything else, Netanyahu's premiership dashed whatever hope
was left for "Greater Israel." His legacy was to strip the very political camp
from which he emerged of its overriding raison d'être and, in doing so, to
seriously weaken it. The ideology of "Greater Israel" which burst onto the
Israeli political scene in the aftermath of the 1967 war and became the issue
around which Israeli politics revolved for the next three decades was effectively laid to rest in the 1999 elections. The results of the Knesset election,
therefore, decisively signaled the ascendancy of identity politics in Israel.

If the Knesset election was driven by identity politics, the prime ministerial election was about personalities, especially Netanyahu's. To those in
Israel and abroad who had watched with growing consternation the deterioration in Israeli-Palestinian relations during Netanyahu's three-year tenure
(1996–1999), his crushing defeat by Barak (who gained almost 400,000
votes more than Netanyahu, winning just over 56 percent of all votes cast)
brought new hope. Barak was Israel's most decorated soldier; he had been
its youngest ever Chief of Staff and had commanded an elite army unit and

participated in some of the Israeli army's most daring exploits (such as the 1975 Entebbe raid). This military background, together with the close relationship he had with the late Yitzhak Rabin, allowed Barak to present himself to Israelis and the international community as Rabin's heir. Like his role model, Barak promised to bring Israelis peace, security, and economic prosperity. He declared his intention to steadfastly pursue the peace process with the Palestinians in order to arrive at a comprehensive final settlement of the conflict, as well as to sign peace treaties with the Syrians and Lebanese. In addition, he vowed to "bring the boys home" and end the highly unpopular guerrilla war that Israeli forces were fighting with their South Lebanese Army (SLA) allies against the Iranian-backed Hizbullah in southern Lebanon. To this end, he declared his willingness to unilaterally withdraw Israeli troops from Southern Lebanon within one year of coming to power if no peace agreements with the Syrians and/or Lebanese could be reached.

But Barak's impressive résumé and bold promises did not win him the election. Rather, it was Netanyahu's flaws. Attacked by some of his own ministers (most notably former defense minister Yitzhak Mordechai, who founded the Center party with other disaffected members of the Likud and ran against Netanyahu for prime minister), abandoned by his coalition allies, and hounded by the press over a series of corruption scandals, Netanyahu's popularity plummeted. He lost support among every group in Israeli society that had previously supported him—poor Mizrahim, new Russian immigrants, the ultra-Orthodox, the settlers.[8] All Barak had to do was to promise change, even without spelling out detailed plans, to capitalize on this disillusionment.[9]

The election for the premiership in 1999 was more about character than about policy. Those policy issues that did feature in the campaign were domestic—the economy, unemployment, education, and government funding of *yeshivot*. The peace process was not a prominent issue. Despite their misgivings, both Netanyahu and Barak were committed to continuing it (Barak had actually opposed the Oslo Accords as Chief of Staff in 1993 and abstained in the vote on the Oslo II Agreement as a member of Rabin's Cabinet in 1995).[10] Furthermore, Barak's impeccable military credentials meant that, unlike his Labor predecessor Peres, he could not easily be depicted as being "soft" on security. After an election campaign largely devoid of policy debates, and without having to fear that Barak would jeopardize their security and confident that the peace process would continue regardless, the vote for prime minister was primarily a referendum on Netanyahu's leadership. The verdict was clear; and in response to the voters' resounding rejection of him, Netanyahu immediately announced his resignation from politics.[11]

Peace First

Barak's solid victory provided him with a clear mandate to rule.[12] But, like all Israeli prime ministers, he had to form a coalition government in order to ensure the support of the Knesset. Barak had a number of coalition options available to him, each offering different benefits and costs. Examining these options and the choices that Barak eventually made in selecting his coalition partners reveals a great deal about Barak's priorities as prime minister and his general political strategy. One option was to assemble a secular coalition with One Israel, Meretz, Shinui, the Center party, Yisrael B'Aliyah, and One Nation. This would be a minority government, however, and would therefore rely upon the tacit support of the Arab parties, as the Rabin/Peres government did from 1992–1996. Barak rejected this potential coalition because he believed that the Rabin/Peres government's unofficial reliance on Arab votes for its parliamentary majority exacerbated tensions among Jewish Israelis, something that Barak was determined to avoid. One way to avoid this was to include the Likud (now led by Ariel Sharon) in this secular coalition. Such a coalition would give Barak a Knesset majority that would enable him to address the major domestic issue of the relationship between religion and state (which might involve the drafting of a written constitution).

But the Likud's presence in his government would restrict Barak's room for maneuver in foreign policymaking, and especially in the peace process with the Palestinians. For this reason, he decided against a National Unity government with the Likud and the other secular parties. Another option was to form a broad coalition including both secular and religious parties, but excluding the Likud, the far-right parties, and the Arab parties. Such a coalition would provide Barak with a comfortable parliamentary majority, give him greater freedom in foreign policymaking and the peace process, but make it harder for him to deal with secular/religious issues. This was the option Barak ultimately favored and after a lengthy period of coalition negotiations, he presented his new government comprising seven parties— One Israel, Meretz, the Center party, Yisrael B'Aliyah, and the three religious parties Shas, the NRP, and United Torah Judaism—to the Knesset on July 6, 1999.

In his speech to the Knesset that day, Barak stated that: "The primary consideration which guided me in composing this government was the need to find the broadest possible common denominator in order to responsibly bring together representatives of parties and sectors from various, even opposing, sides of Israeli society . . . . This government will not turn its back on any group, portion, sector or ideological stream in Israeli society. This will be a government of constant dialogue, openness and attentiveness, a government that will aspire to a 'new national consensus,' but not shirk from decisions or resign itself to paralysis and be stalemated."[13] As this statement suggests, Barak's goal in forming his coalition was not only to ensure himself as much freedom of maneuver as possible in foreign policymaking (especially concerning the peace process with the Palestinians), but also to create a government that would encompass the different groups in Israeli society—with the notable exception of Palestinian Israelis, whose representatives were (as they had always been) left out. In his victory speech on the night of the election, Barak promised to be the prime minister of all Israelis, declaring: "Tonight, we wish to extend a warm and firm hand to the secular, religious, ultra-orthodox, settlers, Sephardim and Ashkenazim, Ethiopian and Russian immigrants, Arabs, Druze, Circassians and the Bedouin. All are part of the Israeli people."[14] And, in his inaugural Knesset speech, Barak described Israeli society as "[A] unique society: a fascinating mosaic of hues and opinions, cultures and creeds— veteran residents and new immigrants, people from different Diasporas, religious and ultra-Orthodox, traditional and secular, Jews and Arabs, Druze and Circassians. Together, equally, they are Israel."[15]

Barak was not simply acknowledging the heterogeneous nature of Israeli society; he was, more importantly, appealing for social unity. He was conveying the message that whatever differences divided Israelis, they were nevertheless "one people."[16] In doing so, Barak was articulating a definition of Israeli national identity that included Jews and non-Jews. According to this, "Israeliness" was divorced from ethnicity, religion, or geographic origin. It was not defined by one culture or social group. Rather, it was a civic, territorial identity shared by all citizens of Israel. This reaffirmed the definition of Israeli national identity espoused by Rabin in the years 1992–1995. But whereas Rabin's conception of Israeli national identity seemed to many to be at odds with an ethno-religious conception of Israeli national identity according to which "Jewishness" was the defining component, Barak also emphasized "Jewishness" and the importance of safeguarding the Jewish identity of Israelis Jews. "It is our mission," he declared to the Knesset, "to prepare the new generation in Israel for the new, open and global era of the 21st Century, while also reinforcing and strengthening the components of its national and Jewish identity, its sense of attachment and its bonds to Israel. The way to this is through deepening historical awareness, acknowl- edging our heritage and faith, building a society based on solidarity, internal cohesion and what is called—with no cause for embarrassment—'national pride.' Not arrogant pride, condescending to others, but pride which rec- ognizes values, and identification with the historical collective memory of all Jewish ethnic groups, with the heritage of the generations and with the awesome contribution that our nation has made to human civilization."[17]

At least rhetorically, then, Barak was careful to defend himself against the kind of accusations that were leveled at Rabin and Peres. They had been

fiercely attacked for neglecting the Jewish identity of Israelis and undermining the Jewish character of the state. In his idealistic embrace of globalization, Peres in particular was assailed by his right-wing critics for blithely
disregarding the threat that it posed to Israel's Jewish culture and identity.
Barak was determined not to make the same mistakes as his Labor predecessors. By paying lip service to Jewish nationalism, by including religious
Zionist and ultra-Orthodox parties in his coalition, and by ensuring that his
government was not dependent on the support of Arab parties in the
Knesset, Barak attempted to avoid the fate that had befallen the Rabin/Peres
government. In their energetic pursuit of peace with the Palestinians, Rabin
and Peres had offended and alienated large segments of the Israeli public—
not only the settlers, but also religious and traditional Israeli Jews who felt
that the peace process was leading to the dissolution of Israeli-Jewish identity
and the eradication of the state's Jewish characteristics. This feeling, however
well founded, contributed to the growing social and political polarization
that occurred during the years of the Rabin government and, ultimately,
helped to foster the climate in which Rabin was assassinated in 1995 and
Peres defeated in the 1996 elections. Barak, therefore, did his best to prevent
the emergence of a similar atmosphere. He made national unity a main
theme of his premiership, regularly calling for it and underlining its importance. His electoral platform for the 1999 elections stated: "The deepening
polarization in our ranks endangers the unity of our society . . . . We are
motivated by our wish to preserve the unity of the nation and the state and
to attain peace among ourselves."[18] And when his new government was officially inaugurated into office he declared that "this day will be chronicled as
a milestone and turning point—a time of reconciliation, unity and peace."[19]

Barak made a concerted effort to strengthen national unity and ensure
against a return to the intensely hostile political climate that prevailed in
Israel in the early years of the Oslo peace process. Not only did he talk of
Jewish "national pride," form a broad-based governing coalition, and
distance himself from the Palestinian Israeli community (despite the fact that
nearly ninety-five percent of Palestinian Israelis voted for him);[20] but also he
expressed a far more sympathetic attitude to the settlers in the West Bank
and Gaza than did Rabin, remarking in one interview: "I'm not a typical
leftist—I have great respect for the pioneering role of the settlers."[21] Whether
sincere or not, this comment was in sharp contrast to the kinds of offensive
remarks that Rabin made about the settlers. Rabin had displayed contempt
and hostility toward the settlers. He did not regard them as pioneers; instead
he considered them an economic burden and a security liability.[22]

Faced with the possibility of having to leave their homes and give up
their way of life and, for some, their dreams of Greater Israel and messianic
redemption, the settler community was further antagonized by Rabin's attitude. Certainly, many would have staunchly opposed the Oslo peace

process under any circumstances, but Rabin only seemed to make matters worse, generating ever more intense settler opposition to his peace policy. This was a lesson that Barak clearly learned from the bitter experience of the Rabin government. Barak established a dialogue with the settlers (something that Rabin had refused to do) and, unlike Rabin, he did not treat the settlers as a bunch of "crazies" (as Rabin had famously called them). Instead, he differentiated between the majority who had settled in the West Bank and Gaza for primarily nonideological reasons (i.e., cheap housing and lifestyle concerns), and the minority of hard-core ideological settlers—religious and secular. Barak tried to appease the former and marginalize the latter. Hence, whereas the Rabin government's 1992 guidelines specified that certain development towns inside pre-1967 Israel should be preferred over certain West Bank and Gaza settlements in terms of government subsidies and support, the guidelines of the Barak government stated that government services to all settlements will be "equal to those offered to residents of all other communities in Israel. The government will offer a response to the ongoing development needs of existing communities. Socioeconomic standards will be equally applied to all communities everywhere." Barak, therefore, refused to re-implement the freeze on the expansion of existing settlements that the Rabin government introduced and which the Netanyahu government revoked.[23] He also insisted that in a final peace agreement with the Palestinians, Israel retain control over the majority of settlers—that is, those who live in the three settlement blocs closest to the 1967 border (Gush Etzion, Ma'ale Adumim, and Ariel). He hoped that this position could win support for the peace process from that settler majority, while isolating the most ideological settlers who tended to live in more distant and scattered settlements.

Barak's general strategy as prime minister was to try to gain the support of as many sections of Israeli society as possible, or at least not to alienate them. Underlying his stated intention to be "everybody's prime minister," was an awareness that he needed to bring as many social groups along as possible for as long as possible in order to carry out his ambitious foreign policy agenda. He would need all the domestic political capital he could muster to gain public and parliamentary support for the concessions he was preparing to make for peace, so why squander it, he seemed to reason, on divisive domestic disputes? For Barak, the strategic imperative of achieving peace treaties with the Palestinians, Syrians, and Lebanese—treaties that were bound to involve "painful concessions" by Israel—made it necessary to postpone dealing with Israeli domestic issues that had the potential to be socially polarizing and politically damaging for him.

Barak's priority was to first solve Israel's external conflicts, before turning to its festering internal conflicts. As he put it in a speech to Israeli officers at the National Security College: "I am convinced that the strongest spring-board for Israel's prosperity and ability to successfully confront its internal problems, lies in a solution to the conflict with our neighbors. Such a solution, as difficult and painful as it may be, will eventually bring an end to our malignant internal rift over the future of the territories and borders, and will enable us to invest all our energies and resources in education, development of infrastructure, bridging the gaps and basic social change."[24] This conviction led Barak to abandon many of the domestic social and economic reforms he proposed during his election campaign for the sake of maintaining his diverse coalition government. One such reform concerned the contentious issue of drafting ultra-Orthodox youth into the army. Barak had promised to abolish their draft exemption, campaigning with the slogan "One nation—one draft." Once in office, however, Barak reversed his position, supporting a piece of legislation (known as the "Tal Bill" after the name of the state commission established to examine the issue) that allowed the practice of granting exemptions from army service to ultra-Orthodox youth to continue. This reversal prevented a rift with the ultra-Orthodox and the loss of one of his coalition partners, United Torah Judaism, but left many secular Israelis feeling that Barak had betrayed them.

Barak's strategy of prioritizing the pursuit of peace over domestic issues encountered a major difficulty, however. Many Israelis, and the political parties representing them, were not willing to put aside or subdue their internal disputes, even if only temporarily. Barak's neglect of contentious domestic issues in favor of foreign policy issues did not make those issues disappear or become less salient—if anything they became more salient as the prime minister appeared to dodge them. This was most evident with Barak's failure to intervene in the long-running dispute between two of his coalition partners, Meretz and Shas, over the allocation of government funds to bail out the bankrupt religious educational network run by Shas (which Meretz, in control of the Ministry of Education, refused to do). At issue was the future of Shas' educational network. For Shas, this network was not just a means of providing patronage and services to its supporters, but also a central component in its broader strategy to religiously transform Israeli-Jewish society from the ground-up through a grassroots "religious revolution."[25] Shas politicians openly expressed this aim. Shas Knesset member David Azoulay, for instance, declared: "Education is the jewel in our crown. What does the Shas movement have without education? Nothing. Only through education can we reach families and their children. Only if education is in our hands, can we generate a revolution in Israeli society."[26]

The conflict between Meretz and Shas, then, was about more than government spending and bureaucratic power. It was, in the words of Shas party spokesperson Itzhak Sudri, part of "a war over culture,"[27] part of the ongoing secular-religious *Kulturkampf* within Israel. The conflict dragged on throughout the first year of Barak's term in office, producing intermittent coalition crises that threatened to bring down the government on numerous occasions. It finally ended with Meretz's departure from the coalition in June 2000 when it seemed that Barak was tilting his support toward Shas in an effort to ensure its support for his peace policy.[28] Barak's poor handling of the Shas-Meretz dispute only served to alienate Meretz and offend Shas.

While his coalition partners squabbled over domestic issues, Barak devoted himself to foreign policy. Initially, he focused on reaching a peace agreement with Syria, rather than with the Palestinians.[29] There were a number of reasons for this. First, a deal with Syria appeared more attainable since the issues at stake in the negotiations with the Syrians seemed easier to resolve than those between the Israelis and Palestinians. Second, the Israeli-Syrian conflict lacked the emotional and historical resonance of the Israeli-Palestinian conflict making it a less explosive public issue in Israel. Syrian President Hafez al-Assad's ill health was another reason for Barak's decision to pursue a peace treaty with Syria first, since it was feared that Assad's successor (most likely his son Bashar) would not enjoy the same degree of domestic authority to allow him to make peace with Israel. Finally, Barak hoped that a peace agreement with Syria would put more pressure on the Palestinian leadership when final status negotiations with the Palestinians got underway.

In accordance with this "Syria first" strategy, in January 2000 Barak met with Syrian foreign minister, Farouk al-Shara, in Shepherdstown, West Virginia, for talks convened by the Clinton Administration. Although the Syrians showed a clear desire to compromise on each of the three sets of issues in dispute (the location of the border, ensuring adequate water supplies, and normalization), Barak hardened Israel's position by insisting on linking a Syrian agreement with an accord on Lebanon, much to the annoyance of the Syrians and President Clinton and his Middle East envoy, Dennis Ross.[30] The talks ended in failure, and by the time Clinton met with President al-Assad in Geneva on March 26, 2000 in a last-ditch effort to rescue the prospects of an Israeli-Syrian peace agreement (a meeting that Barak had requested), the Syrians were no longer willing to compromise.[31] President al-Assad now demanded a Syrian presence on the Sea of Galilee (or Lake Kineret, as the Israelis call it), which Barak refused since that would jeopardize Israel's control of one of its major water sources providing 40 percent of Israel's freshwater needs (by having a presence on it, the Syrians would gain the rights of a riparian state according to international law). Less than three months later, al-Assad was dead and hopes for an imminent Israeli-Syrian peace agreement died with him.

Despite his failure to reach peace agreements with Syria and Lebanon, Barak decided to honor his campaign pledge to "bring the boys home" from southern Lebanon within one year of the inauguration of his government. This now necessitated a unilateral Israeli withdrawal, something that much of Israel's defense establishment (i.e., the intelligence services and the IDF's general staff) were opposed to. But the Israeli public wanted an end to Israel's long and costly occupation of southern Lebanon, even if this meant a unilateral withdrawal. The majority of Israelis had come to regard the IDF's presence in southern Lebanon as pointless and Israel's war of attrition with Hizbullah as unwinnable (the activities of domestic protest groups such as Four Mothers and Red Line had an important affect in this regard). It was this loss of public support for Israel's presence in Lebanon that led Barak to override the advice of his generals and unilaterally withdraw Israeli troops from southern Lebanon in May 2000. As his Deputy Minister Defense Ephraim Sneh bluntly admitted: "We are leaving because of problems with the ability of the Israeli public to stand firm. That is the whole truth. There is no point in pretending."[32] Thus, although the hasty manner of the withdrawal (precipitated by the rapid disintegration of the SLA) and the televised scenes of SLA fighters and their relatives gripped by fear and panic seeking sanctuary in Israel made many Israelis anxious and uncomfortable, it was nonetheless widely welcomed by Israelis for finally bringing an end to what had become Israel's eighteen-year "Vietnam."[33] When the withdrawal was completed on May 24, 2000, Barak expressed the feelings of many Israelis when he declared that Israel's "tragedy" in Lebanon was at last over.[34]

By the summer of 2000, having reached a dead end on the Syrian track, Barak finally turned his attention to reaching a peace agreement with the Palestinians. Time was running out. The Palestinian leadership, in line with their general public, was increasingly impatient with the slow pace of the peace process. They were also disappointed and frustrated with Barak for having postponed talks while he focused on Syria, for not releasing Palestinian prisoners (those imprisoned for actions committed before the signing of the Oslo agreement), for failing to carry out his commitments to implement the third redeployment of Israeli troops and the transfer of three Jerusalem villages, and for allowing the continued expansion of Jewish settlements in the territories. As the Palestinian public grew restive, Israeli intelligence was warning of possible violence in the territories.[35] Moreover, the seventh anniversary of the signing of the Declaration of Principles on September 13, 2000 was fast approaching, when it was feared that the Palestinians would unilaterally declare statehood.

Instead of continuing with the process of piecemeal withdrawals from the West Bank—which Barak believed weakened Israel's negotiating position when permanent status talks got underway (since the Palestinians would already be in control of most of the territories and would consequently be less inclined to compromise), and allowed internal opposition in Israel to mount—Barak wanted to move to permanent status negotiations as soon as possible. In the seven years of the Oslo peace process, there had been no official Israeli-Palestinian negotiations over the issues at the very core of their conflict—the delineation of borders between Israel and a future Palestinian state, the status of Jerusalem, the future of Jewish settlements, the allocation of water resources, and the Palestinian refugees' right of return. A resolution of the conflict necessitated mutual compromises on these crucial permanent status issues. By moving immediately to permanent status negotiations, Barak sought to test Arafat's willingness to make the necessary sacrifices for a lasting peace with Israel.[36] "If Arafat was willing and able to reach a permanent status deal that included compromises in Jerusalem, on refugees and ended the conflict, well and good. If not Barak's strategy would publicly expose this situation thereby maintaining continued legitimacy for Israel to retain some territory as a bargaining chip for future negotiations."[37] Related to this strategy was Barak's awareness of the need for national unity in Israel if a violent conflict with the Palestinians broke out. If permanent status negotiations failed due to Palestinian intransigence, he would have unmasked Arafat's true face (i.e., his hostile intentions toward Israel), the recognition of which would unify Israelis in the event of conflict with the Palestinians—which was likely to come about if negotiations failed. As Barak later explained: "Even if you think you have only a 20 percent chance of achieving peace it is your duty to act . . . You have to try and take the moral high ground. To ensure that if we confront violence we will have both internal unity and moral superiority. Without these two elements, Israel is liable to slide into disaster."[38] For Barak, therefore, it was a "win-win" scenario—he would either achieve peace or ensure Israeli national unity in the case of conflict. Thus, despite the reservations of the Clinton Administration and the reluctance of the Palestinian Authority, Barak pushed hard for permanent status negotiations to get underway.[39] He eventually got his wish when President Clinton convened an Israeli-Palestinian summit meeting at Camp David in July 2000 to conclude the permanent status talks.

The Camp David Summit: The End of the Road

What exactly transpired in the wooded confines of the presidential retreat at Camp David, Maryland, between July 11, the day the summit began, and July 25, the day it acrimoniously ended, remains a subject of much conjecture and controversy to this day.[40] During the two weeks of intensive talks, with a news blackout in place, the details of the negotiations were kept secret. Nor did they become clear afterwards as there was no official transcript of the negotiations, and most of the proposals were only made orally. Thus, journalists and scholars have been left to reconstruct the negotiations at Camp David on the basis of scant, and often unreliable, information provided by members of the Israeli, Palestinian, and American delegations to the summit.

Needless to say, the accounts of what happened substantially differ as each party perceived the negotiations through different lenses and each has different interests that influence their subsequent portrayal of events. By all accounts, however, two issues were the principal causes of deadlock in the negotiations: the issue of sovereignty over the Temple Mount or Noble Sanctuary (Haram al-Sharif—the site containing the Dome of the Rock and the al-Aqsa Mosque as well as the presumed underground remains of King Solomon's and Herod's temples), and the issue of the "right of return" to Israel for Palestinian refugees from the 1948 war. These were perhaps the two most intractable and emotionally charged issues in the Israeli-Palestinian conflict, both of them bound up with the national identities of Israelis and Palestinians. Barak's refusal to allow Palestinian sovereignty over the Temple Mount/Haram al-Sharif and to accept a Palestinian "right of return" to Israel, led Arafat to reject the Israeli offer that was presented to him at Camp David.

Although it did not satisfy Palestinian demands, this offer was nonetheless unprecedented. It was undoubtedly the most ever offered by an Israeli prime minister to the Palestinians. The concessions Barak made at Camp David were far reaching, involving a division of sovereignty in Jerusalem, an Israeli withdrawal from approximately 86 to 91 percent of the West Bank (depending upon how the area is defined) and full Israeli withdrawal from Gaza, an exchange of territory in order to allow Israel to annex the large settlement blocs along the Green Line containing 80 percent of the settlers, and a limited return of Palestinians refugees into Israel.[41] The most controversial of these concessions from an Israeli standpoint was Barak's apparent willingness to "divide" Jerusalem into two cities: a Jewish city to be known as Jerusalem which would remain Israel's capital; and an Arab city to be known as Al-Quds (the Arabic name for Jerusalem), which would serve as the capital of the new Palestinian state.

This was Barak's most symbolically laden concession at the Camp David summit. It broke the long-standing Israeli taboo against partitioning Jerusalem. It effectively challenged Jerusalem's symbolic status for Israeli national identity. "No place in the Land of Israel has greater ethnonational significance for the Jewish people than Jerusalem," one scholar has noted.[42] As the city where the biblical temples were located, the capital of the kingdom of David and Solomon and the subsequent kings of Judea, the only place in Palestine where there had been a continuous Jewish presence, and where

Jews prayed daily to return for millennia, Jerusalem was much more than just Israel's capital city. As Teddy Kollek, the former mayor of Jerusalem, put it: "For three thousand years, Jerusalem has been the center of Jewish hope and longing. No other city has played such a dominant role in the history, culture, religion, and consciousness of a people as has Jerusalem in the life of Jewry and Judaism. Throughout centuries of exile, Jerusalem remained alive in the hearts of Jews everywhere as the focal point of Jewish history, the symbol of ancient glory, spiritual fulfillment and modern renewal. This heart and soul of the Jewish people engenders the thought that if you want one simple word to symbolize all of Jewish history, that word would be 'Jerusalem.' "[43]

Jerusalem, therefore, has a mythic importance for Jewish identity and, by extension, for Israeli national identity, in so far as it is defined by Jewishness. For Israel as a Jewish state, moreover, Jerusalem is its most potent symbol. The city is nothing less than the physical embodiment of the State of Israel's Jewishness, the spatial representation of the Jewish state. Hence, although Israelis accepted the de facto division of the city between 1949–1967 following Israel's War of Independence, Israeli leaders could not renounce Israel's claim to the whole city. In a speech delivered to the Knesset on December 4, 1949, Ben-Gurion made this clear: "And we declare that Israel will not give up Jerusalem voluntarily, just as it did not give up for millennia its religion, its national uniqueness and its hope to return to Jerusalem and Zion . . . . A nation that has maintained loyally for two thousand and five hundred years the oath that the first exiles took on the rivers of Babylon— not to forget thee Jerusalem—this nation will never accept the separation of Jerusalem."[44] Israel's conquest of East Jerusalem from Jordan in the 1967 war, therefore, was one of the state's greatest accomplishments in the minds of many Israeli Jews (as well as Jews around the world). After the war, the idea that Israel would one day agree to a "re-division" of the city was simply inconceivable for them. Israeli Jews could not countenance such an idea. Thus, since 1967 Israeli governments have constantly repeated the official formulation that "Jerusalem is the eternal, undivided capital of the State of Israel and the Jewish people." The unity of Jerusalem became a sacrosanct principle of Israeli politics, one that was incessantly intoned by Israeli politicians.

Barak contravened this principle at Camp David by offering to give the Palestinians sovereignty over parts of East Jerusalem (over the outlying Arab-populated neighborhoods,[45] but not over the more central Arab neighborhoods of East Jerusalem, for which Barak offered the Palestinians functional, but not full, sovereignty). Substantively, Barak's offer merely amounted to an explicit (and long overdue) recognition of the existing state of affairs—namely, that Jerusalem was already a segregated and divided city.[46] Israel's rule over East Jerusalem since 1967 had not fundamentally altered Jerusalem's physical and demographic facts (despite Israeli policies aimed at increasing the Jewish presence in East Jerusalem while reducing the Palestinian presence[47]). Parts of the city remained overwhelmingly Palestinian (especially those areas which were included within Jerusalem after Israel expanded the city's municipal boundaries to include not only the part of Jerusalem that had been under Jordanian rule, but also additional territory from villages in the West Bank), and Israeli Jews seldom entered these areas. Moreover, granting the Palestinians sovereignty over Arab populated areas in the city's periphery, areas that were not part of Jerusalem prior to 1967, would still have allowed Israel to maintain complete sovereignty over "Jewish" Jerusalem (i.e., areas with a predominantly Jewish population).

There was a clear demographic logic behind Barak's offer to give the Palestinians sovereignty over Palestinian populated areas in East Jerusalem. As one member of Israel's negotiating team at Camp David, Elkayim Rubinstein, expressed in discussions with other members of the Israeli delegation: "We have to try to include as few Arabs as possible under our control, both in Jerusalem and in the settlement blocks. We can whole-heartedly accept a formula that would free us of the Arab villages around Jerusalem . . . we should free ourselves of control of 130,000 Arabs [in Jerusalem]."[48] Similarly, former IDF Chief of Staff Amnon Lipkin-Shahak, another Israeli negotiator at Camp David, stated that: "It's in Israel's interest to place as many Palestinian citizens as possible under Arafat's responsibility."[49] Minimizing the number of Palestinians within Israel in order to ensure a long-term Jewish majority in the country—widely accepted as an essential condition for the continued existence of a Jewish state (or at least one that was democratic)—was a major motivation behind Barak's willingness to divide Jerusalem.

But however logical Barak's proposal to divide Jerusalem, it was still a huge departure from more than three decades of Israeli insistence on maintaining the unity of Jerusalem. A unified Jerusalem under Israeli sovereignty had long been an article of faith for most Israeli Jews, not subject to rational considerations. To give up any part of it would be an act of national treachery. In the domestic Israeli context, therefore, the historic significance of Barak's proposal to divide Jerusalem does not lie in its details. More important than the substance of the proposal, was the fact that a proposal had been made. This was the first time any Israeli prime minister had so much as suggested dividing Israel's capital since 1967. It was, in domestic Israeli terms, nothing short of revolutionary. How did this come about? Given the sanctity of the claim to a unified Jerusalem in Israeli public discourse since 1967, this clearly needs some explanation.

Barak's willingness at Camp David to relinquish Israeli sovereignty over some of Jerusalem was not merely the whim of an individual who had completely lost touch with the wishes of Israeli-Jewish society, as some of his critics would later contend. Rather, it was indicative of the profound sociocultural changes that had taken place in Israel over the previous decade. Cumulatively, these changes allowed ideas that were once unthinkable to become conceivable. Israeli national identity and its cultural expression (in music, cinema, and literature, for example) became the subject of open debate and contestation in the 1990s, as discussed in the previous chapter. The rise of identity politics within Israel led to the increasingly vigorous expression of domestic cultural differences. Israeli society was no longer seen as monolithic and homogeneous, but instead as pluralistic and rife with cultural divisions (between religious and secular, Ashkenazim and Mizrahim, Jews and Arabs, Zionists and post-Zionists).

One important element in the sociocultural transformation that took place in Israel in the 1990s was the gradual dissipation of Israeli society's dominant collective narratives, memories, and beliefs. The widely discussed and highly controversial work of Israel's so-called New Historians, which was discussed in the previous chapter, was instrumental in this regard. The demythologizing of Israeli history was part of what Robert Wistrich and David Ohana aptly described as the "new iconoclasm" in Israeli society in the 1990s.[50] Also characteristic of this was the erosion of numerous taboos in Israeli public discourse. It became possible, for instance, to publicly criticize the political manipulation of the memory of the Holocaust and even go as far as to suggest that the Holocaust should be de-emphasized in Israeli collective memory.[51] Criticizing Zionism and suggesting the end of Zionism also became increasingly common and no longer illegitimate. Emigration from Israel was not viewed in the same derogatory, moralistic, and judgmental manner as it had been in the past. Even repealing the Law of Return was openly being advocated by some. Thus, in the 1990s, attitudes and opinions that were once shocking and unspeakable began to openly circulate in the public realm, and steadily became more acceptable, if still often controversial. Public discourse in Israel gradually freed itself from the shackles of Zionist ideology, allowing people to question things that had hitherto been dogma.

Barak's offer at Camp David to divide Jerusalem between Israelis and Palestinians should be placed within this wider Israeli sociocultural context in which the challenging, and sometimes slaughtering, of Zionism's "sacred cows" was taking place. As had happened previously to so many Israeli myths, the myth of the unity of Jerusalem was debunked at Camp David as the reality of a city divided between Israelis and Palestinians, and claimed by both sides, was finally officially acknowledged by an Israeli leader. What ultimately made such an acknowledgement possible was the more open, less ideological public climate that emerged in Israel through the 1990s. In this climate, transgressions from Zionist ideology and the catechisms of Israeli politics became increasingly commonplace, much to the consternation of those who feared the consequences of this new cultural zeitgeist.[52] If it seemed to many by the late 1990s that nothing was sacred anymore in Israel, Barak's proposal to divide Jerusalem was further proof of this. Even Jerusalem was no longer sacred; it was just a piece of valuable real estate to be bargained over. Thus, Jerusalem became one more national symbol whose importance was downgraded and demystified. The ideological axiom—"Jerusalem is the eternal, undivided capital of the State of Israel and the Jewish people"—had apparently lost its hegemonic, taken-for-granted nature along with other once-popular axioms (such as "a people who dwells alone," "the few against the many," and "it is good to die for the homeland"). The unity of Jerusalem ceased to be beyond question. Instead, it became just a slogan, one widely subscribed to, but nonetheless contestable. Hence, the re-partition of Jerusalem, however controversial, became conceivable for growing numbers of Israelis.[53]

Barak's ability to challenge the axioms of Israeli politics, however, only went so far. When it came to the status of the Temple Mount/Haram al-Sharif, Barak firmly refused to accede to the Palestinian demand for sovereignty over the area. The Temple Mount, like Jerusalem at large, had a huge symbolic significance for Israeli Jews, as it was the site on which the first and second Temples had once stood, marking the most sacred spot for the Jewish religion. Dividing Jerusalem would have been difficult enough for Barak to sell to the Israeli-Jewish public; giving the Palestinians sovereignty over the Temple Mount as well would have made his task almost impossible. In effect, by refusing Palestinian sovereignty over the area, Barak was striking a compromise—the Palestinians could have some of Jerusalem, but not the Temple Mount. Thus, the issue of the Temple Mount became the point at which Barak and the Israeli negotiators under him had to draw a line. For the sake of Israeli national identity and the State of Israel's Jewish identity, sovereignty over the Temple Mount had to remain in Israel's hands (even if the Palestinians exercised, as they had long done, de facto control over the site). As Barak told the Israeli delegation: "I don't know a prime minister who would be willing to sign his name to the transfer of sovereignty over the First and Second Temple [the Temple Mount], which is the basis of Zionism;"[54] and in the same discussion, Amnon Lipkin-Shahak stated: "We can't give up sovereignty over the Temple Mount. It's the heart of Jewish culture, whether we control it or not."[55] In a similar vein, Shlomo Ben-Ami, then Israel's public security minister and acting foreign minister, and a leading member of the Israeli delegation at Camp David was reported to have told President Clinton during the summit: "Even in the era of the global village . . . nations do not exist without an anchor of historical identity. The State of Israel represents the accumulation of Jewish memory and we cannot give up sovereignty on the Temple Mount, although we understand that for all appearances the site is Muslim."[56]

While the issue of the Temple Mount was purely symbolic for Israel (as Ben-Ami's statement clearly implies), the issue of a Palestinian "right of return" to Israel was not. For Israelis, it raised the frightening prospect of millions of Palestinians flooding into Israel with a guaranteed admission ticket.[57] This would pose a dire threat to the preservation of Israel's status as a Jewish state. This status was already facing a growing challenge from Palestinian Israelis and post-Zionist Israeli Jewish intellectuals. By dramatically increasing the number of Israel's non-Jewish citizens, and hence their political power, a massive influx of Palestinian refugees would make this challenge almost irresistible. By democratic means, Israel's non-Jewish citizens could simply vote the Jewish state out of existence. Given this perceived danger, the vast majority of Israeli Jews believed that accepting a Palestinian right of return to Israel would be tantamount to national suicide. This was one issue on which there was almost universal agreement among Israelis. Even amongst Israel's left wing, there was broad opposition to a Palestinian right of return. As Yossi Sarid, leader of the left-wing Meretz Party, categorically stated: "Israel can survive without sovereignty over Temple Mount, but it cannot survive with the right of return. If the Palestinians insist on it, there will be no agreement."[58] For the Zionist left,[59] accepting a Palestinian right of return was contrary to the fundamental logic of the Oslo peace process—two states for two peoples (Jewish and Palestinian). Their support for the peace process derived in part from the threat to Israel's Jewishness—demographic and moral—that the left believed Israeli occupation of the territories entailed. Withdrawing from the occupied territories was the only legitimate and practical means in their opinion of ensuring that Israel remained a Jewish and democratic state. The Oslo peace process, then, was conceived and discursively represented by the left as a means to safeguard Israel's Zionist and Jewish identity.[60] More than anything else, a Palestinian right of return represented a threat to this identity, one that had to be resisted at all costs, even at the cost of the peace process itself.

Barak's rejection of a Palestinian right of return at the Camp David summit can be seen, therefore, as a defense of Israel's Zionist and Jewish identity. This was certainly how Barak later presented it to the Israeli public and the international community as he claimed that the Palestinians' insistence upon a right of return to Israel was a "demographic-political tool for subverting the Jewish state."[61] In making this claim—which was widely accepted by Israelis—Barak cast himself as the defender of the Jewish state at Camp David. Such a self-serving depiction, however, distorted the substance of the negotiations with the Palestinians at Camp David over the right of return. In actuality, the Palestinians made an important distinction at Camp David between the right of return, which they would not renounce, and the implementation of this right, which they accepted would have to take into consideration Israel's demographic concerns.[62] As Arafat later put it: "We understand Israel's demographic concerns and understand that the right of return of Palestinian refugees, a right guaranteed under international law and United Nations Resolution 194, must be implemented in a way that takes into account such concerns."[63]

What the Palestinians demanded at Camp David, in other words, was that Israel acknowledge the theoretical right of refugees to return to Israel, in exchange for which the Palestinians would accept significant limitations on the manner in which this right could be exercised—specifically, the number of Palestinians allowed to return to Israel would be limited, and Israel would be able to decide whom to allow to return. This represented a far more moderate and pragmatic Palestinian approach to the refugee issue than their long-standing official demand for an unconditional right of return to Israel. Yet, for the Israeli delegation at Camp David, even this compromise was unacceptable. This was not because they objected to the return to Israel of any Palestinian refugees. They were, in fact, willing to allow a certain number to return (exact numbers were not discussed at Camp David), but under the criteria of family reunification, not a right of return. The disagreement over the issue of Palestinian refugees at the Camp David summit was "about conceptualization rather than outcomes."[64] Both Israeli and Palestinians negotiators accepted that, as an outcome, only a limited number of Palestinian refugees would return to Israel. But whether this return was conceptualized as a Palestinian right or an Israeli humanitarian policy (i.e., family reunification) was the crux of the disagreement.

Although this disagreement may at first appear semantic and trivial, it actually had important ramifications. For the Palestinians, the right of return to Israel was a fundamental tenet of Palestinian nationalism. It was an integral component of their national narrative of dispossession and exile. Just as Jews had always declared their longing to return to Zion during their millennia of exile, Palestinians never abandoned their dream of returning to their lost homes in pre-1967 Israel. In both cases, such desires functioned as constitutive elements of Jewish and Palestinian identity. That is, for both, the desire for an eventual return to the homeland helped sustain a common sense of identity for people scattered in many different parts of the world. For the sake of Palestinian national identity, then, the right of return was a non-negotiable demand. Israel's acceptance in theory of a Palestinian right of return, moreover, was regarded by Palestinians as an essential element in any possible reconciliation between the two peoples. Having caused so much Palestinian suffering and long denied it, an official acknowledgment of this was, for many Palestinians, the very least that Israel could do. Although they may never receive complete justice, an accepted right of return to Israel would provide some compensation, if only symbolically.

From Israel's point of view, accepting a Palestinian right of return carried with it the danger that Israel would not be able to limit the number of returning refugees, whatever assurances the Palestinians, Americans, and international community provided. The fear was that once Israel had opened the floodgates, a trickle of returning Palestinians refugees could easily become an unstoppable wave. But even putting aside this fear, Israel would not accept a Palestinian right of return that entailed an Israeli acknowledgement of responsibility for the creation of the Palestinian refugee problem in 1948. Israel was adamant in its refusal to accept legal or moral responsibility for creating the refugee problem. This was one of the four "red lines" that Barak stipulated to his cabinet he would not cross during negotiations with the Palestinians prior to his departure for the Camp David summit. During the negotiations over the refugee issue at Camp David, Israel declared that it was ready to accept some Palestinian refugees and was prepared to contribute to an international fund that would compensate refugees, but it would not accept responsibility for their displacement in the first place. Elkayim Rubinstein, one of the Israeli negotiators assigned to tackle the refugee issue at Camp David, clearly expressed this position during the negotiations, telling Clinton and the Palestinian negotiator, Nabil Shaath: "On the historical level, we can't agree to be held responsible for the refugee problem. What happened in 1948 is the subject of controversy, and the peace process shouldn't be the arena in which historical truth is pronounced. We want to do our part toward a solution that will put an end to the refugees' suffering, but we're not going to get there by imposing the right of return."[65]

There were two reasons behind Israel's refusal to accept responsibility for the creation of the Palestinian refugee problem. The first was practical; namely that by doing so, Israel could find itself the subject of endless lawsuits seeking reparations from Palestinian refugees and their descendants. The second was emotional; Israelis did not feel that Israel deserved the blame for creating the refugee problem.[66] This is not to say that Israelis believed their country was blameless in the events of 1948–1949. Certainly some continued to cling to this belief, despite all the historical evidence of Israeli expulsions and atrocities against Palestinians that had come to light over the years. But the once dominant belief that the Palestinians had voluntarily left the country (either out of fright or because they were led by their leaders to believe that they would soon return with the triumphant Arab armies) had, like so many other Zionist myths, been demolished over the preceding decade. The fierce public debate over the history of the 1948–1949 war that took place in Israel in the 1990s resulted in greater public awareness that Israel had indeed carried out acts of expulsion against Palestinian civilians (although the extent of such acts and their centralized coordination by Israeli decision-makers remained in dispute). After a great deal of soul-searching, many Israelis had reluctantly come to accept a less glamorous and more nuanced view of their War of Independence. It was for them a just war, to be sure; but like all wars, it involved military abuses against civilians, among them innocent Palestinians who lost their homes, their land, and their livelihoods at the hands of Israeli forces. Yet ultimately, however tragic, the Palestinian refugee problem was not Israel's fault. The Israeli writer, Yossi Melman, summarizes the view of Israelis on this issue: "It took many years until Israeli historiography and public opinion were mature enough to admit that many Palestinians were expelled from their homes by Israeli troops and only a minority left of their own will. Yet most Israelis refuse to accept the Palestinian narrative that it is they who bear responsibility for the Palestinian refugee problem. Israelis put the blame on the Arab leaders who rejected an internationally sanctioned resolution, launched an aggressive war in 1948 and kept the refugees in shantytowns and camps with no attempt to help them resettle."[67]

It was not just historical truth that was at stake for Israelis in their refusal to accept the blame for the Palestinian refugee problem. It was also their own national identity and, specifically, their self-image as "righteous victims" in the Arab-Israeli conflict.[68] From the very beginning of the conflict, Israeli Jews perceived themselves as victims of unjust aggression by the Arabs. It was not until the war in Lebanon and especially the Intifada in the 1980s that Israelis began to seriously question this popular perception. But even after the Lebanon War and Intifada had demonstrated to many Israelis that Israel was not always innocent and moral, thereby challenging Israeli national identity, they did not simply discard their self-image as victims. Instead, they held Israel's occupation of the West Bank and Gaza accountable for their moral decline. Before the occupation Israelis were victims, these Israelis believed, but the occupation turned them into victimizers as well.

This belief enabled them to modify, but still maintain the victim component of Israeli national identity. But if Israel accepted responsibility for the creation of the Palestinian refugee problem, then even this belief was untenable. If Israel was to blame for the suffering of Palestinian refugees, then Israelis were victimizers even at the outset of statehood. If Israelis admitted that Israel was "born in sin," they could no longer nostalgically look back to a time of presumed innocence. They were never simply victims. The Palestinian demand that Israel formally acknowledge its moral responsibility for the creation of the Palestinian refugee problem was, therefore, a direct assault upon the sense of victimhood that is part of Israeli national identity. As such, it went beyond the limits of what Israelis were prepared to acknowledge. It was one thing to express sorrow and regret for the suffering of Palestinian refugees,[69] it was quite another to accept responsibility for this suffering. Although Israeli public discourse concerning the causes of the Palestinian refugee problem had dramatically changed over the course of the 1990s, for the first time openly discussing Israel's culpability and challenging long-held beliefs about Israeli innocence, it would still not countenance the idea that Israel was ultimately to blame. Barak's refusal to do so at the Camp David summit was, therefore, in accordance with Israeli popular sentiment.

In this respect, Israel's position on the refugee issue at Camp David mirrored its position on the issue of Jerusalem and the Temple Mount/Haram al-Sharif. In both cases, Barak and the Israeli negotiators under him, presented positions that went to the limits of what they believed the Israeli public was prepared to accept. What these positions reveal is that as a result of sweeping cultural changes in Israel, proposals that would once have been considered heretical—dividing sovereignty in Jerusalem, allowing some Palestinian refugees to return to Israel—became tolerable, if still, controversial. But what these positions also show is that despite these cultural changes, certain ideas were still beyond the pale—notably, Palestinian sovereignty over the Temple Mount/Haram al-Sharif, and accepting Israel's moral responsibility for the creation of the Palestinian refugee problem. Israeli national identity would not tolerate these things, as the Israeli negotiating team at Camp David was well aware. Even after undergoing a prolonged crisis, therefore, Israeli national identity still effectively placed limits on what Barak could agree to in the negotiations with the Palestinians at Camp David.

The Defeat of Hope

The Camp David summit ended with bitter recriminations from both sides. Both blamed the other for the summit's failure and sought to garner domestic and international support for their positions. In the propaganda campaign it conducted through the media,[70] Israel claimed that Barak had presented the Palestinians with a "generous" offer, and that the Palestinians' rejection of this offer and their failure to make a counter-offer demonstrated their unwillingness to make peace with Israel.[71] It was Arafat's stubborn refusal to compromise, Israel asserted, that prevented a deal from being reached. In this narrative of the Camp David negotiations, put forward by Israel and its supporters, Barak is depicted as the bold, forward-looking peacemaker willing to make a historic compromise with the Palestinians;[72] whereas Arafat is a timid, backward-looking peace-breaker, unable to relinquish the impossible national dreams of the Palestinians and end a conflict to which he had become so comfortably accustomed.[73] This version of the events at Camp David was also supported by some American officials who publicly expressed their exasperation with Arafat.[74] Even President Clinton, who had promised Arafat before the summit that he would not be held accountable if it failed, appeared to place the blame for the summit's failure on the Palestinian leader in an interview on Israeli television a few days after the summit ended.[75] Whether fairly or not, Arafat's intransigence was identified as the chief obstacle to Israeli-Palestinian peace.

This quickly became the conventional wisdom in Israel. The vast majority of Israelis believed that the Palestinians were responsible for the failure of the Camp David summit.[76] Although a comprehensive final peace agreement between Israel and the Palestinians had not been reached, Israelis were at least able to console themselves with the thought that Israel was not to blame, and that it had gone further than ever before in its concessions to the Palestinians and that these concessions were more than reasonable (for many Israelis, Barak had gone too far in his concessions at Camp David[77]). Israel, in short, was in the right. This did not, of course, encourage Israeli hopes for the possibility of peace with the Palestinians. Many Israelis concluded that if the Palestinians were not even willing to accept Barak's "generous" offer at Camp David, then they were not really interested in peace with Israel after all. And, even if they were, the price they were demanding was too high and one that Israel could never accept. Despite Barak's insistence that: "There is still hope for peace. Peace is not dead,"[78] a growing number of Israelis lost hope in the peace process. This loss of hope is clear from a comparison of Israeli public opinion surveys carried out before and after the Camp David summit. In the month before the summit, 46 percent of Israelis believed that the Oslo peace process would bring about peace between Israel and the Palestinians.[79] In the month after Camp David, this number had dropped to 37 percent.[80] In another survey taken in August 2000, 50 percent of Israelis stated that they had grown more pessimistic since Camp David concerning the chances of peace with the Palestinians.[81]

Thus, the failure of the Camp David summit and the popular Israeli belief that the Palestinians were to blame for this failure negatively affected Israelis attitudes toward the peace process with the Palestinians. But this did not destroy the peace process.[82] What did was the eruption of large-scale Palestinian violence on September 30, 2000. The violence, which quickly spread throughout the West Bank and Gaza, came in response to two events. The first was a visit to the Temple Mount/Haram al-Sharif by Ariel Sharon on September 28. This visit, aimed at displaying Israel's control over the site and its attachment to it, generated angry Palestinian protests. The second came the next day, when rioting broke after Friday prayers as thousands of Muslim worshipers were leaving the Haram al-Sharif. As the Israeli police entered the compound, rocks were thrown and the police responded by firing rubber-coated bullets and live ammunition. At least four Palestinians were killed and more than one hundred wounded.

These two events set in motion the second Palestinian Intifada, termed by Palestinians the "al-Aqsa Intifada." But Sharon's provocative visit to the Temple Mount/Haram al-Sharif and the subsequent killing of Palestinian protesters by the Israeli police were only the proximate causes of the second Intifada. Its origin lay in Palestinian disappointment with the Oslo peace process which had been building up for many years, creating an atmosphere of widespread "frustration and hopelessness" in the West Bank and Gaza.[83] In the eyes of many Palestinians, the peace process had simply become a means by which Israel was prolonging "the Occupation" and seizing more Palestinian land.[84] Israel, it seemed to them, had no intention of withdrawing from the West Bank and Gaza and allowing the Palestinians to establish a viable state there. Nor was the peace process bringing the Palestinians the economic benefits they were promised. Living standards had actually declined and unemployment increased during the years of the peace process.[85] To make matters worse, the governing Palestinian Authority (PA) was widely regarded as corrupt and incompetent.[86] These grievances (and many more) were the underlying motivation for the second Palestinian Intifada.[87]

But the second Palestinian Intifada, unlike the first, was not just a popular uprising. It was also an armed campaign against Israel partially directed and funded by the PA, whose security services took an active part in the violent clashes with Israeli troops. Instead of trying to subdue the violence, leaders of the PA, Arafat foremost amongst them, encouraged it and allowed it to escalate. It was the direct involvement of the PA in the Intifada that was most disturbing for Israelis. Their supposed partner for peace had, it appeared, opted instead for violent confrontation. Most Israelis believed, in line with the view of their government, that the second Palestinian Intifada was planned, prepared, and orchestrated by the PA and by Arafat personally. It was intended, in their opinion, to accomplish by force what the Palestinians could not achieve at the negotiating table. In the words of Israel's Foreign Ministry: "The wave of terrorism that began in September 2000 is the direct result of a strategic Palestinian decision to use violence—rather than negotiation—as the primary means to advance their agenda."[88]

This view of the second Intifada led to the inescapable conclusion that the Oslo peace process was dead. By resorting to violence, the Palestinians had killed it. After all, the peace process was fundamentally based upon a mutual agreement to renounce violence and work toward a negotiated settlement of the Israeli-Palestinian conflict. There could be no peace process if one side continued to employ violence in pursuit of its goals. Israel had, in the phrase Barak used and that became a mantra for Israeli officials, "no partner for peace."[89] The overwhelming acceptance of this claim by Israelis eroded whatever hope they had left for the peace process. If the failure of the Camp David summit dented Israeli hopes for peace with the Palestinians, the outbreak of the second Intifada destroyed them altogether.[90]

Israeli optimism in the Oslo peace process was one casualty of the second Intifada. Another casualty, equally if not more disconcerting for Israelis, was the relationship between Israelis Jews and Palestinian Israelis. This already uneasy relationship was severely damaged by the massive protests staged by Palestinian Israelis beginning on October 1 and continuing intermittently for more than a week, and the Israeli police's harsh response to them. These protests, which took place in Palestinian Israeli villages and several towns (including Jaffa, Acre, Nazareth, and Umm al-Fahm), turned violent as some demonstrators (mostly youths) hurled stones and firebombs at the police, set fire to buildings such as post offices, banks, and gas stations, and blocked main highways and junctions around the country. In their effort to quell the violence, the police fired tear gas, rubber-coated bullets, and live ammunition at the demonstrators, killing thirteen and wounding hundreds. The violence was not restricted to clashes between the police and Palestinian Israeli demonstrators. In at least two incidents, Jewish civilians were pulled out of their cars and beaten by Palestinian Israeli mobs. Jewish mobs retaliated by burning mosques and attacking Palestinian Israelis—in the worst mob violence, Jews from Upper Nazareth attacked their Palestinian Israeli neighbors in Nazareth, shooting and killing two. There were even fears that Palestinian Israelis were about to "storm" neighboring Jewish kibbutzim and attempt to "conquer" them and carry out "pogroms" against their residents.[91] Never before in the state's history had there been such inter-communal violence,[92] and for a moment the country seemed to tilter on the edge of civil war between Israeli Jews and Palestinian Israelis.

This was a turning point in the relations between Jewish and Palestinian citizens in Israel. The former felt betrayed by Palestinian Israelis who, by showing their support for the Intifada, had demonstrated to Israeli Jews that their allegiance lay not with their state and their fellow citizens but with their national kin in the West Bank and Gaza. The "Israeli Arab" identity that Israeli Jews had always ascribed to Palestinian Israelis was shown to be a fiction. They were not simply "Arabs," but Palestinians; and they certainly did not regard themselves as "Israeli." This awareness of the national affiliation of Palestinian Israelis heightened concern over their loyalty to the State of Israel. Although this loyalty had always been suspect in the minds of many Israeli Jews, the demonstrations and riots by Palestinian Israelis exacerbated this suspicion. In a public opinion survey of Israeli Jews carried out in their aftermath, 74 percent said that Palestinian Israeli behavior during the first week of the second Intifada amounted to treason.[93] Palestinian Israelis were widely perceived as a security threat, and there was a growing worry that they constituted a potential "fifth column" in Israel's conflict with the Palestinians. Given this worry, some Israeli Jews openly wondered whether Israel could afford to adhere to democratic practices in its treatment of Palestinian Israelis. "Suddenly we are asking ourselves," wrote one Israeli commentator, "Can Israeli democracy survive when 20% of its citizens—who produce nearly one out of every three new babies—identify with our enemies?"[94]

As Israeli Jews fretted anxiously over the loyalty of the minority in their midst, Palestinian Israelis felt ever more alienated from their state and their fellow citizens. This alienation was by no means new, but it deepened considerably in the wake of the events of October 2000 and the Israeli-Jewish public's response to them.[95] The fact that the police had fired live ammunition at Palestinian Israeli protesters, killing twelve of them (the thirteenth fatality was a Palestinian from Gaza), cruelly demonstrated to Palestinian Israelis their second-class status in Israeli society. In the words of Ahmed Tibi, a Palestinian Israeli Knesset member: "We were regarded not as demonstrators but as enemies and treated as such. Before seeing us as citizens, they saw us as Arabs. Jewish citizens demonstrate, but none of them [are] killed."[96] It was this second-class status, as much as feelings of solidarity with Palestinians in the West Bank and Gaza, which led to the demonstrations and riots by Palestinian Israelis in the first place.[97] They were a protest against years of governmental neglect and discrimination against Palestinian Israelis and against their abiding sense of social exclusion and inferiority.[98] The second Intifada just provided the impetus for Palestinian Israelis to express their pent-up frustration and anger at what they saw as their position as second-class citizens in a state constitutionally designed to meet the interests of its Jewish majority.

Another casualty of the second Intifada—in addition to the Israeli public's faith in the Oslo peace process and Jewish-Palestinian relations within Israel—was Barak's premiership. Here too, the Intifada served as the catalyst, rather than simply the cause, of Barak's downfall. Even before he went to the Camp David summit, Barak's coalition was collapsing as his right-wing coalition partners (Shas, the NRP, and Yisrael B'Aliyah) deserted him in protest over the concessions he was preparing to make to the Palestinians. Meretz, another party in Barak's coalition, had left earlier over its dispute with Shas. As a result of these departures from the coalition, Barak was left with a minority government having the support of only forty-two Knesset members. Although the government managed to survive two motions of no-confidence in the Knesset before and after the Camp David summit, it was just a matter of time until Barak's government lost the Knesset's support.

This eventually happened in November 2000 when Shas refused to extend the "safety-net" agreement it had with the government since the month before. Lacking the support of the Knesset, Barak was forced to agree to general elections. Soon after, however, on December 9, 2000, he suddenly announced his resignation, a surprise move that necessitated elections for the premiership within sixty days (but not Knesset elections).[99] Barak's challenger in the election was Likud leader, Ariel Sharon.

The second Intifada and Barak's handling of it dominated the election campaign. Barak was attacked for not responding to the Intifada with the force necessary to quell it. Seizing upon the complaints of some senior IDF officers that their hands were being tied by the political establishment, the right mobilized public opinion against Barak with the slogans "Let the IDF win" and "Barak is humiliating Israel." Barak's critics on the right argued that his unilateral withdrawal of the IDF from Lebanon and his concessions to the Palestinians at the Camp David summit had caused Israel to be viewed as weak and vulnerable by its enemies, and were therefore responsible for inviting Palestinian aggression. The right's accusation that Barak was not using enough military force against the Palestinians presented him with an impossible dilemma. On the one hand, the Israeli public, acutely sensitive to the deterioration in their personal security, demanded an increasingly tough response to Palestinian acts of violence. On the other hand, the international community and the "doves" within Barak's own cabinet, urged restraint in order to prevent the total collapse of the peace process and possibly of the PA itself. Inevitably, the balance between force and restraint that Barak settled on satisfied no one. Whilst Barak was accused abroad (and by some in Israel) of excessive use of force against the Palestinians, he was assailed by the right for insufficient use of force.

Equally problematic for Barak was the issue of continuing negotiations with the PA despite the ongoing Israeli-Palestinian violence. Once again, Barak was caught between conflicting domestic and international pressures, with a majority of Israelis against negotiations whilst the violence continued, while the United States and the international community favored such negotiations. At first, Barak insisted that Israel would not negotiate "under fire," but the failure to achieve a cease-fire in the conflict together with intense international pressure, led Barak to reverse this position and allow peace talks to continue. These talks culminated in a meeting in Taba, Egypt, from January 21 to 27, 2001, during which Israeli and Palestinians negotiators discussed the "bridging proposals" for a comprehensive final status Israeli-Palestinian peace agreement put forward by President Clinton at the end of December 2000.[100] Occurring against a backdrop of continuing Israeli-Palestinian violence and with only days to go before the election in Israel, the Taba talks were a last-ditch, desperate attempt to save the peace process (and, some critics alleged, boost Barak's flagging electoral prospects). Although, once again, no agreement was reached, the Israeli and Palestinian delegations projected an optimistic message, issuing a joint statement at the end of the talks stating: "The sides declare that they have never been closer to reaching an agreement and it is thus our shared belief that the remaining gaps could be bridged with the resumption of negotiations following the Israeli elections."[101]

This optimistic message, however, made little impression upon the Israeli public. They had already given up hope for Israeli-Palestinian peace, and were now more concerned with ensuring their immediate security.[102] When they went to the polls on February 6, 2001, an overwhelming majority of them voted for the candidate they believed was most likely to bring them this security—Likud leader Ariel Sharon. Sharon received 62.4 percent of the vote to Barak's 37.6 percent. This margin of victory—almost 25 points—was the largest in any Israeli election. But it would be a mistake to interpret this as representing a massive public shift to the right in Israel. It was the disintegration of the left, rather than the strengthening of the right, that produced Sharon's huge winning margin over Barak in the February 2001 election. For much of the left in Israel, the second Intifada came as a rude awakening. Until then, they had confidently assumed that the Oslo peace process, despite all its ups and downs, was irreversible and that Israeli-Palestinian peace was within reach. This confidence was shattered as a result of the second Intifada, leaving the left in a state of shock, confusion, and disarray.[103] By the time of the February election, the left had yet to recover. Consequently, not only did much of the left not mobilize public opinion in support of Barak prior to the election, but also many did not bother to vote at all or they cast a blank ballot on the Election Day itself.[104]

The left were not the only ones whose disappointment kept them away from the polls. The vast majority of Palestinian Israelis also did not vote (only 23 percent of Arab Israelis voted—mostly Druze—down from over 70 percent in 1999[105]), heeding the call from their political leaders to boycott the election. The mass boycott of the election by Palestinian Israelis was a protest against Barak's disregard of Palestinian Israeli needs and concerns during his term in office (despite having received 96 percent of the Palestinian Israeli vote in the 1999 election), and his insensitive response to the killing of Palestinian Israelis by the police the previous October. In addition to being a protest, it was also a display of political independence—they were no longer going to automatically support whatever Labor candidate was on the ballot for prime minister. Thus, with many left-wing Israelis staying home in frustration and despair and most Palestinian Israelis boycotting the election, the turnout in the February election was only 62 percent—the lowest voter turnout in Israel's history (on average, voter turnout in previous

Israeli elections was a high 85 percent). This meant that despite winning a large number of the votes cast, Sharon actually only received 36.7 percent of the eligible vote. Nevertheless, for a man who was forced to resign as defense minister (for his role in the Sabra and Shatilla massacre in Beirut in 1982 during Israel's controversial war in Lebanon, for which he was chiefly identified) and who was long considered unelectable, this was a stunning political comeback.

Unity and Separation

If any hope remained for the Oslo peace process after the outbreak of the second Intifada, Sharon's election as Israel's prime minister squashed it completely. A fierce critic of the peace process from the very beginning and a chief architect of Israel's settlement project in the West Bank and Gaza, Sharon was probably the Israeli leader least likely to make peace with the Palestinians (at least, a peace that would satisfy the minimal needs of the Palestinians). Although some optimistically believed that Sharon could become Israel's Charles De Gaulle (France's former general and right-wing nationalist president who extricated it from its bloody colonial war in Algeria), this was simply wishful thinking that completely ignored Sharon's stated goals. Sharon did not disguise his opposition to the Oslo peace process and his belief that a comprehensive settlement of the Israeli-Palestinian conflict was impossible for the foreseeable future. Nor did he prevaricate over his unwillingness to carry out a substantial Israeli withdrawal from the occupied territories. He clearly stated his preference for long-term interim agreements with the Palestinians and expressed his support for the establishment of a Palestinian state in the areas already under Palestinian control—some 42 percent of the West Bank—but he opposed transferring more territory in the West Bank to the Palestinians. He would certainly never agree to any division of Jerusalem or accept a theoretical Palestinian right of return to Israel. There was, therefore, no question that even if peace negotiations with the Palestinians were to resume—which Sharon ruled out as long as Palestinian violence against Israel continued—Sharon was going to offer the Palestinians much less than his predecessor, Barak. And, if the Palestinians had already rejected Barak's "generous" offer at Camp David, they were hardly likely to accept Sharon's much more meager proposal. The prospects for Israeli-Palestinian peace during Sharon's premiership were dim indeed.

For much of the Israeli public, however, this did not seem to matter. Their hopes for peace had already evaporated, their faith in the Palestinian leadership (especially Arafat) as a negotiating partner shattered. Their belief that they lacked a Palestinian partner for peace gave the old popular Israeli slogan "there's no one to talk to" new currency. This had the effect of silencing the public discussion over the concessions Israel should make to achieve peace (as it did in the decade after the 1967 war when it first became conventional wisdom). What was the point of agonizing over the details of peace plans, when the Palestinians were not interested in peace? Thus, Israelis no longer felt the need to continue to angrily debate where the final borders of their state should lie or what the future of Jewish settlements in the West Bank and Gaza should be. The resolution of these once urgent issues was indefinitely postponed as Israelis focused upon their immediate security needs. Sharon might not be able to bring them peace, but Israelis believed he could give them greater security (primarily by implementing a policy of severe military retaliation for Palestinian attacks).

Instead of peace with the Palestinians, what really mattered to Israelis after the outbreak of the second Intifada was peace between themselves (more specifically, between Israeli Jews). National unity became their top priority. To be sure, as I have described in previous chapters, the desire for national unity was not a new phenomenon in Israel.[106] Israeli Jews had long expressed concern over the growing divisions within their midst. Ever since the controversial war in Lebanon, the growing political polarization in the country was a source of public anxiety. This anxiety intensified following the assassination of Prime Minister Rabin, an act that more than any other underscored in the public mind the need for greater national unity. But Rabin's assassination only widened the schisms in Israeli society as the left and right ascribed different meanings to the assassination and argued over how it should be commemorated.[107] With the resurgence of Israeli-Palestinian violence as a result of the second Intifada, the public desire for national unity grew even stronger. Now it was seen as a matter of existential survival.[108] It was not only Israeli democracy that was perceived to be at stake (as many Israelis believed in the wake of Rabin's assassination), but the existence of the state itself. Without national unity, Israelis feared that they would not be able to defend their state against a Palestinian enemy who appeared to be bent upon its destruction. Public dissent was seen by many Israelis as a luxury that Israel could ill afford. What was urgently needed was public and political unity.

The National Unity government comprising Likud and Labor as the main coalition partners that Prime Minister Sharon assembled following the 2001 prime ministerial election was formed in large part in response to this ardent desire for national unity. Sharon himself explicitly recognized this in his first speech after being elected prime minister when he stressed the need for national unity, declaring, "the time has come to reach agreement among us. The public wants unity." He then went on to promise "a new path of peace and unity at home."[109] Similarly, Sharon began his speech to the Knesset presenting his National Unity government in March 2001, saying: "The difficult security situation, and the challenges in the international arena, the deep rupture between the people, baseless hatred—all these call for national unity. Not just a verbal unity. Not just the joining of different political forces and beliefs. We have an urgent need for real unity, unity of the hearts. National reconciliation."[110]

Sharon made the need for national unity a central theme of his premiership. In the context of escalating Israeli-Palestinian violence, he explicitly linked national unity with the physical security of Israelis, stating on one occasion: "Every fissure in our unity is a breach that invites a terrorist, a murderer, a bomber . . . . Therefore the decree of the hour is to stand united and consolidated, and together—only together—to protect our lives . . . . We will stand together because we wish to survive."[111] Nor did the breakup of the National Unity government and its replacement by a Likud-led coalition government following the January 2003 Knesset elections lead Sharon to curtail his appeals for national unity. Speaking to his supporters on the night of his election victory, Sharon stated that, "Israel must not be left [to] split apart internally, eaten up by blind hatred—not at a time of war, not at a time of crisis, not now. Israel needs unity."[112]

In a climate of fear and insecurity produced by Palestinian terrorist attacks, Israeli Jews rallied together as they had done in the past.[113] In this sense, the second Intifada turned the clock back, not only on relations between Israelis and Palestinians, but also on the relations between Israeli Jews. As the sense of siege returned, so too did the sense of togetherness promoted by it. Once again, Israelis felt themselves to be a nation at war, and they united against their common enemy. The Oslo peace process had deprived Israeli Jews of this common enemy; and without the Palestinians as their enemy, they made enemies of each other—secular against religious, left against right, Ashkenazim against Mizrahim, natives against newcomers, et cetera. With the collapse of the peace process and the renewal of Israeli-Palestinian violence, the Palestinians again became the enemy; enabling Israelis Jews to set aside their differences and animosities and focus instead on what they considered to be a fight for their survival.[114]

The perennial Palestinian "Other," therefore, provided Israeli Jews with the unity that they had been lacking for so long. The renewed sense of national unity among Israeli Jews was welcomed by many. In the words of the Israeli journalist, David Landau: "What has been accomplished [by the second Intifada], in effect, is the renewal of the alliance that binds together all (Jewish) sectors of Israeli society . . . . This alliance seemed to be getting weaker and weaker over the years, as theories of post-Zionism and post-Judaism gained headway among the Israeli intelligentsia. The moment of truth, when an Israeli leader finally laid it all out on the table and the Palestinian leader kicked the table over, became a rare moment of Israeli and Jewish unity."[115] Similarly, Meretz Knesset member Amnon Rubinstein took heart from the fact that more Israelis had returned to Israel during the period of the second Intifada than had left the country. For him, this was evidence of the continued resilience and strength of Israeli society. As he put it: "Israeli society is divided on many issues, but is solid in its loyalty and dedication to Israel, even, and especially, in times of trouble."[116] And Israel's president, Moshe Katsav, noted that: "Recent events [have] helped reduce the divisions which exist in Israeli society."[117]

The overwhelming public support for Prime Minister Sharon's policies toward the Palestinians (as consistently reflected in the findings of the Peace Index survey conducted by the Tami Steinmetz Center for Peace Research),[118] revealed the emergence of a new national consensus in Israel. According to Ephraim Yuchtman-Ya'ar, the head of the Tami Steinmetz Center: "This consensus is reflected in widespread mistrust of the Palestinians' commitment to make peace with Israel, and in the common conviction that so long as Palestinian terror continues, Israel must resort to arms in order to protect the lives of its citizens."[119] Indicative of this consensus are the results of the Peace Index survey from March 2001—72 percent of Israeli Jews backed Sharon's refusal to renew the peace talks "under fire" and the same number thought that the Palestinian Authority was not interested in a peace treaty with Israel. A similar percentage also believed that the Palestinians did not accept Israel's existence and that they would destroy Israel if they had the capability to do so.[120]

Convinced of the futility of further negotiations with the Palestinians—at least with its current leadership—and embittered by a seemingly endless series of gruesome suicide bombings targeting innocent civilians, much of the Israeli public continued to back the policies of Sharon, despite their evident failure to bring Israelis the security he promised. In 2001, for instance, 89 percent of Israeli Jews supported the Sharon government's policy of "targeted assassinations" of Palestinian militants involved in terrorism against Israel; the following year the number was 90 percent; and in 2003 it had risen to 92 percent.[121] Three years after the outbreak of the second Intifada, in September 2003, 75 percent of Israeli Jews still supported the policy of not conducting negotiations with the Palestinians as long as Palestinian terrorist attacks continued. The broad support of Israeli Jews for the aggressive military tactics of the Sharon government in combating Palestinian terrorism was also evident in their almost unanimous belief that Israel's military reoccupation of the West Bank carried out in Operation Defensive Shield in March 2002 was justified.[122]

The centerpiece of the new national consensus in Israel was the massive public support for the construction of a security barrier between the West

Bank and Israel.[123] This was supported by those on both the left and right of the political spectrum. The idea of building a wall or fence to separate Israel from the Palestinian territories was not new. A heavily guarded electrified fence between Israel and the Gaza Strip already existed, and in the 1990s official thought had been given to creating one between Israel and the West Bank as well.[124] But it was the second Intifada that propelled the idea to the top of the political agenda. Prime Minister Barak was the first to publicly propose the construction of a security barrier in his campaign for the February 2001 election. By October 2001, a new political movement called "Fence for Life" had come into being with the aim of increasing public support for a security barrier.[125] Despite initially dismissing the idea of a security barrier as "populist,"[126] Prime Minister Sharon eventually relented in the face of mounting public pressure and in June 2002 his government decided to begin building the barrier (although the subsequent delays in its construction suggested to many that Sharon's support was at most lukewarm).[127]

The most obvious explanation for the widespread domestic popularity of building a fence or wall between Israel and the West Bank was the Israeli public's desire for security.[128] Israelis were desperate to find a way to stem the relentless wave of Palestinian suicide bombing attacks. In the first year of the second Intifada, there had been ten suicide bombings within Israel's pre-1967 borders, taking the lives of 49 Israeli civilians and wounding hundreds more.[129] Israel's repeated large-scale military incursions into the West Bank and its temporary reoccupations of Palestinian towns and cities from which the suicide bombers had been dispatched, together with its "targeted" killings of Palestinian militants and reprisals against the families of suicide bombers (demolishing their homes and arresting family members) reduced the number of suicide bombings within Israel, but did not stop them. Moreover, these tough military measures were strongly condemned by most of the international community (with the notable exception of the U.S. administration, except on some rare occasions when tepid criticism was made). Increasingly Israel was again becoming the pariah state that it had been in the 1970s and 1980s.

These measures also frequently incurred Israeli military casualties, something that the Israeli public was less willing to accept than in the past due to the diminished cultural power of the old Zionist values of heroism and self-sacrifice. The steadily mounting death toll from Palestinian suicide attacks, growing international isolation, and a heightened public sensitivity to the loss of Israeli life—civilian and military—all led Israelis to enthusiastically embrace the idea of a security barrier between the West Bank and Israel. They fervently hoped that such a barrier would at least greatly reduce the chances of successful suicide attacks by making it much harder for suicide bombers to enter Israel (not only would there be a high concrete wall or electrified fence for them to surmount, but also ditches, razor wire, electronic motion sensors, and armed guard posts).[130]

Although a desire for greater security was the prima facie reason for the Israeli public's support for the barrier—hence its popular label as a "security barrier"—it was not the only or even the most important motivation behind the construction of the barrier. In fact, high-ranking members of the IDF (in particular, IDF Chief of Staff Moshe Ya'alon) and some prominent retired generals publicly expressed their reservations about the security value of the barrier. It would be almost impossible to hermetically seal the border between Israel and the West Bank due to the close proximity and intermingling of Israeli and Palestinian populations in many places. It would also be futile because Palestinian terrorists would simply find other ways to reach Israeli towns (by air or sea, for example). Nor would a barrier stop rocket attacks like those that hit Israeli towns near the Gaza Strip. Some claimed that it was even more dangerous to erect a barrier and withdraw behind it because it could be construed by Israel's enemies as a retreat "under fire" and a reward for terrorism. This would erode Israeli deterrence, as many believed the withdrawal from southern Lebanon had done. Such arguments against the security value of a barrier made little impression upon Israeli public opinion. Nor were Israelis deterred by its huge financial cost, the slow pace of construction, the international criticism, or the disagreements about its route. The need for a barrier became, in effect, an article of faith for many Israelis. The barrier was a potential salvation they would cling to no matter what.

What lay behind this was not only the public's longing for security, but also a longing by Israeli Jews for separation from the Palestinians. The barrier would accomplish this separation by enabling Israel to withdraw from much of the West Bank even in the absence of a peace treaty with the Palestinians. The collapse of the Oslo peace process turned a unilateral Israeli withdrawal from the West Bank and Gaza from something that was once inconceivable to Israelis into a highly attractive option that the majority steadily came to favor. It did not require a willing Palestinian partner and it dispensed with the need for interminable negotiations. All that was necessary was a political decision and the will to implement it in the face of likely domestic and international opposition. As one Israeli commentator explained the public appeal of "unilateral separation": "It has a soothing ring to it. 'Unilateral'—meaning that Israel can just do what it thinks best, without having to secure the agreement of those impossible, untrustworthy Palestinians. 'Separation'—meaning no more Palestinians."[131] After more than a decade of difficult and frustrating negotiations with the Palestinians and without the prospect of a negotiated settlement to their conflict with the Palestinians in sight, the attraction of unilateral withdrawal for Israeli Jews is not hard to understand. Quite simply, it seemed to be the only way for them to finally separate themselves from the Palestinians. "Us over here, them over there," was how Barak succinctly put it.[132] Erecting a barrier between Israel and the West Bank was thus a physical manifestation of the psychological need of Israelis Jews for separation. The barrier was, in the words of one of Prime Minister Sharon's close advisors, both "a physical and mental wall." The mental dimension was most important—"What we [Israelis] really want," this official disclosed, "is to turn our backs on the Arabs and never deal with them again."[133] Israelis, literally and metaphorically, wanted to wall themselves off from their Palestinian neighbors.

Like their desire for national unity following the outbreak of the second Intifada, the desire of Israeli Jews for separation from the Palestinians was by no means entirely new. From the very beginning of the Oslo peace process, many Israelis supported it as their best hope to finally end their painful entanglement with the Palestinians. Despite all the lofty rhetoric of a new era of peaceful coexistence and Peres' idealistic proposal for a "new Middle East" where Jews and Arabs would progressively integrate econom-ically, politically, and socially; many Israelis Jews—perhaps most—were less inclined toward integration with the Palestinians than toward separa-tion from them. They wished to live in a country that, notwithstanding its location, was as far removed from the Middle East and its "uncivilized" inhabitants as possible. If Israel were to integrate, it would be with Europe and America, not the Middle East. Withdrawing from the West Bank and Gaza Strip would allow Israeli Jews to distance themselves from the Palestinians.

This was essentially the promise that the Oslo peace process held for many Israelis. The apparent failure of the peace process meant that one means of separation from the Palestinians—through mutual agreement—was no longer feasible, at least in the short to medium-term. Hence, Israelis increasingly favored an alternative means toward the same goal—unilateral withdrawal behind a physical barrier. In the words of one Israeli commentator, "many long kilometers of high concrete walls, rolls of barbed wire, deep moats and sophisticated electronic sensors are supposed to make the Palestinians disappear and create a calm, well-defended Israel that, after all the wars and terror, can finally turn into Arkansas if not California."[134]

The majority of Israelis embraced unilateral withdrawal and its promise of separation from the Palestinians. Responding to this Israeli public opin-ion and to growing international pressure to resume negotiations with the Palestinians and find a political solution to the escalating violence (such a solution was proposed in the widely publicized Geneva Agreement drafted by prominent former Israeli and Palestinian officials and made public in

November 2003)—which raised the prospect of an internationally imposed settlement to the Israeli-Palestinian conflict (something that Sharon was anxious to avert[135])—in December 2003, Sharon put forward his own plan for a unilateral Israeli withdrawal from the Gaza Strip and from four small isolated West Bank settlements to be completed by the end of 2005.

This was a dramatic shift in the Sharon government's policy concerning the Israeli-Palestinian conflict, which had hitherto been geared toward militarily defeating the Palestinians and creating an alternative Palestinian leadership to Arafat. It was also a stunning departure for the man who perhaps did more than any other to promote Israel's settlement project in the West Bank and Gaza. Whilst many of his allies and supporters on the far-right were shocked and appalled by Sharon's apparent readiness to dismantle some Israeli settlements in the territories, most Israelis welcomed Sharon's so-called disengagement plan (the international community also welcomed it, albeit reluctantly).[136] Sharon had clearly undergone something of a conversion. The cause of this was his recognition, along with many other leading Likud members (such as his Deputy Prime Minister Ehud Olmert[137]), that a unilateral withdrawal from parts of the West Bank and all of Gaza was necessary to ensure a long-term Jewish majority in Israel and, hence, the future of the Jewish state.[138]

In other words, demography, not security, was the motive for Sharon's disengagement plan. Demographic predictions that within less than ten years there would be more Arabs than Jews in Israel, the West Bank, and Gaza combined (due to the much higher Arab birth rate) seriously called into question Israel's ability to remain a Jewish and democratic state.[139] With a majority of non-Jews under its control, Israel could be Jewish *or* democratic, but not both. Only a Jewish majority could guarantee Israel's identity as a Jewish and democratic state and, with Jewish immigration to Israel slowing to a trickle after the flood of immigrants that arrived from the former Soviet Union in the 1990s, the only feasible way to maintain such a majority was to keep as many Palestinians as possible outside the borders of the state. Disengagement and the construction of a fortified barrier between Israel and the densely populated Palestinian areas in the West Bank and Gaza, therefore, became the means to do this. Compelling evidence that this was the main motive behind Sharon's disengagement plan lies in the circuitous route his government initially chose for the security barrier (before Israel's Supreme Court and pressure from the Bush Administration forced some changes). Instead of hewing closely to the Green Line, the barrier's proposed route jutted deeply into the West Bank to include as many Jewish settlements there as possible. The primary objective was to include the largest number of Jews and the smallest number of Palestinians behind Israel's side of the barrier.[140]

But whatever route the barrier took, Palestinians would still remain within Israel—those who were citizens of Israel, not residents of the West Bank and Gaza. Over time, their number would certainly increase relative to that of Israel's Jewish population,[141] and they were likely to become more politically emboldened and assertive. In light of this, there was a growing public discussion of the "demographic threat" posed to the Jewish state by Israel's Palestinian citizens.[142] Some prominent right-wing politicians went so far as to openly suggest that Israel encourage Palestinian Israelis to leave the country.[143] The concept of "transfer"—an Israeli euphemism for ethnic cleansing—had long been deemed morally reprehensible and calls for it were confined to the margins of Israeli public discourse, made by right-wing extremists like Moledet ("Homeland") party leader Rehavam Ze'evi.[144] Such calls, however, became more frequent and more publicly acceptable following the violent demonstrations by Palestinians Israelis in October 2000.[145] In an interview on Israeli television, for example, Avigdor Lieberman, head of the Russian immigrant party Yisrael Beitenu and a minister in Sharon's government said: "I do not reject the transfer option. We don't have to escape reality. If you ask me, Israel's number one problem . . . is first of all Arab citizens of the State of Israel. Those who identify as Palestinians will have to move to Palestine. Do I consider them citizens of the State of Israel? No! Do we have to settle scores with them? Yes!"[146]

Although the forcible expulsion of Palestinian citizens from Israel was still considered to be morally wrong and politically unfeasible, "voluntary transfer" (as it became known) found increasing support among Israeli Jews (in contrast to the 1990s when support for this declined).[147] In one survey in 2003, for example, 57 percent expressed support for the government encouraging the emigration of Arabs from Israel, and 33 percent favored their expulsion.[148] The greater legitimacy of, and growing support for, policies that would promote the emigration of Palestinian Israelis or even force them to leave Israel, suggested that more and more Israeli Jews were coming to perceive Palestinian Israelis as the enemy. Their loyalty to the State of Israel was widely suspected[149]—something that led Prime Minister Sharon's adviser for Arab affairs to recommend to a special ministerial committee charged with formulating proposals for government policy toward Palestinian Israelis that in order to receive a necessary government-issued identity card, Israeli citizens first take an oath of loyalty to the state (a measure that clearly had Palestinian citizens of Israel in mind).[150] Palestinians were now seen as a threat residing both inside and outside the state to the physical security of Israeli Jews and to the continued existence of the Jewish state.[151] In the mind of the Israeli-Jewish public, the issue of Palestinian Israelis within Israel increasingly merged into the wider Israeli (Jewish)-Palestinian conflict.[152] As a result, "[R]adical new solutions have been formulated that combine measures for the West Bank and Gaza with measures concerning Israeli Arabs and that emphasize the need for national physical separation between Jews and Arabs."[153] One such "solution" which was increasingly advocated was redrawing Israel's borders so that Palestinian-Israeli populated towns and villages along the Green Line would be included in a future Palestinian state, while Israel would annex the large Jewish settlement blocs on the other side of the Green Line in the West Bank.[154] An opinion poll conducted by Israel's daily *Ma'ariv* newspaper in October 2000 showed that 51 percent of Israeli Jews favored this.

Growing intolerance of Palestinian Israelis was evident not only in social attitudes and public discourse, but also in government policies and legislation aimed at them. For example, the new Nationality and Entry into Israel Law passed on July 31, 2003, denied citizenship and residency to Palestinians from the West Bank and Gaza who married Israeli citizens (in the vast majority of cases, Palestinian Israelis)—thereby forcing these married couples to either live separately or leave Israel.[155] The explicit intent of the law was to reduce the number of Palestinians from the occupied territories eligible for naturalization through family reunification.[156] Other pieces of government legislation curtailed the freedom of expression of Arab political parties and Knesset members by allowing the Central Elections Committee to ban parties and individuals that rejected Israel's identity as a "Jewish and democratic state" (not as a Jewish and/or democratic state, as the law was previously worded), or supported (in action or speech) "the armed struggle of enemy states or terror organizations" against the State of Israel.[157] In effect, this meant that, in the words of Nadim Rouhana and Nimer Sultany, "[Knesset] candidates and their parties must submit to the Zionist consensus in order to have the right to be represented in parliament . . . . And because the Zionist hegemony defines which organizations are terrorist and which states are 'enemy,' the law gives the [Central Elections] committee additional leeway to deprive those who deviate from this hegemony of the right to representation."[158] Another law passed on July 22, 2002, lifted the parliamentary immunity of Knesset members who violated these restrictions, thereby allowing them to be legally prosecuted.

All of this amounted to an emphatic reassertion of the Jewishness of Israeli national identity and the Jewishness of the State of Israel. That is, it involved an ethnocentric expression of Israeli national identity that defined this identity in purely ethno-religious terms (i.e., exclusively Jewish)—as Prime Minister Sharon himself put it, "it is Jewishness that gives meaning to our Israeliness"[159]—and a renewed emphasis on Israel's Jewish identity. After a decade in which both the Jewishness of Israeli national identity and the Jewishness of the State of Israel had come under prolonged attack, Israeli Jewish society almost unanimously rallied around these core beliefs.

This was clearly apparent in the "Kineret Declaration" formulated in July 2001 by a group of prominent left- and right-wing, secular and religious Israeli-Jewish writers, scholars, journalists, and public officials (who were members of a larger group called the "Committee for National Responsibility" that was formed in 2001).

Invoking the spirit of Israel's original Declaration of Independence, the Kineret Declaration affirmed Israel's status as both a Jewish and democratic state, stating: "There is no contradiction between Israel's character as a Jewish state and its character as a democracy."[160] It went on to spell out exactly what Israel's Jewish character meant: "The Jewish character of Israel is expressed in a profound commitment to Jewish history and Jewish culture; in the state's connection to the Jews of the diaspora, the Law of Return, and its efforts to encourage *aliya* and absorption; in the Hebrew language, the principal language of the state, and the unique language of a unique Israeli creativity; in the festivals and official days of rest of the state, its symbols, and its anthem; in Hebrew culture with its Jewish roots, and in the state institutions devoted to its advancement; and in the Jewish educational system, whose purpose is to inculcate, along with general and scientific knowledge and the values of humanity, and along with loyalty to the state and love of the land of Israel and its vistas, the student's attachment to the Jewish people, the Jewish heritage, and the book of books."[161] Describing Israel's Jewish citizens, the document stated unequivocally: "We are one people. We share one past and one destiny. Despite disagreements and differences of world-view among us, all of us are committed to the continuity of Jewish life, to the continuity of the Jewish people, and to vouchsafing the future of the State of Israel."[162] The Kineret Declaration was subsequently endorsed by hundreds of well-known Israeli personalities from across the ideological spectrum, among them many leading politicians, intellectuals, and cultural icons. It was praised as "a symbol of Jewish unity," an expression of the "collective Jewish voice" and "a rejection of the idea that a new 'Israeli' people has superseded the Jewish identity."[163]

The reunification of Israeli-Jewish society under the shadow of the second Intifada led, therefore, to a retreat from the more civic and inclusive definition of Israeli national identity that had been articulated during the years of the Oslo peace process (and, especially during the period of the Rabin government). As a result, Israeli national identity ceased to be a focus of societal debate. Likewise, the public controversy over Israel's official identity as a Jewish and democratic state faded away. Those calling for Israel to become a "state for all its citizens" were now just voices in the wilderness, clearly outside the mainstream. The old and dying Zionist consensus was resurrected. The once robust post-Zionist challenge to it appeared to be thoroughly defeated.[164] Post-Zionism became a relic of a bygone age—the age of

Oslo—with just a few die-hard believers left.[165] This reversal of fortune was brought about by the second Intifada. As Tom Segev, the Israeli historian and one of the first people to be associated with post-Zionism, commented: "[T]he intifada forced us to go back into ourselves, into Zionism and ideology. Palestinian terrorism is pushing us back into the Zionist womb .... The matter that was at the heart of the post-Zionist environment was the debate over how to create a Jewish and democratic state. No one is interested in that anymore. We feel as if we must fight for our lives again, because of the Arabs."[166] Although it put an end to the Oslo peace process, therefore, the second Intifada also put an end—at least temporarily—to the crisis of Israeli identity. For Israeli Jews, this was the silver lining on the dark cloud that hung over them.

CONCLUSION: ISRAEL'S IDENTITY
CRISIS IN GLOBAL PERSPECTIVE

At the beginning of the third millennium one senses the coming of a global identity crisis.[1]

—Thomas M. Franck

Thus far, on the basis of the preceding chapters, the impression might have been created that Israelis are peculiarly beset by issues of identity. Perhaps they seem neurotically fixated with their own identity, incessantly examining it, and furiously contesting it. Israeli foreign policy, too, might appear to be singularly bogged down in a quagmire of identity politics, with debates over foreign policy hopelessly entangled in the domestic debate over Israeli national identity. Whereas the foreign policies of other states may reflect the cold calculations of *Realpolitik*, Israeli foreign policy reflects age-old Jewish complexes, and the passions and furies of religious and nationalist zealots. If elsewhere, foreign policy appears to be shaped by reason, in Israel it might seem to be shaped more by emotions, which continually oscillate between undue pessimism and reckless optimism. If this is indeed the impression now in the mind of the reader, it must be immediately dispelled.

The purpose of this book has not been to present Israelis as a people uniquely troubled by divisive issues of identity, and Israel as a state whose foreign policy is uniquely shaped—and hamstrung—by these issues. On the contrary, in so far as this book hopes to contribute toward a general appreciation of the role of national identity in foreign policy, it presents Israel as a case study from which we can derive broader insights about the relationship between national identity and foreign policy. This book claims that national identities shape states' foreign policies, and it has supported this claim by showing how Israeli foreign policy has been influenced by Israeli national identity.

A national identity influences a state's foreign policy in two distinct, though not mutually exclusive, ways. The first way is by shaping the perceptions, beliefs, and attitudes of policy-makers and the general public. In this sense, a national identity can influence the definition of national interests that underlie and motivate a state's foreign policy. In the case of Israel, as chapter 3 argued, Israeli national identity has significantly shaped the foreign policy perceptions, beliefs, and attitudes of Israeli policy-makers and the Israeli public. By far the most influential aspect or component of Israeli national identity in this regard was the Jewish component of Israeli national identity. "Jewishness" has profoundly influenced the worldview of Israeli Jews, their threat perception, their attitudes toward the value of diplomacy and the use of force, and their belief in the primacy of security—all essential ingredients in the formulation of Israeli foreign policy.

The primacy of security in Israeli foreign policy, for example, is not simply a result of the severe threats that Israel has faced. It is also a result of the abiding sense of insecurity felt by Israeli Jews on account of their Jewish identity and the collective historical memories—above all, of the Holocaust—associated with it. The belief that Jewish survival was constantly imperiled and that anti-Semitism was widespread and ever-present fueled the fears and anxieties of Israeli Jews, including Israeli policy-makers, and inclined many to view the conflict with the Arabs not as a conventional struggle for power and territory, but as an existential struggle against the most recent in a long line of anti-Semitic foes. The occasionally acute sensitivities, anxieties, and fears of Israeli politicians and the Israeli public at large are simply inexplicable, therefore, without reference to Jewish historical memories, and especially the traumatic collective memory of the Holocaust.

But the influence of the Jewish component of Israeli national identity upon Israeli foreign policy has not been constant and unwavering. Whilst this influence has been persistent, it has nonetheless varied depending upon the strength of the Jewish component in Israeli national identity at any particular time. The more salient Jewishness was in Israeli national identity (due to both internal and external factors), the more it affected Israeli foreign policy. In the 1950s and early 1960s, when Jewishness was relatively marginal in Israeli national identity (or, put differently, this identity was more civic than ethno-religious), the Jewish component of Israeli national identity had less of an impact upon Israeli foreign policy. This was reflected, for example, in Ben-Gurion's controversial decision to accept monetary reparations for the Holocaust from West Germany. But from the mid-1960s onwards, as Jewishness became increasingly dominant in constituting Israeli national identity, the impact of the Jewish component of Israeli national identity upon Israeli foreign policy increased. This was most evident in the foreign policies of Begin and Shamir, which were geared toward maintaining Israel's control of the West Bank and Gaza, since these areas were considered part of the historical homeland of the Jewish people.

The second way in which a national identity can influence a state's foreign policy is by acting as a constraint upon the kinds of foreign policies that states can pursue. To the extent that they are keen to avoid provoking domestic opposition, policy-makers take national identity into account when deciding upon their foreign policies. Perhaps the clearest single instance of Israeli national identity acting as a constraint on what Israeli policy-makers have been able to do can be seen in Barak's objection at the Camp David summit in July 2000 to Palestinian sovereignty over the Temple Mount/Haram al-Sharif. There was no strategic or material interest at stake, and the area was already under de facto Palestinian control. Thus, it was not the physical control of this area that mattered to Israeli policy-makers— which they openly and readily conceded to the Palestinians—but its symbolic value to Israeli Jews (and indeed, to Jews around the world). If an agreement was reached with the Palestinians at Camp David, Barak already faced an uphill domestic struggle to persuade a skeptical Israeli public to support the concessions he made (most notably, dividing sovereignty over Jerusalem); a further concession over the Temple Mount/Haram al-Sharif was beyond the limits of what Barak could do. The domestic political cost of agreeing to Palestinian sovereignty over the Temple Mount/Haram al-Sharif would simply have been too great.

The domestic opposition Israeli policy-makers can encounter when their foreign policies are perceived to be contrary to the national identity is most apparent in the tragic fate of Prime Minister Rabin. Although his assassination was the action of one individual, it came about within a climate of steadily rising threats and inflammatory verbal denunciations of Rabin and his government. Those opposed to the Oslo Accords did not just campaign against them; they mounted a concerted attempt to delegitimize the Rabin government, seizing upon its reliance on the support of Arab parliamentarians to argue that the government lacked a "Jewish majority" and was therefore illegitimate. The effort to undermine the Rabin government's legitimacy, and the assassination of Rabin himself in the midst of this campaign, starkly testifies to the risk Israeli policy-makers face when their policies are deemed by some to contradict Israeli national identity, and specifically its Jewish component (since Oslo's opponents associated this with Israel's possession of the West Bank and Gaza).

In its effort to explore the relationship between national identity and foreign policy, this book has also examined through the case of Israel the potential impact of a national identity crisis upon a state's foreign policy. It has described how a crisis of national identity can turn foreign policy into a subject of contestation in which competing notions of the national identity vie for supremacy. Foreign policy itself becomes a site of conflict over the identity of the nation. Debates and divisions over national identity are not confined to the domestic arena; instead they are also played out in foreign affairs. This was clearly the case with Israel's policy toward the peace process with the Palestinians in the 1990s as it became entangled in the politics of identity and, consequently, became highly contentious domestically. Although the Oslo peace process was bound to be controversial in Israel since it involved a complete redefinition of Israel's policies toward its historical enemy (the Palestinians), the organization representing them (the PLO), and the occupied territories (the West Bank and Gaza); it became even more controversial as it became publicly associated with divisive cultural issues concerning the definition of Israeli national identity, the relationship between religion and the state, and the future of Zionism and the Jewish state. In the minds of many Israeli Jews on both sides of the political divide, Israel's withdrawal from the occupied territories entailed a new Israel and a new national identity, and the abandonment of many of the beliefs that Israeli Jews had held dear for so long and which had been so central in shaping their national identity. As the Israeli novelist, David Grossman, wrote after the signing of the Oslo Accords: "The Jews living in Israel are now being asked not only to give up on geographical territories. We must also implement a 'redeployment'—or even a complete withdrawal—from entire regions in our soul."[2]

The linkage that emerged between the Oslo peace process and identity politics within Israel made the former even more contentious, and arguably deprived it of some of the public support that it might otherwise have received. Instead of arguing over the strategic and economic costs and benefits of a withdrawal from the territories, Israeli Jews became engaged in a fierce cultural war pitting "Israelis" against "Jews." "Israelis" favored a civic, territorial Israeli national identity, whereas "Jews" supported an ethno-religious definition of Israeli national identity. "Israelis" conceived of Israel as essentially a normal state, bound by the same rules as other states, shaped by the same influences, and sharing the same fate. Jews, by contrast, regarded Israel as the embodiment of the collective Jew and believed that the fate of Israel was no different from that of Jews throughout history. For them, Israel's survival is constantly endangered by anti-Semitic enemies who seek the destruction of the Jews. These two fundamentally different conceptions of the State of Israel and Israeli national identity were at the heart of the Israeli domestic debate over the Oslo peace process.

Although this debate died down by the end of the 1990s and ceased altogether in the wake of the collapse of the peace process and the outbreak of the second Intifada, the division between "Jews" and "Israelis" that underlay it persists to the present day. The renewed sense of national unity that Israeli Jews experienced during the first three years of the second Intifada was severely shaken by the fierce debate that erupted in Israel over Prime Minister Sharon's plan to unilaterally withdraw Israeli settlers and soldiers from Gaza and from four small West Bank settlements—the first removal of

Israeli settlements from the territories since 1967. In the nineteen months that passed between Sharon's first announcement of his disengagement plan and its implementation in August 2005, the passionate campaign mounted by the plan's opponents resembled the intense opposition that the Rabin government encountered during the early years of the Oslo peace process. Once again, large numbers of right-wing and religious Jews denounced the government's "treason," prominent rabbis associated with the settler movement condemned the policy as a sin against God and called upon religious soldiers to disobey their orders in the event of an evacuation, and the prime minister was publicly vilified as an enemy, in a manner that was ominously reminiscent of the right-wing extremist incitement that preceded Rabin's assassination in 1995. This raised fears of an assassination attempt on Prime Minister Sharon, and the possibility of violent resistance by settlers and even a mutiny in the IDF by religious Zionist soldiers.[3] Government ministers, leaders of the settlements, and journalists even warned of an imminent civil war.[4] The Israeli public was equally alarmed—according to one poll in January 2005, 49 percent of Israeli Jews thought that there was a high danger of a civil war.[5]

Thankfully, these fears did not come to pass and the evacuation took place more smoothly and quickly than many had believed possible (it took only six days).[6] But the harrowing televised scenes of fervently religious settlers and their supporters being dragged kicking and screaming out of their homes and synagogues was a searing reminder to Israelis of the divisions in their midst. Although the majority of Israelis supported the withdrawal, the fact that the bulk of the anti-disengagement movement was made up of religious Jews highlighted the overlap between political and religious orientations in Israel. In terms of the categories employed in this book, supporters of the disengagement were likely to be "Israelis," opponents of it were more likely to be "Jews."[7]

Moreover, some of these "Jews" displayed a complete disregard for the will of the majority and a disdain for the state's laws and agents (i.e., the army and police). Although only a small minority, their willingness to engage in civil disobedience and even commit acts of violence directly challenged Israeli democracy and the rule of law. In overcoming this challenge in Gaza, therefore, democracy and the rule of law in Israel passed an important test. But a greater test still lies ahead. Having been defeated in their effort to prevent the withdrawal from Gaza, it is quite likely that some radical right-wing Jews may resort to more extreme measures to stop any larger future withdrawal from the West Bank, territory that is even more precious to them. Notwithstanding the largely peaceful Israeli withdrawal from Gaza, therefore, the probable future withdrawal of Jewish settlers from all but the large blocs of Israeli settlements in the West Bank—whether or not this takes place as a result of an Israeli-Palestinian peace agreement—will almost certainly be met with intense and even violent resistance by this extremist minority. Having successfully confronted militant settlers in Gaza without the nightmare scenario of a civil war materializing, Israeli society is at least better prepared to face this threat in the future than it was during the years of the Oslo peace process.

Resisting the threat posed by extremist right-wing Jews, however, is only one of the challenges that Israeli society faces. Equally important is the need to repair the relationship between the religious Zionist community and the rest of Israeli-Jewish society which has suffered as a result of the disengagement from Gaza, which has left many religious Zionists feeling betrayed by their state and alienated from their society. In addition, the withdrawal from Gaza amounts to a profound and unprecedented challenge to the messianic, redemptive worldview of the religious Zionist community. How they will respond to this ideological crisis and whether this response will widen or narrow the divide between them and Israeli society at large is now a major issue Israel must confront. In seeking to mend the now fractured relationship between the religious Zionist community and the rest of Israeli-Jewish society, the temptation will be to emphasize the Jewish identity that both sides share. Appealing to a common Jewish identity, however contested it may be, has always been and continues to be a chief mechanism for achieving social solidarity in Israel. But while this may prevent a rupture between Israeli Jews, it only exacerbates the division between them and Israel's non-Jewish citizens, especially its Palestinian minority.

Hence, the greatest difficulty for Israeli society lies in sustaining a common sense of identity between Israeli Jews, without further alienating Palestinian Israelis. Already, the reinforcement of the Jewish component in Israeli national identity since the collapse of the peace process and the renewal of Israeli-Palestinian hostilties has strengthened the common denominator shared by Israel's Jewish citizens but widened the divide between them and the country's Palestinian citizens.[8] Bridging this internal divide—the deepest and most persistent of all the cleavages in Israeli society—now ranks alongside the achievement of peace with the Palestinians as the most urgent and critical issue facing Israel in the years ahead. The alienation, exclusion, and discrimination experienced by Palestinian Israelis cannot continue without endangering Israeli democracy and social peace.[9] The inter-communal violence that erupted between Jewish and Palestinian citizens in October 2000 is a stark warning of the danger that lies ahead if Israel fails to accommodate the needs (material and psychological) of its Palestinian minority.

The critical question is whether these needs can be accomodated within the framework of a Jewish state. This question has become a subject of growing debate in Israel in recent years (one that is often framed in terms of the compatibility of Israel's self-definition as both a Jewish and democratic state[10]). What is certain is that as long as the state continues to give preferential treatment to Jews, the Arab-Jewish divide will continue to grow. It is vital, therefore, for the state to abolish all laws and practices (formal and informal) that favor Jewish over Palestinian citizens.[11] Ensuring equal treatment for Arabs and Jews in laws, the provision of state benefits, government funding, and other areas, however, is unlikely to completely alleviate the abiding sense of resentment felt by Palestinian Israelis which is born from a sense of not belonging as much as from perceived discrimination. While some argue that this problem can only be solved by transforming Israel from a Jewish state into a "state for all its citizens," such a solution is opposed by the vast majority of Israeli Jews.[12] A more realistic approach would be to accept as legitimate the desire of the Jewish majority to live in a state with a Jewish ethos and Jewish symbols, while encouraging the development of a civic identity that can be shared by both Jews and Arabs. The rise of such a civic identity need not come at the expense of the ethno-religious national identity held by many Israeli Jews ("Jewishness") nor the national identity of Palestinian Israelis (as Palestinians). Both groups could—indeed must be able to—maintain their separate national identities together with a transcendent Israeli identity based upon their common citizenship.[13]

Promoting a civic identity requires a sustained commitment from future Israeli governments. Since the Rabin government, however, successive Israeli governments have backed away from supporting a civic Israeli identity, preferring instead to strengthen the ethno-religious Jewish identity of the majority of Israeli Jews for the sake of (Israeli-Jewish) national unity. While Israel's conflict with the Palestinians dominates the national agenda, the demands of national unity are likely to continue to trump the need for a stronger civic identity for both Jewish and Palestinian citizens of Israel. Thus, until the confict is resolved, one can expect little progress toward strengthening Israelis' civic identity.

But Israel may not be able to wait until then. There is a real danger that unless significant progress is made in addressing the needs of Palestinian Israelis, they may completely turn away from integrating into Israeli society and embrace greater separatism and demand some form of regional autonomy or even demand the establishment of a democratic binational state in the entire land of Palestine (thereby fusing their struggle with that of Palestinians in the West Bank and Gaza). Such demands will no doubt intensify intolerance toward Palestinian Israelis and increase the calls for their expulsion from Israel that have already been sounded in recent years. Before reaching this dangerous point, therefore, immediate action must be taken to strengthen the civic identity of Israelis.

While a reinvigorated civic identity is necessary for the peaceful coexistence of Jews and Arabs in Israel (as well as other non-Jewish citizens of Israel), it will not settle all the issues of identity that Israelis have been grappling with for so long. Jewish Israelis and Palestinian Israelis will no doubt continue to question and challenge the definition of their respective national identities (for the latter, this may in fact become especially acute following the establishment of a Palestinian state alongside Israel). The meaning of Israel's identity as a Jewish state will also remain unsettled, as it has been since the founding of the state. So too, the perennial question of "who is a Jew" will not be put to rest. More broadly, the cultural tension between individualism and collectivism and between universalism and particularism can never be completely resolved. Whatever social agreements are reached will inevitably be provisional and transient, as they come unstuck by social and political change. It would be naïve, therefore, to expect a future in which questions of identity no longer trouble Israeli society. Identity debates are ongoing, and occasionally they may generate a sense of crisis. An identity crisis is not necessarily a one-off episode. Some authors have presented a crisis of national identity as simply a stage that can occur in the process of social and political development.[14] National identities, however, do not follow a linear path of development. They are never completely secure and are always subject to renewed debate and contestation. Hence, even if Israelis successfully resolve the identity crisis that they have experienced in recent years, they may well face other crises of identity in the future. Israelis will never be entirely free from the challenge of grappling with their many internal divisions and agreeing upon a common identity that can unite a pluralistic and fractious society.

But Israelis will certainly not be alone in this. There is a pervasive anxiety over the future of national identities and widespread fears over the place of national, ethnic, and religious minorities in a host of states. Many societies today are finding it increasingly difficult to agree upon the definition of their collective identity. The crisis of Israeli identity described in this book is not unique. Intense and sustained debates over national identities have been taking place in many different countries around the world—debates that have frequently been interpreted as indicative of a crisis of national identity. Anxiety over European integration in the United Kingdom,[15] over national decline in France,[16] over Islamic extremism in the Netherlands,[17] over Americanization in Japan,[18] over immigration in the United States,[19] over biculturalism in Canada,[20] and over multiculturalism in Australia,[21] have all been interpreted as symptomatic of national identity crises. "Whether in Scotland, Sri Lanka, China, Russia, or Australia, we find potent political debates in which (re)conceptions of national identity are fundamental," one scholar has observed.[22] Notwithstanding the fact that in "different countries debates on national identity involve different kinds of perplexity and agonizing choices," these debates share common features.[23] They often revolve around questions of who should be included within the definition of the nation and who should be excluded, what legacies of the past should be preserved and what should be discarded, and whether "the nation [can] be reconfigured beyond its familiar territoriality and reference to the state, and within a more multinational and multilocational reception?"[24] The definition, content, and future of national identities are highly contentious domestic issues in many states. Undoubtedly, the politics of national identity is at the forefront of contemporary politics in both the developed and developing worlds. Thus, Roxanne Lynn Doty notes that: "National identity is arguably one of the more problematic constitutive elements of contemporary nation-states."[25]

Although national identities have never been totally unproblematic, globalization is making them especially problematic today. Globalization poses a serious challenge to national identities, as it does to many other forms of collective identity.[26] Through ever-expanding information and communication flows and through the mass movement of people and goods, globalization has progressively overwhelmed territorial borders and eroded cultural boundaries.[27] National identities are particularly challenged by the de-territorialization that globalization entails since they have historically been closely bound up with a sense of place.[28] The territorial dimension of national identities finds its greatest expression in the concept of a national "homeland."[29] These homelands are metaphorically "besieged" by globalization, whether in the form of migrant workers, multinational business corporations, or the popularity of transnational consumption and leisure habits. As the "foreign" and the "foreigner" dwell increasingly in our midst, it becomes harder to delineate and sustain the physical and cultural boundaries that are integral in constituting and maintaining national identities. Cultural globalization jeopardizes the distinctiveness of national cultures, and rising immigration alters the demographic makeup of national societies. To the extent that a national identity is defined in terms of shared cultural attributes, the more culturally heterogeneous the population, the harder it becomes to define these cultural attributes.[30] As a result, the definition and even existence of a common national identity is no longer taken for granted, but becomes the subject of explicit debate. Hence, as the populations of states around the world have become increasingly heterogeneous in recent years, such debates have now become commonplace.

Globalization also challenges national identities by undermining the state's central role in creating and sustaining them. Historically, most national identities have been produced and perpetuated by states.[31] As most scholars of nationalism argue, nations did not make states, but rather states made nations. The state's control over education and the media were particularly powerful instruments at its disposal in the construction of a national identity. They provided valuable means by which states inculcated a sense of national belonging in their population (through their ability to disseminate the national history and traditions, for instance).[32] The development and maintenance of a sense of national identity, therefore, has often been intrinsically linked to state practices. As a result of globalization, however, states no longer have the power to define the national identity. More and more states have lost their ability to control the definition of the national identity as globalization empowers new social actors and opens up new discursive spaces beyond the state's authority. The economic liberalization policies associated with globalization have led to the progressive restructuring and contraction of states, creating new social spaces within which social movements can emerge and grow. As states have gradually succumbed to the forces of globalization, their power and prestige have often (but not always) diminished, facilitating the mobilization of new social movements.[33] As a result, there has been a worldwide proliferation of social movements. Many of these social movements are engaged in identity politics, whether their overt agenda is material (for example, to improve the economic welfare of a subnational group by demanding a more equitable distribution of resources), or ideational (for example, to gain official recognition of a group's identity and culture).[34] The identity politics of these social movements often indirectly challenge the state's definition of the national identity—by contradicting the official representation of the nation as unified and homogenous, for instance. Social movements may also directly challenge the state's definition of the national identity by articulating a different definition of the national identity altogether, or simply by denying the state the exclusive right to define the national identity. By weakening the state's capacity to prevent or curtail such challenges, therefore, globalization has effectively empowered new social actors and groups to contest the meaning of the national identity imposed from above by the state. Since the state is no longer able to control the definition of the national identity, different social groups compete to define the national identity, espousing alternative definitions of it.

In addition to empowering new social groups and actors, globalization has also brought about a rapid expansion of media outlets owned by private commercial interests inside and outside state borders (e.g., cable networks). Since the content of these media outlets (television, radio, print publications) is determined by market forces, it can differ markedly from that of state-run media (which tend to reflect official views and ideology). Furthermore, the spread of new communication technologies (such as the Internet and cell phones) has increased the capabilities of non-state actors by providing them with cheap and useful means to mobilize supporters and spread their message. Thus, in so far as the state's control of information through its control of communications was instrumental in the formation and consolidation of national identities, the loss of this control due to the "information revolution" brought about by globalization and new technologies has been instrumental in undermining hegemonic national identities and creating a variety of alternatives to them. As a result: "In place of the harmonized, monologic voice of the Nation, we find a polyphony of voices, overlapping and criss-crossing; contradictory and ambiguous; opposing, affirming, and negotiating their views of the nation."[35] It is in such situations—when there are multiple definitions or conceptions of the national identity circulating and struggling in the public sphere—that crises of national identity are likely to arise. The presence of divergent conceptions of the national identity in fierce competition in the public sphere indicates the lack of a societal consensus over the proper definition of the national identity. The absence of such a consensus is thus often interpreted as a crisis of national identity.

How societies cope with these national identity crises will be one of the most critical issues of the twenty-first century. In our anxious search for secure and stable national identities, one danger is that of trying to erect barriers to keep out threatening or disruptive forces. The desire to "return to our roots," to be "amongst one's own," to renew national "authenticity," is now potent and widespread. But in an age when boundaries are rapidly dissolving, it is impossible for us to retreat into self-enclosed communities. The attempt to resist globalization, international migration, and other transnational forces is doomed to fail. Moreover, the challenge to national identities lies inside as well as outside state borders. The increasing social diversity of national populations and the desire of different substate groups to assert distinct identities will render any attempt to recover a uniform national culture futile. The proliferation of social voices, and the declining ability of states to impose hegemonic national identities means that national identities will remain contested terrains, permanently marked by ambiguity and uncertainty.

If one danger lies in trying to restore a lost certainty to national identities, another danger is that by abandoning national identities altogether in favor either of more global or local identities, we lose the sense of community that holds states and societies together. National identities provide us with an important sense of belonging and communion. For individuals, a national identity is a source of personal dignity, self-respect, and positive social distinctiveness.[36] For societies, a shared national identity facilitates the social trust, solidarity, and mutual responsibility that helps sustain well-functioning democracies and the provision of social justice.[37]

Without them, the risks of social fragmentation and the breakup of states are heightened.

But national identities also pose risks, as the contemporary resurgence of virulent nationalism attests. National identities both unite and divide people. The benefits of national identities come at the price of excluding and marginalizing those outside the boundaries of national belonging. All too often, they can provoke discrimination, oppression, and violence against non-nationals (whether they reside inside or outside the borders of the state). After a decade in which we have witnessed afresh the horrors of genocide, ethnic cleansing, and wars of secession, it is essential that we temper our need for national identities with an awareness of the tragic human consequences that frequently follow from embracing them at all costs. We must find a way, therefore, to nurture national identities while avoiding the exclusionary practices that have traditionally sustained them, and simultaneously develop new collective identities and forms of social cohesion. A prerequisite for this difficult task is a better understanding of the importance of national identities and the role that identity politics plays in world affairs. It is this author's hope that this book may contribute in this regard.

Notes

Introduction

1. Harold R. Isaacs, *Idols of the Tribe: Group Identity and Political Change* (Cambridge, MA: Harvard University Press, 1975), 215.
2. This book is chiefly concerned with the attitudes and views of Israeli Jews, rather than Palestinian Israelis. Palestinian Israelis are largely excluded from this book's analysis since, with few exceptions, they do not participate in the debates over Israeli national identity or Israeli foreign policy this book describes. Arab political parties in the Knesset and Palestinian Israelis in general are still not considered by most Israelis as legitimate participants in the debates over national identity and foreign policy in Israel. As with other public issues in Israel, little attention is paid to the opinions of Palestinian Israelis; and although this is slowly changing with regard to domestic issues; on foreign policy issues, the voices of Palestinian Israelis remain distinctly marginalized.
3. Lee Hockstader, "A Sour Mood Grips Israel As It Prepares to Turn 50," *Washington Post*, February 9, 1998.
4. David B. Green and Peter Hirschberg, "The Jubilee Party Goes Bust," *The Jerusalem Report*, January 22, 1998.
5. Doug Struck, "Israel Celebrates With Mixed Feelings," *Washington Post*, April 30, 1998.
6. This does not mean that the security concerns of many Israelis vis-à-vis the Oslo peace process were not real or deeply felt.
7. Terrell A. Northrup, "The Dynamic of Identity in Personal and Social Conflict," in *Intractable Conflicts and their Transformation*, ed. Louis Kriesberg, Terrell A. Northrup, and Stuart J. Thorson (Syracuse: Syracuse University Press, 1989), 55–82.
8. Jay Rothman, *Resolving Identity-Based Conflict in Nations, Organizations, and Communities* (San Francisco: Jossey-Bass, 1997); Jay Rothman and Marie L. Olson, "From Interests to Identities: Towards a New Emphasis in Interactive Conflict Resolution," *Journal of Peace Research* 38, no. 3 (2001): 289–305.
9. Edward Azar, *The Management of Protracted Social Conflict: Theory and Cases* (Aldershot, UK: Dartmouth, 1990); John Burton, *Conflict: Resolution and Prevention* (New York: St. Martins, 1990).
10. Northrup, "The Dynamic of Identity in Personal and Social Conflict."
11. Daniel Bar-Tal, "From Intractable Conflict through Conflict Resolution to Reconciliation: Psychological Analysis," *Political Psychology* 21 (2000): 360; Yaacov Bar-Siman-Tov, "Dialectics between Stable Peace and Reconciliation,"

in *From Conflict Resolution to Reconciliation*, ed. Yaacov Bar-Siman-Tov (Oxford: Oxford University Press, 2004), 75.

12. This book's claim that national identities are not easily changed or replaced is thus contrary to a view of identities as always being unstable and fluid, a view associated today with postmodernist theory (see, for example, Madan Sarup, *Identity, Culture and the Postmodern World* [Edinburgh: Edinburgh University Press, 1996]; and Stuart Hall and Paul du Gay, eds., *Questions of Cultural Identity* [London: SAGE Publications, 1996]). The postmodernist depiction of identities as always in flux exaggerates the instability of identities. Identities can be deeply rooted, sedimented in people's consciousness over time through a host of cultural and social practices.

13. The term "identity politics" is commonly used to characterize the political and cultural activities of social groups based upon different collective identities (e.g., those based on gender, sexual orientation, race, religion, ethnicity, etc.).

14. Craig Calhoun, "The Problem of Identity in Collective Action," in *Macro-Micro Linkages in Sociology*, ed. Joan Huber (London: SAGE, 1991), 51–75.

15. Craig Calhoun, *Critical Social Theory: Culture, History, and the Challenge of Difference* (Oxford: Blackwell, 1995), 217.

16. This definition of a national identity begs a definition of a nation, which can briefly be defined as "a community whose members share feelings of fraternity, substantial distinctiveness, and exclusivity, as well as beliefs in a common ancestry and a continuous genealogy." Yael Tamir, "The Enigma of Nationalism," *World Politics* 47 (April 1995): 425.

17. The existence of large cultural differences is not necessary for this. As Iver Neumann writes: "[W]hat is at issue in delineation is not 'objective' cultural differences, but the way symbols are activated to become part of the capital of the identity of a given human collective. Any difference, no matter how minuscule, may be inscribed by political importance and serve to delineate identities." Iver B. Neumann, "Self and Other in International Relations," *European Journal of International Relations* 2, no. 2 (1996): 166.

18. Iver B. Neumann and Jennifer M. Welsh, "The Other in European Self-Definition: An Addendum to the Literature on International Society," *Review of International Studies* 17, no. 4 (1991): 327–348.

19. Shibley Telhami and Michael Barnett, "Introduction," in *Identity and Foreign Policy in the Middle East*, ed. Telhami and Barnett (Ithaca: Cornell University Press, 2002), 8.

20. Anthony Smith, *National Identity* (London: Penguin, 1991), 170.

21. Calhoun, *Critical Social Theory*, 231.

22. These are discussed at length in the voluminous scholarly literature on nationalism. In particular see the work of Anthony Smith, *National Identity*; Eric Hobsbawm, *Nations and Nationalism since 1780: Programme, Myth, Reality* (Cambridge: Cambridge University Press, 1990); Ernest Gellner, *Nations and Nationalism* (Ithaca, NY: Cornell University Press, 1983); Walker Connor, *Ethnonationalism: The Quest for Understanding* (Princeton, NJ: Princeton University Press, 1994); Benedict Anderson, *Imagined Communities: Reflections on the Origin and Spread of Nationalism* (New York: Verso Press, 1991); John Breuilly, *Nationalism and the State* (Chicago: University of Chicago Press, 1985); Liah Greenfeld, *Nationalism: Five Roads to Modernity* (Cambridge,

MA: Harvard University Press, 1992); Craig Calhoun, *Nationalism* (Minneapolis, MN: University of Minnesota Press, 1997); and Rogers Brubaker, *Nationalism Reframed: Nationhood and the National Question in the New Europe* (Cambridge: Cambridge University Press, 1996).

23. Michael Billig, *Banal Nationalism* (London: SAGE Publications, 1995).

24. Anthony Smith, "Ethnic Identity and World Order," *Millennium: Journal of International Studies* 12, no. 2 (1983): 156.

25. Smith, *National Identity*, 16.

26. Billig, *Banal Nationalism*, 6.

27. This reminder, however, is so familiar and habitual that it is generally not consciously registered. In his book, Billig analyses the myriad, subtle ways by which our sense of national identity is continually reproduced on a daily basis. Billig, *Banal Nationalism*.

28. For this claim see, James Rosenau, *Turbulence in World Politics: A Theory of Change and Continuity* (New York: Harvester/Wheatsheaf, 1990); Martin Shaw, *Global Society and International Relations* (Cambridge: Polity, 1994); Ken Booth, "Security and Emancipation," *Review of International Studies* 17, no. 4 (1991): 314–315.

29. A process that has been termed "glocalization." Uri Ram, "The Promised Land of Business Opportunities: Liberal Post-Zionism in the Glocal Age," in *The New Israel: Peacemaking and Liberalization*, ed. Yoav Peled and Gershon Shafir (Boulder, CO: Westview, 2000): 217–240.

30. After reviewing data from cross-national public opinion surveys, two scholars found little evidence to support the claim that individuals have shifted their identities away from states toward supranational or subnational entities. Peter Dombrowski and Tom Rice, "Changing Identities and International Relations Theory: A Cautionary Note," *Nationalism & Ethnic Politics* 6, no. 4 (2000): 83–105.

31. Uri Ram, "Postnationalist Pasts: The Case of Israel," *Social Science History* 22, no. 4 (1998): 534.

32. Yosef Lapid and Friedrich Kratochwil, "Revisiting the 'National:' Toward an Identity Agenda in Neorealism?" In *The Return of Culture and Identity in IR Theory*, ed. Lapid and Kratochwil (Boulder, CO: Lynne Rienner, 1996), 105.

33. Jan Jindy Pettman, "Nationalism and After," *Review of International Studies* 24 (December 1998): 151.

34. This effort was heralded by Yosef Lapid and Friedrich Kratochwil's edited volume, *The Return of Culture and Identity in IR Theory*. Another edited volume by Peter Katzenstein published in the same year also drew scholarly attention to the role of collective identities in foreign policy. Peter Katzenstein, ed., *The Culture of National Security: Norms and Identity in World Politics* (New York: Columbia University Press, 1996).

35. Rodney Bruce Hall, *National Collective Identity: Social Constructs and International Systems* (New York: Columbia University Press, 1999), 8.

36. Hall, *National Collective Identity*, 20.

37. George H.W. Bush, "In Defense of Saudi Arabia," speech on August 8, 1990. Quoted in David Campbell, *Writing Security: United States Foreign Policy and the Politics of Identity* (Minneapolis: University of Minnesota Press, 1992), 3.

38. "The President's Message: A Different Battle Awaits," *New York Times*, September 16, 2001.

39. William Wallace, "Foreign Policy and National Identity in the United Kingdom," *International Affairs* 67, no. 1 (1991): 66.

40. Ilya Prizel, *National Identity and Foreign Policy: Nationalism and Leadership in Poland, Russia and Ukraine* (Cambridge: Cambridge University Press, 1998), 19.

41. William Bloom, *Personal Identity, National Identity and International Relations* (Cambridge: Cambridge University Press, 1990).

42. Bloom, *Personal Identity, National Identity and International Relations*, 85.

43. Ibid., 80.

44. Ibid., 81.

45. Constructivism is concerned with exploring the role of cultural meanings, beliefs, understandings, norms, and identities in international politics. The term "constructivism" was coined by Nicholas Onuf in his book, *World of Our Making: Rules and Rule in Social Theory and International Relations* (Columbia: University of South Carolina Press, 1989).

46. Alexander Wendt, "Anarchy is what States Make of It: The Social Construction of Power Politics," *International Organization* 46, no. 2 (Spring 1992): 391–425.

47. Alexander Wendt, *Social Theory of International Politics* (Cambridge: Cambridge University Press, 2000), 231.

48. Michael Barnett, "Culture, Strategy and Foreign Policy Change: Israel's Road to Oslo," *European Journal of International Relations* 5, no. 1 (1999): 10.

49. Shibley Telhami, "Israeli Foreign Policy: A Realist Ideal-Type or a Breed of Its Own?" in *Israel in Comparative Perspective: Challenging the Conventional Wisdom*, ed. Michael Barnett (Albany, NY: State University of New York Press, 1996): 29–51.

50. Marc Lynch, *State Interests and Public Spheres: The International Politics of Jordan's Identity* (New York: Columbia University Press, 1999), 10.

51. Edward Said, "The Phony Islamic Threat," *New York Times Magazine*, November 21, 1993, 62.

52. See, for instance, Yair Sheleg, "Israel's Identity Crisis," *Ha'aretz*, October 11, 1998; Judy Dempsey, "Fault lines at 50," *Financial Times*, April 29, 1998; "Israel's Self-analysis," *Washington Post*, May 16, 1999; Dan Urian and Efraim Karsh, "Introduction," in *In Search of Identity: Jewish Aspects in Israeli Culture*, ed. Dan Urian and Efraim Karsh (London: Frank Cass, 1999), 2; Lilly Weissbrod, "Israeli Identity in Transition," *Israel Affairs* 3, nos. 3–4 (Spring/Summer 1997): 57–61; Eliot A. Cohen, "Israel after Heroism," *Foreign Affairs* 77, no. 6 (November/December 1998): 120.

53. For Erikson's work on identity crises, see Erik H. Erikson, *Identity: Youth and Crisis* (New York: W.W. Norton, 1968); and Erik H. Erikson, *Identity and the Life Cycle: Selected Papers by Erik H. Erikson. Psychological Issues*, vol. 1 (New York: International Universities Press, 1959).

54. Lucian Pye, "Identity and the Political Culture," in *Crises and Sequences in Political Development*, ed. Leonard Binder et al. (Princeton: Princeton University Press, 1971), 110–111.

55. Ibid., 111.

Chapter 1   The Construction of Israeli National Identity: From Jews to Israelis and Back Again

1. Quoted in Tom Segev, *1949: The First Israelis* (New York: The Free Press, 1986), xvii.
2. Gershom Scholem, "Israel and the Diaspora," in *On Jews and Judaism in Crisis: Selected Essays*, ed. Werner J. Dannhauser (New York: Schocken Books, 1976), 257.
3. Walter Laquer, *A History of Zionism* (New York: MJF Books, 1972), 3.
4. Arthur Hertzberg, *The Zionist Idea* (New York: Greenwood, 1970), 21.
5. Michael A. Meyer, *Jewish Identity in the Modern World* (Seattle: University of Washington Press, 1990), 35.
6. Gideon Shimoni, *The Zionist Ideology* (Hanover, NH: Brandeis University Press, 1995), 47–48.
7. Initially the Jewish intelligentsia of Western Europe viewed anti-Semitism either as a vestige of an older, passing age, or else as a reasonable gentile punishment for incomplete assimilation of the individual Jew. This later view, however, was contradicted by the fact that anti-Semitism was also directed against completely assimilated Jews—most notoriously, in the 1895 trial for treason of the French Jewish military officer Alfred Dreyfuss, which came to be known as the "Dreyfuss Affair." In reaction to this, the "rational" explanation for anti-Semitism changed and was explained by Western European Zionists as a reasonable gentile response to the "strangeness" of the Jewish nation, its incomplete assimilation. They simply substituted the Jewish nation for the Jewish individual, and hence advocated collective national assimilation rather than individual assimilation.
8. Shimoni, *The Zionist Ideology*, 390.
9. Ibid., 390.
10. Quoted in Nissim Rejwan, *Israel in Search of Identity: Reading the Formative Years* (Gainesville, FL: University Press of Florida, 1999), 62.
11. Ibid., 61.
12. The Uganda proposal was formally rejected at the seventh Zionist Congress in 1905 after Herzl's death (he died on July 3, 1904, shortly after his forty-fourth birthday).
13. The leading figures of the movement were Nahman Syrkin, Berl Katznelson, Yitzhak Tabenkin, and David Ben-Gurion, the latter becoming the chairman of the Jewish Agency in charge of the *Yishuv* during the years of the British mandate in Palestine and later Israel's first prime minister.
14. Uri Ram, "Zionist Historiography and the Invention of Modern Jewish Nationhood: The Case of Ben Zion Dinur," *History and Memory* 7, no.1 (Spring/Summer 1995): 115–116.
15. Quoted in Meyer, *Jewish Identity in the Modern World*, 69.
16. Quoted in Segev, *1949: The First Israelis*, 292.
17. Quoted in Uri Ben-Eliezer, "A Nation-in-Arms: State, Nation, and Militarism in Israel's First Years," *Comparative Studies in Society and History* 37, no. 2 (April 1995): 264.
18. Anderson, *Imagined Communities*.
19. Eric Hobsbawm and Terence Ranger, eds., *The Invention of Tradition* (Cambridge: Cambridge University Press, 1982).

20. Ram, "Zionist Historiography and the Invention of Modern Jewish Nationhood," 100.
21. The term "ethnie" is used by Anthony Smith, see his book *National Identity*.
22. Benjamin Beit-Hallahmi, "Naming Norms and Identity Choices in Israel," in *Jewish Survival: The Identity Problem at the Close of the Twentieth Century*, ed. Ernest Krausz and Gitta Tulea (New Brunswick: Transaction, 1998), 191.
23. Charles S. Liebman, "Religion and Modernity: The Special Case of Israel," in *The Jewishness of Israelis: Responses to the Guttman Report*, ed. Charles S. Liebman and Elihu Katz (Albany, NY: State University of New York Press, 1997), 89.
24. Baruch Kimmerling, "Between the Primordial and the Civil Definitions of the Collective Identity: *Eretz Israel* or the State of Israel?" in *Comparative Social Dynamics: Essays in Honor of S.N. Eisenstadt*, ed. Erik Cohen, Moshe Lissak, and Uri Almagor (Boulder, CO: Westview, 1985), 271.
25. Baruch Kimmerling, "Between Hegemony and Dormant *Kulturkampf* in Israel," in Urian and Karsh, eds. *In Search of Identity*, 60.
26. Quoted in Ze'ev Tzahor, "Ben-Gurion's Mythopoetics," in *The Shaping of Israeli Identity: Myth, Memory and Trauma*, ed. Robert Wistrich and David Ohana (London: Frank Cass, 1995), 66. Ben-Gurion believed that the Bible was a text accepted by all Jews, and could therefore serve as a basis for unity of the Jewish people returning to their homeland.
27. Beit-Hallahmi, "Naming Norms and Identity Choices in Israel," 193.
28. Yael Zerubavel, *Recovered Roots: Collective Memory and The Making of Israeli National Tradition* (Chicago: University of Chicago Press, 1995), 6–7.
29. Ram, "Zionist Historiography and the Invention of Modern Jewish Nationhood," 93.
30. Quoted in Zerubavel, *Recovered Roots*, 18.
31. In the 1930s and 1940s, "sabra" and "Hebrew" were both used to make this distinction, but beginning in the 1950s "sabra" replaced the term "Hebrew." Oz Almog, *The Sabra: The Creation of the New Jew*, trans. by Haim Watzman (Berkeley: University of California Press, 2000), 4.
32. Quoted in Segev, *1949: The First Israelis*, 292.
33. Zerubavel, *Recovered Roots*, 26.
34. Quoted in Amnon Rubinstein, *The Zionist Dream Revisited: From Herzl to Gush Emunim and Back* (New York: Schocken, 1984), 4.
35. Quoted in Zerubavel, *Recovered Roots*, 20.
36. Ibid., 21.
37. Beit-Hallahmi, "Naming Norms and Identity Choices in Israel," 193.
38. Rubinstein, *The Zionist Dream Revisited*, 6.
39. Quoted in Laurence J. Silberstein, *The Postzionism Debates: Knowledge and Power in Israeli Culture* (London: Routledge, 1999), 39.
40. Ibid., 41.
41. Zionism's opposition to Yiddish resulted in it quickly becoming identified with movements that opposed Zionism, such as those based upon socialism (e.g., the *Bund*) or Jewish cultural autonomy in the Diaspora (e.g., the ideas of the Jewish historian Simon Dubnov). The *Haredi* community in Israel continues to use Yiddish and educate their children in Yiddish to this day, indicating their opposition to Zionism and their attempt to preserve the Jewish culture of the Diaspora.
42. Beit-Hallahmi, "Naming Norms and Identity Choices in Israel," 195.

43. Ibid., 193.

44. Quoted in Shimoni, *The Zionist Ideology*, 291.

45. Ibid.

46. Quoted in Rubinstein, *The Zionist Dream Revisited*, 34.

47. Quoted in Segev, *1949: The First Israelis*, 287–288.

48. Gershom Scholem, interview with Ehud Ben Ezer in *Unease in Zion* (New York: Quadrangle Books, 1974), 273, 275. Quoted James S. Diamond, *Homeland or Holy Land? The "Canaanite" Critique of Israel* (Bloomington: Indiana University Press, 1986), 12.

49. Zerubavel, *Recovered Roots*, 27.

50. "Canaanism" was actually the name given to this ideology by its opponents, but it became generally known by this term. For an examination of Canaanism, see Diamond, *Homeland or Holy Land?*; Yaacov Shavit, *The New Hebrew Nation: A Study in Israeli Heresy and Fantasy* (London: Frank Cass, 1987); and Boas Evron, " 'Canaanism': Solutions and Problems," *The Jerusalem Quarterly*, no. 44 (Fall 1987): 51–72.

51. Yonatan Ratosh was his pen name. His real name was Uriel Halpern.

52. The Canaanite movement first started as a literary movement in Paris in the 1920s. It became a political movement in 1944 with the establishment of the "Committee for the Formation of Hebrew Youth."

53. Diamond, *Homeland or Holy Land?*, 3.

54. Shavit, *The New Hebrew Nation*, 5.

55. Quoted in Diamond, *Homeland or Holy Land?*, 61.

56. Ibid., 4.

57. Hannan Hever, "Territoriality and Otherness in Hebrew Literature of the War of Independence," in *The Other in Jewish Thought and History: Constructions of Jewish Culture and Identity*, ed., Laurence J. Silberstein and Robert L. Cohn (New York: New York University Press, 1994), 239.

58. Baruch Kurzweil, "The Nature and Origins of the Young Hebrews (Canaanite) Movement," in *Our New Literature—Continuation or Revolution?* [Hebrew] (Tel Aviv: Schocken Books, 1960), 274.

59. Akiva Orr, *Israel: Politics, Myths and Identity Crises* (London: Pluto, 1994), 51.

60. Arthur Koestler, *Promise and Fulfillment: Palestine 1917–1949* (London, 1949), 331. Quoted in Harold Fisch, *The Zionist Revolution: A New Perspective* (New York: St. Martin's, 1978), 105.

61. Isaiah Berlin, "The Origins of Israel," in *The Power of Ideas*, ed. Henry Hardy (London: Chatto and Windus, 2000), 158.

62. The term comes from the Hebrew word *tzabar*, the name of a local pear cactus, which has a prickly exterior hiding a soft heart, a characteristic supposedly shared by native Israelis.

63. Almog, *The Sabra*, 5.

64. Ibid., 262.

65. Ibid., 121–123.

66. Ibid., 233–244.

67. Ibid., 8. The use of the masculine pronoun in this sentence is intentional since the classic, idealized, sabra was male.

68. Ibid., 258.

69. Cited in Meyer, *Jewish Identity in the Modern World*, 74.

70. Ibid.
71. Liebman, "Religion and Modernity," 89.
72. Quoted in Urian and Karsh, "Introduction," in Urian and Karsh, *In Search of Identity*, 1.
73. On the website of Israel's Ministry of Foreign Affairs <http://www.israel.org/peace/independ.html>
74. By the end of the 1948 war, approximately 156,000 Arabs were left inside Israel's new borders. The wave of Jewish immigration in the first years of the state reduced the percentage of Arabs in the population from about 14 percent in 1949 to about 11 percent in 1955. Avraham Selah, "Arabs of Israel," in *Political Dictionary of the State of Israel*, 2nd ed., ed. Susan Hattis Rolef (New York: Macmillan, 1993), 40.
75. They also had their land expropriated by the state, much of it given to Jewish settlements in government attempts to increase the Jewish presence in northern and western Galilee, the centers of Palestinian population. For a detailed examination of the Israeli government's use of legal instruments to confiscate Arab lands between 1948–1960 see Geremy Forman and Alexander Kedar, "From Arab Land to 'Israel Lands': The Legal Dispossession of the Palestinians Displaced by Israel in the Wake of 1948," *Environment and Planning D: Society and Space* 22 (2004): 809–830.
76. Ilan Peleg, "Israel's Constitutional Order and *Kulturkampf*: The Role of Ben-Gurion," *Israel Studies* 3, 1998, no. 1: 240–241.
77. Rebecca B. Kook, *The Logic of Democratic Exclusion: African Americans in the United States and Palestinian Citizens in Israel* (Lanham, MD: Lexington Books, 2002), 57–73.
78. Joel Migdal, *Through the Lens of Israel: Explorations in State and Society* (Albany, NY: State University of New York Press, 2001), 158.
79. Yossi Shain, "Israel's State and Civil Society after 50 Years of Independence," *Palestinian Academic Society for the Study of International Affairs* (December 1997): 226.
80. Almog, *The Sabra*, 29.
81. Quoted in Segev, *1949: The First Israelis*, 268.
82. Knesset Protocol, August 19, 1952. Quoted in Ben-Eliezer, "A Nation-in-Arms," 265.
83. Peter Y. Medding, *Mapai in Israel* (Cambridge: Cambridge University Press), 1972.
84. For a detailed analysis of the doctrine of *mamlachtiyut* and its application in the period 1948–1967 see, Peter Y. Medding, *The Founding of Israeli Democracy, 1948–1967* (Oxford: Oxford University Press, 1990), 134–177.
85. Quoted in Ram, "Zionist Historiography and the Invention of Modern Jewish Nationhood," 107.
86. Charles S. Liebman and Eliezer Don-Yehiya, *Civil Religion in Israel: Traditional Judaism and Political Culture in the Jewish State* (Berkeley: University of California Press, 1983), 84.
87. Ibid., 84.
88. David Biale, *Power and Powerlessness in Jewish History* (New York: Schocken, 1986), 152.
89. Quoted in Segev, *1949: The First Israelis*, 287.
90. Shmuel Sandler, *The State of Israel, the Land of Israel: The Statist and Ethnonational Dimensions of Foreign Policy* (Westport, CT: Greenwood, 1993), 101.

91. Quoted in Sandler, *The State of Israel, the Land of Israel*, 101.
92. This inevitably gave rise to a debate, which continues to this day, over the question of "who is a Jew?"
93. Eliezer Schweid, "Judaism in Israeli Culture," in Urian and Karsh, eds., *In Search of Identity*, 18.
94. For an extensive discussion of Israel's relationship with the Holocaust see, Tom Segev, *The Seventh Million: The Israelis and the Holocaust* (New York: Hill and Wang, 1993).
95. Yechiam Weitz, "Political Dimensions of Holocaust Memory in Israel During the 1950s," in *Wistrich and Ohana*, eds., *The Shaping of Israeli Identity*, 142–143.
96. Zerubavel, *Recovered Roots*, 76.
97. On the website of Israel's Ministry of Foreign Affairs <http://www.israel.org/peace/independ.html>
98. Schweid, "Judaism in Israeli Culture," 18.
99. Ibid.
100. Ibid., 19.
101. Robert Wistrich and David Ohana, "Introduction," in Wistrich and Ohana eds., *The Shaping of Israeli Identity*, xii.
102. Amos Elon, *A Blood-Dimmed Tide: Dispatches from the Middle East* (New York: Columbia University Press, 1997), 272.
103. Eichmann was found guilty and sentenced to death—the first and only death sentence to be passed in Israel (carried out in 1962).
104. Zerubavel, *Recovered Roots*, 195.
105. Liebman, "Religion and Modernity," 89–90.
106. Kimmerling, "Between the Primordial and the Civil Definitions of the Collective Identity," 268–269. Kimmerling cites survey results examining the collective identity of Jewish youth in Israel carried out in 1965 and 1974 that reveal the growth of "Jewish" as opposed to "Israeli" identity. Between these dates, those youth of western origin identifying themselves as "Israeli" dropped from 50 to 41 percent, and those of eastern origin identifying themselves as "Israeli" dropped from 30 to 24 percent. Even amongst those who defined themselves as "non-religious," Jewish identity rose from 4 to 14 percent among the youth of western origin, and from 5 to 21 percent among the youth of eastern origin. Thus since the mid-1960s, there was a clear increase in self-identification as "Jewish" and a decrease in "Israeli" identification.
107. Erik Cohen, "Citizenship, Nationality and Religion in Israel and Thailand," in *Comparative Social Dynamics*, ed. Erik Cohen, Moshe Lissak, and Uri Almagor: 90. Boulder, CO: Westview, 1985.
108. Bernard Susser, "Commentary," in Liebman and Katz, eds., *The Jewishness of Israelis*, 168.
109. Liebman, "Religion and Modernity," 94.
110. Charles S. Liebman and Bernard Susser, "Judaism and Jewishness in the Jewish State," *The Annals of the American Academy of Political and Social Science* 555 (January 1998): 23.
111. Seliktar, *New Zionism and the Foreign Policy System of Israel*, 124.
112. Liebman, "Religion and Modernity," 91.
113. Aronoff, *Israeli Visions and Divisions*, 6.

114. Alan Dowty, "Is there a Jewish Politics?" in *The Role of Domestic Politics in Israeli Peacemaking*, ed. David Hornik (Jerusalem: The Leonard Davis Institute for International Relations, September 1997), 8.
115. Cited in Seliktar, *New Zionism and the Foreign Policy System of Israel*, 121.
116. Cohen, "Citizenship, Nationality and Religion in Israel and Thailand," 90.
117. *Davar*, October 5, 1979. Quoted in Rubinstein, *The Zionist Dream Revisited*, 97.
118. The distribution of religious observance amongst Israeli Jews has remained basically unchanged since the 1960s. Fourteen percent define themselves as "strictly observant," 24 percent as "observant to a great extent," 41 percent as "somewhat observant," and 21 percent as "totally non-observant." Figures cited in Shlomit Levy, Hanna Levinsohn, and Elihu Katz, "Beliefs, Observances and Social Interaction Among Israeli Jews: The Guttman Institute Report," in Liebman and Katz, eds., *The Jewishness of Israelis*, 16.
119. A watershed in this process was the emergence in early 1971 of the "Black Panthers" movement among disaffected, poor, urban Mizrahi youth. Sami Shalom Chetrit, "Mizrahi Politics in Israel: Between Integration and Alternative," *Journal of Palestine Studies* 29, no. 4 (2000): 53.
120. In the 1981 election, around 70 percent of the Labor vote was Ashkenazi and about 70 percent of the Likud vote was Mizrahi and a similar distribution occurred in the 1984 election. Seliktar, *New Zionism and the Foreign Policy System of Israel*, 145.
121. Ibid., 131.
122. Quoted in Joseph Massad, "Zionism's Internal Others: Israel and the Oriental Jews," *Journal of Palestine Studies* 25, no. 4 (1996): 57.
123. Raphael Cohen-Almagor, "Cultural Pluralism and the Israeli Nation-Building Ideology," *International Journal of Middle East Studies* 27 (1995): 464.
124. The political dominance of the Labor party had been steadily eroding for some time before the 1977 election. Since the 1959 Knesset elections when Mapai received forty-seven seats (the most it ever received and this still only amounted to just over a third of the total seats in the Knesset), it lost seats in every subsequent election (despite merging with Ahdut Ha'avodah in 1965 and with Mapam in 1968). For an analysis of the rise and fall of the "dominant party system" led by Mapai/Labor that was established in the 1930s and lasted until 1977 election, see Myron J. Aronoff, *Power and Ritual in the Israel Labor Party* (Armonk, NY: M.E. Sharpe, 1993).
125. Don Peretz and Sammy Smooha, "The Earthquake: Israel's Ninth Knesset Elections," *Middle East Journal* 31 (Summer 1977): 251–266.
126. Alan Dowty, "Zionism's Greatest Conceit," *Israel Studies* 3, 1998, no. 1: 17.
127. Segre, *A Crisis of Identity*, 150.
128. Jacob Abadi, *Israel's Leadership: From Utopia to Crisis* (Westport, CT: Greenwood, 1993), 97.

Chapter 2   Between Isolation and Integration: Foreign Policy and Israeli National Identity

1. Quoted in Myron J. Aronoff, "Myths, Symbols and Rituals of the Emerging State," in *New Perspectives on Israeli History: The Early Years of the State*, ed. Laurence J. Silberstein (New York: New York University Press, 1991): 178.

2. Menachem Begin, *The Revolt*, trans. by Shmuel Katz (New York: Henry Schuman, 1951), 26–46.
3. Quoted in Alan Dowty, *The Jewish State: A Century Later* (Berkeley: University of California Press, 1998), 186.
4. Aaron Klieman, *Israel & The World After Forty Years* (McLean, VA: Pergamon-Brassey's, 1990), xiii.
5. The only book to offer a theoretically rigorous examination of Israeli foreign policy in its entirety is Michael Brecher's landmark study, *The Foreign Policy System of Israel: Setting, Images, Process* (New Haven: Yale University Press, 1972).
6. Shibley Telhami, "Israeli Foreign Policy: A Realist Ideal-Type or a Breed of Its Own?" In *Israel in Comparative Perspective*, ed. Michael Barnett: 30.
7. Ibid., 32.
8. Ibid., 30.
9. Avner Yaniv, *Dilemmas of Security: Politics, Strategy, and the Israeli Experience in Lebanon* (Oxford: Oxford University Press, 1987), 11.
10. See, Avi Shlaim, "Conflicting Approaches to Israel's Relations with the Arabs: Ben-Gurion and Sharett, 1953–1956," *The Middle East Journal* 37, no. 2 (1983): 280–311; Yaacov Bar-Siman-Tov, "Israel's Peace-Making with the Palestinians: Change and Legitimacy," in *From Rabin to Netanyahu: Israel's Troubled Agenda*, ed. Efraim Karsh (London: Frank Cass, 1997), 170–186.
11. For a bureaucratic politics account see, Lewis Brownstein, "Decision Making in Israeli Foreign Policy: An Unplanned Process," *Political Science Quarterly* 92, no. 2 (1977): 259–279. For a party political analysis see, Avi Shlaim and Avner Yaniv, "Domestic Politics and Foreign Policy in Israel," *International Affairs* 56, no. 2 (1980): 242–262; Uri Bialer, *Between East and West: Israel's Foreign Policy Orientation 1948–1956* (Cambridge: Cambridge University Press, 1990).
12. Yagil Levy, *Trial and Error: Israel's Route from War to De-escalation* (Albany, NY: State University of New York Press, 1997).
13. For example, Samuel J. Roberts, *Party and Policy in Israel: The Battle between Hawks and Doves* (Boulder, CO: Westview, 1990); and Sasson Sofer, *Zionism and the Foundations of Israeli Diplomacy* (Cambridge: Cambridge University Press, 1998).
14. Roberts, *Party and Policy in Israel*.
15. Quoted in Shlomo Avineri, "Ideology and Israel's Foreign Policy," *The Jerusalem Quarterly*, no. 37 (1986): 11.
16. Quoted in Brecher, *The Foreign Policy System of Israel*, 236.
17. Ibid., 232 (emphasis in original).
18. Ibid.
19. Ibid., 229.
20. Ibid., 230.
21. Ibid., 229.
22. Ibid., 231.
23. Ibid., 276 (emphasis in original).
24. Sofer, *Zionism and the Foundations of Israeli Diplomacy*, 365.
25. Seliktar, *New Zionism and the Foreign Policy System of Israel*, 107.
26. Ibid.
27. Quoted in Asher Arian, *Security Threatened: Surveying Israeli Opinion on Peace and War* (Cambridge: Cambridge University Press, 1995), 163.

28. Eban was Israel's first and long-serving ambassador to the UN as well as to the United States, and was also Israel's foreign minister at the time of the 1967 war. Abba Eban, *My Country* (Jerusalem: Weidenfeld and Nicolson, 1972), 180.
29. Arian, *Security Threatened*, 161.
30. Ibid., 164.
31. Ibid., 186. Arian finds that this belief crossed over demographic divisions in the population, whether in terms of ethnicity, religiosity, class, education, age or gender. The fact that it is shared by both young and old suggests that it has not been diminished by generational change and testifies to powerful processes of attitudinal socialization. Levels of education and religiosity, however, were more closely related to the strength of this belief, with the most educated and secular most likely to reject it. Ibid., 182–186.
32. Rubinstein, *The Zionist Dream Revisited*, 80.
33. Klieman, *Israel & The World After Forty Years*, 53.
34. Stewart Alsop, "Again, the Masada Complex," *Newsweek*, March 19, 1973, 104. Quoted in Yael Zerubavel, "The Multivocality of a National Myth: Memory and Counter-Memories of Masada," *The Shaping of Israeli Identity*, in Wistrich and Ohana, ed., 123.
35. *Ha'aretz*, April 29, 1973. Quoted in Zerubavel, "The Multivocality of a National Myth," 128.
36. Rejwan, "Israeli Attitudes to the Arab World," 26. Quoted in Brecher, *The Foreign Policy System of Israel*, 301.
37. Quoted in Silberstein, *The Postzionism Debates*, 216, note 15.
38. Quoted in Brecher, *The Foreign Policy System of Israel*, 302.
39. Bernard Lewis, *Semites and Anti-Semites: An Inquiry into Conflict and Prejudice* (London: Phoenix, 1997), 192–235.
40. One prominent dissenter from this policy was Moshe Sharett, foreign minister from 1948–1956 and prime minister from 1954–1955. Sharett urged a more moderate Israeli policy and a more active pursuit of peace believing that Israeli policy could induce Arab moderation and promote conciliation and compromise between the two peoples. His view, however, was strictly a minority one.
41. Quoted in Joel Benin, "Israel at Forty: The Political Economy/Political Culture of Constant Conflict," *Arab Studies Quarterly* 10, no. 4 (1988): 436.
42. Quoted in Brecher, *The Foreign Policy System of Israel*, 284.
43. "Interview with Yitzhak Rabin," *Bamahane*, December 28, 1965, 4. Quoted in Efraim Inbar, *Rabin and Israel's National Security* (Baltimore: Johns Hopkins University Press, 1999), 11.
44. *Maariv*, September 25, 1974. Quoted in Efraim Inbar, "Israeli National Security, 1973–1996," *The Annals of the American Academy* 555 (January 1998): 66.
45. Efraim Inbar, "Attitudes toward War in the Israeli Political Elite," *Middle East Journal* 44 (1990): 431–445.
46. Ibid., 438.
47. Ibid.
48. *Parliamentary Minutes*, June 8, 1982, 2746. Quoted in Inbar, "Attitudes toward War in the Israeli Political Elite," 438.
49. *Parliamentary Minutes*, June 28, 1982, 2915. Quoted in Inbar, "Attitudes toward War in the Israeli Political Elite," 439.
50. *Parliamentary Minutes*, June 29, 1982, 2961. Quoted in Inbar, "Attitudes toward War in the Israeli Political Elite," 439.

51. Mead, *Mind, Self and Society.*
52. G.H. Mead, *Mind, Self and Society* (Chicago: University of Chicago Press, 1934).
53. On the role of "significant others" in helping to define a national identity, see Anna Triandafyllidou, "National Identity and the 'Other,'" *Ethnic and Racial Studies* 21, no. 4 (July 1998): 593–612.
54. Quoted in Efraim Inbar, "Israeli National Security 1973–1996," 66.
55. Sandler, *The State of Israel, the Land of Israel,* 106.
56. Quoted in Ilan Peleg, *Begin's Foreign Policy, 1977–1983: Israel's Move to the Right* (Westport, CT: Greenwood, 1987), 33.
57. Quoted in Eric Silver, *Begin: The Haunted Prophet* (New York: Random House, 1984), 118.
58. Peleg, *Begin's Foreign Policy,* 66.
59. Press Conference with Prime Minister Begin, IDF Chief of Staff Eitan, IAF (Israel Air Forces) Commander Ivri and Director of Military Intelligence Saguy, June 9, 1981, in *Israel's Foreign Relations: Selected Documents 1981–1982,* vol. 7, ed. Meron Medzini (Jerusalem: Ministry of Foreign Affairs, 1988), 74–80.
60. Quoted in Scott Atran, "Stones against the Iron Fist, Terror within the Nation: Alternating Structures of Violence and Cultural Identity in the Israeli-Palestinian Conflict," *Politics & Society* 18, no. 4 (1990): 498.
61. Peleg, *Begin's Foreign Policy,* 67.
62. Ibid., 56–57 (emphasis in original).
63. Ibid., 63.
64. Quoted in Abadi, *Israel's Leadership,* 97–98.
65. Sandler, *The State of Israel, the Land of Israel,* 267.
66. Avineri, "Ideology and Israel's Foreign Policy," 3.
67. Amos Oz, "The Power and the Purpose," in *The Slopes of Lebanon,* trans. by Nicholas de Lange (London: Vintage, 1991), 75.
68. Amos Oz, "He Raises the Weak from the Dust and Lifts the Poor Out of the Dirt," in Nicholas de Lange, *The Slopes of Lebanon,* 236.
69. Amos Oz, "Whose Holy Land? Divided Israel in Palestine," in *Israel, Palestine and Peace,* trans. by Nicholas de Lange (New York: Harcourt Brace, 1995), 83.
70. Address to the Knesset by Prime Minister Begin, October 18, 1982, in *Israel's Foreign Relations, Selected Documents 1982–1984,* vol. 8, ed. Meron Medzini (Jerusalem: Ministry of Foreign Affairs, 1988), 234.
71. Address by Prime Minister Begin to Israel Bonds Conference, August 14, 1983, in *Israel's Foreign Relations,* vol. 8, ed. Medzini, 442.
72. Statement in the Knesset by Prime Minister Begin on the Reagan Plan, December 8, 1982, in *Israel's Foreign Relations,* vol. 8, ed. Medzini, 204.
73. The settlement activities, land control, economic, administrative, and legal arrangements designed by the Begin government to ensure total Jewish control over the West Bank and Gaza are well documented in a number of sources. Perhaps the fullest account is provided by the former deputy mayor of Jerusalem Meron Benvenisti in *The West Bank Data Project: A Survey of Israel's Policies* (Washington, DC: American Enterprise Institute, 1984).
74. Peleg, *Begin's Foreign Policy,* 110–111.
75. Ian S. Lustick, *Unsettled States, Disputed Lands: Britain and Ireland, France and Algeria, Israel and the West Bank-Gaza* (Ithaca: Cornell University Press, 1993), 352–395.

76. Ian S. Lustick, "Hegemony and the Riddle of Nationalism: The Dialectics of Religion and Nationalism in the Middle East," *Logos: A Journal of Modern Society and Culture* 1, no. 3 (2002): 38.
77. Ibid., 39.
78. Amos Perlmutter, "Begin's Rhetoric and Sharon's Tactics," *Foreign Affairs* 61, no. 1 (1982): 71.
79. Dayan and Weizman were instrumental, for instance, in moderating Begin's position in the negotiations over the Camp David Accords and the Egyptian-Israeli peace treaty, and persuading him to make significant concessions.
80. Perlmutter, "Begin's Rhetoric and Sharon's Tactics," 74.
81. Ibid., 71.
82. The basic assumption of Begin, Sharon, and IDF Chief of Staff Eitan was that the PLO's political strength rested upon its military capabilities.
83. *Maariv*, July 2, 1982. Quoted in Gad Barzilai, *Wars, Internal Conflicts, and Political Order: A Jewish Democracy in the Middle East* (Albany, NY: State University of New York Press, 1996), 143.
84. Statement in the Knesset by Prime Minister Begin, June 8, 1982, in *Israel's Foreign Relations*, vol. 8, ed. Medzini, 9–10.
85. Statement in the Knesset by Prime Minister Begin, 1 June 1983, in *Israel's Foreign Relations*, vol. 8, ed. Medzini, 425–426.
86. Barzilai, *Wars, Internal Conflicts, and Political Order*, 146–147.
87. Interview with Defense Minister Arens in *Davar*, May 17, 1983, in *Israel's Foreign Relations*, vol. 8, ed. Medzini, 423–424.
88. Colin Shindler, *Israel, Likud and the Zionist Dream: Power, Politics and Ideology from Begin to Netanyahu* (London: I.B. Tauris, 1995), 101.
89. Ibid.,136.
90. Ibid.
91. Yoram Peri, "Coexistence or Hegemony? Shifts in the Israeli Security Concept," in *The Roots of Begin's Success: The 1981 Israeli Elections*, ed. Dan Caspi, Abraham Diskin, and Emanuel Gutman (New York: St. Martin's, 1984), 202. See also, Dan Horowitz, "Israel's War in Lebanon: New Patterns of Strategic Thinking and Civilian-Military Relations," in *Israeli Society and its Defense Establishment: The Social and Political Impact of a Protracted Violent Conflict*, ed. Moshe Lissak (London: Frank Cass, 1984), 83–102.
92. Peri, "Coexistence or Hegemony?," 203.
93. Mira Sucharov, "Types and Roles in International Relations: Beyond the Green Room," paper presented at the annual meeting of the International Studies Association, February 1999, Washington DC.
94. Efraim Inbar, "The 'No Choice War' Debate in Israel," *Journal of Strategic Studies* 12 (1989): 22–37.
95. Ibid., 25.
96. In essence, Begin tried to redefine the concept of "war of no choice" in much narrower terms as referring solely to a war directly initiated by the Arabs. In so doing, he sought to empty the concept of its normative connotations. Ibid., 27.
97. Ibid.
98. Address by Prime Minister Begin at the National Defense College, August 8, 1982, in *Israel's Foreign Relations*, vol. 8, ed. Medzini, 136.
99. Inbar, "The 'No Choice War' Debate in Israel," 28.

100. George Simmel, *Conflict* (New York: Free Press, 1955).
101. Muzafer Sherif and Carolyn Sherif, *Groups in Harmony and Tension: An Integration of Studies on Intergroup Relations* (New York: Harper, 1953).
102. Yitzhak Rabin, *The Rabin Memoirs*, 2nd ed. (Berkeley: University of California Press, 1996, reprint).
103. Rabin, *The Rabin Memoirs*, 335.
104. The far-right Tehiya party, for instance, gained a 74 percent increase in electoral support in the 1984 election compared to the one in 1981. Barzilai, *Wars, Internal Conflicts, and Political Order*, 154.
105. Ram, "Postnationalist Pasts," 525.
106. Ephraim Lapid, interview by author, July 21, 2000, Tel Aviv, Israel. Lapid was IDF spokesman and member of the General Staff between 1984 and 1989.
107. Some of these individuals later attained positions of power and influence within Israeli politics, such as Avraham Burg who was a leader of the Peace Now movement at the time of the war in Lebanon and went on to become speaker of the Knesset and a leading figure in the Labor party. Other prominent Labor doves like Yossi Beilin and Yael Tamir were also involved in opposition to the war.
108. Shimon Peres, *The New Middle East* (New York: Henry Holt, 1993), 56.
109. Michael Keren, *The Pen and the Sword: Israeli Intellectuals and the Making of the Nation-State* (Boulder, CO: Westview, 1989), 94.
110. In 1982, there were about 3,000 volunteer associations and interest groups officially registered with the Israeli Ministry of the Interior. By 2000, that number had spectacularly grown to 30,000. Angelika Timm, "Israeli Civil Society Facing New Challenges," *Israel Studies Forum* 17, no. 1 (Fall 2000): 47.
111. Peleg, *Begin's Foreign Policy*, 170.
112. Israel's parliamentary democracy is based on a system of proportional representation in which the entire country represents one constituency and ballots are cast for parties rather than individuals. Parties thus gain seats in the Knesset directly in accordance with their share of the national vote (with a 1 percent parliamentary threshold in the 1980s which was later raised to 1.5 percent). This electoral system means that the composition of the Knesset closely mirrors the social and political divisions within the country at large. As such, election results serve as reliable indicators of the degree of the population's social and political cohesion or fragmentation.
113. Prime Minister Peres to the United Jewish Appeal Leadership Conference, September 16, 1984, in *Israel's Foreign Relations: Selected Documents, 1984–1988*, vol. 9, ed. Meron Medzini (Jerusalem: Ministry of Foreign Affairs, 1992), 17.
114. Statement in the Knesset by prime minister designate Shamir, October 20, 1986, in *Israel's Foreign Relations*, vol. 9, ed. Medzini, 516.
115. Statement in the Knesset by Prime Minister Shamir, December 23, 1988, in *Israel's Foreign Relations: Selected Documents, 1988–1992*, vol. 11, ed. Meron Medzini (Jerusalem: Ministry of Foreign Affairs, 1992), 11.
116. Lustick, *Unsettled States, Disputed Lands*, 368–373.
117. Ibid., 372.
118. Poll conducted by *Dahaf*. Ibid., 415.
119. Interview with Defense Minister Arens in *Davar*, May 17, 1983, in *Israel's Foreign Relations*, vol. 8, ed. Medzini, 423–424.

120. Interview with Prime Minister Shamir on Israel radio, May 7, 1984, in *Israel's Foreign Relations*, vol. 8, ed. Medzini, 562–563.
121. Lustick, *Unsettled States, Disputed Lands*, 359.
122. Lustick, "Hegemony and the Riddle of Nationalism," 42. Ibid., 352–395.
123. Yossi Ahimeir, Shamir's political advisor and spokesman (1984–1992) and director-general of the Prime Minister's Office under Shamir (1988–1992), claims that Shamir would not compromise over his principles, at most he would make temporary compromises in order to achieve his goals. Moreover, according to Ahimeir, Shamir strongly believed that Israel could have peace and keep possession of the territories. Yossi Ahimeir, interview by author, August 9, 2000, Ramat Gan, Israel.
124. Another example of Likud's attempt to project a moderate public image was Shamir's refusal to enter a coalition government with the far-right parties after the 1988 election. Shamir wanted to define the Likud as Israel's centrist party and therefore avoided associating it with the far-right parties. Yossi Ahimeir, interview by author.
125. Shindler, *Israel, Likud and the Zionist Dream*, 211.
126. Ian S. Lustick, "The Fetish of Jerusalem: A Hegemonic Analysis," *Israel in Comparative Perspective*, in Michael Barnett, ed., 147.
127. Yaron Ezrahi, *Rubber Bullets: Power and Conscience in Modern Israel* (New York: Farrar, Straus and Giroux, 1997), 207–209.
128. In order to suppress the uprising without killing too many demonstrators, Israeli soldiers were issued with rubber and plastic bullets that were designed to cause minimal injury.
129. Ezrahi, *Rubber Bullets*, 216.
130. Mark Tessler, "The Intifada and Political Discourse in Israel," *Journal of Palestine Studies* 19 (1990): no. 45.
131. This principle has long been a central aspect of Israeli military culture. Broadly speaking, it refers to ethical military conduct (such as restraint in the use of force, and minimizing harm to enemy civilians).
132. Yoram Peri, "Afterword: Rabin: From Mr. Security to Nobel Peace Prize Winner," in Rabin, *The Rabin Memoirs*, 355.
133. Daniel Bar-Tal and Neta Oren, *Ethos as an Expression of Identity: Its Changes in Transition from Conflict to Peace in the Israeli Case*, Davis Occasional Papers, no. 83, November 2000, The Leonard Davis Institute for International Relations, Hebrew University, Jerusalem, pp. 13–14.
134. Ezrahi, *Rubber Bullets*, 234.
135. *Maariv*, February 3, 1988. Quoted in Inbar, *Rabin and Israel's National Security*, 9.
136. Statement in the Knesset by Prime Minister Shamir, March 29, 1988, in *Israel's Foreign Relations: Selected Documents, 1984–1988*, vol. 10, ed. Meron Medzini (Jerusalem: Ministry of Foreign Affairs, 1992), 902.
137. Quoted in Klieman, *Israel & the World after 40 Years*, 51.
138. Arian, *Security Threatened*, 174.
139. Quoted in Klieman, *Israel & the World after 40 Years*, 63.
140. Jewish suffering was viewed theologically as an affirmation of the Jewish people's "chosenness" (thereby reinforcing the Jews' commitment to the preservation of Judaism and Jewish tradition).

141. Benny Morris, *Righteous Victims: A History of the Zionist-Arab Conflict, 1881–1999* (New York: Alfred A. Knopf, 2000).
142. Lustick, "The Fetish of Jerusalem," 147.
143. Arian, *Security Threatened*, 68.
144. Lustick, "The Fetish of Jerusalem," 147.
145. *The Jerusalem Post*, May 9, 1989. Quoted in Lustick, "The Fetish of Jerusalem," 147.
146. Lustick, "The Fetish of Jerusalem," 148.
147. Tessler, "The Intifada and Political Discourse in Israel," 48.
148. Interview with Prime Minister Shamir in the *Jerusalem Post*, January 13, 1989, in *Israel's Foreign Relations*, vol. 11, ed. Medzini, 22.
149. Statement in the Knesset by Prime Minister Shamir, March 29, 1988, in *Israel's Foreign Relations*, vol. 10, ed. Medzini, 902.
150. Interview with Prime Minister Shamir on Israel Radio, February 19, 1989, in *Israel's Foreign Relations*, vol. 11, ed. Medzini, 48.
151. Interview with Prime Minister Shamir on Israel Television, March 26, 1989, in *Israel's Foreign Relations*, vol. 11, ed. Medzini, 96.
152. David Kimche, director-general of Israel's Foreign Ministry from 1979 to 1986, claims that Shamir was a very suspicious person. He did not trust the Arabs, the Europeans, or even the United States. The only people he trusted were the Jews. David Kimche, interview by author, August 8, 2000, Ramat Hasharon, Israel.
153. Interview with Prime Minister Shamir in the *Jerusalem Post*, January 13, 1989, in *Israel's Foreign Relations*, vol. 11, ed. Medzini, 19–20.
154. The "Jordanian option" referred to the desire of leading Labor party figures such as Rabin and Peres to resolve the Palestinian issue by returning the West Bank to Jordanian rule (as it had been under between 1948–1967), rather than allow the establishment of a separate Palestinian state in the area. The hope of negotiating a territorial settlement with the Hashemite regime in Jordan rather than with the Palestinians, however, was extinguished after King Hussein renounced Jordan's claim to the West Bank in 1988 and accepted the PLO as the sole legitimate representative of the Palestinians.
155. Moshe Arens, Israel's foreign minister at the time, cites this as Shamir's chief motivation for proposing the Shamir-Rabin peace plan in 1989. Moshe Arens, interview by author, September 20, 2000, Jerusalem, Israel.
156. Concern about the emerging rift between Diaspora Jewry and Israel as a result of the Intifada led the Shamir government to organize a "Conference on Jewish Solidarity with Israel" in March 1989. The aim was to underline the unity of world Jewry and the continued backing of Diaspora Jewry for the positions of the Israeli government.
157. Yossi Ahimeir, interview by author.
158. Statement in the Knesset by Prime Minister Shamir on the Peace Initiative, May 17, 1989, in *Israel's Foreign Relations*, vol. 11, ed. Medzini, 1.

Chapter 3   Out of the Ghetto: The Oslo Peace Process and Israeli National Identity

1. Yitzhak Rabin, "What Kind of Israel Do You Want?" speech reprinted in English in Rabin, *The Rabin Memoirs, appendix D*, 396.

2. From the text of the address by Yitzhak Shamir at the inaugural ceremony of the 13th Knesset, *BBC Summary of World Broadcasts*, July 15, 1992.

3. Haim Barkai, "Economic Policy," *Political Dictionary of the State of Israel*, in Rolef, ed., 362.

4. For a detailed analysis of the events that produced the 1993 Oslo Accords, see David Makovsky, *Making Peace with the PLO: The Rabin Government's Road to the Oslo Accord* (Boulder, CO: Westview, 1995). For first-hand accounts by the leading Israeli participants in the negotiations leading to the Oslo Accords see, Yossi Beilin, *Touching Peace: From the Oslo Accord to a Final Agreement* (London: Weidenfeld and Nicolson, 1999); Shimon Peres, *Battling for Peace: Memoirs* (London: Orion, 1995); Uri Savir, *The Process: 1,100 Days That Changed the Middle East* (New York: Random House, 1998).

5. Although the Oslo Accords would not have come about were it not for the PLO's willingness to denounce terrorism, recognize Israel, and accept a Palestinian state in the West Bank and Gaza, the PLO had already expressed a readiness to accept a two-state solution and to negotiate with Israel by the late 1980s. Thus, the major policy shift that occurred prior to the Oslo Accords concerned Israel, not the PLO.

6. Operation Desert Storm began at 7 p.m. Eastern Standard Time on January 16, which was 3 a.m. January 17, Baghdad time.

7. Sharon, Weizman, and Arens all advocated an Israeli military response. Moshe Arens, interview by author.

8. Gad Barzilai and Efraim Inbar, "Do Wars Have an Impact?: Israeli Public Opinion After the Gulf War," *The Jerusalem Journal of International Relations* 14, no. 1 (1992): 49.

9. Jacob Abadi, "The Gulf War and its Implications for Israel," *Journal of South Asian and Middle Eastern Studies* 17, no. 3 (1994): 56.

10. Arian, *Security Threatened*, 87.

11. Eitan Haber, director-general of the Office of the Prime Minister under Rabin (1992–1995), interview by author, July 17, 2000, Ramat Gan, Israel.

12. *Ha'aretz*, July 20, 1993.

13. Barzilai and Inbar, "Do Wars Have an Impact?," 49.

14. Officially, the Palestinian representatives in Madrid and in the subsequent rounds of talks in Washington were part of a joint Jordanian-Palestinian delegation.

15. The United States was the chief sponsor of the conference as it was eager to take advantage of the new strategic environment in the Middle East after the end of the Cold War and the Gulf War to bring peace and stability to the region.

16. David Kimche, interview by author.

17. Bar-Siman-Tov, "Israel's Peace-Making with the Palestinians," 171.

18. Savir, "The Process," 5.

19. Yossi Ahimeir, interview by author.

20. Clyde Haberman, "Shamir Admits Plan to Stall Talks For 10 Years," *New York Times*, June 27, 1992.

21. Yossi Ahimeir, interview by author.

22. Interview with Prime Minister Shamir in the *Jerusalem Post*, April 6, 1991, in *Israel's Foreign Relations*, vol. 11, ed. Medzini, 493.

23. Independence Day Message by Prime Minister Shamir, May 7, 1992, in *Israel's Foreign Relations*, vol. 11, ed. Medzini, 735.

24. Address by Prime Minister Shamir to B'nai B'rith Conference, May 11, 1988, in *Israel's Foreign Relations*, vol. 11, ed. Medzini, 924–925.

25. Michael Barnett, "Who Lost Judea and Samaria? *Israel's National Identity Debate After Peace*," paper presented at the conference, "Identities in Transition from War to Peace," Hebrew University of Jerusalem, November 30–December 1, 1999, Jerusalem, Israel.

26. Inbar, *Rabin and Israel's National Security*.

27. Ibid., 137.

28. This possibility was heightened as a result of the "loan crisis" in the fall of 1991 when the Shamir government requested $10 million in loan guarantees from the United States. In response, the Bush Sr. administration insisted that such a loan would only be granted if the money was not used for settlement activities in the territories, a condition that Shamir opposed. The subsequent standoff between Shamir and the Bush Sr. administration (principally, U.S. Secretary of State, James Baker) led to a crisis in U.S.–Israeli relations and worries in Israel that the once unshakeable U.S.–Israeli relationship had weakened.

29. Eitan Haber, interview by author.

30. Ibid.

31. Ibid.

32. For instance, in a speech to the Knesset on October 3, 1994, outlining his government's peace policy, Rabin stated that: "We have already encountered, ad nauseam, the expression 'window of opportunity'—but what can we do? This is the correct expression for these times." Policy Statement by Prime Minister Yitzhak Rabin to the Knesset, October 3, 1994. Official transcript reprinted in Inbar, *Rabin and Israel's National Security*, 179–190.

33. Rabin referred to the PLO as the "so-called PLO" (thereby denying its claim to be a liberation movement) and to its leader, Yasser Arafat, as "a man to be mentioned often with disgust." Inbar, *Rabin and Israel's National Security*, 26.

34. Labor won 44, Meretz (composed of the former parties Mapam, Shinui, and the Civil Rights Movement) won 12. The Likud won 32 seats, Tzomet 8, the National Religious Party 6, and Moledet 3.

35. Leon T. Hadar, "The 1992 Electoral Earthquake and the Fall of the 'Second Israeli Republic,'" *Middle East Journal* 46, no. 4 (1992): 594.

36. The last Labor-led government (then named the "Alignment") was elected on December 31, 1973, and was headed by Yitzhak Rabin. It remained in power until Likud's victory in 1977.

37. Avi Diskin, "Elections to the Knesset," *Political Dictionary of the State of Israel*, in Rolef, ed., 365.

38. Arian, *Security Threatened*, 144.

39. In a 1994 survey, only 17 percent of Israeli-Jewish respondents cited either of these as reasons for Israel to withdraw from the territories. Arian, *Security Threatened*, 30–31.

40. Ibid., 154.

41. Ibid., 259. In 1986, almost 50 percent of respondents cited the belief that Israel had a "right to the land" as the main reason to hold onto the territories, whereas by 1993 only 30 percent gave this as the main reason. Ibid., 30–31.

42. Ezrahi, *Rubber Bullets*, 103.

43. Rafael Medoff and Chaim Waxman, *Historical Dictionary of Zionism* (Lanham, MD: Scarecrow Press, 2000), 176.

44. Yael Zerubavel, " 'Death on the Altar': Transforming Representations of Patriotic Sacrifice in Israeli Culture," paper presented at 16th annual meeting of the Association for Israel Studies, Tel Aviv University, June 25–27, 2000, Tel Aviv, Israel.

45. Ezrahi, *Rubber Bullets*, 163–164.

46. Arian, *Security Threatened*, 262.

47. Then IDF Chief of Staff Amnon Shahak later referred to this development in explaining the apparent rise in the number of young Israelis who sought to avoid military service, stating that: "The problem is a preference for individualism over the collective in an age of liberalism." Quoted in Clyde Haberman, "Israel's Army, Once Sacrosanct, Is Now Becoming deglamourized," *New York Times*, May 31, 1995.

48. Yoel Marcus, "Ideology Is Taking Off for Anatolia," *Ha'aretz*, July 4, 1995.

49. Erik Cohen, "Israel as a Post-Zionist Society," *The Shaping of Israeli Identity*, in Wistrich and Ohana, eds., 210.

50. Kimmerling, "Between Hegemony and Dormant *Kulturkampf* in Israel," 61.

51. Wistrich and Ohana, "Introduction," viii.

52. Ephraim Kleiman, "The Waning of Israeli *Etatisme*," *Israel Studies* 2, no. 2 (1997): 146–71.

53. Ezrahi, *Rubber Bullets*, 6.

54. The Intifada, no doubt, played a role in this development.

55. Arian, *Security Threatened*, 269.

56. Quoted in Ezrahi, *Rubber Bullets*, 71.

57. "Not a Peace Process, But Peacemaking," speech reprinted in Rabin, *The Rabin Memoirs*, 390–391.

58. Eitan Haber, interview by author.

59. *BBC Summary of World Broadcasts*, July 15, 1992.

60 Ibid.

61. Address by prime minister designate Yitzhak Rabin at the 13th Knesset, July 13, 1992. *Foreign Broadcast Information Service* (FBIS), FBIS-NES-92-135, July 14, 1992: 24.

62. Address by Prime Minister Rabin to Keren Hayesod Conference, June 23, 1993, in *Israel's Foreign Relations, 1992–1994*, vol. 13, ed. Meron Medzini (Jerusalem: Ministry of Foreign Affairs, 1995), 248.

63. Address by Prime Minister Rabin at the Central Memorial Assembly in Warsaw, April 19, 1993, in *Israel's Foreign Relations*, vol. 13, ed. Medzini, 209.

64. Savir, *The Process*, 312.

65. Aaron Klieman, "New Directions in Israel's Foreign Policy," in *Peace in the Middle East: The Challenge for Israel*, ed. Efraim Karsh (London: Frank Cass, 1994), 96.

66. Klieman, "New Directions in Israel's Foreign Policy," 109.

67. Arian's attitude survey of Israeli Jews revealed declining support for the beliefs that, "world criticism of Israeli policy stems mainly from antisemitism," "Israel is and will continue to be 'A people dwelling alone,' " and "the whole world is against us." In 1991, the year of the Gulf War and Madrid talks, 68 percent of respondents agreed with the first two statements, and 43 percent agreed with the third statement. By 1994, however, 50 percent agreed that "world criticism

of Israeli policy stems mainly from antisemitism," 54 percent that "Israel is and will continue to be 'A people dwelling alone,' " and only 35 percent that "the whole world is against us." Between the years 1991 to 1994, therefore, Israelis' perennial sense of isolation and persecution diminished. Arian, *Security Threatened,* 174–175. The Arab-Israeli peace process and improving relations with the rest of the world appear as the most likely causes for this important change in attitude. This is clearly related to the parallel shift of Israeli public opinion during the years 1991–1994 toward a more conciliatory stance vis-à-vis the Palestinians.

68. *Jerusalem Post,* January 27, 1994.
69. Remarks by Foreign Minister Peres to the diplomatic community in Israel, August 5, 1992, in *Israel's Foreign Relations,* vol. 13, ed. Medzini, 32.
70. During this time, Israel established full diplomatic relations with a host of countries from the former Soviet Union, Eastern Europe and the developing world, including China and India. In 1994, it had active diplomatic relations with 142 countries—more than it had ever had before, and a huge improvement from the 1970s when at one point it only had diplomatic relations with 65 countries. Klieman, "New Directions in Israel's Foreign Policy," 98.
71. Klieman, "New Directions in Israel's Foreign Policy," 101–102.
72. This was reflected in the restructuring of the Foreign Ministry, enlarging its policy planning staff, and elevating its offices for cultural relations, for international organization and cooperation, and for overseas information services. A new human rights division, and a department for overseeing the peace process were also set up, and the ministry's personnel and budget were increased. Klieman, "New Directions in Israel's Foreign Policy," 100–101.
73. In June 1993, Israel was nominated to its first UN committee, and in 1994 Israelis participated in a UN-sponsored peacekeeping mission in Angola and joined the UN team monitoring elections in South Africa. Israelis also began to be elected to influential UN agencies such as the International Court of Justice, the World Health Organization, and the Committee on Human Rights.
74. "What Kind of Israel Do You Want?" Rabin, *The Rabin Memoirs,* 396–399.
75. Policy Statement by Prime Minister Yitzhak Rabin to the Knesset, October 3, 1994. Official transcript reprinted in Inbar, *Rabin and Israel's National Security,* 188.
76. For example, the Rabin government ensured equal access to healthcare for Arab and Jewish citizens and equal child benefit allowances (by removing the extra benefits for families of those who had served in the IDF).
77. Quoted in Myron J. Aronoff and Pierre M. Atlas, "The Peace Process and Competing Challenges to the Dominant Zionist Discourse," in *The Middle East Peace Process: Interdisciplinary Perspectives,* ed. Ilan Peleg (Albany, NY: State University of New York Press, 1998), 45.
78. Eitan Haber, interview by author.
79. "What Kind of Israel Do You Want?" speech reprinted in Rabin, *The Rabin Memoirs,* 396–399.
80. Eitan Haber, interview by author.
81. Ibid.
82. Savir, *The Process,* 22–23.
83. This was not the only way they attempted to publicly legitimize the peace process. They also often cited economic and security rationales for their peace policy.

84. Statement in the Knesset by Prime Minister Rabin on the Hebron Murders, February 28, 1994, in *Israel's Foreign Relations, 1992–1994*, vol. 14, ed. Meron Medzini (Jerusalem: Ministry of Foreign Affairs, 1995), 502–505.

85. Address by Foreign Minister Peres at the United Nations World Conference on Human Rights, Vienna, June 15, 1993, in *Israel's Foreign Relations*, vol. 13, ed. Medzini, 245.

86. Remarks by Foreign Minister Peres to the Diplomatic Community in Israel, August 5, 1992, in *Israel's Foreign Relations*, vol. 13, ed. Medzini, 31–32.

87. Address by Foreign Minister Peres at the Israel-PLO Agreement Signing Ceremony, Cairo, May 4, 1994, in *Israel's Foreign Relations*, vol. 14, ed. Medzini, 617.

88. This point is noteworthy because, somewhat ironically, it was Peres who was later widely condemned for his alleged neglect of Israel's Jewish identity and its Jewish culture.

89. Address by Foreign Minister Peres to the Zionist Actions Committee, June 23, 1993, in *Israel's Foreign Relations*, vol. 13, ed. Medzini, 254.

90. On the concept of "framing," see Barnett, "Culture, Strategy and Foreign Policy Change," 15.

91. Ilan Pappé, "Post-Zionist Critique on Israel and the Palestinians," *Journal of Palestine Studies* 26, no. 3 (1997): 38.

92. Address by Foreign Minister Peres at the Meeting of the Council of the Socialist International, Lisbon, October 6, 1993, in *Israel's Foreign Relations*, vol. 13, ed. Medzini, 350.

93. Amnon Raz-Krakotzkin, "A Peace Without Arabs: The Discourse of Peace and the Limits of Israeli Consciousness," in *After Oslo: New Realities, Old Problems*, ed. George Giacaman and Dag Jørund Lønning (London: Pluto, 1998): 60.

94. Arian, *Security Threatened*, 89.

95. Bar-Tal and Oren, *Ethos as an Expression of Identity*, 13.

96. For example, in a 1994 survey of the attitudes of Israeli youth conducted by the Carmel Institute for Social Research and commissioned by the Ministry of Education, 37 percent of Jewish respondents said they hate Arabs, and less than a third said they would be willing to host an Arab in their home. *Jerusalem Post*, November 26, 1996.

97. Ilan Peleg, "Otherness and Israel's Arab Dilemma," in Silberstein and Cohn, *The Other in Jewish Thought and History*, 258–280. See also, Herbert Kelman, "The Interdependence of Israeli and Palestinian National Identities: The Role of the Other in Existential Conflict," *Journal of Social Issues* 55, no. 3 (1999): 581–600.

98. Dan Bar-On, "Israeli Society between the Culture of Death and the Culture of Life," *Israel Studies* 2, 1997, no. 2: 99.

99. David Grossman, "Suddenly, Human Contact," in *Death as a Way of Life*, trans. by Haim Watzman, ed. Efrat Lev (London: Bloomsbury, 2003), 6–7.

Chapter 4   The Crisis of Israeli Identity

1. Quoted in "Israel's Self-analysis," *Washington Post*, May 16, 1999.

2. Naomi Chazan, speech at a conference on "Identities in Transition from War to Peace," Hebrew University of Jerusalem, December 1, 1999, Jerusalem, Israel.

3. Peter B. Evans, Harold K. Jacobson, and Robert D. Putnam, eds., *Double-Edged Diplomacy: International Bargaining and Domestic Politics* (Berkeley, CA: University of California Press, 1993).

4. Israel's economic structure converged with that of other post-industrial societies. According to statistics published by Israel's Central Bureau of Statistics in 1998, for instance, 70 percent of the Israeli workforce was employed in the service sector. Figure cited in Ram, " 'The Promised Land of Business Opportunities,' " 221.

5. Ibid., 224–225.

6. Yair Sheleg, "Israel's Identity Crisis," *Ha'aretz*, October 11, 1998.

7. "*Too* like other nations?" *Jerusalem Post*, April 20, 1999.

8. Unlike in the past, the Israeli media was no longer deferential and subservient to Israeli governments on issues concerning the Palestinians.

9. Sofer, *Israel in the World Order*, 4.

10. Rosemary Hollis, *Israel on the Brink of Decision: Division, Unity and Crosscurrents in the Israeli Body Politic* (London: Research Institute for the Study of Conflict and Terrorism, May 1990), 28.

11. The Oslo I agreement was supported by 53 percent of Israelis, and opposed by 45 percent, with 2 percent having no opinion, according to a poll conducted by the Israeli newspaper *Yediot Aharonot* in late August 1993. The Oslo II agreement was supported by 51 percent of Israelis, and opposed by 47 percent, with 2 percent having no opinion, according to a poll conducted in late September 1995. *Yediot Aharonot*, August 30, 1993, September 28, 1995.

12. See, for instance, the monthly results of the Peace Index survey conducted by the Tami Steinmetz Center for Peace Research at Tel Aviv University <http://www.tau.ac.il/peace/Peace_Index/>

13. Bar-Siman-Tov, "Israel's Peace-Making with the Palestinians," 180.

14. Only 61 MKs voted to ratify the Oslo I agreement, 50 voted against, 8 abstained, and 1 did not take part in the vote. The Oslo II agreement was also ratified by 61 votes with 59 votes against it.

15. Yaacov Bar-Siman-Tov, *Peace Policy as Domestic and as Foreign Policy: The Israeli Case* (Jerusalem: The Leonard Davis Institute for International Relations, The Hebrew University, June 1998), 23.

16. The opposition argued that on issues so vital to the Jewish people a referendum was necessary or at least a special majority in the Knesset to neutralize the Arab vote.

17. Yehiel Leiter, *Crisis in Israel: A Peace Plan to Resist* (New York: S.P.I. Books/Shapolsky, 1994), 109.

18. Quoted in *The Jerusalem Post*, April 14, 1995.

19. Ibid.

20. Interview with Foreign Minister Peres in *Jerusalem Post*, July 1, 1994, in *Israel's Foreign Relations*, vol. 14, ed. Medzini, 672–673.

21. Briefing to the Foreign Press by Foreign Minister Peres, June 28, 1993, in *Israel's Foreign Relations*, vol. 13, ed. Medzini, 260.

22. The settlers in particular felt abandoned by the Rabin government and perceived Prime Minister Rabin to be cold, aloof, and completely unsympathetic to their plight. Ehud Sprinzak, "Israel's Radical Right and the Countdown to the Rabin Assassination," in *The Assassination of Yitzhak Rabin*, ed., Yoram Peri (Stanford, C.A.: Stanford University Press, 2000), 108.

23. Hillel Halkin, "Israel & the Assassination: A Reckoning," *Commentary* 101, no. 1 (1996): 29.

24. Arian, *The Second Republic*, 7.

25. Eva Etzioni-Halevy and Rina Shapira, *Political Culture in Israel: Cleavage and Integration among Israeli Jews* (New York: Praeger, 1977), 159–162.

26. This was shown in a study of Israeli high school students and their parents (Simon N. Herman, *Israelis and Jews: The Continuity of an Identity* [New York: Random House, 1970]); and in a study of Israeli university students (Eva Etzioni-Halevy and Rina Shapira, "Jewish Identification of Israeli Students: What Lies Ahead," *Jewish Social Studies* 37 [1975]: 251–266).

27. Sammy Smooha, *Arabs and Jews in Israel: Change and Continuity in Mutual Intolerance*, vol. 2 (Boulder, CO: Westview, 1992), 81.

28. The determination of one's Jewishness became a major issue in the wake of the massive influx of immigrants from the former Soviet Union. A large number of these immigrants were not Jewish according to strict orthodox criteria, raising the perennial question of "who is a Jew?"

29. Studies of immigrants from the former Soviet Union found that a majority of them emphasized their Jewish identity over their Israeli identity. Reported in Elazar Leshem and Moshe Sicron, "The Soviet Immigrant Community in Israel," in *Jews in Israel: Contemporary Social and Cultural Patterns*, ed. Uzi Rebhun and Chaim I. Waxman (Lebanon, NH: Brandeis University Press, 2004), 107.

30. Kimmerling and Moore, "Individual Strategies of Adopting Collective Identities," 398–400.

31. The Canaanite movement that emerged in Israel during the 1940s and early 1950s most clearly and provocatively articulated a new territorially based Israeli national identity, in opposition to an ethno-religious Jewish national identity.

32. Eva Etzioni-Halevy, "Collective Jewish Identity in Israel: Towards an Irrevocable Split?" in Krausz and Tulea, eds., *Jewish Survival*, 67.

33. According to an unpublished survey of Jews in Israel conducted in 1996 by the Tami Steinmetz Center, 95 percent of religious Jews evinced a very strong sense of Jewish identity, whereas only 65 percent of secular Jews did. Etzioni-Halevy, "Collective Jewish Identity in Israel," 70. See also, Etzioni-Halevy and Shapira, *Political Culture in Israel*, 170–173.

34. Kimmerling and Moore, "Individual Strategies of Adopting Collective Identities," 398–400.

35. Liebman and Susser, "Judaism and Jewishness in the Jewish State."

36. Ibid., 24. According to Baruch Kimmerling: "Israeli traditionalism is an incoherent set of values, norms, beliefs and practices mainly borrowed from the codified 'high' Jewish religion, but is mixed with many folkloric and 'popular' religious elements (such as cults and holidays dedicated to local ethnic 'saints')." Kimmerling, "Between Hegemony and Dormant *Kulturkampf* in Israel," 54.

37. Two broad sociological studies on the "Beliefs, Observances and Social Interactions Among Israeli Jews" conducted by the Guttman Institute in 1991 and 1999 revealed a decline in the number of people who identified themselves as "traditional" and an increase in those identifying themselves as "nonreligious" and "ultra-Orthodox." Shlomit Levy, Hanna Levinsohn, and Elihu Katz, "The Many Faces of Jewishness in Israel," in Rebhun and Waxman, eds., *Jews in Israel*, 279.

38. This trend had been underway for many years. Already in the 1970s, two Israeli scholars described an "intergenerational decline in religiosity" and warned that "the

prospects seem to be for a gradual decline of Jewish identification from generation to generation." Etzioni-Halevy and Shapira, *Political Culture in Israel*, 174.

39. The survey of Jews in Israel conducted by the Tami Steinmetz Center in 1996 indicated that Jewish identity declined with each successive generation of secular Jews. Eva Etzioni-Halevy explains this "intergenerational distancing from religion" in the following manner: "People who are first-generation secular still remember the religious atmosphere from their home and, even though they reject religion, they still want to retain some of its flavor. By contrast, those who are second generation secular or more, no longer remember sights, sounds and smells from a religious past. They have no flavor to retain." Eva Etzioni-Halevy, *The Divided People: Can Israel's Breakup Be Stopped* (Lanham, MD: Lexington, 2002), 117–118.

40. Alan Dowty characterizes it as a "secularism of convenience," as opposed to the "nationalist secularism" associated with Labor Zionism. Dowty, *The Jewish State*, 173.

41. The values of secular Israelis corresponded to what Ronald Inglehart famously labeled "postmaterialist" values (such as self-fulfillment and personal autonomy). See, Ronald Inglehart, *Culture Shifts in Advanced Industrial Society* (Princeton, NJ: Princeton University Press, 1990).

42. Charles S. Liebman, "Cultural Conflict in Israeli Society," in Liebman and Katz, eds., *The Jewishness of Israelis*, 113.

43. Etzioni-Halevy, *The Divided People*, 7.

44. Ibid., 118.

45. Ibid., 118–119.

46. Ibid., 55–61.

47. Charles S. Liebman and Eliezer Don-Yehiya, *Civil Religion in Israel: Traditional Judaism and Political Culture in the Jewish State* (Berkeley: University of California Press, 1983).

48. Gershon Shaked, "Israeli Society and Secular-Jewish Culture," in Liebman and Katz, eds., *The Jewishness of Israelis*, 165.

49. Levy, Levinsohn, and Katz, "Beliefs, Observances and Social Interaction Among Israeli Jews," 1–37.

50. Ibid., 30.

51. Only 40 percent of those who described themselves as "totally nonobservant" answered "definitely yes" to the question of whether they considered themselves Zionists, compared to around 60 percent for the rest of the Israeli Jewish population; 43 percent of the totally nonobservant said that feeling part of the Jewish people was very important as a guiding principles in their lives compared to over 80 percent of the more observant; and 52 percent of the totally nonobservant felt that living in Israel was very important as a guiding principle in their lives, whereas around 85 percent of more observant Israelis felt so. Liebman, "Cultural Conflict in Israeli Society," 109. Other studies have produced similar evidence linking levels of religiosity to commitment to Zionism, attachment to Israel, and affinity with Jews abroad. For a discussion of these studies, see Etzioni-Halevy and Shapira, *Political Culture in Israel*, 172–173.

52. Liebman, "Cultural Conflict in Israeli Society," 110.

53. From an interview with Amos Oz quoted in, Amos Oz, *In the Land of Israel*, trans. by Maurie Goldberg-Bartura (New York: Harcourt Brace, 1993), 115–116.

54. Orr, *Israel: Politics, Myths and Identity Crises*, 52.
55. Empirical research has confirmed this strong correlation between identities and orientations toward the territories and the Arab-Israeli conflict. Those Israeli Jews who fall into the category of doves are far more likely to identify themselves primarily as "Israeli" rather than "Jewish." Conversely, those Israeli Jews who fall into the category of hawks are far more likely to identify themselves primarily as "Jewish" rather than "Israeli." Doves, therefore, tend to be "Israelis" whereas hawks tend to be "Jews" in terms of their primary identification. Michal Shamir and Asher Arian, *Collective Identity and Electoral Competition in Israel* (Unpublished manuscript, Tel Aviv University, May 1997), 25.
56. According to Yehiel Leiter, spokesperson for YESHA, those who support the "normalization" of Israel "wish to escape obligations and historic responsibilities by replacing Israel's Jewish identity with a general cosmopolitan world culture, and all too often the worst of that culture." Leiter, *Crisis in Israel*, 110.
57. Eliezer Schweid, "Judaism in Israeli Culture," in Rebhun and Waxman, eds., *Jews in Israel*, 262.
58. According to Ehud Sprinzak, Amir became convinced that "the killing of the prime minister [Rabin] was an order from God" which he was required to undertake. Sprinzak, "Israel's Radical Right and the Countdown to the Rabin Assassination," 121.
59. Quoted in Marc H. Ellis, "Murdering Rabin And The Jewish Covenant," *Middle East Policy* 4, no. 3 (March 1996): 76.
60. *Din Moser* refers to a Jew who turns other Jews, or their property over to an oppressor; theoretically the punishment for such an act can be death. *Din Rodef* refers to a person pursuing another to kill him, and Jewish law requires a bystander to stop the pursuer by taking his life if necessary.
61. This symbolic interpretation of the Rabin assassination was evident in the wording of the original inscription that appeared on the memorial in Tel Aviv marking the spot where Rabin was killed which described Amir as "a young Jewish man wearing a kippa." The word "kippa" was subsequently removed after religious Israelis took offense to this reference to Amir's religiosity. *Ha'aretz*, November 29, 1999.
62. Quoted in Dina Shiloh, "An Open Wound," *Jerusalem Post*, October 31, 1997.
63. Avi Katzman, "Grandfather of a New Israeli Identity," *Ha'aretz*, November 3, 2000.
64. Baruch Kurzweil made this description of secular Israelis. Quoted in Orr, *Israel: Politics, Myths and Identity Crises*, 23.
65. Yoram Peri, "The Assassination: Causes, Meaning, Outcomes," in Peri, ed., *The Assassination of Yitzhak Rabin*, 49.
66. Peri, ed., *The Assassination of Yitzhak Rabin*, 54.
67. Yoram Peri, "The Media and Collective Memory of Yitzhak Rabin's Remembrance," *Journal of Communication* 49, no. 3 (1999): 116. Public pressure eventually led the Knesset to pass a law in the summer of 1997 to institute an official memorial day.
68. Peri, "The Media and Collective Memory of Yitzhak Rabin's Remembrance," 109–110.
69. The NRP, for instance, campaigned on the slogan "Zionism with a soul," and attracted the votes of around 50,000 secular Israelis. Elazar and Sandler,

"Introduction: The Battle over Jewishness and Zionism in the Post-Modern Era," *Israel Affairs* 4, no. 1 (Autumn 1997): 19.

70. Shamir and Arian, *Collective Identity and Electoral Competition in Israel*, 20.

71. The Meretz minister of Education in the Rabin government, for instance, suggested the removal of references to religion from war memorial services, and the adoption of a new code of ethics for the IDF in which the defense of democracy would be emphasized and references to Judaism de-emphasized.

72. Elazar and Sandler, "Introduction: The Battle over Jewishness and Zionism in the Post-Modern Era," 19.

73. David Nachmias and Itai Sened, "The Bias of Pluralism: The Redistributive Effects of the New Electoral Law," in *The Elections in Israel 1996*, ed., Asher Arian and Michal Shamir (Albany: State University of New York Press, 1999), 269–94.

74. Labor received 34 Knesset seats and the Likud list (which included an electoral alignment with David Levy's Gesher and Raphael Eitan's Tsomet) received 32 seats.

75. Also important in contributing to Netanyahu's narrow defeat of Peres was the abstention of many Israeli Arab voters in the election (who would otherwise most likely have voted for Peres) in protest over what they saw as the slaughter of innocent Lebanese as a result of the "Grapes of Wrath" operation against Lebanese targets authorized by then Prime Minister Peres shortly before the 1996 election, which led to the death of 100 Lebanese civilians in the village of Kana.

76. Peres, *The New Middle East*.

77. In the words of Itamar Rabinowitz, Israel's ambassador to the United States and the chief Israeli negotiator with Syria under the Rabin government: "There was a grand strategy, [but] there wasn't a grand vision." Itamar Rabinowitz, interview by author, July 19, 2000, Tel Aviv, Israel.

78. Eitan Haber, interview by author.

79. Nissim Rejwan, *Israel's Place in the Middle East: A Pluralist Perspective* (Gainesville, FL: University Press of Florida, 1998), 174–176.

80. Quoted in Massad, "Zionism's Internal Others," 54.

81. Edward Said, *Orientalism* (New York: Vintage, 1979).

82. *Le Monde*, March 9, 1966. Quoted in Rejwan, *Israel's Place in the Middle East*, 144.

83. According to a 1995 survey, 56 percent of Israeli Jews preferred Israel to integrate politically into Europe-America compared to 22 percent favoring political integration into Asia-Africa. Even more, 76 percent preferred Israel to integrate financially and economically into Europe-America, compared to 15 percent favoring economic integration into Asia-Africa. The greatest discrepancy, however, concerns integration with regard to culture and lifestyle, with 74 percent favoring Europe-America and only 10 percent favoring Asia-Africa. Cited in Smooha, "The Implications of the Transition to Peace for Israeli Society," 32.

84. Shimon Shamir, interview by author, July 20, 2000, Tel Aviv, Israel.

85. The main group of people to which Peres' vision of a "New Middle East" was attractive was Israel's new upper class who was the primary beneficiary of globalization. Uri Ram, "The New Upper Class and its New Middle East," paper presented at 16th annual meeting of the Association for Israel Studies, Tel Aviv University, June 25–27, 2000, Tel Aviv, Israel.

86. Peres, *The New Middle East*, 80–81.

87. See, for instance, Yoram Hazony, "The End of Zionism?" *Azure: Ideas for the Jewish Nation*, no. 1 (Summer 1996).

88. Yoram Hazony, *The Jewish State: The Struggle for Israel's Soul* (New York: Basic/New Republic Books, 2000), 62.
89. Benjamin Netanyahu, *A Place Among the Nations: Israel and the World* (New York: Bantam Books, 1993).
90. Netanyahu, *A Place Among the Nations*, 376.
91. Peres, *Battling for Peace*, 417–418.
92. Numerous Israeli commentators have decried what they perceived as the "Americanization" of Israel. See, Michael Arnold, "The 51st state?" *Jerusalem Post*, April 23, 1999. For scholarly analyses of this, see the special issue on "The Americanization of Israel" in *Israel Studies* 5, no. 1 (2000).
93. Quoted in Dan Perry, "Israel's Identity Crisis: Hi-Tech Modernity or Jewish Tradition?" *Associated Press*, June 11, 1996.
94. When he later presented his government to the Knesset, Netanyahu declared that: "The new government will nurture the values of the Jewish heritage in education, culture and the media." Quoted in Danny Ben-Moshe, "Elections 1996: The De-Zionization of Israeli Politics," *Israel Affairs* 3, nos. 3–4 (1997): 69.
95. Thomas L. Friedman, "For Orthodox Jews, the Choice was Netanyahu or Pizza Hut," *International Herald Tribune*, September 23, 1996.
96. Quoted in *International Herald Tribune*, September 23, 1996.
97. Liebman and Susser, "Judaism and Jewishness in the Jewish State," 24.
98. The posters were distributed by the ultra-Orthodox Lubavitch movement.
99. Quoted in Thomas L. Friedman, "The Morning After," *New York Times*, October 25, 1998.
100. Arian, *The Second Republic*, 7–9.
101. Quoted in Perry, "Israel's Identity Crisis."
102. *Ma'ariv*, June 18, 1996.
103. Interview with Benjamin Netanyahu for "Shattered Dreams of Peace: The Road From Oslo," *PBS*, 2002.
104. Interview with Benjamin Netanyahu for "Shattered Dreams of Peace."
105. "Report on Israeli Settlement in the Occupied Territories," *The Foundation for Middle East Peace*, vol. 8, no. 5, September 1998.
106. Except for the periods 1929–1931 and 1936–1968, there has been a significant Jewish presence in Hebron since Biblical times. In Jewish tradition, Hebron is one of the four "sacred communities"—ancient cities that were sites of Jewish religious activity. During the British Mandate in Palestine, Hebron was the site of one of the worst anti-Jewish riots in which Arab mobs killed sixty-seven Jews in 1929 resulting in the evacuation of the remaining Jews from the city. After the 1967 war, the first Jewish settlement was established next to Hebron in a place named Kiryat Arba.
107. This led Benjamin Begin, the son of Menachem Begin and the minister of Science and Technology in Netanyahu's government, to resign in protest.
108. Dore Gold, Israeli Ambassador to the UN during Netanyahu's government (1997–1999), and a close foreign policy advisor to Netanyahu, claims that Netanyahu attempted to move the Likud away from the ideological fervor and rigidity of the Shamir period to a position of "pragmatic conservatism." Dore Gold, interview by author, September 17, 2000, Jerusalem, Israel.
109. Charles Enderlin, *Shattered Dreams: The Failure of the Peace Process in the Middle East, 1995–2002* (New York: Other Press, 2003), transl. by Susan Fairfield, 96.

110. Netanyahu refused to carry out the two subsequent withdrawals called for in the Wye River Memorandum on the grounds that the Palestinians were not keeping the commitments they made to combat anti-Israel terrorism and incitement.

111. Uzi Benziman, "Time to Come Clean," *Ha'aretz*, March 30, 1997.

112. David Makovsky, "Netanyahu Presents Allon-Plus Plan," *Ha'aretz*, June 5, 1997.

113. David Makovsky, "We May Accept a Limited Palestinian State," *The Jerusalem Post*, December 20, 1996; Yoel Marcus, "And You Shall Beat Your Swords," *Ha'aretz*, June 10, 1997; Ze'ev Schiff, "Netanyahu's Map," *Ha'aretz*, August 19, 1997.

114. The *Kulturkampf* between secular and religious Jews in Israel in the 1990s can be traced all the way back to the late eighteenth century, when the Jewish enlightenment movement—the *Haskalah*—began challenging the Orthodox Rabbinical establishment and its traditional religious definition of Jewish identity.

115. Quoted in Deborah Sontag, "Israeli Politicians Urge Ultra-Orthodox Leaders to Cancel Sunday Rally," *New York Times*, February 12, 1999.

116. Figures cited in *Maariv*, September 19, 2000.

117. In a landmark decision in December 1998, the Supreme Court declared the blanket exemption illegal, sparking furious protests from the ultra-Orthodox community. Lee Hockstader, "Israeli 'Yeshiva Boys' Lose Draft Exemption: Ultra-Orthodox Jews Vow to Defy Ruling," *Washington Post*, December 10, 1998.

118. Quoted in Sara Helman, "Militarism and the Construction of Community," *Journal of Political and Military Sociology* 25 (Winter 1997): 317–318.

119. In particular, army experience is perceived as a prerequisite for political opposition. Helman, "Militarism and the Construction of Community," 323.

120. This is reflected in the "one nation-one draft" campaign slogan used by Ehud Barak in the run-up to the 1999 elections when he promised to pass a law to draft yeshiva students into the army. Such a slogan clearly reflected the equation drawn between the IDF and the Israeli nation.

121. Thus, Stuart Cohen argues that rather than bolstering national cohesion, Israel's system of military service actually accentuates societal divides since it creates a stratification within Israeli society between those who serve in the IDF and those who do not serve (whether their non-service is volitional or non-volitional). Stuart A. Cohen, "Military Service in Israel: No Longer a Cohesive Force?" *The Jewish Journal of Sociology* 39, nos. 1–2 (1997): 10.

122. As a result, there is a social distinction between the Arabs who serve in the IDF (the Druze who do compulsory military service and the Bedouin who volunteer for military service), and those that do not (Palestinian Israelis—who are exempted from military service on security grounds). It is not a coincidence, therefore, that the first non-Jew ever to become a minister in an Israeli government was a Druze Arab (in the Sharon government).

123. The IDF had earlier performed this role in the 1950s with regard to the new immigrants from North Africa and the Middle East. The IDF used numerous means, such as lectures and study camps, to "educate" the new immigrants and "Israelize" them. See, Zvi Zameret, "A Truly National Service," *Ha'aretz*, March 16, 2001.

124. Doron Rosenblum, "Could Induction Induce Fears of a Vacuum?" *Ha'aretz*, July 7, 2000.

125. Ibid.

126. Popular Mizrahi singers were Zehava Ben, Sarit Hadad, Chaim Moshe, Yitzhak Kala, and Avihu Medina and most well-known, Ofra Haza. Popular Mizrahi writers were Shimon Ballas, Sami Michael, Eli Amir, Amnon Shamosh, and Albert Suissa, to name just a few.

127. Sami Shalom Chetrit, "Mizrahi Politics in Israel: Between Integration and Alternative," *Journal of Palestine Studies* 29, no. 4 (2000): 60.

128. Charles Taylor, *Multiculturalism: Examining the Politics of Recognition* (Princeton: Princeton University Press, 1994).

129. Yehouda Shenhav, "Fragments of a Mosaic, or a Fragmented Mosaic?" *Ha'aretz*, June 8, 2000.

130. Nissim Calderon, *Multiculturalism versus Pluralism in Israel* (Haifa: Haifa University Press, 2000). Quoted in Yossi Yonah, "East is East, West is West, and That's That," *Ha'aretz*, June 30, 2000.

131. Thus, Sammy Smooha writes that: "Israel has remained a society with cultural diversity or multiplicity of cultures but without multiculturalism." Sammy Smooha, "Jewish Ethnicity in Israel: Symbolic or Real?" in Asher Arian and Michal Shamir, eds., *Jews in Israel*, x, 71–72.

132. See for instance, Deborah Sontag, "Talk of a 'Multicultural' Label Sets Off an Emotional Debate in Israel," *International Herald Tribune*, December 7, 1999.

133. Yair Sheleg, "Changing the Melting Pot," *Ha'aretz*, February 16, 2001.

134. Zohar Shavit et al., "A Position Paper on Cultural Policy in Israel in the 21st Century" (The Israeli Ministry of Science, Culture, and Sport: Jerusalem, 2000). Quoted in Shenhav, "Fragments of a mosaic."

135. Gideon Samet, "The Collapse of the Common Denominator," *Ha'aretz*, April 10, 1998.

136. Amnon Rubinstein, "We all feel like minorities," *Ha'aretz*, August 29, 2000.

137. Ofir Haivry, "The First Israelis," *Azure* (Winter 1999): 1.

138. Gershon Shaked, "Shall We Find Sufficient Strength? On Behalf of Israeli Secularism," in Urian and Karsh, eds., *In Search of Identity*, 85.

139. See, for example, Allison Kaplan Sommer, "Who is an Israeli?" *Jerusalem Post*, May 11, 1997.

140. Quoted in Sommer, "Who is an Israeli?"

141. Dafna Lewy-Yanowitz, "Undercooked in the Melting Pot," *Ha'aretz*, October 15, 1999.

142. The survey was carried out by Yochanan Peres and Sabina Lissitsa of Tel Aviv University and cited in Thomas O'Dwyer, "Left, Right, Inside, Out," *Ha'aretz*, June 30, 2000.

143. Quoted in Herb Keinon, "Changing Faces," *Jerusalem Post*, December 2, 1999.

144. Rochelle Furstenberg, "A Culture Apart," *Jerusalem Post*, December 10, 1999.

145. Yair Sheleg, "Changing the Melting Pot," *Ha'aretz*, February 16, 2001.

146. Part of the reason for this failure was the decision by Israeli authorities to abandon the traditional absorption policy, and "privatize" absorption by directly providing resources to immigrants including housing subsidies, living allowances, job search assistance, and vouchers for Hebrew classes and job training.

147. The failure to integrate new immigrants into Israeli culture was also apparent in statistics released in late 1999 by the absorption ministry which revealed that three-quarters of Israel's 74,000 Ethiopian immigrants could not write in basic Hebrew and 45 percent could not hold a simple conversation in Hebrew. Yair Sheleg, "Report: Ethiopian Immigrants Poorly Integrated," *Ha'aretz*, November 17, 1999.

148. Eliahu Salpeter, "The Danger of Tinkering with the Law of Return," *Ha'aretz*, December 9, 1999.

149. Sheleg, "Changing the Melting Pot."

150. Salpeter, "The Danger of Tinkering with the Law of Return." See also, Dan Margalit, "The Jewish People's Right of Return," *Ha'aretz*, December 6, 1999.

151. Israel's Law of Return embodies a different conception of Jewish identity from that of Orthodox religious law. The former defines a Jew as anybody descended from at least one Jewish grandparent, whereas the rabbinical definition limits it to those born to Jewish mothers.

152. Statistic cited in Yair Sheleg, "Absorption Ministry Considers Limiting Non-Jewish Aliyah," *Ha'aretz*, November 29, 1999.

153. Ibid.

154. Lily Galili, "The New Wave of Immigration and the Jewish State," *Ha'aretz*, September 30, 1999. Thus, somewhat ironically, the Law of Return, which was originally intended to enshrine and express Israel's identity as a Jewish state, came to be perceived by some as a danger to the preservation of this identity.

155. Ian Lustick, "Israel as a 'Non-Arab' State: The Political Implications of Mass Immigration of Non-Jews," *Middle East Journal* 53, no. 3 (1999): 417–433.

156. There were also roughly 160,000 foreign workers living in Israel who were also not Jewish, but this group lacks citizenship and hence cannot vote.

157. Quoted in Joseph Algazy, "Arab MKs Plan to Introduce Bills to Abolish Jewish Agency, Zionist Federation, Others," *Ha'aretz*, October 6, 1999.

158. For instance, on the front cover of *Ha'aretz*'s Independence Day supplement in 2000 were photographs of four young, modern-looking Palestinian Israelis, beneath which were the words: "One In Six: They're young, they're professional, they're Israeli. But for 18 percent of the country's citizens who are Arab, Independence Day is no cause for celebration." *Ha'aretz magazine*, May 5, 2000. For a study of the problem of Palestinian citizens in Israel, see Nadim Rouhana, *Palestinian Arabs in an Ethnic Jewish State: Identities in Conflict* (New Haven: Yale University Press, 1997).

159. For an extensive discussion of Israeli policy toward Palestinian Israelis, see Ian S. Lustick, *Arabs in the Jewish State: Israel's Control of a National Minority* (Austin, University of Texas, 1980).

160. An example of this discrimination was the fact that in 1994, government funding to Arab and Druze localities amounted to 1,050 shekels per person, whereas government funding to Jewish localities amounted to 2,400 shekels per person. "Facts about the Arab Citizens of Israel" (New York: The Abraham Fund, 2001).

161. Rebecca B. Kook, *The Logic of Democratic Exclusion: African Americans in the United States and Palestinian Citizens in Israel* (Lanham, MD: Lexington Books, 2002), 183.

162. In the late 1990s, the per capita GNP of the Palestinian and Druze sector in Israeli society was two-thirds that of the Jewish sector, and over 50 percent of the Palestinian and Druze population in Israel lived below the poverty line, compared to 16 percent of the Jewish population. "Facts about the Arab citizens of Israel."

163. See, for instance, Zvi Bar'el, "It's Identity, not Fundamentalism, that the Arabs are Talking About," *Ha'aretz*, September 24, 1999.

164. For example, in a 2001 survey into their attitudes, only 33 percent of Palestinian Israeli respondents said the label "Israeli" accurately described their identity, compared to 63 percent who said so in 1995. Ori Nir, "Israeli Arab Alienation Intensifies," *Ha'aretz*, May 21, 2001.

165. Quoted in Uriya Shavit, "Talk is Cheap," *Ha'aretz*, October 20, 2000.

166. Abdel Hakim Mufid, the editorial secretary of the Islamic movement's weekly newspaper *Saut al-Haqq wal-Hurriya* ("Voice of Truth and Freedom"). Quoted in Shavit, "Talk is Cheap."

167. For this argument see, Nadim Rouhana, "Israel and its Arab Citizens: Predicaments in the Relationship between Ethnic States and Ethnonational Minorities," *Third World Quarterly* 19, no. 2 (1998); Nadim Rouhana and Assad Ghanem, "The Crisis of Minorities in Ethnic States: The Case of the Palestinians in Israel," *International Journal of Middle East Studies* 30 (1998).

168. In the 1999 elections, Azmi Bisharah, the leader of the Palestinian Israeli political party Balad, ran for prime minister, the first ever Palestinian Israeli candidate (he withdrew his candidacy just before the election). The demand to redefine Israel as a "state for all its citizens" was the centerpiece of his campaign.

169. Jacob M. Landau, *The Arab Minority in Israel, 1967–1991: Political Aspects* (Clarendon Press, Oxford, 1993), 167–170.

170. Kook, *The Logic of Democratic Exclusion*, 172–173.

171. Anton Shammas, "Us? Who is Us?" *Koteret Rashit*, May 13, 1987 (Hebrew). Quoted in Shuki Mairovich, "Post-Zionist Blues—and Reds and Greens," *Ha'aretz*, April 19, 2000.

172. The term "post-Zionist" has often been used in a very loose and careless way to describe anyone with critical attitudes to Zionism and Israeli history. For a discussion of the different uses of the term and its varied meanings see, Ephraim Nimni, "Introduction," in *The Challenge of Post-Zionism: Alternatives to Israeli Fundamentalist Politics*, ed., Ephraim Nimni, (London: Zed Books, 2003), 3–4; and Nira Yuval-Davis, "Some Thoughts on Post-Zionism and the Construction of the Zionist Project," in Nimni, *The Challenge of Post-Zionism*, 183.

173. Although post-Zionism first emerged in Israel in the mid-1980s, it did not receive widespread public attention until the 1990s.

174. Although often labeled post-Zionist, this view would be more accurately described as anti-Zionist.

175. For an example of this latter view see, Amos Elon, "Israel and the End of Zionism," *New York Review of Books*, December 19, 1996, 22–30.

176. The *Ha-Tikvah* contains phrases such as "so long as still within our breasts the Jewish heart beats true," "to Zion looks the Jew" and "our land of Zion and Jerusalem."

177. Evron, *Jewish State or Israeli Nation?*, 243.
178. Ram, "Postnationalist Pasts," 526.
179. Meyrav Wurmser, "Can Israel Survive Post-Zionism?" *Middle East Quarterly* 6, no. 1 (1999): 3.
180. The "post-Zionist" label was usually applied to characterize this scholarly work, even though some of the scholars involved did not actually identify themselves as post-Zionists (such as the historian Benny Morris).
181. These works began appearing in the 1980s. Some notable examples were, Benny Morris' book *The Birth of the Palestinian Refugee Problem, 1947–1949* (Cambridge: Cambridge University Press, 1987), which reexamined the origins of the Palestinian refugee problem and claimed that Israel bore a large share of the responsibility for it; Avi Shlaim's book *Collusion Across the Jordan: King Abdullah, the Zionist Movement, and the Partition of Palestine* (Oxford: Clarendon Press, 1988), which presented a new view of the relations between the Yishuv and Transjordan arguing that the Jewish Agency colluded with King Abdullah of Transjordan to partition Palestine at the expense of the Palestinians; Tom Segev's book *The Seventh Million: The Israelis and the Holocaust*, which asserted that the rescue of European Jewry was never a primary concern for Zionism as a movement and that Ben-Gurion and other Zionist leaders reacted with indifference to the Holocaust; and Zeev Sternhell's book, *The Founding Myths of Israel: Nationalism, Socialism and the Making of the Jewish State* (Princeton: Princeton University Press, 1998), which debunked the myth that the Zionist leaders who founded Israel were attempting to establish a new type of society based upon egalitarian principles.
182. Ram, "Postnationalist Pasts," 519.
183. Ilan Pappé, "Critique and Agenda: The Post-Zionist Scholars in Israel," *History and Memory* 7, no. 1 (1995): 85.
184. Perhaps the fiercest public attack on the New Historians was made by the Labor Zionist intellectual Aharon Megged in his article "The Israeli Suicide Drive," *Ha'aretz Magazine*, June 10, 1994. Other highly publicized attacks came from the "traditional" historian Shabtai Teveth (see for instance, Shabtai Teveth "Charging Israel with Original Sin," *Commentary* 88, no. 3 [1989]: 24–33); and Efraim Karsh in his book, *Fabricating Israeli History: The "New Historians"* (London: Frank Cass, 1997).
185. Israel adopted the British thirty-year rule for the review and declassification of foreign policy documents. Under this rule, a vast amount of primary source material was released for research in the Central Zionist Archives, the Israel State Archives, the Haganah Archive, the IDF Archive, the Labor Party Archive, and the Ben-Gurion Archive.
186. Quoted in Relly Sa'ar, "Who is Threatening the History Inspector?" *Ha'aretz*, September 14, 1999.
187. Ibid.
188. Ibid.
189. Dan Margalit, "It *Was* a Case of the Few Against the Many," *Ha'aretz*, September 16, 1999.
190. Yoram Hazony, for example, denounced what he described as the "de-Judaization of Israeli schools." Yoram Hazony, "Antisocial Texts: Who removed Zionism from Israel's textbooks?" *The New Republic*, April 17, 2000.

191. In the words of Michael Head, professor of history at the Hebrew University and head of the Education Ministry's professional committee under the Barak government: "It is precisely from a self-confident Zionist point of view that we can learn about the less attractive sides of the history of the Yishuv, such as the War of Independence." Quoted in Sa'ar, "Who is Threatening the History Inspector?"

192. Elie Podeh, "History and Memory in the Israeli Educational System: The Portrayal of the Arab-Israeli Conflict in History Textbooks (1948–2000)," *History & Memory* 12, no. 1, (2000): 65–100.

193. Uri Ram, "From Nation-State to Nation—State: Nation, History and Identity Struggles in Jewish Israel," in Nimni, ed., *The Challenge of Post-Zionism*, 20–41.

Chapter 5   The Return of the Other

1. Ariel Sharon, *Warrior: The Autobiography of Ariel Sharon*, with David Chanoff (New York: Simon and Schuster, 1989), 533.

2. Yossi Beilin, "Moving forward after Oslo," *Ha'aretz*, November 7, 2000.

3. Labor's Knesset seats declined from 44 in 1992 to 34 in 1996 to 26 in 1999. Likud's seats in the Knesset dropped from 40 in 1992 to 32 in 1996 to 19 in 1999.

4. Quoted in Ari Shavit, "He Will Be Back," *Ha'aretz magazine*, July 21, 2000.

5. Shinui had been a political party in the 1980s and it won seats in the Knesset in 1981, 1984, and 1988, but subsequently disappeared until 1999.

6. All three parties called for the separation of religion and state and for a written constitution.

7. The NRP lost nearly half its Knesset seats, winning only five seats; the National Union party received only four seats.

8. Of all these groups, the loss of support for Netanyahu among new immigrants from the former Soviet Union was the most damaging. This group had played a major role in Netanyahu's victory in 1996 with 70 percent voting for Netanyahu. In 1999, by contrast, 60 percent voted for Barak. Barak's preelection promise to transfer control of the important Ministry of the Interior (which controls citizenship, residency, housing, welfare benefits, and other key issues for immigrants) from Shas to the Russian party Yisrael B'Aliyah was perhaps the decisive factor for him in attracting the votes of the new immigrants.

9. His election slogan was "Israel wants a change."

10. For a discussion of Barak's attitude toward the Oslo peace process see, Jonathan Rynhold, "Making Sense of Tragedy: Barak, the Israeli Left and the Oslo Peace Process," *Israel Studies Forum* 19, no. 1 (2003): 9–33.

11. Netanyahu's "retirement" from politics was brief. In 2002, he returned to the fray, becoming foreign minister in Ariel Sharon' government.

12. Barak received a majority of the Jewish vote, safeguarding him from the accusations that were leveled against the Rabin government that it lacked a Jewish majority.

13. "Speech by Prime Minister Ehud Barak on the Presentation of the Government to the Knesset Jerusalem, July 6, 1999." http://www.mfa.gov.il/MFA/Government/Speeches

14. "Victory Speech by Prime Minister Elect Ehud Barak, Tel-Aviv, May 18, 1999." http://www.mfa.gov.il/MFA/Government/Speeches
15. "Speech by Prime Minister Ehud Barak on the Presentation of the Government to the Knesset Jerusalem, July 6, 1999."
16. "Victory Speech by Prime Minister Elect Ehud Barak."
17. "Speech by Prime Minister Ehud Barak on the Presentation of the Government."
18. "Ehud Barak's Plan for a Better Israel," <http://www1.knesset.gov.il/elections/pm/ematza_pm_0.htm>
19. "Speech by Prime Minister Ehud Barak on the Presentation of the Government."
20. In the opinion of the Palestinian–Israeli politician Azmi Bishara who ran as a candidate for prime minister in the 1999 election until dropping out from the race just two days before the election. "He's [Barak] a right-winger. He wants to bring about a reconciliation among the Jewish public, not with the Arab public." Larry Derfner, "The Taboo That Won't Be Broken," *The Jerusalem Post*, June 16, 1999.
21. Lally Weymouth, "The Peace of the Brave," *Newsweek* 134, no. 19 (November 1999).
22. After visiting two settlements each containing thirty families, Rabin remarked that they "will cost us $250,000 per family to protect, even though the contribution to security is absolutely nil." *The Jerusalem Post*, June 22, 1995.
23. Barak also made Yitzhak Levy, the leader of the NRP that represents many of the settlers, minister of Housing in his government—a position responsible for housing construction in the settlements.
24. "Prime Minister Barak Remarks to the National Security College, August 17, 2000." http://www.mfa.gov.il/mfa/go.asp?MFAH0hv30.
25. Ricki Tessler, "Public Finance in Shas's Religious Revolution Service," paper presented at 16th annual meeting of the Association for Israel Studies, Tel Aviv University, Tel Aviv, Israel, 25–27 June 2000.
26. Quoted in Daniel Ben Simon, "A Maternity Dress for Every Woman, and a Synagogue on Every Ship," *Ha'aretz*, April 14, 2000.
27. Quoted in R. Jeffrey Smith, "In 'War over Culture,' Israeli Party Sees Its Schools as Front Line," *International Herald Tribune*, May 4, 2000.
28. Ultimately, this was to no avail as Shas later withdrew from the government on the eve of Barak's departure to the Camp David Summit in July 2000 in protest over Barak's refusal to reveal the so-called red lines beyond which he would not offer any more concessions to the Palestinians.
29. In preferring to pursue the Syrian track to the Palestinian one, Barak was following in the footsteps of his mentor, Rabin, who only supported the Israeli-Palestinian negotiations in Oslo after negotiations with Syria had reached a dead-end.
30. See, Clinton's account of the failed Shepherdstown talks in his autobiography *My Life* (New York: Knopf, 2004), 885–886; and Dennis Ross' account in his memoir *The Missing Peace: The Inside Story of the Fight for Middle East Peace* (New York: Farrar, Straus and Giroux, 2004), 549–565. Both Clinton and Ross blame Barak for the failure of the Shepherdstown talks.
31. Ross speculates that the ailing Assad was no longer interested in a peace agreement with Israel and was focused instead on managing his succession. See, Ross, *The Missing Peace*, 588–589.
32. Zvi Zinger, "The IDF pullout—Due to Problems in the Israeli Staying Power," *Yediot Aharonot*, May 19, 2000. Similarly, Major General Moshe Ya'alon, in a

speech at the National Defense College in December 2000 before he became the IDF's Chief of Staff, stated that: "We withdrew from Lebanon because we were vanquished above all by the consciousness of Israeli society." Quoted in Ha'aretz, March, 22, 2002.

33. In a poll taken on the evening after Israel's withdrawal, 72 percent of the respondents believed that leaving Lebanon unilaterally was the correct decision. Yehuda Ben-Meir, The Withdrawal from Lebanon and the Israeli Domestic Scene, Strategic Assessment 3, no. 1 (June 2000), Jaffee Center for Strategic Studies, Tel Aviv University.

34. William A. Orme Jr., "Retreat From Lebanon: The Israelis; Barak Declares End to 'Tragedy' as Last Troops Leave Lebanon," *The New York Times*, May 24, 2000.

35. Gilad Sher, *Within Touching Distance* (Tel Aviv: Yediot Achronot, 2001) [Hebrew], 121.

36. "Ehud Barak on Camp David: 'I Did Not Give Away A Thing,'" *Journal of Palestine Studies* 33, no. 1 (2003): 86–87.

37. Jonathan Rynhold, "Making Sense of Tragedy," 17.

38. Ari Shavit, "Eyes Wide Shut," Interview with Barak, *Ha'aretz*, September 9, 2002.

39. Rob Malley and Hussein Agha, "Camp David: The Tragedy of Errors," *The New York Review of Books*, August 9, 2001.

40. Jeremy Pressman, "Visions in Collision: What Happened at Camp David and Taba?" *International Security* 28, no. 2 (2003): 5–43.

41. Pressman, "Visions in Collision," 8.

42. Sandler, *The State of Israel, the Land of Israel*, 63.

43. Teddy Kollek, *Jerusalem* (Washington, DC: Washington Institute For Near East Policy, 1990), 19–20.

44. Quoted in Sandler, *The State of Israel, the Land of Israel*, 69.

45. These included Abu Dis, al-Aysawiyah, Shu'fat, Bayt Hanina, Qalandiya, al-Thuri, Umm Tuba, al-Sawahirah al-Gharbiyah, Kafr Aqb, and Samir Amis. Pressman, "Visions in Collision," 18.

46. Mick Dumper, "Jerusalem and the Illusion of Israeli Sovereignty," *Middle East Report*, August 4, 2000. http://www.merip.org/mero/mero080400.html

47. Such policies included, severely restricting Palestinian building in East Jerusalem, revoking Palestinians' residency and social benefits, and neglecting infrastructure in Palestinian neighborhoods. "Injustice in the Holy City," *B'Tselem Journal* (December 1999). http://www.btselem.org/English/Publications/Full_Text/Injustice_in_the_Holy_City/index.asp

48. Quoted in Enderlin, *Shattered Dreams*, 222.

49. Ibid., 220.

50. Wistrich and Ohana, "Introduction," in Wistrich and Ohana, eds., *The Shaping of Israeli Identity*, viii.

51. Avirama Golan, "Strippers in the Shadow of the Holocaust," *Ha'aretz*, November 23, 1999.

52. See, for instance, the alarm over the erosion of Zionist ideology sounded by Yoram Hazony. Hazony, *The Jewish State*.

53. Evidence for this claim is the fact that in a public opinion survey carried out shortly after the Camp David summit ended, 38 percent of Israelis were in favor of accepting Palestinian sovereignty over the Arab neighborhoods in East

Jerusalem (58 percent were opposed). Ephraim Ya'ar and Tamar Hermann, "Peace Index—July 2000." http://www.tau.ac.il/peace

54. Quoted in Enderlin, *Shattered Dreams*, 223.

55. Ibid., 221.

56. Quoted in "The At Odds Couple," *Ha'aretz*, July 28, 2000.

57. According to the United Nations Relief and Works Agency for Palestine Refugees (UNRWA), as of 2003 there were 4.1 million registered Palestinian refugees. http://www.un.org/unrwa/overview/index.html

58. "The Palestinian Right of Return," *The Economist*, January 6, 2001.

59. For the distinction between the Zionist and non-Zionist left see, Pappé, "Post-Zionist Critique on Israel and the Palestinians," 38.

60. As Yossi Beilin, one of Oslo's chief architects, later explained: "[T]he Oslo act was a Zionist act that was aimed at saving the Jewish nation-state." Quoted in Ari Shavit, "Mister ice guy," *Ha'aretz*, June 14, 2001.

61. Benny Morris, "Camp David and After: An Exchange (1. An Interview with Ehud Barak)," New *York Review of Books*, June 13, 2002. See also Barak's interview with Newsweek magazine. Lally Weymouth, "Barak's View of the Future: Die or Separate," *Newsweek*, July 23, 2001.

62. Pressman, "Visions in Collision," 30.

63. Yasser Arafat, "The Palestinian Vision of Peace," *New York Times*, February 3, 2002.

64. Jerome Segal, "Clearing Up The Right-Of-Return Confusion," *Middle East Policy* 8, no. 2 (2001): 24.

65. Quoted Enderlin, *Shattered Dreams*, 197–198.

66. In a poll taken in late 1999 on the question, "who is responsible for the creation of the refugee problem in 1948—Israel or the Arabs," only 9.5 percent of Israelis answered that Israel was to blame, 25 percent said that both sides were to blame, and almost half (47.5 percent) placed the blame on the Arabs. Ya'ar and Hermann, "Peace Index—December 1999."

67. Yossi Melman, "We Cannot Have Them Back," *The Guardian*, September 20, 2002.

68. Morris, *Righteous Victims*.

69. Israel was prepared to issue a statement of some sort that would announce its regret, sorrow and compassion for the plight of Palestinian refugees.

70. For details of the Israeli propaganda campaign that began even before the summit ended, see Aluf Benn, "The Selling of the Summit: How Ehud Barak took Advantage of the Isolation and Blackout Imposed by the Americans at Camp David to Win the Israeli-Palestinian Propaganda Battle," *Ha'aretz* July 27, 2001.

71. For this claim see, Morris, "Camp David and After." For a rebuttal of it, see Malley and Agha, "Camp David: The Tragedy of Errors."

72. This flattering portrayal of Barak was made by President Clinton when he told reporters after the summit ended that Barak "showed particular courage, vision, and an understanding of the historical importance of this moment." With regard to Arafat, by contrast, Clinton merely said that, "Arafat made it clear that he, too, remains committed to the path of peace." "President, William J. Clinton Statement on the Middle East Peace Talks at Camp David. The White House, The James S. Brady Press Briefing Room, Washington, DC, July 25, 2000," http://www.state.gov/www/regions/nea/000725_clinton_stmt.html

73. For this negative view of Arafat see, Dennis Ross, "Yasir Arafat: Think Again," *Foreign Policy* (July–August 2002). For the Palestinian version of the events at Camp David see, Akiva Eldar, "What Went Wrong at Camp David—The Official Palestinian Version," *Ha'aretz*, July 24, 2001. See also, Lee Hockstader, "A Different Take on the Camp David Collapse," *Washington Post*, July 24, 2001.

74. See, for instance, Dennis Ross, "Camp David: An Exchange," *New York Review of Books*, September 20, 2001.

75. In the interview, Clinton stated that he "thought that the Prime Minister was more creative and more courageous" than Arafat. "Clinton Interview by Israeli Television on Peace Talks," Office of International Information Programs, U.S. Department of State, July 28, 2000, http://usinfo.state.gov

76. In a poll conducted soon after the summit, 67 percent of Israelis held the Palestinians responsible for its failure. Ephraim Yuchtman-Ya'ar, "The Oslo Process and Israeli-Jewish Public: A Story of Disappointment?" *Israel Studies Forum* 18, 1 (Fall 2002): 16.

77. In a survey conducted soon after the Camp David summit, 44 percent of Israeli Jewish respondents felt that Barak has been "too conciliatory" in the negotiations. Ya'ar and Hermann, "Peace Index, July 2000."

78. Quoted in Suzanne Goldenberg, "Barak rushes to blame unyielding Arafat in Jerusalem," *The Guardian*, July 26, 2000.

79. Ya'ar and Hermann, "Peace Index—June 2000."

80. Ya'ar and Hermann, "Peace Index—July 2000."

81. Ya'ar and Hermann, "Peace Index—August 2000."

82. Israeli and Palestinian negotiators continued to meet privately in August and early September 2000 in an attempt to overcome the impasse that was reached at Camp David.

83. "Preliminary Submission of the Palestine Liberation Organization to the International Commission of Inquiry," December 8, 2000: 10. Quoted in Pressman, "Visions in Collision," 36.

84. Between 1994 and 2000, the Israeli government confiscated approximately 35,000 acres of Palestinian land in the West Bank for the construction of bypass roads and settlements. Sara Roy, "Decline and Disfigurement: The Palestinian Economy After Oslo," in Roane Carey, ed., *The New Intifada: Resisting Israel's Intifada* (New York, 2001), 95.

85. Between 1992 and 1996, the average unemployment rate in the West Bank and Gaza rose from 3 percent to 28 percent. During the same period, real Gross National Product (GNP) declined 18.4 percent, and real per capita GNP fell by 37 percent. UNSCO, *Economic and Social Conditions in the West Bank and Gaza Strip, Quarterly Report*, prepared by Salem Aljuni et al. (Gaza: United Nations Office of the Special Coordinator in the Occupied Territories, April 1, 1997), i. & 6, cited in Sara Roy, "Decline and Disfigurement," 91–92.

86. Khalil Shikaki, "Palestinians Divided," *Foreign Affairs* 81, no. 1 (Jan/Feb2002).

87. See the "Mitchell Commission Report" at www.fmep.org/documents/ Mitchell_commission.html.

88. "Israel, the Conflict and Peace: Answers to Frequently Asked Questions," November 2003, http://www.mfa.gov.il/MFA/MFAArchive/ 2000_2009/2003/ 11/Israel-+the+Conflict+and+Peace-+Answers+to+Frequen.htm#cause

89. "Statement by Prime Minister Ehud Barak, Jerusalem, October 7, 2000," http://www.shanghai.mfa.gov.il/mfa/go.asp?MFAHOil 30

90. A public opinion poll carried out by the School of Education at Tel Aviv University showed that it was the violence that broke out in September 2000 far more than the failure at Camp David that eroded Israeli faith in the peace process. Akiva Eldar, "The revolutionary road to 194," *Ha'aretz*, July 22, 2002.

91. Ori Nir, "The Conquerors from Kafr Manda," *Ha'aretz*, June 18, 2001.

92. There had of course been far worse inter-communal violence between Jews and Arabs in 1947–1948 (in the period immediately preceding the establishment of the State of Israel).

93. Nadim Rouhana and Nimer Sultany, "Redrawing the Boundaries of Citizenship: Israel's New Hegemony," *Journal of Palestine Studies* 33, no. 1 (2003): 9.

94. Jonathan Rosenblum, "A Different Kind of Unity," *Jerusalem Post International Edition*, October 20, 2000.

95. The extent of this alienation and the impact of the events of October 2000 upon it were revealed in a survey conducted by the Israel Democracy Institute, which showed that in February 2001 only 21 percent of Palestinian Israelis felt proud to be an Israeli, whereas the year before (in April 2000) this number was 55 percent. Asher Arian, Shlomit Barnea, and Parzit Ben-Nun, *The 2004 Israeli Democracy Index* (The Israel Democracy Institute: Jerusalem, 2004), 30.

96. Quoted in International Crisis Group, "Identity Crisis: Israel and its Arab Citizens," *ICG Middle East Report* no. 25 (March 4, 2004): 9.

97. See, Zvi Bar'el, "It's not about the Temple Mount; say Israeli Arabs," *Ha'aretz*, October 3, 2000.

98. "Identity Crisis: Israel and its Arab Citizens."

99. Barak's motive was to prevent Netanyahu from running against him in the election for prime minister (which Netanyahu was expected to win), since Netanyahu was not a Knesset member and therefore without new Knesset elections he was not eligible to run for prime minister.

100. For details of these proposals see, "President Bill Clinton, Proposals for a Final Settlement, Washington, 23 December 2000," *Journal of Palestine Studies* 30, no, 3 (2001): 171–173.

101. "Israeli-Palestinian Joint Statement, 27 January 2001," http://www.mfa.gov.il/MFA/MFAArchive/2000_2009/2001/1/Israeli-Palestinian+Joint+Statement+-+27-Jan-2001.htm

102. In a poll taken at the end of January 2001, 54 percent of Israeli Jews responded that they did not believe that the Oslo peace process would bring about peace between Israel and the Palestinians in the coming years. Ya'ar and Hermann, "Peace Index-January 2001."

103. Neve Gordon, "The Israeli Peace Camp in Dark Times," *Peace Review* 15, no. 1 (2003): 39–45.

104. Just over 20 percent of those who voted for Barak in the 1999 elections did not vote in the 2001 election. Yuchtman-Ya'ar, "The Oslo Process and Israeli-Jewish Public," 16.

105. International Crisis Group, "Identity Crisis: Israel and its Arab Citizens," 10.

106. According to a Gallup poll released in January 2000, for instance, 47 percent of Israelis felt that "preventing a rift in the nation" was more important than

signing peace agreements with the Arabs, compared to 34 percent who believed the opposite. *Ha'aretz*, January 21, 2000. Similarly, in a survey conducted shortly after the Camp David summit, 37 percent of Israeli Jews ranked "internal tension between the various sectors of the public" as the most important problem on Israel's national agenda, while only 18 percent considered the peace process to be the most important problem. Ya'ar and Hermann, "Peace Index, August 2000."

107. Peri, "The Assassination: Causes, Meanings, Outcomes," 25–62.
108. The desire for internal unity is common to societies faced with external threat. Underlying this desire is the belief that unity strengthens national resolve in responding to threats and prevents the adversary from exploiting internal divisions. It also promotes the willingness of individuals to make sacrifices for the sake of the national struggle.
109. "PM-Elect Makes Unity his Theme," *Ha'aretz*, February 7, 2001.
110. "Inauguration Speech of Prime Minister Ariel Sharon in the Knesset, Jerusalem, March 7, 2001." Israel Ministry of Foreign Affairs, http://www.israel-mfa.gov.il/MFA/Government/Speeches
111. "Excerpts from Speech by Prime Minister Ariel Sharon to the Likud Congress, Jerusalem, October 23, 2002." Israel Ministry of Foreign Affairs, http://www.israel-mfa.gov.il/MFA/Government/Speeches
112. "Text of Prime Minister Ariel Sharon's Victory Address." Israel Ministry of Foreign Affairs, http://www.israel-mfa.gov.il/MFA/Government/Speeches
113. A public opinion survey taken in March 2002, posed the question: "In your opinion have recent events, including terrorist attacks and operation 'Defensive Shield,' strengthened or weakened the sense of national unity in the Israeli-Jewish public?" Eighty-six percent of Israeli Jewish respondents answered that the events strengthened national unity, and only 9.5 percent responded that it was weakened. Tamar Hermann, "Tactical Hawks, Strategic Doves: The Positions of the Jewish Public in Israel on the Israeli-Palestinian Conflict," *Strategic Assessment* 5, no. 2 (August 2002).
114. In a Ma'ariv poll from October 2001, for example, only 2 percent of respondents said the religious-secular divide should be central to the national agenda. Cited in Yossi Klein Halevi, "The New Patriots," *The Jerusalem Report*, November 5, 2001.
115. David Landau, "Rejected We Stand," *Ha'aretz*, February 16, 2001.
116. Amnon Rubinstein, "In Fact, We Are Closing Ranks," *Ha'aretz*, November 20, 2000.
117. *Ha'aretz*, October 5, 2000.
118. http://www.tau.ac.il/peace/
119. Yuchtman-Ya'ar, "The Oslo Process and Israeli-Jewish Public," 23.
120. *Ha'aretz*, April 4, 2001.
121. Asher Arian, *Israeli Public Opinion on National Security 2004* (Tel Aviv: Jaffee Center for Strategic Studies, October 2003), 29.
122. Yuchtman-Ya'ar, "The Oslo Process and Israeli-Jewish Public," 17.
123. According to an opinion poll conducted in January and February 2004, 80 percent of Israelis supported this. Arian, *Israeli Public Opinion on National Security 2004*.
124. Jonathan Rynhold, "Constructing the Fence and Deconstructing Disengagement: Identity, Norms and Security in Israel," paper presented at the annual conference of the Association of Israel Studies, Jerusalem, June 2004.

125. David Rudge, "New Movement Calls for Unilateral Separation from Palestinians," *The Jerusalem Post*, October 15, 2001.

126. Amit Ben-Aroya, "Sharon: The Separation Fence is a Populist Idea," *Ha'aretz*, April 12, 2002.

127. Mazal Mualem, "Smart Fence, Stupid Politics," *Ha'aretz*, August 30, 2003.

128. There is no agreed upon description of the barrier Israel began building in the summer of 2002. Israelis and pro-Israel supporters abroad tend to describe it as a "fence," whereas Palestinians and their supporters abroad often describe it as a "wall." In actuality, it is both—in some parts it is a fence and in others a wall (according to the plan submitted by Israel's Ministry of Defense which is responsible for its construction, less than 5 percent of the final barrier will take the form of a wall ["The Seam Zone," Israel Ministry of Defense, www.seamzone. mod.gov.il/Pages/ENG/]). Given this dispute over terminology, I prefer to use the more neutral description "barrier."

129. "Erased In A Moment: Suicide Bombing Attacks Against Israeli Civilians," *Human Rights Watch*, October 2002.

130. Some 63 percent of Israelis Jews believed that the barrier could significantly reduce the number of Palestinian terrorist attacks against Israel, and another 19 percent believed that it could stop terrorism altogether. Ya'ar and Hermann, "Peace Index-October 2003."

131. Larry Derfner, "The Separation Option," *The Jerusalem Post*, August 10, 2001.

132. Ibid.

133. Quoted in James Bennet, "Sharon's Wars," *The New York Times Magazine*, August 15, 2004, 67–68.

134. Emuna Elon, "Beyond the Illusion of the Fence," *The Jerusalem Report*, August 26, 2002.

135. See his remarks in Bennet, "Sharon's Wars," 52.

136. In the Peace Index survey of April 2004, 59 percent of Israeli Jews expressed support for the plan compared to only 34 percent who opposed it. Ephraim Yaar and Tamar Hermann, "Peace Index / The Majority Wants Disengagement," *Ha'aretz*, April 7, 2004.

137. See the interview with Ehud Olmert in Joseph Berger, "How a Zionist Hawk Grew His New Dovish Feathers," *The New York Times*, August 13, 2004.

138. Thus, after gaining his cabinet's final approval on February 20, 2005, for his plan to withdraw Jewish settlers from Gaza, Sharon stated that the withdrawal "ensures the future of the State of Israel as a Jewish and democratic state." Quoted in Greg Myre, "Cabinet in Israel Ratifies Pullout From Gaza Strip," *The New York Times*, February 21, 2005.

139. Lilly Galili, "Jewish Demographic State," *Ha'aretz*, June 30, 2002.

140. Amir Rapaport, "The Fence," *Ma'ariv*, October 24, 2003.

141. The Palestinian Israeli community's growth rate was around 3.4 percent, compared to 1.4 percent for Israeli Jews. *Identity Crisis: Israel and its Arab Citizens*: 19.

142. In a widely publicized speech Netanyahu, for example, described Palestinian Israelis as a "demographic problem." Aluf Benn and Gideon Alon, "Netanyahu: Israel's Arabs are the Real Demographic Threat," *Ha'aretz*, December 18, 2003.

143. Sari Makover, "Danger: No Border Ahead," *Ma'ariv*, February 21, 2002.

144. The political platform of Moledet includes a chapter entitled, "Separation of the Peoples and Population Transfer." Significantly, Moledet was a member of

Sharon's National Unity Government and Ze'evi was the minister of Tourism before his assassination by members of the Popular Front for the Liberation of Palestine in October 2001.

145. In January 2002, for example, huge posters declaring "Only transfer will bring peace" appeared around the country. Makover, "Danger: No Border Ahead."

146. Israeli television Channel Two's "Meet the Press" program, December 2001, quoted in *Identity Crisis: Israel and its Arab Citizens*: 20.

147. *Identity Crisis: Israel and its Arab Citizens*: 20.

148. In 2002, these figures were 53 percent and 31 percent, respectively. Arian, *Israeli Public Opinion on National Security 2004*, 30.

149. In 2003, two-thirds of Israeli Jews felt that Palestinian Israelis were disloyal to the state. Arian, *Israeli Public Opinion on National Security 2004*, 34.

150. Yair Ettinger, "PM's Arab Adviser Urges Mandatory Flag Waving and loyalty Oaths," *Ha'aretz*, November 5, 2003.

151. Nearly two-thirds of Israeli Jews saw Palestinian Israelis as a security threat in 2001, and over 70 percent did so in 2002. Rouhana and Sultany, "Redrawing the Boundaries of Citizenship," 15. Israeli Jews became particularly alarmed when a handful of Palestinian Israeli citizens were linked to suicide bombings in 2002. This stoked public fears of Palestinian Israelis as a "fifth column." Consequently, in the summer of 2002, the Interior Ministry proposed taking steps to establish a new policy that revoked citizenship from Palestinian Israelis charged with involvement in terrorism (this did not apply to non-Arab Israelis).

152. Yossi Alpher, "An Israeli View: Coming to Terms," *Bitter Lemons*, http://www.bitterlemons.org/previous/bl111102ed41.html

153. Yossi Alpher, "An Israeli View."

154. In an interview in April 2002, former Prime Minister Barak noted that this "makes demographic sense and is not inconceivable," and Labor MK and then transportation minister in Sharon's National Unity government, Ephraim Sneh expressed his support for the proposal. Rouhana and Sultany, "Redrawing the Boundaries of Citizenship," 18.

155. The law effectively discriminated against Palestinian Israelis as they are the ones most likely to marry Palestinians; their spouses are barred from entering Israel, unlike non-Jewish spouses from anywhere else.

156. Nadim Rouhana and Nimer Sultany, "Redrawing the Boundaries of Citizenship," 13.

157. *Identity Crisis: Israel and its Arab citizens*: 10. Oren Yiftachel, "The Shrinking Space of Citizenship: Ethnocratic Politics in Israel," *Middle East Report*, no. 223 (2002): 40–41.

158. Nadim Rouhana and Nimer Sultany, "Redrawing the Boundaries of Citizenship," 11.

159. Quoted in *Ha'aretz*, April 27, 2001.

160. "Appendix: The Kineret Declaration," *Azure* (Summer 2002), http:// www.azure.org.il/13-editors.htm

161. Ibid.

162. Ibid.

163. David Hazony, "Miracle on the Sea of Galilee," *Azure* (Summer 2002), http://www.azure.org.il/13-editors.htm

164. A small indication of this was the rejection by the Knesset's Education Committee of the high school history textbook "A World of Changes" which had sparked much debate when it was introduced in 1999 for its revisionist treatment of Israel's War of Independence. Jonathan Rosenblum, "The Great Awakening," *Jerusalem Post*, February 23, 2001.

165. Neri Livneh, "Post-Zionism only rings once," *Ha'aretz*, February 12, 2005.

166. Quoted in Dalia Shehori, "Post-Zionism is Dead or in the Deep Freeze," *Ha'aretz*, April 20, 2004.

Conclusion: Israel's Identity Crisis in Global Perspective

1. Thomas M. Franck, "Tribe, Nation, World: Self-Identification in the Evolving International System," *Ethics and International Affairs* 11 (1997): 151.

2. Quoted in Hazony, *The Jewish State*, 72.

3. "Dichter Meets with Settlers," *The Jerusalem Post*, July 6, 2004. "Lapid Cautions Right against Incitement," *The Jerusalem Post*, September 9, 2004.

4. "Lapid Cautions Right against Incitement." Uri Avnery, "On the Road to Civil War," *Maariv International*, November 22, 2004.

5. Ephraim Yaar and Tamar Hermann, "Peace Index: January 2005," http://www.tau.ac.il/peace

6. "Israel Completes Pullout Ahead of Schedule, Without Serious Violence," *The New York Times*, August 24, 2005.

7. According to statistical analyses of the demographic profiles of supporters and opponents of the disengagement plan based on polling conducted by the Tami Steinmetz Center, ultra-Orthodox Jews were fourteen times more likely to be opposed to the disengagement plan than secular Israeli Jews, while those who defined themselves as religious were nine times more likely to oppose the disengagement plan than secular Israeli Jews. Ephraim Yaar and Tamar Hermann, "Peace Index: July 2005," http://www.tau.ac.il/peace.

8. Evidence of this appears in a study conducted by the Givat Havivah Center for Arab-Jewish Coexistence. The study found that only 27 percent of Israel's Arab population call themselves "Arab Israelis" or "Israelis"—down from 46 percent in 1995. Instead, most identified themselves as "Palestinians in Israel" or simply as "Arabs." Cited in Yossi Klein Halevi, "The New Patriots," *The Jerusalem Report*, November 5, 2001.

9. Some scholars contend that Israel is not a democracy because of its discriminatory treatment of its Palestinian citizens (see, Oren Yiftachel, "The Concept of 'Ethnic Democracy' and Its Applicability to the Case of Israel," *Ethnic and Racial Studies* 15 (January 1992): 125–136; Asad Ghanem, Nadim Rouhana, and Oren Yiftachel, "Questioning 'Ethnic Democracy': A Response to Sammy Smooha," *Israel Studies* 3, no. 2 (1998): 253–267). Although the unequal treatment of Palestinians in Israel certainly damages the quality of Israeli democracy, many states that are considered democratic have poor records in their treatment of minorities (national, ethnic, racial, etc.). Hence, it is better to consider Israel to be a flawed democracy, but a democracy nonetheless (for this argument see, Jeff Spinner-Halev, "Unoriginal Sin: Zionism and Democratic Exclusion in Comparative Perspective," *Israel Studies Forum* 18, no. 1 [Fall 2002]: 26–56).

10. For a review of this debate see, Alan Dowty, "Is Israel Democratic? Substance and Semantics in the 'Ethnic Democracy' Debate," *Israel Studies* 4, no. 2 (Fall 1999): 1–14.

11. For a similar proposal see, Ilan Peleg, "Israel between Democratic Universalism and Particularist Judaism: Challenging a Sacred Formula," *Report of the Oxford Center for Hebrew and Jewish Studies* (2002–2003): 17.

12. In a national survey of Israeli Jews carried out in 1999, 78 percent expressed the belief that the state should have a Jewish character, albeit not necessarily a religious one. Levy, Levinsohn, and Katz, "The Many Faces of Jewishness in Israel," 276.

13. Herbert Kelman, "The Interdependence of Israeli and Palestinian National Identities: The Role of the Other in Existential Conflict," *Journal of Social Issues* 55, no.3 (1999): 586. In the United Kingdom, for example, the Scots, Welsh, and English maintain their distinct national identities as well as a common civic identity. One can therefore be both Scottish (a national identity) and British (a civic identity).

14. This developmentalist view draws heavily upon Erik Erikson's usage of the term identity crisis in his work on the maturation of children and adolescents. See, for instance, Sidney Verba's statement: "The question of national identity is the political version of the basic personal problem of self-identity. Erik Erikson has argued that 'the crisis of identity' must be resolved if a mature and stable personality is to develop. Similarly one can argue that the first and most crucial problem that must be solved in the formation of a political culture if it is to be capable of supporting a stable yet adaptable political system, is that of national identity." Sidney Verba, "Comparative Political Culture," in *Political Culture and Political Development*, ed., Lucian W. Pye and Sidney Verba (Princeton: Princeton University Press, 1965), 529.

15. Wallace, "Foreign Policy and National Identity in the United Kingdom," 68.

16. Amelia Gentleman, "Summertime, and Living Is Not Easy for French Racked with Self-doubt," *The Guardian*, August 10, 2004.

17. Stryker McGuire, "Clash of Civilizations," *Newsweek International*, November 22, 2004.

18. John Nathan, *Japan Unbound: A Volatile Nation's Quest for Pride and Purpose* (Houghton Mifflin: New York, 2004).

19. Francis Fukuyama, "Identity Crisis: Why We Shouldn't Worry about Mexican Immigration," *Slate*, June 4, 2004. http://slate.msn.com/id/2101756

20. Conrad Black, "Canada's Continuing Identity Crisis," *Foreign Affairs* 74, no. 2 (1995): 99–115.

21. "A National Identity Crisis," *The Economist*, December 14, 1996.

22. Shearman, "Nationalism, the State, and the Collapse of Communism," 92.

23. Bhikhu Parekh, "Discourses on National Identity," *Political Studies* 42 (1994): 501.

24. Pettman, "Nationalism and After," 164.

25. Roxanne Lynn Doty, "Immigration and National Identity: Constructing the Nation," *Review of International Studies* 22 (1996): 240.

26. M.J. Shapiro and H.R. Alker, eds., *Challenging Boundaries: Global Flows, Territorial Identities* (Minneapolis: University of Minnesota Press, 1996).

27. David Morley and Kevin Robins, *Spaces of Identity: Global Media, Electronic Landscapes and Cultural Boundaries* (London: Routledge, 1995). See also,

Robert J. Lieber, and Ruth E. Weisberg, "Globalization, Culture, and Identities in Crisis," *International Journal of Politics, Culture and Society* 16, no. 2 (2002): 273–296.

28. Daniel Deudney, "Ground Identity: Nature, Place, and Space in Nationalism," in Lapid and Kratochwil, eds., *The Return of Culture and Identity in IR Theory*, 129–145.

29. Anthony Smith, "States and Homelands: The Social and Geopolitical Implications of National Territory," *Millennium: Journal of International Studies* 10, no. 3: 187–202.

30. See, for instance, Samuel Huntington's analysis of the threat of Hispanic (and particularly Mexican) immigration to American national identity in his book *Who Are We?: The Challenges to America's National Identity* (Simon & Schuster: New York, 2004).

31. Anthony Smith, "The Nation: Invested, Imagined, Reconstructed?" *Millennium: Journal of International Studies* 20, no. 3 (1991): 353–368. John Breuilly, *Nationalism and the State*, 2nd ed. (Chicago: University of Chicago Press, 1994), 390.

32. Geoff Eley and Ronald Grigor Suny, "Introduction: From the Moment of Social History to the Work of Cultural Representation," in Eley and Suny, eds., *Becoming National*, 9.

33. Ollapally and Cooley, "Identity Politics and the International System," 482.

34. Alberto Melucci claims that all social movements have an identity dimension. Alberto Melucci, *Nomads of the Present: Social Movements and Individual Needs in Contemporary Society* (Philadelphia: Temple University Press, 1989).

35. Prasenjit Duara, "Historicizing National Identity, or Who Imagines What and When," in Eley and Suny, eds., *Becoming National*, 161–162.

36. This claim is based upon optimal distinctiveness theory and social identity theory in social psychology. See, respectively, Marilynn B. Brewer, "The Social Self: On Being the Same and Different at the Same Time," *Personality and Social Psychology Bulletin* 17 (1991): 475–482; and Henri Tajfel, *Differentiation between Social Groups: Studies in the Social Psychology of Intergroup Relations* (London: Academic, 1978).

37. For this argument see, Yael Tamir, *Liberal Nationalism* (Princeton: Princeton University Press, 1993); David Miller, *On Nationality* (Oxford: Clarendon Press, 1995); Margaret Moore, "Normative Justifications for Liberal Nationalism: Justice, Democracy and National Identity," *Nations and Nationalism* 7, no. 1 (2001): 1–20.

INDEX